Language Learning Strategies and Individual Learner Characteristics

Also Available From Bloomsbury

Foreign Language Learning with Digital Technology, edited by Michael Evans
Language Learner Strategies, Michael James Grenfell and Vee Harris
Learning Strategies in Foreign and Second Language Classrooms,
Ernesto Macaro
Teaching and Learning a Second Language, Ernesto Macaro
Teaching English to Young Learners, edited by Janice Bland

"With publication of this landmark volume, language learning strategies are fully established on the cutting edge of language teaching and research. It marks an evolution in the field from the conceptualization and applications of strategies to innovative research designs. The text features eminent researchers along with emerging voices that are taking the work on strategies in exciting new directions. The chapters will re-shape how students, teachers, researchers, and policy-makers think about strategies for language learning."

Peter MacIntyre, Professor of Psychology, Cape Breton University, Canada

"This collection represents the future for language learning strategy (LLS) research, building on solid theoretical foundations but looking ahead to new directions for the field. Drawing on a diverse set of studies and contexts, the chapters elaborate on our understanding of the critical role strategies play in language learning processes and how LLSs interconnect with many personal and contextual factors. While offering valuable theoretical, methodological, and empirical insights, this book also impressively manages to keep the discussions connected to practice. This collection will be pivotal in defining future directions for the field and helping us to better appreciate the ways in which LLSs contribute to and connect with language learning processes."

Sarah Mercer, Head of ELT, University of Graz, Austria

"An excellent resource for language learning researchers and teachers alike. It helps clarify critical methodological issues for researchers. It also provides practical pedagogical ideas for teachers to enhance language learners' strategic learning capacity."

Xuesong Gao, Associate Professor, University of New South Wales, Australia

"A highly readable, insightful, and innovative book for teachers and researchers interested in language learning strategies and individual learner characteristics. Its careful editing and global reach make the book an invaluable compendium for an international readership."

Werner Delanoy, Professor of English Language Teaching,
Alpen-Adria-Universität Klagenfurt, Austria

"Oxford and Amerstorfer 'walk their talk' as they contextualize language learning strategy use and self-regulation in a dynamic approach and deliver a volume that does not shy away from such complexity. Their contributors hail from a myriad of different countries, are both seasoned and up-and-coming, and address theory,

practice, research and assessment from both tried-and-true as well as innovative mindsets. This book is a must-have for all language practitioners!"

Tammy Gregersen, Professor of English, University of Northern Iowa, USA

"[This book] provides a current research foundation on language learners' strategy use. One great strength of this publication is that the contributors include both internationally recognized researchers of language learning strategies, including names that everyone will recognize (for example Chamot, Cohen, Oxford, Griffiths, and Gu), along with a cast of newer researchers whose names will soon be synonymous with language learning strategy research. The book provides all language teaching professionals interested in strategy-based research a current perspective of classroom applications and research ideas for the use of language learning strategies in a wide variety of learning contexts."

Neil Anderson, Professor, Department of English Language Teaching and Learning, Brigham Young University-Hawaii, USA

Language Learning Strategies and Individual Learner Characteristics

Situating Strategy Use in Diverse Contexts

Edited by Rebecca L. Oxford and Carmen M. Amerstorfer

Bloomsbury Academic
An imprint of Bloomsbury Publishing Plc

B L O O M S B U R Y
LONDON · OXFORD · NEW YORK · NEW DELHI · SYDNEY

Bloomsbury Academic

An imprint of Bloomsbury Publishing Plc

50 Bedford Square	1385 Broadway
London	New York
WC1B 3DP	NY 10018
UK	USA

www.bloomsbury.com

BLOOMSBURY and the Diana logo are trademarks of Bloomsbury Publishing Plc

First published 2018

British Library Cataloguing-in-Publication Data

A catalogue record for this book is available from the British Library.

ISBN:	HB:	978-1-3500-0504-4
	ePDF:	978-1-3500-0505-1
	ePub:	978-1-3500-0506-8

Library of Congress Cataloging-in-Publication Data

Names: Oxford, Rebecca L., editor. | Amerstorfer, Carmen M., editor.
Title: Language learning strategies and individual learner characteristics : situating strategy
use in diverse contexts / edited by Rebecca L. Oxford and Carmen M. Amerstorfer.
Description: London, UK ; New York, NY : Bloomsbury Academic, 2018. | Includes
bibliographical references and index.
Identifiers: LCCN 2017019669| ISBN 9781350005044 (hb) |
ISBN 9781350005068 (epub)
Subjects: LCSH: Language and languages–Study and teaching–Methodology. | English
language–Study and teaching–Foreign speakers. | Second language acquisition.
Classification: LCC P53 .L367 2017 | DDC 418.0071–dc23 LC record available at
https://lccn.loc.gov/2017019669

Typeset by RefineCatch Limited, Bungay, Suffolk

To find out more about our authors and books visit www.bloomsbury.com.
Here you will find extracts, author interviews, details of forthcoming
events and the option to sign up for our newsletters.

Contents

List of Figures   ix

List of Tables   x

Notes on Contributors   xii

Preface: About This Book *Rebecca L. Oxford and Carmen M. Amerstorfer*   xviii

Foreword *Stephen Ryan*   xxi

Introduction: The State of the Art in Language Learning Strategies and
Individual Learner Characteristics *Rebecca L. Oxford and Carmen M.
Amerstorfer*   xxiii

Part I   Theoretical Foundations of Individuals' Situated, Self-Regulated
Language Learning Strategies in Authentic Contexts

1   Understanding Language Learning Strategies in Context: An
    Innovative, Complexity-Based Approach *Rebecca L. Oxford,
    Roberta Z. Lavine, and Carmen M. Amerstorfer*   5

2   Moving from Theory to Practice: A Closer Look at Language
    Learner Strategies *Andrew D. Cohen*   31

3   How Individual Differences Relate to Successful Strategy Use:
    Self-Regulated Language Learners Around the World *Carol Griffiths*   55

Part II   Research Methodologies for Exploring Learning Strategies and
Individual Differences

4   Listening to Highly Anxious EFL Learners through the Use of
    Narrative: Metacognitive and Affective Strategies for Learner
    Self-Regulation *Christina Gkonou*   79

5   Modeling a Prototypical Use of Language Learning Strategies:
    Decision Tree-Based Methods in Multiple Contexts
    Atsushi Mizumoto and Osamu Takeuchi   99

6   Mixing Methods: Investigating Self-Regulated Strategies in a
    Cooperative EFL Learning Environment *Carmen M. Amerstorfer*   123

Part III   Studies of Learning Strategies Emphasizing Diverse Contexts and
Individual Difference Factors

7   Making Language Learning Strategies Research Useful: Insights
    from China *Peter Yongqi Gu*   145

8   Language Learning Strategies in Greek Primary and Secondary
    School Learners: How Individual Characteristics Affect Strategy
    Use *Angeliki Psaltou-Joycey and Zoe Gavriilidou*   167

9   Contextual and Individual Difference Variables: Pronunciation
    Learning Strategies in Form-Focused and Meaning-Focused
    Activities *Mirosław Pawlak*   189

Part IV   Preparing Teachers and Presenting Strategy Instruction
to Learners

10 Preparing Language Teachers: New Teachers Become Ready to Teach
    Learning Strategies in Diverse Classrooms *Anna Uhl Chamot*   213

11 Investigating English Majors' Affective Strategy Use, Test Anxiety,
    and Strategy Instruction: Contextual Influences *Jakub Bielak and
    Anna Mystkowska-Wiertelak*   237

12 Young Language Learners in Classroom Contexts: The Development
    of Strategy Assessment Methods and Tools *Pamela Gunning and
    Carolyn E. Turner*   261

Conclusion: Lessons Learned and the Future of Situated Learning
    Strategies *Carmen M. Amerstorfer and Rebecca L. Oxford*   287

Appendices   299
Index of Names   309
Subject Index   315

Figures

I.1	Bronfenbrenner's theory of contexts	xxix
1.1	AIMS slide: Person on the moon	13
1.2	AIMS slide: Building blocks	13
1.3	AIMS slide: Flower	13
2.1	Example from the CARLA website	40
5.1	A database search of language learning strategies research and questionnaire use during the period 1971 to 2015	100
5.2	An example of a five-point Likert scale strategy questionnaire result	105
5.3	A profile plot in cluster analysis (Mizumoto and Takeuchi 2008)	109
5.4	The concept of decision trees	110
5.5	The result of decision tree analysis	115
5.6	Error rate and the number of grown trees (*top*); variable importance plot (*bottom*)	116
8.1	Greece's current administrative areas according to Law 3852/2010	173
11.1	The use of *all strategies* before and after the intervention by high-TA, medium-TA, and low-TA participants	249
11.2	The use of *different strategies* before and after the intervention by high-TA and low-TA participants	250
11.3	The use of *cognitive, metacognitive*, and *affective strategies* before and after the intervention by high-TA, medium-TA, and low-TA participants	251
12.1	Model of a good oral presentation	274

Tables

I.1   The systems in Bronfenbrenner's theory of contexts   xxx

1.1   Post-AIMS questionnaire (adapt as needed)   16

3.1   Participant details   58

3.2   Individual and median (M) ratings from the good language learner questionnaire   61

4.1   Information about the participants   85

4.2   Strategies for coping with language anxiety reported by learners   88

5.1   Cronbach's alpha coefficients, descriptive statistics, and correlations of measures ($n = 711$)   113

6.1   Key to determine high, medium, and low frequency of LLS use   133

6.2   Overview of the participants' *SILL* profiles   134

6.3   Example of a strategy with identical purposes in two situations   136

6.4   Example of a strategy with different purposes in two situations   136

7.1   Number of publications by year (1997–2012)   147

7.2   Learning strategy standards by level   155

7.3   Strategy boxes in Unit 11 of *Senior High English*   157

8.1   Unemployment rate and GDP in Greek peripheries   174

8.2   Descriptive data and *t*-test comparisons by LLS and gender   177

8.3   Descriptive data and *t*-test comparisons by LLS and level of education   177

8.4   Descriptive statistics of the LLS use according to proficiency level   178

8.5   Descriptive statistics of the LLS use according to region of residence   178

10.1   Question 4: High-, mid-, and low-level rankings of learning strategy activities/assignments (2008–2012; N = 61)   227

10.2   Question 5: LLSI challenges and solutions (2008–2012; N = 61)   229

11.1   Three components of the treatment (affective SI)   241

11.2   The instruments   243

11.3   Data collection procedures   244

11.4   Correlations (Pearson) between trait TA (*RTT*) and strategy use (*SILL*) at Time 1   247

11.5   Correlations (Pearson) between state TA (*anxometers*) and
       strategy use (two surveys) at Time 2   247
11.6   Descriptive statistics and dependent-samples *t*-tests for strategy
       use by the whole sample (*n* = 41) at Times 1 and 2   248
11.7   Descriptive statistics for strategy use by low-TA (*n* = 14), medium-
       TA (*n* = 13), and high-TA (*n* = 14) participants at Times 1 and 2 249
11.8   RM ANOVA of the means for affective strategies across the three
       groups and at Times 1 and 2   252
11.9   One-way ANOVAs of the strategy use means of low-TA, medium-
       TA and high-TA groups at Time 2   252
11.10 RM ANOVA of the affective strategies means for the three groups
       separately across Time 1 and Time 2   253
12.1   Teacher SA template   273
12.2   Bottom-up development of strategy table (column 1)/Top-down
       use of strategy table (column 2)   276
12.3   Operationalizing the coding of the phases of SI   277
12.4   Task-based questionnaire: Reading strategies   278

Contributors

Carmen M. Amerstorfer works as a researcher and teacher trainer for the Department of English at Alpen-Adria-Universität Klagenfurt (AAU), Austria. She has teaching experience in EFL and ESP at educational institutions in Austria, the Netherlands, and China. She has taught foreign language learners of all ages and at educational levels from pre-K to tertiary. Carmen's main research interests include learner-centered teaching approaches, strategic language learning, and psychology in language learning. In 2015 Carmen organized an international conference on language learning strategies that is hosted bi-annually throughout the world. In her position as Chair of the School of Education at AAU, Carmen works on improving teacher training programs and cooperation among educational institutions in Austria and across the globe.

Jakub Bielak is Assistant Professor at the Department of English Studies of the Faculty of Pedagogy and Fine Arts at Adam Mickiewicz University, Poznań/Kalisz, Poland as well as Senior Lecturer at the Institute of Modern Languages of the State University of Applied Sciences in Konin, Poland. His major interests include form-focused instruction, individual learner differences, language learning strategies, and applications of cognitive linguistics to language teaching. Among his publications there are a book (*Applying Cognitive Grammar in the Foreign Language Classroom: Teaching English Tense and Aspect*, 2013, co-authored with Mirosław Pawlak), several articles in edited volumes and journals, and two co-edited volumes. Jakub has been Assistant to the Editor of the journal *Studies in Second Language Learning and Teaching* since 2011 and Head of the university press in Konin since 2015.

Anna Uhl Chamot is Professor Emerita of Curriculum and Pedagogy at the Graduate School of Education and Human Development, George Washington University, USA, where she directed the National Capital Language Resource Center (NCLRC). Dr. Chamot has conducted research that investigated language learning processes of both second and foreign language students. Her research interests are in language learning strategies, content-based language instruction, and literacy development in adolescent English learners. She co-designed the *Cognitive Academic Language Learning Approach* (*CALLA*), an instructional model for English language learners and has adapted this model for students learning English and other languages as foreign languages. Her publications include articles and books on research, methodology, and instructional materials. Dr. Chamot holds a PhD in Applied Linguistics from the University of Texas at Austin, an MA in Foreign Language Education from Teachers College, Columbia University, and a BA in Spanish Literature from the George Washington University.

Editors' Note
Shortly before this book's publication, Dr. Chamot suddenly passed away. Scholars around the world who are interested in learning strategies are deeply saddened. We are all grateful to Dr. Chamot for the guidance, inspiration, and love that she gave to us and to the field.

Andrew D. Cohen was a Peace Corps Volunteer in rural community development with the Aymara Indians on the High Plains of Bolivia. As a professor, he taught ESL at UCLA, USA, language education at the Hebrew University of Jerusalem, Israel, and second language studies at the University of Minnesota, USA, before retiring in 2013. He was also Secretary General of AILA (1996–2002). Cohen is co-editor of *Language Learning Strategies* (2007), author of *Strategies in Learning and Using a Second Language* (2011), and co-author of *Teaching and Learning Pragmatics* with Noriko Ishihara (2014). He has also published numerous book chapters and journal articles, and has written a guide for young language learners, with a companion guide for teachers. He piloted the guide with 5th and 6th-grade Spanish immersion students at a charter school in Forest Lake, MN. Copies of most of his papers are available for download on his website: https://z.umn.edu/adcohen.

Zoe Gavriilidou (BA, D.E.A., PhD) is Professor of Linguistics and Head of the Department of Greek at the Democritus University of Thrace, Greece. She has participated in research projects and was the supervising coordinator of the THALES 379335 Project on Language Learning Strategies (total budget €600,000). She is the author of several monographs and papers and has organized international conferences such as the International Conference of Greek Linguistics (September 2011), Language Learning Strategies: Current Issues and Future Perspectives (June 2015), and the 2nd International Conference on Situating Strategy Use: Present Issues and Future Trends (September 2017). In 2000 she submitted a proposal for elaborating the *Textbook for Teaching Greek Language* in the second grade of Greek public schools and her proposal was accepted by the Greek Ministry of Education. She is also a member of the experts' committee for the revision of curricula in Greece and Cyprus in primary and secondary education. Her main areas of research interest include language learning strategies, pedagogical lexicography, linguistic testing, language teaching, and morphology.

Christina Gkonou is Lecturer in TEFL and MA TEFL/TESOL Course Director at the Department of Language and Linguistics, University of Essex, UK. She leads postgraduate modules on teacher training and education, and the psychology of language learning and teaching. Her main research interests are in all areas of the psychology of learners and teachers, but more specifically in language anxiety and emotions, teacher identity and agency, and emotion-regulation strategies for language learning. She is the co-editor of *New Directions in Language Learning Psychology* and *New Insights into Language Anxiety: Theory, Research and Educational Implications*, and co-author of the *MYE (Managing Your Emotions) Questionnaire*.

Carol Griffiths has been a teacher, manager and teacher trainer of ELT for many years. She has taught in many places around the world, including New Zealand, Indonesia, Japan, China, North Korea, UK, and Turkey. She has also presented at numerous conferences and published widely, including her books *Lessons from Good Language Learners* and *The Strategy Factor in Successful Language Learning*. Learner issues (e.g., individual differences, such as strategies, style, gender, age, culture, motivation, identity), teacher education and support (e.g., methodology, error correction), language issues (e.g., EFL), and using literature to teach language are her major areas of research interest.

Peter Yongqi Gu is Associate Professor at the School of Linguistics and Applied Language Studies, Victoria University of Wellington, New Zealand. He is also adjunct Research Fellow at the National Research Centre for Foreign Language Education at Beijing Foreign Studies University, China. His main research interests include learner autonomy and learning strategies, vocabulary acquisition, language testing, and assessment.

Pamela Gunning lectures at Concordia University, Canada. She has vast experience as an elementary ESL teacher and has co-authored several ESL textbooks for children. She is the author of the strategy questionnaire *Children's SILL*, the first adaptation of Oxford's *SILL* for YLLs. Under the auspices of the Ministry of Education of Québec, she has also co-authored a strategy training module, "Strategies for Success in ESL," to help teachers incorporate learning strategy instruction into their ESL teaching. She has been a consultant on strategies to the Ministry of Education of Québec. She has also published articles in journals and chapters in books. Her teaching and research focus on primary pedagogy, strategies, and classroom-based assessment. Her current research examines inter-disciplinary strategy instruction, in particular, L1–L2 cross-linguistic teacher collaboration in teaching reading strategies to YLLs.

Roberta Z. Lavine is Associate Professor of Spanish/Director of Undergraduate Studies in the Department of Spanish and Portuguese, in the School of Languages, Literatures and Cultures at the University of Maryland (UMD), USA. She teaches Spanish for specific purposes and cross-cultural communication at the undergraduate level and language learning and disabilities at the graduate level. Her interests include educational technology and second language pedagogy. She was a Fulbright scholar in Chile and co-edited a volume on technology and teacher training, *Preparing and Developing Technology-Proficient L2 Teachers*. She co-directed a program for educational reform in Latin America, where she implemented the *Diplomado en Educación Universitaria*, the first of its kind in Ecuador. She was named Professor Emerita at the Universidad Tecnológica Equinoccial, Ecuador, for her efforts on behalf of Ecuadorean education. Lavine has also been presented with numerous teaching awards and grants including the "UMD Award for Innovation in Teaching with Technology."

Atsushi Mizumoto, PhD in Foreign Language Education, is Associate Professor at the Faculty of Foreign Language Studies and the Graduate School of Foreign Language Education and Research, Kansai University, Japan. His current research interests include learning strategies, language testing, corpus use for pedagogical purposes, and research methodology. He has published articles in journals such as *Applied Linguistics*, *Language Teaching Research*, *Reading in a Foreign Language*, *ReCALL*, *RELC Journal*, and *System*. He was the recipient of the Best Academic Paper Award from the Japan Society of English Language Education in 2014 and the Research Encouragement Award from the Japanese Association for English Corpus Studies in 2016.

Anna Mystkowska-Wiertelak is Assistant Professor at the Department of English Studies of the Faculty of Pedagogy and Fine Arts at Adam Mickiewicz University, Poznań/Kalisz, Poland as well as Senior Lecturer at the Institute of Modern Languages of the State University of Applied Sciences in Konin, Poland. Her main interests comprise, apart from teacher education, second language acquisition theory and research, language learning strategies, learner autonomy, form-focused instruction, willingness to communicate and motivation. Her recent publications include *Production-Oriented and Comprehension-Based Grammar Teaching in the Foreign Language Classroom* (with Mirosław Pawlak 2012) and *Willingness to Communicate in Instructed Second Language Acquisition* (with Mirosław Pawlak 2017). Anna Mystkowska-Wiertelak is Assistant to the Editor of the journal *Studies in Second Language Learning and Teaching* (http://www.ssllt.au.edu.pl).

Rebecca L. Oxford is Professor Emerita and Distinguished Scholar-Teacher at the University of Maryland and currently teaches at the University of Alabama at Birmingham. She directed language teacher education programs at the University of Maryland, the University of Alabama, and Columbia University, as well as coordinating an intensive English program at the Pennsylvania State University. She has presented keynotes and workshops at language conferences in more than 40 countries and has published over 250 articles and chapters on language learners, psychology, culture, and teaching methods. Among her best known books are *Language Learning Strategies: What Every Teacher Should Know, Language Learning Strategies around the World,* and *Teaching and Researching Language Learning Strategies: Self-Regulation in Context.* She co-edited special issues on strategies in *System, Studies in Second Language Learning and Teaching,* and *International Review of Applied Linguistics in Language Teaching.*

Mirosław Pawlak is Professor of English in the English Department, Faculty of Pedagogy and Fine Arts at Adam Mickiewicz University, Kalisz, Poland, and Department of Research on Language Learning and Teaching, Faculty of Philology, State University of Applied Sciences, Konin, Poland. His main areas of interest are SLA theory and research, form-focused instruction, corrective feedback, pronunciation teaching, classroom discourse, learner autonomy, communication and learning strategies, grammar learning strategies, motivation, and willingness to communicate. His recent publications include *Error Correction in the Foreign Language Classroom: Reconsidering the Issues* (2015) and several edited collections on learner autonomy, language policies of the Council of Europe, form-focused instruction, speaking in a foreign language, classroom-oriented research, and individual learner differences. He is Editor of the journals *Studies in Second language Learning and Teaching* and *Konin Language Studies,* as well as the book series "Second Language Learning and Teaching," published by Springer.

Angeliki Psaltou-Joycey, BA, Dip TEFL, MA, PhD, is Professor Emerita of the School of English, Aristotle University of Thessaloniki, Greece. Her research interests and publications focus on SLA, language learning strategies and styles, English/Greek as an S/FL, and multilingualism. In the field of theoretical linguistics, her interests focus on tense/aspect. She has authored *Language Learning Strategies in the Foreign Language Classroom* (2010), co-authored *The Temporal System of Modern Greek: Studies from the Perspective of Greek as a Foreign Language* (in Greek) (2011), co-edited *Cross-Curricular Approaches to Language Education* (2014), and edited *Foreign Language Learning Strategy Instruction: A Teacher's Guide* (2015). She is Editor of *Journal of Applied Linguistics*.

Osamu Takeuchi, PhD in Education, is Professor of Applied Linguistics in the Faculty of Foreign Language Studies/Graduate School of Foreign Language Education & Research, Kansai University, Osaka, Japan. His research interests include L2 learner strategies, L2 affective factors, and self-regulation in L2 learning. He was the recipient of the JACET Award for Outstanding Academic Achievement in 2004 and of the LET Award for Outstanding Academic Achievement in 2009. He is currently on the editorial boards of *System* and *Turkish Online Journal of English Language Teaching*.

Carolyn E. Turner is Associate Professor, Retired, of Second Language Education in Integrated Studies in Education at McGill University, Canada. Her research examines language testing/assessment in educational settings and in healthcare contexts. She is Past President of the International Language Testing Association (ILTA) and served as Associate Editor of *Language Assessment Quarterly*. In 2009 she was a founding member of the Canadian Association for Language Assessment/Association canadienne d'évaluation des langues. She has been involved with language assessment issues/research in organizations including the International Civil Aviation Organization (ICAO); Ministry of Education of Québec; Educational Testing Service (ETS), Princeton, NJ. Her publications are in journals such as *Language Testing, Language Assessment Quarterly, TESOL Quarterly, Canadian Modern Language Review, Health Communication*, and chapters in edited collections. She is presently co-authoring *Learning-Oriented Assessment in Language Classrooms: Using Assessment to Gauge and Promote Language Learning* with James Purpura.

Preface

About This Book

Rebecca L. Oxford
University of Maryland, USA

Carmen M. Amerstorfer
Alpen-Adria-Universität Klagenfurt, Austria

This book is about foreign and second language learning strategies and individual learner characteristics (e.g., anxiety and motivation), which are situated in particular contexts.

1. Who will find this book useful?

If you are in any of the following groups, you will likely find this volume highly valuable. It is especially to you that we offer this book, though others might also learn much from it.

a. Teachers of university students in areas such as languages, language teaching methods, second language acquisition, learning strategies, individual differences, language learning theory and practice, psychology, cross-cultural studies, self-regulation, emotions or affect, or other subjects.
b. Teachers of languages for adult students, university students, K–12 students, or others.
c. Researchers and theorists.
d. Graduate students or upper-level undergraduates interested in any of the topics above.
e. Authors and designers who want to include strategies in language textbooks or language instruction websites.

For all these readers, this volume offers state-of-the-art chapters in which research and theory are tied to practice. It provides a vast array of resources and references, as well as a dedicated website.

2. Are global perspectives present in this book?

Internationality is a fundamental quality of every contributor. The contributors currently live and work in Austria, Canada, Greece, Japan, New Zealand, Poland, Turkey, the United Kingdom, and the United States. In addition, some contributors were born in or spent their childhoods in countries (e.g., China, Colombia, Greece, and Jamaica) that are not their current countries of residence. Many contributors had major professional or academic experiences in countries—e.g., Bolivia, Cambodia, China, Chile, Costa Rica, Ecuador, Estonia, France, Indonesia, Israel, Japan, Latvia, Lithuania, the Netherlands, North Korea, Qatar, Russia, Scotland, and Singapore—that are neither their original homelands nor their current countries of residence. This list of countries is illustrative rather than exhaustive; our authors have traveled to many additional countries in the world to make presentations, give workshops, and get to know other cultures. We note all these international linkages to emphasize the importance and presence of global perspectives in this book. Such international views benefit all readers of this book.

3. What else is important about the contributors?

The book includes two major groups of contributors. The first group consists of internationally known experts, while the second group consists of relatively new scholars—the next-generation of leaders in situated strategies and individual learner characteristics. In his Foreword to this book, Stephen Ryan correctly notes that the established scholars bring a continuity of insight and that the less familiar voices point to the vitality and health of this field, which he sees as having a global reach.

4. What are some general themes in this book?

Theory, research and assessment, and practice are listed below as separate thematic threads, but actually they are tightly interwoven.

4.1. Theory

Theories about the following are mentioned briefly or explained in depth: self-regulation, agency, autonomy, mediation, and cognitive modifiability/instrumental enrichment; the synergy among teaching, learning, assessment, and research; the task cycle; complex (dynamic) systems; context, environment, situatedness, and the person-in-context relational view; a human development system (ranging from microsystem through macrosystem and chronosystem); cognitive information processing; creative imagination; language use and pragmatics; metastrategies and other strategies; consciousness; cultural iceberg, large and small cultures, and cultural values; positive psychology; states, such as emotional states; and long-term individual differences, such as emotional traits, willingness to communicate, and cognitive styles.

4.2. Research and assessment

This book's research and assessment strand is rich. One chapter calls for researchers to provide more usable strategy research and suggests how to do so. Some valuable approaches for strategy assessment discussed in this volume are general strategy questionnaires, think-aloud protocols, retrospective interviews, diaries and other narratives, scenario-based questionnaires, observations, and a decision-tree approach. The book presents qualitative, quantitative, and mixed-methods research. Various chapters explore researching and assessing strategies for pronunciation, pragmatics, listening, reading, speaking, writing, and test-taking.

4.3. Practice

Every part of this book ultimately has implications for practice. Most obviously, the book's practical aspects include teacher preparation; differentiated strategy instruction for highly diverse learners; and realistic, classroom-based ways to gather and analyze data and report results for optimal educational use. The book will be of practical value in the print form, as well as the digital form. Go to the SSU1 conference website (https://conference.aau.at/event/9/) for a link to strategy materials, ideas, and suggestions.

Foreword

Stephen Ryan
Waseda University, Tokyo

There is a classic scene in one of the *Godfather* films in which the protagonist summarizes his on-off relationship with the mafia by exclaiming "Just when I thought I was out they pull me back in!" While in no way wishing to draw a comparison between the worlds of academic research and organized crime, the sentiment of the scene in many ways resonates with my own relationship with the concept of strategies. There have been times when strategies have appeared as a key focal point linking my research to teaching; there have been other times when the concept has seemed so slippery and elusive that I have shunned it in frustration. Yet I always come back and, over the years, I have come to realize that I am not alone in this experience. Despite interest and attention taking us in other directions, for many researchers and teachers, strategies always seem to "pull us back in." This new volume goes a long way to explaining that persistent fascination.

The field of strategies research is one born out of a creative tension between theory and practice. In effect, strategies researchers are simultaneously investigating the surface manifestations of learner behavior while attempting to delve beneath that surface to explore the inner mental worlds of learners, the underlying processes and volitional roots of strategy use. Surely, this represents the core of the teaching experience and, as such, will always be a key concern for anybody with an interest in education. Nevertheless, this dual perspective is not without its conflicts, as more theoretically oriented researchers look to build solid theoretical frameworks while the more practice-oriented strive to maintain enough flexibility in those frameworks to withstand the demands of the classroom. The organization of the current volume demonstrates the editors' determination to resolve this tension by considering the theoretical and the practical as a whole. The book aims to help readers not only understand, but also investigate and teach strategies.

The first part of the book explores some of the definitional issues surrounding the concept of strategies and provides an authoritative overview of current thinking, creatively melding established concepts with refreshing new ideas. The theme of integrating the old and the new is continued into the next part of the book, which investigates some of the methodological issues associated with researching strategies. The chapters in this part demonstrate that there is room, and a clear need, for conventional methods to co-exist with more innovative approaches to research. The second part of the book moves on to focus on strategies in practice, and one of the most welcome aspects of this new volume is how it highlights the complex, situated nature of strategies. Early strategies research, influenced by the good language learner literature and the broader academic climate of the era, sought to categorize strategies in a widely generalizable manner. This approach made a huge contribution to our understanding of foreign and second language (L2) learning, but in doing so inadvertently created categorization schemes that could be, and were, interpreted in a rigid, inflexible way. This new book appears to draw a line under that approach, recognizing strategic learning as a flexible, dynamic, and highly situated process. The editors describe the final part of the book—concerned with the teaching of strategies—as a "gold mine for L2 teachers" and I concur with this evaluation. The chapters here are firmly rooted in the classroom experience and generously share materials for readers to develop within their own teaching contexts.

Personally, the most refreshing and satisfying aspect of this book comes in the sheer range of perspectives on display. On the one hand, there is a pleasing sweep in the familiarity of the voices. It is always a pleasure, and a learning experience, to hear from some of the most established, pioneering figures in the field, and in this book their presence offers a valuable sense of continuity and authority. On the other hand, the newer, less familiar voices are a testament to the health and vitality of the field. Furthermore, there is a welcome range in the geographic and cultural diversity of the various contributions, taking in North America, Europe, and East Asia. From a technical standpoint, I can only admire how the editors have skillfully woven this diversity into a coherent whole.

Rebecca L. Oxford and Carmen M. Amerstorfer have collaborated to provide a timely reminder of the relevance and vitality of strategies research. Some of us will always find our heads being turned by newer, more glamorous concepts, but the chapters in this book serve as an illustration of the centrality of strategies research to our understanding of L2 learning and its power to always "pull us back in."

Introduction

The State of the Art in Language Learning
Strategies and Individual Learner Characteristics

Rebecca L. Oxford
University of Maryland, USA

Carmen M. Amerstorfer
Alpen-Adria-Universität Klagenfurt, Austria

Tell me, what is it you plan to do with your one wild and precious life?

Mary Oliver

1. Keys

Imagine that poet Mary Oliver is talking to foreign and second language (L2) learners about their lives and learning. L2 learning ideally opens a special space beyond learners' current understandings and sometimes even beyond their imaginations. The space is filled not just with vocabulary and grammar but also with new perceptions, conceptions, places, people, customs, and cultures—perhaps even new worlds. How can learners move toward and take advantage of these growth opportunities? One answer is self-regulated language learning strategies (LLS), chosen and implemented by L2 learners in individualized ways to address complex contexts around them and to deal with their own inner states.

Fathi, a refugee in the U.K., for instance, who needs help in understanding street signs and in stores, has developed a polite routine for asking strangers for help. Hand gestures, shrugging with shoulders, and single words in the L2 (English) help him to get by at the beginning. When people stop and explain something, Fathi pays attention to learn a little English every day. He uses a dictionary, takes notes in a pocket notebook, and looks at pictures and words to guess the gist of simple magazine articles. He progresses quickly when he attends refugee language classes and starts talking to people at the shops. He is a strategic learner.

Rhea, a linguist, is learning two languages simultaneously. Her social situation is different from Fathi's, but like him, she is highly strategic. She has problems in remembering the tones of various Chinese words and in understanding the long, multi-syllabic words she hears in Russian. To deal with Chinese tones, she creates mental pictures of the tones of a word and practices them aloud. She mentally breaks down a long Russian word and imagines it as a linked set of small train cars with Cyrillic writing for a syllable on the side of each train car. As she goes on, Rhea changes her learning strategies somewhat, crafting new ones that give her greater power.

Fathi and Rhea employ LLS to develop competence in their new languages. As they become more strategic, they learn more effectively. Thus, slowly but surely, they open the door to new opportunities, selves, and cultures. These are just two examples of learners whose lives are enhanced through LLS.

This introduction presents and explains the six goals of the volume. Specific descriptions of the chapters are contained elsewhere (see introductions to each part of the book).

2. Goals of the book

The overall goals (A–F) of the book are explained here. Chapters typically address multiple goals.

2.1. Goal A: To define LLS in an encompassing, theoretically satisfactory way

Below is the first theoretically integrated LLS definition, adapted from a definition by Oxford (2017).

> LLS are mental actions that are sometimes also manifested in observable behaviors. They are complex, dynamic, teachable, and at least partially conscious. LLS can be orchestrated to meet immediate learning needs in specific contexts.

> LLS can involve various self-regulation functions (e.g., cognitive, emotional/affective, motivational, social, and metastrategic) to (a) accomplish current language tasks, (b) improve language learning and performance, and/or (c) enhance long-term proficiency.

The functions named above—cognitive, emotional/affective, motivational, social, and metastrategic[1]—are flexible and fluid (see Goal C). We could call them "categories," but that term connotes specific, rather rigid *types* of strategies, while the term "functions" seems more fluid, creative, and process-oriented, in short, more realistic.

2.2. Goal B: To explain the linkage between self-regulation and LLS

A succinct, useful definition of self-regulation comes from Panadero and Alonso-Tapia (2014, 451): "the control that students have over their cognition, behaviour, emotions and motivation through the use of personal *strategies* to achieve the goals they have established" (emphasis added) in real contexts. This definition does not mention the role of teachers or others in mediating learning and helping learners develop strategic self-regulation.

Donato and McCormick (1994) researched portfolio assessment in a French class to uncover the important relationship between LLS and mediation (by the teacher or another more capable other), which is a major part of the sociocultural theory of self-regulation (Vygotsky 1978, 1981). Oxford (1999) went further to show that self-regulation, developed, as Vygotsky said, through mediation, could be a key theoretical base for LLS. In Vygotsky's theory, the more able person (teacher, parent, more advanced peer), mediates learning by holding rich, contextualized dialogues with the learner. During these dialogues the more capable other mediates by modeling mental functions (we justifiably call them strategies), such as analyzing, synthesizing, planning, summarizing, and monitoring, and guides the learner through the zone of proximal development or ZPD, i.e., the area the learner can traverse with assistance. The learner actively internalizes and transforms mental functions through stages: social speech, egocentric speech, and inner speech, or true self-regulation. Mediation can also occur when the learner interacts with cultural tools (e.g., books, technologies, or language itself).

Vygotskian self-regulation continued in the development of Instrumental Enrichment (IE), Reuven Feuerstein's instructional model for producing "cognitive modifiability" in language learners, learners with disabilities, and others (Feuerstein et al. 2006). The LLS / self-regulation linkage for language learners was also emphasized by Chamot (2014), Griffiths (2013), Oxford (2017), and Rose (2012). In addition, many scholars have studied self-regulation's close theoretical cousins, such as agency, autonomy, self-determination, self-direction, and self-efficacy (for a review, see Oxford 2017).

Zimmerman and Schunk (2011) designed a task-cycle model of self-regulated learning with strategies. This model developed in social cognitive psychology. In the task cycle, learners use strategies in the forethought phase, the task implementation phase, and the self-reflection phase. After the task is done, learners evaluate their own performance and assess the value of the strategies they used. Bandura (1997) discovered that the development and use of learning strategies was positively affected by modeling by peers, parents, and teachers.

2.3. Goal C: To demonstrate how LLS are employed in flexible, fluid ways

Strategic learners, especially those who are experienced in using LLS, tend to use strategies with flexibility and fluidity. Learners might move back and forth among strategic functions, i.e., cognitive, affective, motivational, social, and metastrategic (Oxford 2017).

L2 learners in authentic contexts use LLS flexibly due to their own shifting interests, motivations, perceptions of task difficulty, emotional states, and energy levels. These changeable, internal aspects are part of what Mercer (2014) called the "context within." Fleeting internal factors like emotional states are not often considered individual differences (see Goal D) because they vary so quickly.

Jorge is a strategic L2 learner who uses the strategy of analyzing fluidly and flexibly. For him, analyzing in the cognitive mode means dividing a difficult or confusing concept, essay, paragraph, or word into parts for better learning. Jorge uses the analyzing strategy in its affective or motivational function by momentarily separating an emotion or motivation from the element that sparks it, thus understanding and regulating the emotion or motivation. Similarly, when Jorge is socially uncomfortable, he uses analyzing to understand the social situation and effectively regulate his social behavior.

LLS flexibility and fluidity are also partly in response to ever-fluctuating demands within learning contexts (e.g., classroom, home, online, a friend's house, or a workplace). Donato and McCormick (1994) commented that both LLS and contexts are under constant development.

2.4. Goal D: To show the linkages between individual differences and LLS

Goal C concerned internal factors that are part of the "context within" but are so changeable that they are not usually viewed as individual differences. Goal D focuses on what might more typically be called individual differences (Dörnyei 2005; Dörnyei and Ryan 2015; Ehrman, Leaver, and Oxford 2003; Griffiths 2008; Oxford 2012; Oxford and Ehrman 1993; Robinson 2002; Skehan 1989). The "context within" includes not only fleeting factors (Goal C), but also *longer-term, personal learner qualities*, such as general self-esteem and self-concept, long-term interests, deep-seated motivation, overall willingness to communicate, emotional traits, aptitudes (e.g., cognitive, social, artistic), cognitive styles, personality traits, and long-standing personal beliefs, all of which are part of the patterns of individual differences among learners. Longer-term qualities do not necessarily mean permanent qualities, because with effort and strategies some of these features can be shifted. LLS use can help to improve self-esteem, remold self-concept in positive ways, strengthen aptitude (perhaps via "cognitive modifiability"), make cognitive styles more flexible, increase willingness to communicate, and alter personal beliefs—although some scholars see these internal factors as more permanent.

Individual differences also include the learner's *personal demographics* (e.g., age, gender, sexuality, age, religion, socioeconomic status, and education level), which affect LLS use. Some demographics are more changeable than others. Age changes unceasingly in one direction: upward. Gender was formerly a given but has become alterable as transgender people are increasingly acknowledged. With motivation, effort, and learning strategies, learning can improve, and education level might lead to a higher socioeconomic status. Individual differences are connected to the learning contexts, leading to Goal E.

2.5. Goal E: To explore the relationships among contexts, complexity, and strategic learners

L2 learners are "plunged into the maelstrom of the world with its demands and mixed messages" (Grenfell and Harris 1999, 41). Learners constantly influence their contexts and are influenced by them. We start with cultural aspects.

2.5.1. Cultural beliefs and values

A culture is a group with a common history, as well as generally common beliefs, values, symbols, and behavioral expectations. Metaphorically speaking, culture is often depicted as an iceberg with a visible tip above the water line and an unseen, immensely influential, and more massive part—including cultural beliefs and values (CBV)—below the water line. CBV are aspects of external culture and directly or indirectly affect many learners' autonomy and LLS use. Some CBV have concerns about power (or whether power should be shared) in relationships among races, genders, ages, and regions and in learner-teacher relationships. Other CBV focus on family, respect, honor, compassion, education, communication, careers, money, and marriage. Many CBV become internalized, unconscious, and unquestioned, leading to automatic behavior. Certain ones, often automatic, have huge effects on an individual's inclination (or disinclination) to employ LLS and use the new language.

Classroom contexts are small cultures (Holliday 1999).[2] For a given learner, classroom contextual elements include task demands, assessments, materials, desks, books, "climate" (invitational quality, physical and emotional safety), and the teacher's and other students' actions and beliefs, all of which can influence a person's LLS use. Conversely, LLS use affects the classroom, especially the teacher's actions after witnessing LLS use: subsequent praise, mediation, classroom-climate efforts, and evaluation of learners (as strategic or not, capable or not, motivated or not).

2.5.2. *Person-in-context relational view*

Ushioda's (2009, 220) "person-in-context relational view" is related to LLS use, because it centers on "the agency of the individual person as a thinking, feeling human being, with an identity, a personality, a unique history and background, a person with goals, motives and intention." Ushioda brought attention to contexts, as did Dörnyei, MacIntyre, and Henry (2015) and Mercer (2015, 2016). In 2015 Amerstorfer initiated a bi-annual, international conference called "Situating Strategy Use" (i.e., within contexts).

2.5.3 *Bronfenbrenner's view of contexts*

Bronfenbrenner (1995, 2005; Bronfenbrenner and Morris 2006) described contexts or systems, nested one inside the other (see Figure 1.1), as influencing the developing person. In his theory, five systems foster human development: microsystem, mesosystem, exosystem, macrosystem, and chronosystem (Table 1.1; see Oxford 2017 for details).

Everything we have said so far about contexts and systems suggests that we live in webs of complex systems. For several decades *complexity theory* has been applied to L2 learning, starting with Larsen-Freeman's (1997) work on chaos. However, the LLS field is only now beginning to pay attention to complexity concepts (for the first in-depth treatment, see Oxford 2017). Complexity theorists defy the post-positivist worldview, which argues that research should be conducted in a primarily linear fashion with isolated variables. Research that is based on complexity theory takes a holistic, dynamic, nonlinear, connected view and rejects fragmentation, stasis, linearity, and unconnectedness. Chapter 1 will further discuss this topic.

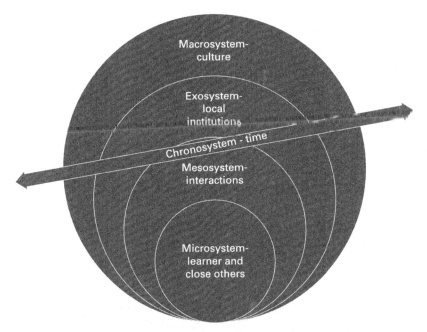

Figure I.1 Bronfenbrenner's theory of contexts
Source: R. Oxford

2.6. Goal F: To discuss traditional and new methods for LLS research, assessment, and instruction.

2.6.1. LLS research and assessment

Many people assess and investigate LLS as an individual difference variable (see Goal D) including dozens, hundreds, or more learners per study in general, frequency-based terms ("highest in cognitive strategies, lowest in affective strategies," often in relation to gender, university, or country). This research is usually done with Likert-scaled surveys, which are sometimes criticized on statistical grounds, but some chapters in this book justify such survey use on several counts. Likert-scale surveys often offer a broad picture of LLS use. When researching LLS with a survey, researchers could offer caveats about (a) the existence of diverse contexts and tasks for LLS use and (b) the fluidity and complexity of LLS. Unfortunately, (a) and (b) are not usually reflected in ordinary Likert-scale questionnaires, nor are caveats about these factors typically included in reports of results.

Recognition of a high degree of complexity in LLS use often calls for mixed-methods assessment and research. Qualitative measurements are used along

Table I.1 The systems in Bronfenbrenner's theory of contexts

Microsystem

Microsystem = learner + immediate environment (e.g., peers, family, educational and religious institutions, neighborhood, and workplaces). In microsystems, LLS are among learner "resource factors," as are intelligence, creativity, emotions, skills, material resources, and past experiences.

Mesosystem

Mesosystem = interrelationships among aspects of the microsystem or between two or more microsystems. These interrelationships might occur between (a) the learner and (b) a teacher, a peer, a school, or a family, for instance. LLS choice is influenced by the mesosystem (and also influences it, we add).

Exosystem

Exosystem = larger social system, which has an indirect, short- or long-term effect on individuals. Exosystem includes decisions, laws, government reform, policies, and contingencies. Individuals usually have little immediate influence on exosystem.

Macrosystem

Macrosystem = long-lasting, major elements with significant effects on individuals. Examples of these elements: ongoing socioeconomic factors, national/international organizations, and cultures and subcultures (groups with common history, beliefs, values, symbols, and behavioral expectations).

Chronosystem

Chronosystem = time system, a late addition to Bronfenbrenner's model. Time operates across all systems.

---

with quantitative ones, and these instruments are administered sequentially or in other ways. In contrast, a *single* measurement instrument in a mixed-methods study can, by itself, include both qualitative and quantitative items, as in a new scenario-based emotion regulation questionnaire for affective LLS measurement (Gkonou and Oxford 2016).

Many other options also exist for LLS assessment and research methodologies. Narratives (e.g., diaries, interviews, and auto-ethnographies) have helped learners to identify their LLS as rapidly fluctuating, contextualized, self-regulated actions and to explore and understand their related thoughts and feelings. The idiodynamic method holds promise for identifying rapid-fire changes in strategy use or purpose. Retrodictive qualitative modeling starts at an outcome phase and traces back the dynamics in time, providing a new way of assessing and identifying LLS in context. Decision-tree-based methods are statistically valuable and highly innovative for the LLS field. This book shows many of the possibilities regarding assessment and research methods, traditional and new, that can explore LLS use.

2.6.2. Strategy Instruction (SI)

The intertwining of multiple factors—self-regulated LLS, contexts, and individual differences—can be brought together in strategy instruction (SI) that is differentiated to meet the needs of diverse learners. Well-focused, learner-oriented SI facilitates learning effectiveness and, correspondingly, teaching effectiveness. Some leaders are differentiating SI to meet individual learners' goals and characteristics: sensory preferences, cognitive styles, current strategy knowledge and use, proficiency levels, interests, social background, personality, motivation, age, and gender (Chamot and Harris 2018; Oxford 2017).

Content-based instruction (CBI), also known as Content and Language Integrated Learning (CLIL), is now popular on many continents. Chamot's (2009, 2014) Cognitive Academic Language Learning Approach (CALLA) is a form of CBI/CLIL that smoothly integrates content learning, language learning, and the use of self-regulatory LLS. LLS are teachable, and expertly planned SI is valuable (Chamot 2009, 2014; Chamot and Harris 2018). CBI/CLIL, like technology-based L2 learning, is cognitively demanding, and LLS can help lower that load (Oxford and Lin 2011).

SI effectiveness studies are often said to be optimally conducted with a classic experimental or quasi-experimental design, typically using quantitative questionnaires. In these designs, certain controls are exerted, and (traditionally speaking) only one group out of two receives the SI treatment. One-group SI research designs, with some caveats, can be useful, especially as precursors to experimental or quasi-experimental studies that are more controlled. See Plonsky (2011) for a meta-analysis of selected SI studies using such designs and measurements. On the other hand, very different SI studies can be done using mixed-methods (see earlier); ethnographic or self-ethnographic methods; analysis of learner and/or teacher journals; video-based observations; and a range of other methods (Oxford 2017).

3. Conclusion

This chapter began with a quotation from poet Mary Oliver, who brought imagination and attention to individuals' lives. In the subsequent discussion, we indicated that L2 learning is a key to new possibilities, selves, and cultures beyond a learner's current imagination. In turn, LLS are a key to L2 learning.

The focus then turned to the six goals of the book: (a) to define LLS; (b) to link LLS and self-regulation; (c) to explain the fluidity of LLS; (d) to show the association between individual differences and LLS; (e) to explore the relationships among contexts, complexity, and strategic learners; and (f) to provide insights on methods for strategy research, assessment, and instruction. The discussions related to each of these goals open the door for the twelve chapters in the book.

Notes

1 The metastrategic function includes planning, organizing, monitoring, and evaluating. This function is, by definition, above ("meta") the other four functions in the sense that it generally amplifies or aids those other functions (see Oxford 2017).
2 Holliday argued that in small cultures, cohesive behavior occurs, and there is freedom from "culturist" stereotypes (e.g., ethnic, national, and international). However, we see diverse behavior and serious stereotyping in some classrooms.

References

Bandura, Albert. 1997. *Self-efficacy: The Exercise of Control.* New York: Freeman.
Bronfenbrenner, Urie. 1995. "Developmental Ecology through Time and Space: A Future Perspective." In *Examining Lives in Context: Perspectives on the Ecology of Human Development,* edited by Phyllis Moen, Glen H. Elder, and Kurt Lüscher, 619–47. Washington, DC: American Psychological Association.
———. 2005. *Making Human Beings Human: Bioecological Perspectives on Human Development.* Thousand Oaks, CA: SAGE.
Bronfenbrenner, Urie, and Pamela A. Morris. 2006. "The Bioecological Model of Human Development." In *Handbook of Child Psychology, Vol. 1,* 793–828. doi: 10.1002/9780470147658.chpsy0114
Chamot, Anna Uhl. 2009. *The CALLA Handbook: Implementing the Cognitive Academic Language Learning Approach.* 2nd edition. White Plains, NY: Pearson Education/ Longman.
———. 2014. "Developing Self-Regulated Learning in the Language Classroom." In *Knowledge, Skills and Competencies in Foreign Language Education.* Proceedings of the Sixth International CLS Conference (CLaSIC), Singapore, 78–88.

Chamot, Anna Uhl, and Vee Harris, eds. 2018. *Learning Strategy Instruction in the Language Classroom: Issues and Implementation.* Bristol: Multilingual Matters.

Donato, Richard, and Dawn E. McCormick. 1994. "A Sociocultural Perspective on Language Learning Strategies: The Role of Mediation." *Modern Language Journal* 78: 453–64.

Dörnyei, Zoltán. 2005. *The Psychology of the Language Learner: Individual Differences in Second Language Acquisition.* Mahwah, NJ: Lawrence Erlbaum Associates.

Dörnyei, Zoltán, and Stephen Ryan. 2015. *The Psychology of the Language Learner Revisited.* New York: Routledge.

Dörnyei, Zoltán, Peter D. MacIntyre, and Alistair Henry, eds. 2015. *Motivational Dynamics in Language Learning.* Bristol: Multilingual Matters.

Ehrman, Madeline E., Betty Lou Leaver, and Rebecca L. Oxford. 2003. "A Brief Overview of Individual Differences in Second Language Learning." In *Individual Differences: Research Advances*, special issue, edited by Madeline E. Ehrman, Betty Lou Leaver, and Rebecca L. Oxford. *System* 31: 313–30.

Feuerstein, Reuven, Louis Falik, Yaacov Rand, and Raphael S. Feuerstein. 2006. *The Feuerstein Instrumental Enrichment Program: Creating and Enhancing Cognitive Modifiability.* Jerusalem: ICELP Press.

Gkonou, Christina, and Rebecca L. Oxford. 2016. "Managing Your Emotions for Language Learning Questionnaire." Version 4.1. In *Teaching and Researching Language Learning Strategies*, Rebecca L. Oxford 2017, 317–33. New York: Routledge.

Grenfell, Michael, and Vee Harris. 1999. *Modern Languages and Learning Strategies: In Theory and Practice.* London: Routledge.

Griffiths, Carol, ed. 2008. *Lessons from Good Language Learners.* Cambridge: Cambridge University Press.

——. 2013. *The Strategy Factor in Successful Language Learning.* Bristol: Multilingual Matters.

Holliday, Adrian. 1999. "Small Cultures." *Applied Linguistics* 20 (2): 237–64. doi: 10.1093/applin/20.2.237

Larsen-Freeman, Diane. 1997. "Chaos/Complexity Science and Second Language Acquisition." *Applied Linguistics* 18 (2): 141–65.

Mercer, Sarah. 2014. "The Self from a Complexity Perspective." In *Multiple Perspectives on the Self in SLA*, edited by Sarah Mercer and Marion Williams, 160–76. Clevedon: Channel View Publications.

——. 2015. "Learner Agency and Engagement: Believing You Can, Wanting to, and Knowing How to." *Humanizing Language Teaching*, 17 (4). Accessed 15 August, 2016. http://www.hltmag.co.uk/aug15/mart01.rtf

——. 2016. "The Contexts within Me: L2 Self as a Complex Dynamic System." In *The Dynamic Interplay between Context and the Language Learner*, edited by Jim King, 11–28. London: Palgrave Macmillan. doi: 10.1057/9781137457134_2

Oxford, Rebecca L. 1999. "Relationships between Second Language Learning Strategies and Language Proficiency in the Context of Learner Autonomy and Self-regulation." *Revista Canaria de Estudios Ingleses* 38: 108–26.

——. 2012. "Individual Differences." In *Routledge Encyclopedia of Second Language Acquisition*, edited by Peter Robinson, 302–8. 2nd edition. London: Routledge.

——. 2017. *Teaching and Researching Language Learning Strategies: Self-Regulation in Context.* 2nd edition. London: Routledge.

Oxford, Rebecca L., and Madeline E. Ehrman. 1993. "Second Language Research on Individual Differences." In *Annual Review of Applied Linguistics*, edited by William Grabe, 188–205. Cambridge: Cambridge University Press.

Oxford, Rebecca L., and Chien-Yu Lin. 2011. "Autonomous Learners in Digital Realms: Exploring Strategies for Effective Digital Learning." In *Independent Language Learning: Where Innovation Meets Application*, edited by Bruce Morrison, 157–71. Hong Kong: Independent Learning Association / Hong Kong Polytechnic University Press.

Panadero, Ernesto, and Jesús Alonso-Tapia. 2014. "How Do Students Self-Regulate? Review of Zimmerman's Cyclical Model of Self-Regulated Learning." *Anales de Psicología* 30 (2): 450–62.

Plonsky, Luke. 2011. "The Effectiveness of Second Language Strategy Instruction: A Meta-analysis." *Language Learning* 61 (4): 993–1038.

Robinson, Peter. 2002. *Individual Differences and Instructed Language Learning*. Amsterdam: John Benjamins.

Rose, Heath. 2012. "Reconceptualizing Strategic Learning in the Face of Self-Regulation: Throwing Language Learning Strategies out with the Bathwater." *Applied Linguistics* 33 (1): 92–98.

Skehan, Peter. 1989. *Individual Differences in Second-language Learning*. London: Edward Arnold.

Ushioda, Ema. 2009. "A Person-in-Context Relational View of Emergent Motivation, Self and Identity." In *Motivation, Language Identity and the L2 Self*, edited by Zoltán Dörnyei and Ema Ushioda, 215–28. Bristol: Multilingual Matters.

Vygotsky, Lev S. 1978. *Mind in Society: The Development of Higher Psychological Processes*. London: Harvard University Press.

——. 1981. "The Genesis of Higher Mental Functions." In *The Concept of Activity in Soviet Psychology*, edited by James V. Wertsch, 144–88. Armonk, NY: Sharpe.

Zimmerman, Barry J., and Dale H. Schunk. eds. 2011. *Handbook of Self-Regulation of Learning and Performance*. New York: Routledge.

Part I

Theoretical Foundations of Individuals' Situated, Self-Regulated Language Learning Strategies in Authentic Contexts

Every research area requires a degree of standardization regarding terminological definitions and explanations of core concepts in order to create a basis for meaningful scholarly discussion. In the past forty-two years, abundant attempts have been made at defining language learning strategies (LLS) and other key issues related to foreign and second language (L2) learning. Regardless of inconsistencies in strategy definitions, which Oxford (2017) analyzes in much detail, the field has never ceased to exist. LLS research is "alive and kicking" on a global scale (Mizumoto and Takeuchi, Chapter 5 in this volume).

Variations regarding terminology and conceptual definitions proliferated wildly, but some early, influential categorization schemes for LLS (for example, Rubin 1975; O'Malley and Chamot 1990; Oxford 1990) dominated the field. In recent years, however, a few strategy scholars have started to pay less attention to metaphorical boxes that are labelled according to certain features of LLS (e.g., "cognitive strategies" or "vocabulary learning strategies"). These scholars have begun to analyze strategy data to emphasize functions rather than categories and to show rapid fluidity and flexibility of strategies in use. A hoped-for development will be a widespread moving away from rigid categorization schemes toward the recognition of strategic L2 learning as a flexible and dynamic process.

Oxford (2017) is the first scholar to seriously examine LLS through the lens of the scientific theory of complexity. She learned much about complexity through scholarship and collaborative interactions with several major figures in the complexity area, such as Diane Larsen-Freeman, Phil Hiver, and Peter

MacIntyre. Complexity theory suggests that learning strategies, learners, language learning, personalities, emotions, motivations, contexts, and related aspects are all complex systems and that they are bound together into larger complex systems. Besides complexity theory, specific focus areas have developed in LLS research, such as strategy assessment and strategy instruction (see Part IV).

Part I in this book contains three chapters, each offering various facets of the prism of second and foreign language learning strategies. In Chapter 1, Oxford, Lavine, and Amerstorfer apply numerous tenets of complexity theory to a special kind of strategy-awareness raising, known as Amazing IMages of Strategies, or the AIMS process. Their studies used lively and colorful photographs to elicit responses to open-ended questions from participating in-service and future L2 teachers in different parts of the world. The participants often commented on the complexity of L2 learning processes and of strategies. In all locations, the participants' motivation toward strategy use and strategy instruction was heightened by the photos and the related questions.

In Chapter 2, Cohen explains how LLS can be categorized. Instead of one fixed scheme, Cohen provides multiple possibilities to classify strategies. Chapter 2 enables a view of multiple angles, each of which encourages new perspectives on strategic language learning. Specific examples of LLS and strategy-enhancing activities are available on the CARLA website, which is a very useful resource and worth a visit for L2 learners and teachers. Cohen furthermore shares insights into strategy instruction with a specific emphasis on the roles of teachers in strategy instruction. Finally, he reports on his personal experience of learning Chinese as one of his many foreign languages.

Chapter 3, by Griffiths, takes a holistic view of self-regulated language learners from around the globe. The group of participants in the reported study comes from an impressive variety of nations and jointly possesses a great cultural wealth. Griffiths underscores how important it is to respect and take into account L2 learners' individual differences. The author explains how individual learner characteristics relate to successful strategic L2 learning and focuses her analyses on a selection of features. Griffiths' comprehensive perception of situated L2 learning is reflected throughout the study and enriches the latest developments in LLS research.

The chapters in Part I were selected because they present theoretical (and yet practical) foundations for contextualized, self-regulated learning strategies. Readers of these chapters will gain a sense of theoretical underpinnings of strategies, multiple types and aspects of strategies, actual strategy use in varied settings and for different purposes, and teachers' perceptions of strategies across cultures.

References

O'Malley, J. Michael, and Anna Uhl Chamot. 1990. *Learning Strategies in Second Language Acquisition*. Cambridge: Cambridge University Press.

Oxford, Rebecca L. 1990. *Language Learning Strategies: What Every Teacher Should Know*. Boston: Heinle & Heinle.

——. 2017. *Teaching and Researching Language Learning Strategies: Self-Regulation in Context*. 2nd edition. New York: Routledge.

Rubin, Joan. 1975. "What the 'Good Language Learner' Can Teach Us." *TESOL Quarterly* 9 (1): 41–51.

CARLA   website

1

Understanding Language Learning Strategies in Context

An Innovative, Complexity-Based Approach

Rebecca L. Oxford
Roberta Z. Lavine
University of Maryland, USA

Carmen M. Amerstorfer
Alpen-Adria-Universität Klagenfurt, Austria

Imagination is "a process of expanding our self by transcending our time and space and creating new images of the world and ourselves."

Etienne Wenger 1998, 176

To understand language learning strategies *in context* (for instance, analyzing, paying attention, using positive self-talk, or finding resources for learning), we need to consider some specific characteristics of second and foreign language (L2) learning strategies.

Language learning strategies (LLS[1]) ...

- are purposeful mental actions (sometimes also manifested as observable behaviors) that the learner creatively implements to meet learning-related needs;
- aid the learner in developing self-regulation, completing L2 tasks, and moving toward L2 proficiency;
- are complex, dynamic, and fluidly employed in specific sociocultural contexts.
- are used consciously or at least partially consciously;
- can be discussed in terms of functions, such as "metastrategic,"[2] cognitive, emotional/affective, motivational, and social;
- can be taught.

This chapter presents an innovative, complexity-based approach to understanding LLS. They are complex systems embedded in systems that are even more complex (Oxford 2017). Understanding LLS in all their richness and complexity calls for imagination. The contextualized, complex nature of LLS is the topic of Section 1. Section 2 briefly focuses on the importance of imagination in strategic learning. Section 3 introduces imaginative, strategy-related photographs, provides guidelines for using them to help learners develop their strategy awareness, and presents descriptions of several such sessions. Section 4, the conclusion, includes a summary, a list of ideas for future research, and possible activities for the future.

1. The contextualized, complex nature of LLS

This part of the chapter explains how LLS are contextualized (situated in specific environments) and why strategies are complex systems embedded in even more complex systems.

1.1. Context

Strategy users are embedded in their *contexts* (*environments*) and are constantly influencing and being acted upon by elements of their contexts. "A person is coupled with his or her environment," said Diane Larsen-Freeman (2015, 30). The word *system,* or an organized whole with interconnected parts, is an important key to context. *Ecology* is the science of the relationships of life forms to each other and their surroundings. Therefore, an *ecosystem* is a group of interconnected components created by the interaction of a community of organisms with their environment. LLS are part of a *learner-context ecosystem,* in which complex processes occur within learners and between learners and their sociocultural environment (Kramsch 2002; Oxford 2017; Ushioda 2015; van Lier 2004).

1.1.1. *Person-in-context relational view*

Ushioda's (2009) "person-in-context relational view" centers on "the agency of the individual person as a thinking, feeling human being, with an identity, a personality, a unique history and background, a person with goals, motives and intention" (2009, 220). This person, whom we will call Ileana, uses LLS, which are intentional, are spurred by motives, and serve learning goals. Ileana interacts with "the fluid and complex system of social relations, activities, experiences and multiple micro- and macro-contexts in which [she] is embedded ..." (ibid.).

1.1.2. Bronfenbrenner's theory of contexts

The most famous theorist of the ecology of human development was Urie Bronfenbrenner (1979, 1989, 2005; Bronfenbrenner and Morris 2006). He revealed that contexts are nested one inside the other and influence the developing person. In Bronfenbrenner's theory, five systems foster human development: microsystem (the learner and his or her immediate social environment, such as family, peer group, and neighborhood), mesosystem (interactions within one microsystem or between two microsystems, e.g., teacher and student working together), exosystem (local networks and institutions that influence the person indirectly), macrosystem (cultural beliefs and values, major social conditions, national/international governments or organizations), and chronosystem (the system of time). See *Introduction: The State of the Art in Language Learning Strategies and Individual Learner Characteristics* and Oxford (2017) for more details.

Any aspect or element of Bronfenbrenner's model (e.g., student, a classroom of students, a local mosque full of worshippers, or a national government or set of cultural values, as well as the historical chronosystem) can easily be thought of as a complex system.

1.2. Complexity

For several decades *complexity theory* has been applied to L2 learning, starting with Larsen-Freeman's (1997) work on chaos, although the L2 learning strategy field is only now beginning to pay attention to complexity concepts (Oxford 2017). Research that is based on complexity theory uses a holistic, dynamic, nonlinear, connected lens (Bailly 2012; De Bot 2008; Larsen-Freeman 1997, 2015, 2017; Ortega and Han 2017; Oxford 2017).

1.2.1. A few complex systems

The L2 learner is a complex system. As a complex system, the learner is "developing and changing through contact with other systems (parents, classmates, [teachers], friends, TV, computer games, Internet sites, movies, religion), and demonstrating a unique collection of needs, intelligences, learning preferences, learning styles, [learning strategies], beliefs, perceptions and attitudes" (Finch 2004, 3). A learning strategy or set of learning strategies can be viewed as a complex system within the learner and situated in the extremely complex environment. In addition, as noted by Dörnyei (2009), L2 learners' three mental domains—cognition, affect (emotion), and motivation—are also complex systems. "Complex systems are everywhere we look" (Oxford 2017, 113), in fact.[3]

1.2.2. *Some features of complex systems*

A primary feature of a complex system is *situatedness (contextualization)* within an environment, as mentioned earlier. A second feature is *nestedness*. A complex system involves "a hierarchical structure of nested levels" (Larsen-Freeman 2015, 29); see the Bronfenbrenner discussion earlier. No one has neatly configured a nested set of levels for LLS. Such a set might include levels like the following, although we have not put them in any specifically nested order: personal factors influencing strategy choice (e.g., age, gender, interests, self-esteem, motivation, degree of self-regulation), contextual factors influencing strategy choice (e.g., task purpose and requirements, social context, teacher–student interactions and expectations, peer interactions and expectations, cultural values), nature of strategy, situational orchestration of strategies in chains or clusters, and strategy success.

The third feature is *openness*. A complex system, such as a class or a learner, is open to a larger web of systems, which help it grow and change. Complex systems take in energy, information, and/or matter from other complex systems (Larsen-Freeman 2015, 2017). This does not eliminate the system's own *self-modification*, i.e., the complex system under development operates as a resource for its own further development (Larsen-Freeman 2017).

The fourth characteristic is *emergence*, meaning that patterns emerge from system components that interact. Connections among complex systems are unpredictable and can lead to the emergence of new forms that are more than the sum of the parts. For instance, new LLS can emerge for a given learner (or for a group) in a specific context, even without formal SI (strategy instruction).

The fifth feature is *interconnectedness*, i.e., relationships among multiple components of a complex system are connected in nonlinear, organic, holistic, and causally bidirectional ways (for instance, cognition and emotion influence each other). *Multiple causes*, the sixth feature, include a range of influences, such as main causes, secondary causes, and hidden or distant causes. Think about the following examples of multiple causes: (a) the learner is theoretically in charge of his or her own strategy use, but there are influences from the teacher, the task, the general situation, and even cultural beliefs; and (b) the success of SI is not just due to a brilliant and sensitive teacher and willing students but also to factors such as good weather, a good lunch, students' general alertness, good materials, enough time in the academic schedule, family and institutional support, and lack of major academic headaches during an SI session.

The seventh aspect is *multiplicity*, which refers to the incredible diversity of learners' needs, behaviors, motivations, and aptitudes, as well as the amazing range of contexts in which learning occurs and the diverse developmental pathways are followed by varied learners. SI must be designed and adapted to deal with this multiplicity. Another aspect of multiplicity is the different forms of assistance that a strategy offers the learner: assistance for developing self-regulation, completing immediate tasks, and increasing proficiency. Yet another aspect of multiplicity is the multiple functions that a single strategy can serve for a given learner within the same lesson or even within a matter of moments: helping the learner cognitively, affectively, motivationally, socially, and in other ways.

The eighth and ninth features are *nonlinearity* and *dynamism*. Nonlinearity refers to disproportionate outcomes that cannot be predicted, partly because of dynamism (changeability, fluctuation) and sensitivity in the system. Learners dynamically orchestrate strategies in combinations, such as chains or clusters, with varied, sometimes unexpected outcomes. Regarding linearity, a given event might have different outcomes for different people at the same time or for the very same person at different times. For example, even when SI is well tailored to the group, we cannot expect this instruction to work equally for every student in the group or for any specific student across time and in all circumstances; fluctuations often occur in a complex system. In certain cases, a very small amount of SI might lead to a huge payoff in student achievement. In other cases, a strong investment in SI (through new textbooks containing strategies, for instance) might result in disappointingly few student improvements during the trial period. Some remarkably positive results might occur later, but since studies are often cut off after a short, intensive period, some key changes can be missed.

A different trend from dynamism is *stability* (the attractor state, Hiver 2015), which is the tenth feature. A system's organized pattern of stability can occur from time to time. Certain feedback reinforces stability, while other feedback amplifies change in the system. Stability in a system does not usually last long, and big change is possible at any time (Larsen-Freeman 2017). Even in stability there is constant activity in the students' interactions with each other, the teacher, the materials, the language, and their own LLS.

Finally, *adaptiveness* is the eleventh characteristic. Adaptiveness means that a complex system learns from experience and changes in response to novel changes in the environment (Larsen-Freeman 2017). Subsystems are also co-adaptive. For example, students' emerging strategy use after a recent SI session influences the teacher's willingness to conduct SI in the future.

So far we have demonstrated that LLS are situated in contexts and that they have the characteristics of complex systems. We now turn to a different but related part of LLS: imagination.

2. The importance of imagination for strategic L2 learning

The word *imagination* is based on the word *image*, or picture, conception, idea, impression, or graphic or vivid representation or description (Merriam-Webster 2016a). An *image*, or *imagery* in general, need not be related to the sense of sight but can involve other modalities as well (Dörnyei and Chan 2013). *Imagination* relates to the ability to form a picture in the mind of something one has not experienced by the senses; creative ability; ability to deal with a problem; and the act of forming an image in the mind (Merriam-Webster 2016b). The famous physicist Albert Einstein saw himself as an artist because of his imagination, which he believed to be a central force in his creative work. He stated, "I am enough of the artist to draw freely upon my imagination. Imagination is more important than knowledge. Knowledge is limited. Imagination encircles the world" (cited by Nilsson 2010). In addition to meaning the physical ability to see, *vision* refers to something that is imagined (Merriam-Webster 2016c). A vision can come to any of the senses, i.e., hearing, sight, smell, taste, and touch.

Imagination and vision help learners mentally contact their "possible selves," e.g., future selves, present and past selves, and ought-to selves (see Dörnyei 2009; Dörnyei and Chan 2013; Dörnyei and Ryan 2015). With the aid of their own imaginations and SI, L2 learners can feel their motivation, identify their learning needs, select from a range of LLS to meet those needs, implement those strategies, recognize when they have made progress, and keep the cycle going.

3. Imagining strategies: Seeing context and complexity

This part of the chapter employs imagination and vision to reveal strategies' contexts and complexity. It does so by means of strategy-focused photographs known as AIMS, "Amazing IMages of Strategies." Here we offer guidelines for using AIMS to develop learners' strategy awareness, which emerges during the first stage of SI. However, some highly perceptive, self-knowing learners are already somewhat aware of their own strategies even without SI.

The photos in this section are in black and white, although our homepage[4] contains them in full color. The homepage also contains an array of other AIMS photos for your use, always copyright free. From now on we use "AIMS" to refer to both the photographs and the strategy awareness process that employs the photos.

3.1. Some guidelines for using AIMS

Here are some flexible guidelines for employing AIMS.

- *Who should be involved?* Let's assume you are the AIMS leader, i.e., the knowledgeable person who wants to help L2 learners or L2 teachers become aware of LLS. The same general AIMS guidelines apply when you are working with current and future L2 teachers who know little about strategies. However, you might want to speak to them differently.[5]
- *Should teachers and students be included in the same AIMS session?* It is possible, but it is probably not a good idea.
- *What if some AIMS participants are already quite aware of strategies?* If some AIMS participants are more familiar than other participants with strategies, it is fine. AIMS can then be used as an entertaining way to help them understand their strategies more deeply. If it is a mixed group, those who are more aware of strategies can serve as mentors or add more to the conversation.
- *In what language should the session be conducted?* If possible, the session should be conducted in the native language of the participants or a language that they know well. When it is necessary to use a language that participants are currently learning, be sure to give all the support necessary. One benefit of an AIMS session is the communication that occurs through photos.
- *What should be the tone of an AIMS session?* Avoid lecturing about LLS and discussing any technical categories (cognitive, affective, and such). Never link AIMS to a test situation. An AIMS session should be warm, welcoming, exciting, understandable, and nonthreatening. It should encourage participation by all.
- *What if people from one gender or certain cultures are silent during the discussions?* Depending on the group, be sure to include photos that are appealing to men, to women, and to both, as well as photos that reflect the

cultures in your group. There are many online outlets for obtaining copyright-free, free-of-charge photos that are relevant to your AIMS participants.[6] Be aware, though, that some participants will likely be less talkative than others no matter what.

- *What are some activities in the first AIMS session?* See the reports of AIMS sessions that we have conducted. You might use the photos in Figures 1.1 through 1.3, which show a person on the moon, building blocks, and a flower. Other photos we have used are a group of penguins, a person juggling, ice crystals, a person climbing a mountain, a sailboat on the water, and tunnels. Hundreds more photos are possible for use as AIMS. Include questions as shown on the slides, along with the photos. We have found that the questions and the photos, when used together, stimulate a flow of discussion that helps AIMS participants become increasingly aware of LLS. Many participants are intrigued, especially upon recognizing that they already use some helpful strategies. This discovery learning process often captivates participants.

- *Open with a warm-up or "hook" activity.* One very effective way to do this is to ask students to learn quickly ten words that you give them in a rare language, and then ask them to explain how they did this (the strategies they used). A different "hook" activity consists of rapid-fire brainstorming. Ask participants to brainstorm what they think "strategy" or "learning strategy" means. (They usually say things like this: "A strategy is an action," "A strategy has a goal," "A strategy helps me achieve something," or "I use a strategy to make things easier.") You could also remind participants that they use strategies all the time, for learning and many other purposes. Ask them what they use strategies for. (Participants might mention strategies for getting to work on time, strategies for winning in sports or games, strategies for finishing tasks on the job, strategies for getting along with a spouse or boyfriend/girlfriend, or even strategies for trying to get a winning lottery ticket.)

- *Now use the photos to start a deeper discussion about strategies.* Present six to twelve photos (see Figures 1.1–1.3, as well as any photos from the large selection on our homepage) to participants in an easy, relaxed, non-stressful way, usually by projecting them onto a large screen or wall. Although these photos at first seem to have little or nothing to do with strategies, they have been selected to illustrate very specific features of LLS—characteristics that would not be instantly obvious to participants but which they could soon understand.

AIMS – **A**mazing **IM**ages of **S**trategies

Person on the Moon

Sample questions:

- What is happening in this photo?
- What physical senses or emotions arise when you look at the photo?
- How does this photo relate to learning strategies?
- What is complex about this photo?

Figure 1.1 AIMS slide: Person on the moon
Source: photorack.net, copyright-free

AIMS – **A**mazing **IM**ages of **S**trategies

Building Blocks

Sample questions:

- What is happening in this photo?
- What physical senses or emotions arise when you look at the photo?
- How does this photo relate to learning strategies?
- What is complex about this photo?

Figure 1.2 AIMS slide: Building blocks
Source: Martin Bagar, with permission

AIMS – **A**mazing **IM**ages of **S**trategies

Flower

Sample questions:

- What is happening in this photo?
- What physical senses or emotions arise when you look at the photo?
- How does this photo relate to learning strategies?
- What is complex about this photo?

Figure 1.3 AIMS slide: Flower
Source: Clifford Stocking, with permission

Tell participants, "Now you will be using photos to brainstorm the features of strategies. There are no correct or incorrect answers. No one will be judged. I am interested in your responses as a group. To help you, I will ask you some questions." The questions on the figures are: *What is happening in this photo? What physical senses or emotions arise when you look at this photo? How does this photo relate to learning strategies? What is complex about this photo?* In response to the last question, participants might point out some elements of complexity, though they will not use any technical terms and have not generally had any training in complexity theory. They might mention the way an object or person is situated in the environment in the photo; the interconnections among multiple, diverse elements; patterns emerging from interactions; dynamism (movement, change, fluctuation, surprises, unpredictability) or moments of stability; and the openness of the system to growth and modification with information from other systems. Not all these features will be mentioned, but AIMS participants in the past have thought of at least some of them when looking at the photos. If your participants mention any complexity-related features, be sure to point out why these features are important.

- *Provide scaffolding if participants need it.* We have never encountered a situation in which participants could not answer the questions creatively and with interest. However, if participants need help on the first slide, which might be the astronaut walking on the moon, you could say something like this, leading the participants by the hand: *Let's think about what is happening in this photo. This person is walking on the moon. How do you think the person feels emotionally or physically (lost, overwhelmed, tired, excited, etc.)? What strategies could the person use to help himself or herself walk on the moon more effectively? Have you ever felt like the person on the moon when you are learning your new language? How did you feel exactly? What strategies do you usually use for learning your new language? What seems complex about this photo?* As soon as possible, move to having participants just answer the questions on the next slide. You will want the participants to give all the information (their responses to the questions on the slides) more independently.

- *Consider what participants are doing.* In talking about the photos and answering the questions on the slides, participants are developing their own personalized, inventive, imaginative meanings about LLS purposes and features. Their strategy awareness is increasing, sometimes dramatically. Ask someone in the group to take notes or record if desired.

- *Organize participants' contributions and give feedback.* Toward the end of the AIMS session, systematize what the participants have said about the photos. To do this, summarize aloud what the participants have said. For example, you might say something like this, but you must tailor it to what the participants actually stated and to the specific photos you used: *While we were looking at the photos, this group said that strategies give us power, strength, and light. Strategies let us swim in the sea of learning. Strategies take us places we have never gone before. They take us up the stairs of understanding. They help us maneuver in difficult spots. They help us learn, explore, and grow. They make us feel lighter because we are more successful. They are sometimes complex to help us in hard, complex situations. We can learn them from people who know more than we do.* Do not merely read these statements aloud. Express them with feeling and interest! Build your own statements on what participants have said when they looked at the photos. Explain to the participants that they have just uncovered the main features of LLS. If you have time, open up a participant discussion about what they learned.
- *Alternatively, ask participants to summarize their contributions.* If you have a mature group that takes initiative, ask participants to identify their overarching learnings based on reactions to the photos. Then ask them to explain these learnings aloud or act out these learnings, always with feeling and meaning.
- *Ask students to complete a simple questionnaire* (Table 1.1) *to consolidate their learning from the first AIMS session.*

3.2. Informal AIMS studies

Rebecca Oxford used online photos (prior to the current AIMS photo set) to increase the strategy awareness of university EFL learners, university EFL teachers, and teacher education students in four workshops in Poland and Turkey and other workshops in the U.S. Very few participants were aware of the term *learning strategies.* The photos included: (a) a giant tree with a twisted trunk, (b) a toolbox, (c) a jockey and horse jumping over a barrier, (d) a man walking on the moon, (e) a woman jumping across a dangerous gap between mountains, (f) a swirling piece of multicolored cloth, (g) a plane breaking the sound barrier, (h) a key, (i) a strong person carrying a heavy load, (j) a shining prism, (k) a woman triumphant after a race, and (l) an arrow. Informal

Table 1.1 Post-AIMS questionnaire (adapt as needed)

Date and Location (or Institution)

Dear AIMS Participant,

We are delighted that you came today to learn about language learning strategies. We would like to ask you to answer a few questions about your experience. You do not have to give your name. Please answer all the questions.

1. How much did you know about strategies *before* the session today? Put an X or a check mark somewhere on the line.

    A lot _____ Not much

2. How much did you learn about strategies *during* the session today? Put an X or a check mark somewhere on the line.

    A lot _____ Not much

3. How much did you like the session today? Put an X or a check mark somewhere on the line.

    A lot _____ Not much

4. How much did you like the photographs? Put an X or a check mark somewhere on the line.

    A lot _____ Not much

5. What are the three things you liked the most about the session?

6. What, if anything, do you suggest for us to change?

7. What other comments would you like to share?

---

observations indicated that the photos and the discussions touched participants' imaginations and sparked their interest in strategies. Typical examples of learners' comments (as they described LLS based on the photos) included: *Strategies help me do things, help me go new places, open doors, are tools, are keys, are bright, help me speak,* and *make me feel good.* EFL teachers and teacher education students used similar descriptions but also gave others: *Strategies have to fit the task, Strategies have many facets. Strategies help learners go where they have never gone before, put the choice in learners' hands, help learners overcome obstacles, help learners achieve difficult things, ease the load,* and *are not an extra burden. You might not need a strategy if you have done the same thing many times. Learners shift strategies as needed. One strategy does not fit all circumstances. You've got to be awake and motivated to use strategies, and strategies make you more motivated.*

Oxford also conducted a formal, 90-minute AIMS session with ESL teachers and one Chinese teacher, all studying in a master's program at the University of Alabama at Birmingham (USA). Due to space limitations in this chapter, a different publication will report on this AIMS session and its outcomes.

3.3. AIMS at Alpen-Adria-Universität Klagenfurt, Austria (AAU)

A formal AIMS session was conducted at the English Department at the Faculty of Humanities at Alpen-Adria-Universität Klagenfurt (AAU) in Austria. AAU is a national university with a current enrollment of 10,319 students, of whom 113 are studying to become EFL teachers at secondary level.

3.3.1. *Purposes*

The purposes were to raise awareness of LLS and to collect reactions to AIMS from a group of European EFL learners.

3.3.2. *Context*

The AIMS session occurred in the introductory lesson of a language teaching methodology course. It was led by Carmen Amerstorfer.

3.3.3. *Participants*

The participants were thirteen female and two male EFL teacher education students. Two participants were exchange students from Spain and Serbia (with respective L1s) who were studying to become EFL teachers in their countries of origin. The rest were Austrian (L1 German) and enrolled in the teacher education program at the Department of English. Most participants were in their early twenties; however, two participants were experienced classroom teachers (one primary school teacher and one teacher of Spanish and French as a foreign language at secondary level) and approximately 30 years of age. The participants' minimum EFL proficiency level was B2 (CEFR), and all knew at least one other foreign language.

3.3.4. *Methodology of the AIMS session*

The 120-minute session started with a warm-up activity, in which the participants memorized ten Quechua (a South American language) words within two minutes. After an informal exchange of the memorization strategies used, the group discussed definitions of LLS.

Then the participants were invited to verbally express their thoughts about ten AIMS, i.e., the images of a person on the moon (Figure 1.1), building blocks (Figure 1.2), a flower (Figure 1.3), and the following figures found on the homepage: penguins, a person juggling, a person climbing on a mountainside, a sailboat, ice crystals, a tortoise, and tunnels.

One after the other, the ten images were projected onto a screen. The participants used the guiding questions on the slides smoothly and flexibly as the basis for an enthusiastic conversation about strategies. They talked without much interference by the instructor and finally completed the post-AIMS questionnaire.

Amerstorfer invited participants to do a follow-up activity outside of the session: taking and explaining their own strategy-related photos, which could be used as part of future AIMS sessions.

3.3.5 *Results of the AIMS discussion*

The AIMS inspired the participants' imagination and caused a lively group discussion about different strategy functions, contextual influences, and the complexity and dynamic nature of the topic. For example, movement was detected in the image of the *flower* (the first slide shown) because it "opens and closes every day." One student imagined herself at the center of a water lily floating in a pond (i.e., context) with the petals symbolizing influencing factors. One student said, "You look at the image and your brain starts searching for the English word for it [the water lily]." Some students tried to translate the German word rather than think about strategies. Another said, "The image triggers memories of when you've seen water lilies before." At that stage in the AIMS session (the showing of the first slide), the students had not yet started thinking about strategies and did not link the flower to strategies.

The *ice crystals* presented on the second slide were described as "unique" with a sense of "simple complexity." One participant noted that "ice crystals grow and develop further, which shows learning strategies. They get more specific and more beautiful."

The third slide offered *building blocks*, which were associated with a solid foundation required for L2 learning. LLS, symbolized by building blocks in different shapes and colors, can be ordered and re-ordered as necessary in specific situations.

The photo of *a person juggling* (the fourth slide) was associated with learner agency, "being in charge" and "being in control." The image was described as "balancing strategies and deciding and weighing out which strategy to use when."

The image of *a person climbing*, shown on the fifth slide, triggered comments about physical and mental effort, risk taking, "moving forward in a step-by-step process," strategic planning, and changing the plan "so you don't get stuck."

About the image of a *sailing boat*, the sixth slide presented, one participant cited multiple strategies when saying, "You have to have the right position of the sail to get the most force to go forward. Sometimes you have to adapt to environmental circumstances. If it's a bigger boat, you have to work together with other people [...] You're a part of a team."

The *penguins* on the seventh slide were mainly related to social and coping strategies. One student said, "This picture expresses adapting strategies from other people or from the environment." Another explained, "It shows coping strategies in difficult situations. The inner penguins move towards the outer circle where it is cold, and inside it is warm. And the ones who are on the outer edge move inside. They move all the time so that they keep warm. It's a great strategy! And it's all dynamic."

The *tortoise*, included as the eighth slide, was understood as "a symbol for being strong" and for "resilience." Participants suggested, "continue learning even if it's hard," "never give up," and "take some time to develop your own strategies." One participant noted that through evolution the tortoise "has adapted to its environment" and "is perfectly fitted to exist." Another student, who usually avoids speaking in a group, mentioned that a tortoise can hide in its shell.

The *person on the moon*, seen as the ninth slide, was understood as a metaphor for exploring new strategies. Like exploring outer space requires team support, foreign language learning requires a teacher and other speakers of the language. Other associations were being brave and continuing to try regardless of temporary failure.

The *tunnels*, offered as the tenth slide, demonstrated motivation, the metaphorical "light at the end of the tunnel," and that "everything will be fine in the end." They were further associated with taking shortcuts, i.e., to "go through the mountain instead of over it." One participant emphasized the process of learning a foreign language: "You shouldn't only think about the goal but also about *how* you get there." Another one analyzed that driving through a dark tunnel is like trying to solve a problem. With "learning strategies, you can get to the light." Their comments were abundant. Interestingly, this image took the longest to elicit any comments. The AIMS leader already wanted to skip it, but the participants asked to go back, and then the comments came flooding in.

Concluding their AIMS discussion, the group emphasized that strategic language learning requires learning from others, similar to learning how to sail, juggle, or climb. Participants noted that strategic learning also involves knowing where they are going, deciding best strategies to take, and flexibly moving to new strategies if current ones do not work. Being strategic in learning necessitates responsibility, confidence, resilience, coping, and hoping for a good outcome.

3.3.6. Highlights of the post-AIMS questionnaire

The questionnaire showed that the participants had different knowledge about LLS *before* the AIMS session (Q1) but all of them learned something *during* the session (Q2). On a continuum graph from "a lot" to "not much", all participants made marks in the top third when asked how much they liked the AIMS session (Q3) and the images (Q4). Comments about their learning gains during the AIMS session (Q5) included complexity, awareness, and teachability. The participants further highlighted that individual preferences influence strategy choice and that strategies can be learned, improved, and shared. The participants were genuinely interested in learning more about strategies, particularly about SI, individual learner characteristics (e.g., age, learner types), and how strategies can be adapted to different learning situations (Q6). The general feedback about the AIMS session was very positive (Q8). The only recommendation for improvement was to include more images (Q7).

Specific results of the post-AIMS questionnaire are available from the chapter authors.

3.4. AIMS at the University of Maryland (USA)

An AIMS session was conducted in a Spanish class in the Department of Spanish and Portuguese in the School of Languages, Literatures and Cultures at the University of Maryland College Park (UMD) in the United States. UMD is a Carnegie I Research University with more than 38,000 students. There are approximately 140 undergraduate Spanish majors and 264 undergraduate Spanish minors. Roberta Lavine led the AIMS session, assisted by Rae Lan.[8]

3.4.1. Purposes

The purposes were to raise awareness of LLS and to collect reactions to AIMS from a group of Spanish language and literature learners.

3.4.2. Context

The AIMS session occurred during one class session in a 400-level Spanish literature class after two months of the semester. Although the class is taught in Spanish, the AIMS training session was conducted in English for consistency.

3.4.3. Participants

The participants were ten female and two male Spanish language students. All were bilingual and at least three were trilingual. The participants' Spanish proficiency levels were in the B2—C2 (CEFR) ranges.

3.4.4. Methodology of the AIMS session

The 75-minute session started with introductions, followed by the same warm-up activity previously described for AAU, the memorization of ten Quechua words within two minutes. Students worked in groups of three to informally discuss the strategies they used to memorize the words, after which they reported them to the class.

Learners then worked in groups of three to discuss examples of how they used strategies in one of the following areas: their everyday life, to learn languages, or to understand literature. The whole class then discussed the idea of strategies vs. strategy and ways to explore strategies as an interrelated and complex system.

In a whole class context, students discussed an image of an astronaut (the person walking on the moon) while using the sample questions as a guide. The participants were then invited to verbally express their thoughts about specific AIMS. In different groups of three, each triad explored one of the following: building blocks, a person juggling, penguins, and a tunnel. Showing their image, each group presented the members' ideas, and a short class discussion followed.

Lavine announced a follow-up "photo search" activity involving participants in looking for online photos that reminded them of LLS. These photos could contribute to future AIMS awareness sessions. Finally, the participants took the post-AIMS questionnaire.

3.4.5. *Results of the AIMS warm-up activities and discussion*

In the Quechua warm-up activity, interesting strategies arose. A few were association, sounds, context, location, and visual images. Students generated their own definition of LLS: "conscious processes we use to learn with deliberate actions."

For the question of how the photo of the *person on the moon* relates to LLS, there were many valuable comments, such as: taking steps, exploring new territories, discovering something new, using trial and error to succeed or fail, being able to be out of one's comfort zone, and looking beyond a shared context. The AIMS motivated an extensive group discussion about different strategies, the process of learning and succeeding and its complexity.

The *building blocks*, presented next, were described as essential pieces that provide the flexibility to move parts of language around to express individual thoughts. Students talked about needing stability (stable blocks) to help them analyze literature (build higher).

Juggling, presented as the third slide, inspired a discussion about multitasking and keeping everything going at once. In terms of strategies, the students reflected on how they must employ all parts of language (e.g., grammar, vocabulary, content, and pragmatics) needed to "juggle" in order to communicate.

The *penguins*, offered as the fourth image, generated responses quite similar to those in the AAU AIMS session. Participants in Maryland, as in Austria, viewed penguins as related to social interaction strategies, as well as strategies to understand culture. Learners examined the idea of a social group and how hard it is to understand another culture. They commented on the collective nature of the picture, how the penguins appeared to support one another and the pairs were situated close to each other, drawing parallels with norms of Spanish-speaking environments.

The *tunnel* was presented as the fifth and final image of this AIMS session. The tunnel elicited feelings of light and peacefulness. Students talked about the open road and the lack of traffic bringing ease. They talked about seeing the light at the end of the tunnel (the process in the dark before seeing the light) and equating it to the hard work of finally understanding something.

Almost every student commented about AIMS leading to discussion and collaboration, actions that they thought could help them understand the deeper meaning of the literature read for class. They also remarked that naming some of the strategies reminded them of what they already do and that listening to their classmates built new strategies for success.

3.4.6. Highlights of post-AIMS questionnaire

The questionnaire showed that the participants had varying amounts of knowledge about L2 LLS *before* the AIMS session (Q1). All participants learned something during the session (Q2). Participants indicated that they liked the AIMS session and the images very much (Q3 and Q4). The next question (Q5) asked participants for three things they liked the most about the AIMS session. A few highlights focus on how the images and a visual context encourage analysis and making connections; how using the images as a basis for collaboration motivates new ideas and interactions; and how working with the images assists in concretizing learning as a complex process. The final query (Q6) simply asked for comments. The comments were very positive, focusing on the relationship between analyzing the pictures and opportunities for creativity. One student said, "The photos are a bit abstract, and make you really think how it can relate to the questions asked. It is an opportunity for discussion groups to come up with really good and creative ideas and thoughts." Another learner stated, "Excellent project. [I] never thought a simple penguin picture could have so much to analyze!" Feedback from participants showed that they thought AIMS was a great way to connect with students.

Additionally, Rae Lan made the following suggestions for the future concerning the Maryland AIMS session: (a) Allow students more time for sharing the strategies that they used for memorizing the Quechua words. (b) When participants share their answers to the questions on a given slide, ask them to come to the front to discuss the slide. (See other suggestions by Lan in section 4.3.)

4. Conclusions

Here we share a summary of the chapter, followed by ideas for future AIMS research and suggestions for future AIMS activities.

4.1. Summary

This chapter aimed at imagining and envisioning LLS in ways that reveal their situatedness in authentic contexts and their complex interrelationships with other aspects of learning and the learner. To some degree participants mentioned features of complexity when analyzing the photos, although not, of course, using technical terms. The visual sense has been extremely important in this chapter; in fact, photographs have been the focal point for intensive discussions and entertaining activities. This chapter is intended to encourage readers to keep expanding the strategic vision and imagination, work toward greater understanding of the role of strategies as a complex system within other complex systems, and help students use their imagination as they discern their own needs and decide which strategies to use. Though we designed AIMS primarily to awaken strategy awareness in L2 learners, in some cases the photographs and the process could be used for the professional development of L2 teachers.

Our experimentation with AIMS has shown that a combination of strategy-focused instructional actions (warm-up activities, use of images and questions simultaneously, an intensive discussion, possible small group work, and a concluding, reflective questionnaire) proved to be very helpful in increasing participants' strategy awareness. Participants were future EFL teachers in the Austrian AIMS session and students of Spanish language and literature in the Maryland AIMS session, as well as a range of people and ages in the informal AIMS sessions in Poland and Turkey. The similarity of some of the comments in AIMS sessions in distant sites was remarkable. Some comments in the discussions indicated an awareness of (a) the tremendous complexity and difficulty of learning languages and cultures and (b) the aid that LLS offer to deal with those issues. Participants felt energized and inspired by the AIMS sessions and believed that images were a spark to strategy awareness.

4.2. Future AIMS research ideas

In-depth research with AIMS in the future could include questions such as the following:

- How do participants respond to AIMS? What do they learn from it?
- What do they like or dislike about the photos? What do they like or dislike about the discussions and other activities?
- Which specific combinations of instructional activities might work most effectively for which kinds of participants, and why?
- To what extent and in what ways do participants use their imaginations through AIMS to understand the general concept of strategy (purpose, nature, contexts of use, complexity, etc.)?
- To what extent and in what ways are participants already using LLS? Do participants want to go further to learn about strategies and find out how to use them?
- How can AIMS, as a strategy-awareness process, ease the way for more detailed SI?
- How would someone effectively describe the AIMS process to a colleague who knows very little about LLS? How would the person explain AIMS to a colleague who knows a significant amount about LLS?
- How could technology be optimally deployed in an AIMS session?
- How can AIMS be adapted for different situations and groups?
- How do existing strategy-awareness practices on various continents compare with AIMS?
- What would need to be adapted in order to use AIMS in professional development for L2 teachers who are unfamiliar with LLS?

Well-crafted observation scales, learner diaries, AIMS leader diaries, interviews, video analyses, and quantitative and qualitative surveys could be useful to answer these questions.

4.3. Suggestions for future AIMS activities

First, ask one of the participants in an AIMS session to write down all the strategies mentioned during the session. The list could then be thematically arranged, shared with all participants in the session, and used later for AIMS sessions or SI sessions. Second, conclude an AIMS session by giving students an interesting handout to take home with them, thus enhancing their interest in strategies, helping them to organize their thinking, and encouraging them to learn more about strategies. These recommendations came from Rae Lan.

Third, if you wish to increase the focus on complexity, explain a few features of complex systems (e.g., situatedness, openness, dynamism, interconnectedness, and adaptiveness) in relation to the first couple of AIMS slides. However, use these terms sparingly, if at all; it might be better to employ terms that are less technical (e.g., for dynamism, use "movement" or "change"). With some background in complexity gained from such discussions about the first couple of slides, participants will be more able to identify complexity features in other slides.

Fourth, ask participants to bring in drawings, photos, or videos that remind them of LLS. These are new additions to the AIMS bank! Please send us copies to increase our shareable, global bank of AIMS materials.[7] Variations on this theme were done with groups in Austria (the post-AIMS photo shoot) and Maryland (the post-AIMS online photo search). If possible, ask participants to discuss their new AIMS contributions online or at the AIMS group's next session. If you desire, ask students to mention the strategy principle, feature, or connection that they recognize in their innovative contribution.

Fifth, ask participants to discuss strategies they often use, how they decide to use those strategies, and what the outcomes are. Ask them to make attractive posters with those three topics (strategies, reason, and outcome).

Sixth, consider the following two drama-related options. Option A: AIMS participants role-play someone from an image, e.g., a moonwalker, someone passing through a tunnel, a juggler, or a mountain climber, and then discuss how strategies relate to the action. Option B: Participants act out the use of specific strategies inspired by their favorite AIMS images.

Seventh, conduct a "Dear Abby" or "Agony Aunt" LLS activity, which was created by the first author and typically works very well. In this activity, each AIMS participant writes a letter about his or her greatest problems in L2 learning and signs a creative name, such as "Gary Loves German," "Curious Carmen," "Forever Seeking Strategies," "Confused in Cincinnati," "Romeo," "Theresa of Downing Street," "Sherlock," or "ESL Ellie." The zanier the name, the better. Participants put their letters in a "mailbox" (any box or table top will do). Everyone then becomes a Dear Abby or Agony Aunt, picks up a problem letter from the mailbox, and writes back to the original sender, making suggestions about strategies that could be used to solve the learning problem. (If the participants are teachers, it is possible to adapt this activity so that they write letters about problems that their students have in L2 learning. Then each Dear Abby / Agony Aunt writes back to suggest the strategies the teacher should teach the students to solve the problem.) Lead a discussion to help participants think about what they learned.

Eighth, show participants a large picture of the three-phase task triangle (in Oxford 2017). It contains these phases: forethought, performance, and self-reflection. Ask participants to brainstorm specific strategies that would go into each part.

Ninth, ask participants to spend three to five minutes at the end of each day writing down their LLS for that day in a strategy diary. Ask them to discuss their strategy diaries during an AIMS session. Working together, participants in the session could create color-coded posters to organize their strategies. Example: red for reading strategies, yellow for listening strategies, green for writing strategies, and so on. A different way to divide strategies might be used, but *avoid technical terms* such as "affective," "cognitive," and so on.

Tenth, conduct any of the large array of strategy-awareness activities in Oxford (1990).

Eleventh, find images of strategies that are free and unrestricted for personal and commercial purposes. Describe in your own words how the images show strategies. Remember to provide the source and access date for all images. Save these images for the next AIMS session you conduct.[8]

Notes

1   As we use it, the abbreviation LLS can be either singular or plural.
2   The metastrategic function includes planning, organizing, monitoring, and evaluating. This function is *above* ("meta") the other four functions in the sense that it generally amplifies or aids those other functions (see Oxford 2017). For a given strategy, such as analyzing, these functions can change rapidly, even while the learner is working on a specific L2 task. The strategy of analyzing can be used for multiple functions. Examples: to solve a cognitive-linguistic problem, to help the learner address an emotional (affective) problem, and to analyze a task as part of metacognitive planning.
3   Some complex systems, such as the universe or multiple universes, are so large that the mind can hardly comprehend them; other complex systems, such as body cells, are too small to be visible without special equipment (Oxford 2017).
4   Our homepage, managed by Alpen-Adria-Universität Klagenfurt, is https://conference.aau.at/event/9/
5   Some teachers, but not all, might not want to talk about their own LLS. They might feel more comfortable talking about their students' strategies.
6   Some include: http://photorack.net/index.php and https://www.shopify.com/blog/17156388–22-awesome-websites-with-stunning-free-stock-images
7   For ease of contact, use email: rebeccaoxford@gmail.com, carmen.amerstorfer@aau.at

8 Rae Lan, PhD, is Associate Professor and the Director of the Language Center at the Department of Foreign Languages and Applied Linguistics at National Taipei University, Taipei, Taiwan.

References

Bailly, Sophie. Guest Editor. 2012. "Numéro Spécial: Didactique des Langues et Complexité: en Hommage à Richard Duda" [Special issue: Language Teaching and Complexity—in Honor of Richard Duda]. *Mélanges CRAPEL*, 33.

Bronfenbrenner, Urie. 1979. *The Ecology of Human Development: Experiments by Nature and Design*. Cambridge, MA: Harvard University Press.

——. 1989. "Ecological Systems Theory." In *Annals of Child Development Vol. 6: Theories of Child Development: Revised Formulations and Current Issues*. 6th edition, edited by Ross Vasta. Hoboken, NJ: Wiley.

——. 2005. *Making Human Beings Human: Bioecological Perspectives on Human Development*. Thousand Oaks, CA: SAGE.

Bronfenbrenner, Urie, and Pamela A. Morris. 2006. *The Bioecological Model of Human Development*. Handbook of Child Psychology, Vol. 1, 793–828. doi: 10.1002/9780470147658.chpsy0114

De Bot, Kees, ed. 2008. Special Issue: Second Language Development as a Dynamic Process. *Modern Language Journal* 92: 166–78.

Dörnyei, Zoltán. 2009. *The Psychology of Second Language Acquisition*. New York: Oxford University Press.

Dörnyei, Zoltán, and Letty Chan. 2013. "Motivation and Vision: An Analysis of Future L2 Self Images, Sensory Styles, and Imagery Capacity across Two Target Languages." *Language Learning* 63(3): 437–62. doi: 10.1111/lang.12005

Dörnyei, Zoltán, and Stephen Ryan. 2015. *The Psychology of the Language Learner Revisited*. New York: Routledge.

Finch, Andrew. 2004. "Complexity and Systems Theory: Implications for the EFL Teacher/Researcher." *Journal of Asia TEFL* 1(2): 27–46. http://www.finchpark.com/arts/complexity-and-systems-EFL.pdf

Hiver, Phil. 2015. "Attractor States." In *Motivational Dynamics in Language Learning*, edited by Zoltán Dörnyei, Peter D. MacIntyre, and Alastair Henry, 20–28. Bristol: Multilingual Matters.

Kramsch, Claire. 2002. "Introduction: How Can We Tell the Dancer from the Dance?" In *Language Socialization and Acquisition: Ecological Perspectives*, edited by Claire Kramsch, 1–30. London: Continuum.

Larsen-Freeman, Diane. 1997. "Chaos/Complexity Science and Second Language Acquisition." *Applied Linguistics* 18 (2): 141–65.

——. 2015. "Ten 'Lessons' from Complex Dynamic Systems Theory: What Is on Offer." In *Motivational Dynamics in Language Learning*, edited by Zoltán Dörnyei, Peter D. MacIntyre, and Alastair Henry, 24–43. Bristol: Multilingual Matters.

——. 2017. "Complexity Theory: The Lessons Continue." In *Complexity Theory and Language Development: In Honor of Diane Larsen-Freeman*, edited by Lourdes Ortega and ZhaoHong Han. Amsterdam: John Benjamins.

Merriam-Webster Dictionary. 2016a. "Image." Accessed August 15, 2016. http://www.merriam-webster.com/dictionary/image

——. 2016b. "Imagination." Accessed August 15, 2016. http://www.merriam-webster.com/dictionary/imagination

——. 2016c. "Vision." Accessed August 15, 2016. http://www.merriam-webster.com/dictionary/vision

Nilsson, Jeff. 2010. "Imagination Is More Important Than Knowledge." *The Saturday Evening Post*, March 20. http://www.saturdayeveningpost.com/2010/03/20/history/post-perspective/imagination-important-knowledge.html

Ortega, Lourdes, and ZhaoHong Han, eds. 2017. *Complexity Theory and Language Development: In Honor of Diane Larsen-Freeman*. Amsterdam: John Benjamins.

Oxford, Rebecca L. 1990. *Language Learning Strategies: What Every Teacher Should Know*. Boston: Heinle & Heinle.

——. 2017. *Teaching and Researching Language Learning Strategies: Self-Regulation in Context*. 2nd edition, New York: Routledge.

Ushioda, Ema. 2009. "A Person-in-Context Relational View of Emergent Motivation, Self and Identity." In *Motivation, Language Identity and the L2 Self*, edited by Zoltán Dörnyei and Ema Ushioda, 215–28. Bristol: Multilingual Matters.

——. 2015. "Context and Complex Dynamic Systems Theory." In *Motivational Dynamics in Language Learning*, edited by Zoltán Dörnyei, Peter D. MacIntyre, and Alastair Henry, 64–71. Bristol: Multilingual Matters.

van Lier, Leo. 2004. *The Ecology and Semiotics of Language Learning: A Sociocultural Perspective*. New York: Springer.

Wenger, Etienne. 1998. *Communities of Practice: Learning, Meaning, and Identity*. Cambridge: Cambridge University Press.

2

Moving from Theory to Practice

A Closer Look at Language Learner Strategies

Andrew D. Cohen
University of Minnesota, USA

1. Introduction

This chapter provides an overview of some key issues with regard to theoretical notions of language learner strategies and then segues into more practical applications. As always, my underlying concern is with language learning and the language learner. So, first the focus will be on theoretical issues regarding language learner strategies, followed by the issue of how to conduct strategy instruction. The next concern will be the role of teachers in strategy instruction, and by extension, the part that strategy instruction research plays in the equation. Finally, I will take a personal look at my own language learner strategies in learning my thirteenth language, Mandarin.

2. Theoretical issues concerning language learner strategies

The construct *language learner strategies* (LLS) has been defined—and consequently researched—in numerous ways over the years. My own current working definition is:

> thoughts and actions, consciously chosen and operationalized by language learners, to assist them in carrying out a multiplicity of tasks from the very onset of learning to the most advanced levels of target-language (TL) performance.
>
> Cohen 2011, 7[1]

In my mind, the element of consciousness is what distinguishes strategies from processes that are not strategic. The element of choice is crucial because this is what gives a strategy its special character. Macaro (2006) offered a level of rigor uncommon in describing and discussing LLS, not only linking them to specific tasks, but also raising the issue of whether LLS function in isolation or rather as part of a sequence or cluster. My opinion about LLS definitions: they should clarify, not obfuscate. It helps move the action along into the realm of practice to use definitions that lay language learners can understand.

Dörnyei and others resoundingly criticized the LLS field for not having an adequate theoretical basis. Oxford (1999, 2011, 2017) linked LLS with individual students' autonomy and self-regulation,[2] and Griffiths (2013) tied LLS to individual differences, learning context, goals, and the real world of the classroom. Most recently, in his new joint volume with Ryan, Dörnyei now asserts that in the new individual differences landscape, LLS appear to sit much more comfortably than they did a decade ago, and so he feels that their role warrants careful re-examination, which is what he and Ryan offered in their 2015 book (Dörnyei and Ryan 2015).

Since strategies can be viewed as theoretically multifaceted, LLS enthusiasts are admonished not to indulge in attempts at clarification that oversimplify and thereby reduce the richness and predictive potential of what by its very nature is highly complex (Griffiths and Oxford 2014). It is ironic then how simplistically various strategies are actually labeled and referred to in practice. The LLS literature abounds with vague labels or statements like "I use inference" intended to convey a strategy, but actually referring more generally to a skill. *Skills* are the ability to do something. So "inference" as a skill is the ability to derive the meaning of something. The *strategies*, then, are the operationalization of the skill—that is, selected processes to actualize the skill. *Inferencing*, for example, takes a number of conscious strategies to pull off effectively. As an aside, when a *move* is no longer consciously selected, it is still a *process*, but in my view no longer a *strategy*. Research on the strategies associated with inferencing has identified no fewer than twelve types: analyzing, associating, repeating, using textual clues, using prior knowledge, paraphrasing, making inquiry, confirming/disconfirming, commenting, stating failure or difficulty, suspending judgments, and reattempting (Hu and Nassaji 2014).

As a language learner, I am mindful of what "operationalizing strategies" means. Each week I provide a series of ten journal entries on my life in Chinese, which I share with my three Chinese tandem partners (in *pinyin*, rather than in Chinese characters, which my 73-year-old brain is unable to cope with readily at this stage in my life). Dealing with Mandarin keeps me humble, and it keeps me in touch with the reality of LLS in the trenches, where it is crucial for me to use a host of reading and writing strategies. With regard to LLS labels, "use a dictionary" does not begin to get at the strategies that I use to journal about my life in Mandarin—rather, it entails a complicated back and forth between Google Translate, an online two-way dictionary, and feedback from my tandem partner to arrive at accurate word meanings, which are stored electronically in BYKI (a program by Transparent Language) according to word categories—nouns, verbs, adjectives, function words (adverbs, conjunctions, etc.), and measure words. I now have approximately 3,550 words (1,850 nouns, 800 verbs, 500 adjectives, 350 function words, and 50 measure words) entered into my own personal electronic English–Chinese dictionary. I draw on these regularly to write my weekly blog.

2.1. Ways to classify learner strategies

I have realized over the years that part of the difficulty in interpreting the LLS literature is that there are numerous different and often competing systems for classifying language strategies. Here are just three of these:

1. *By goal:* Strategies for *learning* the TL—for example, identifying, distinguishing, grouping, and memorizing strategies—and strategies for *using* the TL material that has already been learned—that is, strategies for performing your knowledge, such as retrieval, rehearsal, communicative, and cover strategies. The last are strategies for looking good, even when you do not have a clue as to what you are hearing, saying, reading, or writing.

2. *By function:* These are what have been referred to extensively in the literature as metacognitive, cognitive, affective, and social strategies. When addressing non-academics such as learners, I have referred to metacognitive strategies as "strategies for supervising the learning and use of the TL" (i.e., strategies for planning ahead, monitoring your performance, evaluating how it went). The important thing to notice here is that these four main functions are actually functions of what might be the very same strategy. So, for example, you use the strategy of "interrupting a conversation in the TL" when you are feeling left out. At any split second, the function of this interruption may be metacognitive (you are monitoring your behavior and have determined it is necessary to be more engaged in a conversation), cognitive (you are searching for the language material to use in order to interrupt the conversation), social (you are checking whether it is socially appropriate for you to be interrupting the speakers), or affective (you are feeling left out and want to do something about it). Note that the function can truly shift at a moment's

notice. So it is not necessarily the case that a strategy is immutably a metacognitive one but rather it takes on a metacognitive function.[3]

3. *By skill*: Listening, speaking, reading, writing, vocabulary, grammar, or translation strategies with regard to the TL. As with the function approach, the skill approach provides a popular way to classify strategies, especially with regard to the two productive and two receptive skills, plus the skill of vocabulary learning. Less attention is given to the skill areas of dealing with grammar and the use of translation, both of which can benefit greatly from well-placed strategies.

2.1.1. *Other ways to classify strategies*

- by age level and stages in life—with the implication that certain strategies may best be used by learners at different age ranges over a lifetime (e.g., strategies for younger learners, for teenagers, for adults, and for seniors).
- according to learners' proficiency levels—a rather difficult categorization since higher- and lower-proficiency learners may use the very same strategies, but employ them in sometimes subtly different ways with regard to the nature of their use and the quality derived from the use.
- by specific TLs where special strategies need to be mobilized by learners/ users. For examples, learners of Hebrew and Arabic need strategies for correctly marking the gender of verbs in all tenses in Hebrew and Arabic. This means, for instance, that speakers of Hebrew need to correctly perceive the gender of young children when addressing them.
- by strategy use reserved for interactions in the school culture, such as strategies for use in a lycée in France or in a pre-university cram school in Taiwan.
- according to their use with speakers of different varieties of the TL, such as by gender, age, socioeconomic status, occupation, religious sect, or geographic region.

2.2. The good language learner issue

Are strategies used in special ways by good language learners? My personal view is that whereas strategies are, in principle, available to everyone, super-learners take strategizing to a new level—so as to:

- have people think their pronunciation is native or nearly so in the TL,
- get the pragmatics right in numerous situations in the TL,
- have only negligible grammar errors in their oral language,

- have the vocabulary trip off their tongue relatively effortlessly in the TL,
- read effortlessly and then insightfully critique high-level reading material of keen interest in the TL,
- express themselves in written language at a native-like level in the TL (perhaps with some editing), and
- take a major role in a presentation and discussion about an academic topic entirely in the TL.

Especially in the U.S., there is the widespread phenomenon of language learners reaching a plateau with regard to their language proficiency, where they remain or attrite. They do not attain anything close to the levels that I enumerated above.

2.3. Individual differences in LLS use

What causes individual differences in LLS use? The truth is that there are a host of factors. The easy part is listing them. The real challenge is determining the extent to which any one of these factors is responsible for a learner's relative success at using a strategy or strategy sequence/cluster in a given TL instance:

- language proficiency (as suggested above),
- learning style preferences—since it is likely that having a propensity to prefer certain approaches to dealing with given language tasks will bring with it certain preferred strategies (see Cohen 2012a),
- the selection of just the right strategies for dealing with the task at hand and the relative success at using these strategies effectively,
- the learner's language aptitude configuration, since the relative aptitude of learners with regard to strategy use on given tasks can be influenced by how strong learners are with regard to working memory, associative memory, long-term memory retrieval, implicit learning, processing speed, and auditory perceptual acuity (see Linck et al. 2013),
- the learners' motivational configuration—that is, the interaction of motivation with numerous internal, social, and contextual factors (Dörnyei and Ushioda 2010),
- the learners' personality (see the narratives of Mark and Wanda in Oxford 2014),
- the impact of home life—such as the possibility of richer strategy development in a multilingual home (e.g., inference strategies becoming well-honed by incessantly having to distinguish two or more languages being spoken in a multilingual home; Grenfell and Harris 2015),[4] and

- the learners' own subjectivity with regard to the use or non-use of strategies from their repertoire (given the individual learners' sense of identity/agency; see Ishihara and Cohen 2014, 106).

So, given the array of individual differences named above (as well as gender), is it any wonder that learners differ in their selection and use of LLS? One can see how valuable a research project it would be to determine the extent to which each of these factors influences the use of given strategies in the completion of designated tasks.

3. How to conduct strategy instruction

In this section, we will consider strategy instruction (SI) handbooks, short courses and materials, the role of SI in TL pragmatics performance, the use of technology in SI, and strategies for enhancing test performance. It is important to note that what is referred to as SI in this volume was originally referred to as *styles- and strategies-based instruction* (SSBI) for two reasons: The first was that Oxford and I wanted to emphasize that it was important to view learning styles and strategies as being in partnership. Currently, while styles are addressed in most SI materials and courses, it is deemed unnecessary to include "styles" in the title. In addition, the use of the term "based" was to underscore the crucial role of strategies in instruction. Eventually, it was considered unnecessary to stress this issue.

3.1. SI Handbooks

It is inspiring to see that as of now there are some fine handbooks available for learners, replete with strategies for dealing with certain language skills. One such handbook was developed as a guide for reading and writing strategies for pupils in public schools in Singapore (Gu, Zhang, and Bai 2011). This guide provides instances of teachers modeling, for example, the specific strategies that help to operationalize the skill of inferencing: namely, identifying the problem, using contextual information to guess, using linguistic knowledge (i.e., "this is because . . ."), using world knowledge to guess, and evaluating the resulting inference.[5]

Anna Chamot, a strategy instruction pioneer, has recently called for differentiation in SI (Chamot 2012; also Chapter 10 in this volume). In her 2012 model, pupils describe the learning strategies that they used in doing a task. The teacher then writes each example on the board and gives a brief label for the learning strategy it illustrates. Students individually complete a grid in which they identify the strategies that they use most often and provide examples of how they have used each strategy. In principle, it is a noble aim to have SI cater to each and every learner. Note that the Chamot model reduces the plethora of strategies to brief labels. It is an empirical question as to how effective this approach actually is over time. These labels are meant to remind learners of the actual strategies that they had used in the past as they tackle new tasks. In reality, it is probably a tall order for teachers to refine SI to a highly differentiated level. In reality, while teachers can play a valuable role (for more on this see Oxford 2017 and Chamot, Chapter 10 in this volume), it is likely that a fair amount of the onus still falls on the learners themselves to individualize the SI process. Again, this issue needs to be explored empirically.

Another SI handbook is an outgrowth of extensive LLS work being done in public schools in Greece (Psaltou-Joycey 2015). The second portion of the book is devoted to describing SI tasks: activities for mainstream primary pupils (Agathopoulou et al. 2015), activities for mainstream lower-secondary school (Kantaridou and Papadopoulou 2015), and activities for minority primary and lower-secondary schools (Mitits and Sarafianou 2015). Included in these chapters are strategies for the following:

- analyzing vocabulary (e.g., parts of words; cognates in L1, L2, and L3) and classifying words,
- dictionary use,
- reading comprehension: reading for the gist/general understanding/details, visualization, filling in the gaps, summarizing, making mind maps as graphic organizers, and guessing what comes next,
- observing and making inferences about similarities and differences in schools, cultures, and countries, and about signage,
- mobilizing short-term memory as well as long-term memory, such as through memorizing people's faces,
- understanding grammar—for example, simple present vs. present continuous,
- expressing emotions, and
- evaluating the effectiveness of strategy use—for example, after making an error.

3.2. Short courses and materials

The first CARLA summer institute on LLS took place in 1998 with Susan Weaver, Rebecca Oxford, and the author as co-instructors. The 20th SI summer institute for teachers (entitled *Improving Language Learning: Styles- and Strategies-Based Instruction* (SSBI)) took place on July 17–21, 2017 at the University of Minnesota, Minneapolis, with Martha Nyikos of Indiana University as the long-time instructor.[6] Here is the outline of the current course:

- Day 1
  Defining, Integrating, and Working with Styles and Strategies
  Raising Awareness of Current Strategy Use
  Resolving Style/Strategy Conflicts
- Day 2
  Ways to Assess How Styles and Strategies Affect Learning
  Intersection of Style, Strategy, and Task
  Hands-On SSBI Activities and Lesson Planning
- Day 3
  Frameworks for SSBI
  Teaching vs. Learning Strategies
  Teacher and Student Roles in Challenging Learning Contexts
- Day 4
  Motivation for Language Learning
  Creating SSBI Lesson Plans in Three Frameworks
  More Hands-On SSBI Activities
  Review of SSBI Research and Implication
- Day 5
  Participant Presentations and Peer Feedback of SSBI Lessons and Project Design
  Style/Strategy Review and Debate
  Goal-Setting for the Future

The SSBI Instruction Manual (Cohen and Weaver 2006) used in these summer institutes is available for purchase from the University of Minnesota Bookstore. There is also extensive coverage of SI in Cohen (2011).

3.3. The role of SI in TL pragmatics performance

The literature has usually favored general approaches to SI, without being adequately attuned to the culturally and situationally grounded aspects of the language. It was this insight that motivated me to create a classification system for strategies dealing with the learning and use of TL pragmatics (Cohen 2005, 2014), with the express purpose of supporting learners in being strategic about pragmatics:

- speech acts like greetings, thanks, compliments, requests, apologies, complaints, criticism,
- being polite and impolite,
- recognizing humor, teasing, sarcasm,
- understanding and use of cursing,
- engaging in small talk,
- dealing with listener responses and turn taking, and
- knowing how to recognize and use discourse markers like "well," "you know," "so," "I think," "on the other hand," "frankly," and "as a matter of fact."

The classification system includes two types of strategies and what I now see as use of the metapragmatic function (as well as the cognitive, social, and affective) in strategy use:

1. *Strategies for the INITIAL LEARNING of TL pragmatics—for example, taking practical steps to gain knowledge of how, say, specific speech acts work*—gathering information (through observation, interview, and written material) on how certain speech acts are performed by members of one or more "communities of practice" within a given speech community (e.g., at the workplace: making requests of age mates, refusing requests made by higher-status people, and thanking people in service—e.g., cafeteria workers, custodians).

2. *Strategies for PERFORMING pragmatics—for example, devising and then utilizing a memory aid for retrieving the pragmatics material that has already been learned*—visualizing a listing of the specific strategies for the given pragmatics material—possibly remembered through an acronym— and then scanning down this list in order to select the members of, say, a given speech act set that seem appropriate for the given situation.

3. Aside from assuming a cognitive, a social, or an affective function, a strategy for learning or performing TL pragmatics may also take on a metacognitive function—for *PLANNING, MONITORING, AND EVALUATING* the use of the strategy. For example, in an effort to avoid pragmatic failure, learners may monitor for the level of directness or indirectness in the delivery of TL pragmatics (e.g., a request of a stranger on an airplane); the appropriateness of the selected term of address (e.g., referring in the L2 to Dr. Stephen Blake as "Doc," "Steve," or "you"—either tu or vous); tone, facial expressions, and gestures. (Whereas an actor usually gets coached in such matters, language learners are invariably left to figure it out by themselves.)

3.4. The use of technology in SI

Perhaps the most detailed approach to strategies and strategizing available on the web is the Spanish Grammar Strategies Website: http://www.carla.umn.edu/strategies/sp_grammar/index.html

The strategies were obtained on a bottom-up basis through collecting 36 hours of videotaping of University of Minnesota undergraduate students explaining the strategies that they used to successfully learn Spanish grammar. I personally went into Spanish language classes and recruited students who felt that they had successful grammar learning and grammar using strategies to share. The students were given coupons at the university bookstore in exchange for their time and effort. Seventy-two strategies were identified and validated from the many hours of videotaping. These strategies were meticulously included in a website that took two years to construct. The approach taken in the design of the website was to have those who would access it be able to choose strategies according either to some need to bolster a specific grammar rule or according to their learning style preferences.

Once the website was operative, a study was conducted to track the selection and use of strategies by fifteen University of Minnesota undergraduates over six

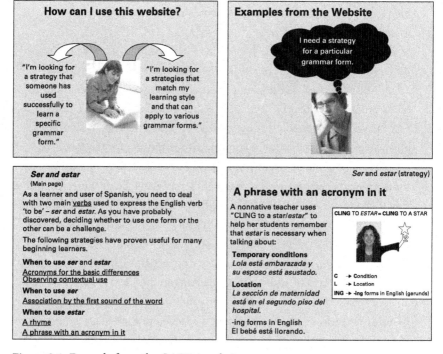

Figure 2.1 Example from the CARLA website

to eight weeks. Students' responses on the strategy tracking forms and in the interviews over the course of study indicated that the learners generally benefited to some extent and in some cases greatly from use of the website, suggesting its potential for supporting learners of Spanish in remembering and correctly using various grammatical forms that had previously been problematic for them (Cohen et al. 2011). A strategies website such as this one—whether focused on grammar or some other skill—could support learners in performing language skills more effectively. As reflected in this study, learners may be aware of, in this case, grammatical problems but without deriving a dependable way to deal with them when left to their own devices. Having strategies readily available through a website such as this can help to remediate some of these problem areas.

3.5. Strategies for enhancing test performance

Test-taking strategies can be crucial for learners taking high-stakes tests. Test-management strategies can be crucial in navigating the test and responding effectively. Students can benefit from good guidance materials. The Education Testing Service deserves praise for supporting research on strategies students used on the iBT TOEFL test (e.g., Cohen and Upton 2007), and the findings provide important input for SI sessions.

Three types of test-taking strategies have been identified (see Cohen 2012b):

1. *Language learner strategies*—the ways that respondents operationalize the basic skills of listening, speaking, reading, and writing, as well as the related skills of vocabulary learning, grammar, and translation. So, for example, with regard to reading skills associated with summarizing, strategies would include distinguishing key points from lesser ones, as well as being able to paraphrase material at a higher level of generality.

2. *Test-management strategies*—strategies for responding meaningfully to the test items and tasks. So strategies on a reading test could deal with how respondents return to the question to obtain more information, how they compare multiple-choice options rigorously to determine the most plausible response, and how they crosscheck with the reading text to make sure their choice seems appropriate.

3. *Test-wiseness strategies*—strategies for using knowledge of test formats and other peripheral information to answer test items without going through the expected linguistic and cognitive processes. Again, with regard to a

reading test, it would mean using the process of elimination rather blindly (i.e., selecting an option without really understanding it at all, but rather out of a vague sense that the other options are not likely to be correct), using clues in other items to answer an item under consideration, and selecting the option because it appears to have a word or phrase from the passage in it—possibly a keyword.

Consequently, in responding to a reading comprehension item, the respondents may draw from their repertoire of reading strategies (e.g., looking for markers of meaning in the passage, such as definitions, examples, indicators of key ideas, guides to paragraph development), test-management strategies (e.g., selecting options through the measured elimination of other options as unreasonable based on paragraph/overall passage meaning), and test-wiseness strategies (e.g., selecting the option simply because it has a word from the passage in it). Clearly, language educators would want to discourage using test-wiseness strategies (see Cohen 2013a, about how to do this).

4. The role of teachers in SI

How can teachers support learners in being better strategizers? It was suggested by Peter Yongqi Gu (personal communication, August 2015) that an ideal situation would be one in which teachers are knowledgeable about:

- the strategies being targeted altogether and those likely to be elicited by any given TL task,
- options for how to use a given strategy in a given task,
- the proficiency level of the students,
- the students' cultural and educational background,
- their motivation level,
- their cognitive/learning style preferences, and
- when to engage in explicit SI.

Consistent with Butler (2002), Gu recommends a situation in which students arrive at their own strategies, with teacher support but without the teacher feeding them strategies—a bottom-up approach; this provides greater credibility for students than if strategies are supplied by teachers.

Rebecca Oxford (personal communication, August 2015) also sees the role of the teacher in SI as demanding, given the learners' contextualized, situated, complex, and fluctuating needs. She would recommend (as would I) that teachers formally assess learning style preferences, LLS, and language proficiency. To assist in this effort, Oxford (1990) constructed the *Strategy Inventory for Language Learning (SILL)* and a task-based reading strategy assessment (Oxford et al. 2004). Along with Julie Chi, we constructed a skill-based strategy inventory (Cohen, Oxford, and Chi 2002). In addition, Oxford (2011) also recommended that teachers become knowledgeable about the other variables in the lives of each learner by using informal observation, dialogue journals, narratives, or other tools. She suggested that teachers be cognizant of the contexts in which students live, interact, and learn—that strategies need to be contextualized. He (2002) and Gao (2010) documented how learners use different strategies at different points in their life. Much of the strategy work has not tended to contextualize strategy use, but rather has relied on a more generalized model.

To what extent are teachers' efforts at strategy instruction picked up on and operationalized by learners? One of the very early strategy instruction efforts involved research on the effect of SI regarding mnemonic devices. The aim was to investigate the impact of teaching learners how to use the mnemonic keyword strategy for remembering specific words (Cohen and Aphek 1981). The findings were that some learners used the teacher's suggested strategies and it helped, that other learners used the teacher's strategies and it did not help, and still other learners ignored the teacher's strategy suggestions. These early results motivated me to favor separate websites for learners. Teachers can make suggestions but should not be offended if learners ignore them.

Other than sending learners to websites, what can teachers do to help students use learner strategies? There are lots of ideas in "The Practice of Strategy Instruction" (Cohen 2011, Chapter 4). If possible, teachers could conduct SI as part of their regular instruction. But how do language educators get this to happen? One way is to send key language teachers to the CARLA institute on Styles and Strategy Instruction offered every summer at the University of Minnesota, usually in July.[7] It is also possible for institutions to develop their own local LLS institutes.

5. Research on SI

The following are four representative studies of SI over the last decade:

- Gu (2007) exhibited rigor both in administering SI to 5th-grade ESL students on writing strategies, and also in procedures for conducting research, including a delayed posttest.

- Gu, Hu, and Zhang (2009) worked with 4th to 6th-grade ESL students to improve their listening strategies.
- Nguyen and Gu (2013) administered SI for academic writing with 3rd-year university English majors in Vietnam.
- Gunning and Oxford (2014) conducted a study with 6th-grade ESL students to get them to be more strategic in their speaking.

In light of the continual appearance of studies like those above in the LLS research literature, it has been pointed out that it is difficult to do cross-study comparisons of such SI because of differences in the interventions. Plonsky's (2011) meta-analysis of SI found a small to medium overall effect for SI, with type and number of strategies, learning context (second versus foreign language), and length of intervention serving as moderator variables. In addition, an earlier study (Harris 2007) noted that differences in setting, in duration (i.e., from one 50-minute period to an entire year), and importantly in the nature of the SI led to differences in the results. It is noted that little information is provided in SI studies as to the following:

- the choice of skill area(s),
- how the strategies were tailored to learners' age, stage, and proficiency level, and the learners' views regarding the SI intervention (i.e., what was best for the given learners as opposed to what was most convenient for the given researchers).

Harris (2007) provided some of this information in her own SI study focusing on listening and reading.

5.1. How to evaluate the effectiveness of SI?

While the triangulation of measures is potentially beneficial, rather than just adding instruments for their own sake, it would probably have a greater impact on the results to find ones that truly complement the others. So, for example, let us say there is a functional inventory for describing the range of strategies reportedly used in performing a series of specific tasks. If there were also an effective instrument for describing the sequencing, pairing, or clustering of strategies in accomplishing these tasks, then it could behoove the study to use both of these measures for obtaining a more robust description of the strategies involved. In addition, I would want to see whether and how strategies are used over time, as we did when studying the use of strategies from the Spanish

Grammar Strategies Website (Cohen et al. 2011). Since many factors are involved in LLS research, our instruments need to be task-related, instructionally relevant, and creative.

In addition, the more focused the SI, the more likelihood that the results will provide genuine insights. An early SI study involving French and Norwegian learners, for example, provided SI on speaking and measured SI impact on the performance of a series of speaking tasks. Immediately upon completion of each task, the respondents were asked to provide retrospective verbal reports on the strategies that they had used (Cohen 2011). In that study, a checklist of strategies was provided to help prompt the recollection of strategies deployed.

5.2. What about research on the quality of strategy use?

Aside from the frequency of strategy use, are there any measures that can tap into the quality of strategy use? One way is through verbal report with learners to see if the strategy is working. While getting feedback from the learners about how they have used strategies in actual real-world tasks is crucial, it is a challenge to obtain. Checking out whether a given strategy does really give the learners control over language material is a way to monitor for quality. Just because learners say that a strategy has a certain positive effect does not ensure that this is the case. It is possible to engage learners in language activities that test them on their ability with the subjunctive, gender agreement, or whatever, as was done in the Cohen et al. (2011) study. In that study systematic verification was performed to ensure that the use of strategies earmarked as "successful" by students had, in fact, produced the desired outcome.

5.3. Issues in SI research

The following are some questions worthy of being asked with regard to SI research:

- What are the so-called strategies in the study? Are they actually more skill-like (e.g., I use a dictionary) than strategy-like (I use Google Translate but then cross-check every unknown vocabulary work in my online bilingual dictionary)?
- Are students actually taught strategies for dealing with, say, grammatical forms (e.g., distinguishing one from another)? How vague/specific is the SI?

- How similar are learners in their pattern of strategy use by task? To what extent are they deploying single strategies, strategy sequences, strategy pairs, strategy clusters, or some combination of these?[8]
- To what extent is SI implicit and to what extent explicit—that is, are pupils expected to internalize various strategies associated with tasks that they do or are they explicitly taught to use these strategies?
- Is there follow-up to see if pupils have transferred the strategies to other tasks?

Another whole area of concern with regard to SI research is that of survey questionnaire design for LLS and of coding. Gu, Hu, and Zhang (2009) pointed out the following with respect to LLS survey instruments:

- The instruments were not able to get at the mechanisms behind strategy learning,
- The items tended to be decontextualized,
- The self-report used in the questionnaires did not necessarily reflect actual behavior,
- The questionnaire approach did not get at the orchestration of strategies (e.g., sequences and clusters).

With regard to the coding of these LLS survey questionnaires, Gu (2014) contended that results of SI research might be questionable on the grounds of problematic coding alone. Gu noted that incidences of strategy use might very well be coded and tallied according to a classification system of learner strategies that did not reflect the quality of the strategy use. In such a case, then, statistical analyses run to find out whether groups of learners differed in the number of strategies used and/or types of strategy used might reveal differences that distorted the true picture. In addition, Gu suggested gathering other types of information, such as what motivated learners to use a particular strategy, the quality of the strategy use, the level of flexibility displayed in the use of the given strategy, and the efficiency with which the strategy was used.

While much of the research methodological literature has only caveats about what is likely wrong with LLS research, there are also studies that underscore the positive side of certain research techniques like verbal report, that have been around for many years (see Cohen 2013b). One such study (De Silva and Graham 2015) found the use of stimulated recall to be very beneficial. The researchers reported gaining insights into strategy orchestration of both high- and low-proficiency learners (twelve Sri Lankan college EFL learners). Their protocol data showed that different writers used strategies in different combinations and that these strategy clusters interacted in writing. In addition, the recall data helped reveal how the students' use of strategies developed—in a way that quantitative data collection methods alone (e.g., questionnaires) would not have been able to.

6. Strategies for learning my thirteenth language

People have often called me a consummate language learner and strategy user, although I do not typically use such terminology to describe myself. What strategies work best for me in learning Mandarin (see Cohen and Li 2013)? Here is a small sampling of strategies I currently use:

- Creating my own curriculum around what interests me.
- Making an electronic dictionary by word categories—at present, over 3,550 nouns, verbs, adjectives, function words, and measure words. (At the outset of the chapter, I shared some of the vocabulary strategies that I use for attaining my own dictionary entries.)
- Getting tandem partners and coaching them on how to give feedback. I write a personal blog on ten topics per week. I review the corrections from my partner before our Skype session. They also send me more feedback after the session. I further correct my sentences. I make vocabulary entries based on the feedback, but as I do so, I invariably become aware of necessary fine-tuning of word meanings. So, I send an email requesting information on semantic distinctions. I find electronic dictionaries woefully inadequate at providing me with such information.
- What makes them truly tandem sessions is that, in return, my tandem partners get feedback from me on their oral and written English. Depending on the tandem partner, the feedback has been on English conversation, on papers for publication, or on course assignments.

Whereas I started learning Mandarin with every intention to develop my listening and speaking skills to a reasonable degree, instead I have found that I am mostly developing my ability to read and write in *pinyin*. Here is a sample entry from September 10, 2015, in my weekly journaling with my tandem partner:

> *Shang ge xingqier women qu youtaihuitang canjia guanyu Yiselie zōngjiào jíduānzhǔyì de yanjiang. Tanhua de ren shi yige Meiguoren de labi shi Yiselie yìhuì de yimíng qián chéngyuán. Ta zhèngzài jíjí tuīdòng lìfǎ dǎjī zōngjiào jíduānzhǔyì.*

(This past Tuesday we went to our synagogue to hear a talk about religious extremism in Israel. The speaker was an American-born rabbi, who was a former member of parliament. He was actively engaged in promoting the enactment of laws to crack down on religious extremism.)

As a cognitive strategy, I make sure that I understand semantic distinctions in learning vocabulary: *gonzuo*—a person working, *yunzhuan*—a machine working. My efforts to cluster words by tone in order to help remembering word tone failed. I found words like *liànxí* "practice, exercise" (4th and then 2nd tone) and *liánxì* "connection" (2nd and then 4th tone) to be daunting to learn. At present, while I mark correctly the tones of all new words I enter into my electronic dictionary, I cannot say I have learned and can properly do any of them by heart. While I am continuing to work on my Chinese, I only use *pinyin*, as noted earlier. Consequently, I have to deal with homonyms like *nán* (2nd tone) for both "south" and "male." Such ambiguities would be resolved instantly if I were learning vocabulary through the use of Chinese characters.

7. Conclusions

Learners can be more proactive in their own language learning. They need not be dependent on the teacher. After all, during much of their lives, they will not have access to a teacher. Teachers can be more proactive in coaching learners to use LLS more effectively. Perhaps it is a tall order to expect teachers to be truly mindful of the LLS factors (as identified by Gu and listed in section 4 above) as they apply to every student. Nonetheless, teachers can support their learners in being better strategizers. Finally, research has an important role to play in LLS work, and ideally the issues raised in this chapter will help to stimulate fresh thinking about how to do such research. Along these lines, a recent article provided suggestions from over twenty LLS experts concerning research they would like to see conducted (Cohen and Griffiths 2015).

Notes

1   Editors' note: Cohen (2011) and Macaro (2006) find the distinction between language learner strategies and language learning strategies to be useful. Of 33 strategy definitions mostly from the language learning field, nearly 10% address strategies that the definers explicitly call language learner strategies (see study in Oxford 2017). The acronym LLS, which Cohen explains as language learner

strategies, is sometimes applied to phenomena that other experts cited by Cohen in this chapter call language learning strategies (e.g., Griffiths 2013, Griffiths and Oxford 2014, Gu 2014, Gunning and Oxford 2014). There is still a need for discussions about strategy terminology in our field. We are grateful to Cohen for his efforts to clarify language learner strategies.

2 Editor's historical note by Oxford: There was interesting, potentially valuable theoretical work in the LLS field well before Dörnyei (2005) and other external critics in the early 2000s leveled the guns at inadequate LLS theory. The early link between LLS and self-regulation was evident, but indirect, with my 1990 and 1996 books (showing strategic self-direction and autonomy, closely tied to self-regulation), O'Malley and Chamot's 1990 book (including autonomy in the cognitive information-processing model), Rubin's 2001 article (on learner self-management), and Wenden's 1991 book (on strategies and autonomy). The direct link between strategies and self-regulation occurred when I strongly proposed, in a 1999 article in a small, international journal, that self-regulation and autonomy should become a joint theoretical base for strategies. The powerful linkage between self-regulation and strategies became better known in my 2011 and 2017 books. None of the LLS theoretical contributions noted here were stimulated by criticisms from Dörnyei or others, because nearly two decades ago some of us understood LLS and self-regulation to be strongly linked, and nearly three decades ago we grasped that LLS, autonomy, and self-direction were related. A note from educational psychology: The association between strategies and self-regulation or autonomy in educational psychology and social cognitive psychology started early and remains strong (Panadero and Alonso-Tapia 2014; Winne and Perry 2000; Zimmerman and Martinez-Pons 1986; Zimmerman and Schunk 2011). Thanks to Cohen for raising issues like this that need discussion.

3 Findings from a recent study would support the notion that a given strategy may assume different functions on a moment-to-moment basis (Cohen and Wang 2017).

4 My three Aventura, Florida (USA) grandchildren are growing up in a trilingual environment where their Venezuelan mother only speaks Spanish with them, their Israeli-American father only speaks Hebrew with them, and the community at large (the media, the local schools, and most public venues) provides ample English input, along with Spanish input as well.

5 As mentioned earlier, at least 12 types of strategies contribute to inferencing (Hu and Nassaji 2014).

6 See http://carla.umn.edu/institutes/index.html for specifics.

7 See http://carla.umn.edu/institutes/index.html for specifics.

8 As noted above, a recent study (Cohen and Wang 2017) explored this issue. Results revealed complex strategy patterns among six Chinese students in completing a vocabulary task in English. There was a fluctuation in strategy functions when strategies were used either alone, in pairs, or clusters.

References

Agathopoulou, Eleni, Thomaï Alexiou, Vassilia Kazamia, and Areti-Maria Sougari. 2015. "Activities for Mainstream Primary Pupils." In *Foreign Language Learning Strategy Instruction: A Teacher's Guide*, edited by Angeliki Psaltou-Joycey, 52–115. Kavala: Saita Publications.

Butler, Deborah L. 2002. "Individualizing Instruction in Self-regulated Learning." *Theory into Practice* 41 (2): 81–92.

Chamot, Anna Uhl. 2012. "Differentiated Instruction for Language and Learning Strategies: Classroom Applications." In *Perspectives on Individual Characteristics and Foreign Language Education*, edited by Wai Meng Chan, Kwee Nyet Chin, Sunil Bhatt, and Izumi Walker, 115–29. Boston: DeGruyter Mouton.

Chapelle, Carol A., ed. 2013. *The Encyclopedia of Applied Linguistics*. Oxford: Wiley-Blackwell.

Cohen, Andrew D. 2005. "Strategies for Learning and Performing L2 Speech Acts." *Intercultural Pragmatics* 2 (3): 275–301.

——. 2011. *Strategies in Learning and Using a Second Language*. Abingdon: Routledge/Pearson Education.

——. 2012a. "Strategies: The Interface of Styles, Strategies, and Motivation on Tasks." In *Psychology for Language Learning: Insights from Research Theory and Practice*, edited by Sarah Mercer, Stephen Ryan, and Marion Williams, 136–50. Basingstoke: Palgrave Macmillan.

——. 2012b. "Test-taking Strategies." In *The Cambridge Guide to Second Language Assessment*, edited by Christine Coombe, Peter Davidson, Barry O'Sullivan, and Stephen Stoynoff, 96–104. Cambridge: Cambridge University Press.

——. 2013a. "Using Test-wiseness Strategy Research in Task Development." In *The Companion to Language Assessment: Approaches and Development*, edited by Anthony J. Kunnan. Volume 2. Hoboken, NJ: Wiley and Sons.

——. 2013b. "Verbal Report." In *The Encyclopedia of Applied Linguistics*, edited by Carol A. Chapelle. Oxford: Wiley-Blackwell.

——. 2014. "Strategies for Learning and Performing Speech Acts." In *Teaching and Learning Pragmatics: Where Language and Culture Meet*, edited by Noriko Ishihara and Andrew D. Cohen, 227–43. New York: Routledge.

Cohen, Andrew D., and Edna Aphek. 1981. "Easifying Second Language Learning." *Studies in Second Language Acquisition* 3 (2): 221–36.

Cohen, Andrew D., and Carol Griffiths. 2015. "Revisiting LLS Research 40 Years Later." *TESOL Quarterly* 49 (2): 414–29.

Cohen, Andrew D., and Ping Li. 2013. "Learning Mandarin in Later Life: Can Old Dogs Learn New Tricks?" *Contemporary Foreign Language Studies* 396 (12): 5–14.

Cohen, Andrew D., Rebecca L. Oxford, and Julie C. Chi. 2002. *Language Strategy Use Survey*. Minneapolis, MN: Center for Advanced Research on Language Acquisition, University of Minnesota.

Cohen, Andrew D., Angela Pinilla-Herrera, Jonathan R. Thompson, and Lance E. Witzig. 2011. "Communicating Grammatically: Evaluating a Learner Strategies Website for Spanish Grammar." *CALICO Journal* 29 (1): 145–72.

Cohen, Andrew D., and Thomas A. Upton. 2007. "'I Want to Go Back to the Text:' Response Strategies on the Reading Subtest of the New TOEFL." *Language Testing* 24 (2): 209–50.

Cohen, Andrew D., and Isobel Wang. 2017. "Fluctuation in the Function of Language Strategies Function." Under review for publication in a journal.

Cohen, Andrew D., and Susan J. Weaver. 2006. *Styles and Strategy-based Instruction: A Teachers' Guide.* Minneapolis, MN: Center for Advanced Research on Language Acquisition, University of Minnesota.

De Silva, Radhika, and Suzanne Graham. 2015. "The Effects of Strategy Instruction on Writing Strategy Use for Students of Different Proficiency Levels." *System* 53: 47–59.

Dörnyei, Zoltán. 2005. *The Psychology of the Language Learner: Individual Differences in Second Language Acquisition.* Mahwah, NJ: Erlbaum

Dörnyei, Zoltán, and Stephen Ryan. 2015. *The Psychology of the Language Learner Revisited.* New York: Routledge.

Dörnyei, Zoltán, and Ema Ushioda. 2010. *Teaching and Researching Motivation.* 2nd edition. Harlow: Longman/Pearson Education.

Gao, Xuesong Andy. 2010. *Strategic Language Learning: The Roles of Agency and Context.* Bristol: Multilingual Matters.

Grenfell, Michael, and Vee Harris. 2015. "Learning a Third Language: What Learner Strategies do Bilingual Students Bring?" *Journal of Curriculum Studies* 47 (4), 553–76.

Griffiths, Carol. 2013. *The Strategy Factor in Successful Language Learning.* Bristol: Multilingual Matters.

—— and Rebecca L. Oxford. 2014. "The Twenty-first Century Landscape of Language Learning Strategies: Introduction to this Special Issue." *System* 43: 1–10.

Gu, Peter Yongqi. 2007. "Strategy-based Instruction." In *Proceedings of the International Symposium on English Education in Japan: Exploring New Frontiers*, edited by Tomoko Yashima and Toshiyo Nabei, 21–38. Osaka: Yubunsha.

——. 2014. "To Code or Not to Code: Dilemmas in Analyzing Think-aloud Protocols in Learning Strategies Research." *System* 43: 74–81.

Gu, Peter Yongqi, Guangwei Hu, and Lawrence J. Zhang. 2009. "Listening Strategies of Singaporean Primary Pupils." In *Language Learning in New English Contexts*, edited by Rita E. Silva, Lubna Alsagoff, and Christine C. M. Goh, 55–74. London: Continuum.

Gu, Peter Yongqi, Lawrence J. Zhang, and Rui Bai. 2011. *Strategy-based Instruction: Focusing on Reading and Writing Strategies.* Beijing: Foreign Language Teaching and Research Press.

Gunning, Pamela, and Rebecca L. Oxford. 2014. "Children's Learning Strategy Use and the Effects of Strategy Instruction on Success in Learning ESL in Canada." *System* 43: 82–100.

Harris, Vee. 2007. "Exploring Progression: Reading and Listening Strategy Instruction with Near Beginner Learners of French." *Language Learning Journal* 35 (2): 189–204.

He, An E. 2002. "Learning English in Different Linguistic and Socio-cultural Contexts." *Hong Kong Journal of Applied Linguistics* 7 (2): 107–21.

Hu, Hsueh-chao Marcella, and Hossein Nassaji. 2014. "Lexical Inferencing Strategies: The Case of Successful Versus Less Successful Inferencers." *System* 45: 27–38.

Ishihara, Noriko, and Andrew D. Cohen, eds. 2014. *Teaching and Learning Pragmatics: Where Language and Culture Meet.* New York: Routledge.

Kantaridou, Zoe, and Iris Papadopoulou. 2015. "Activities for Mainstream Lower Secondary Schools." In *Foreign Language Learning Strategy Instruction: A Teacher's Guide*, edited by Angeliki Psaltou-Joycey, 116–74. Kavala: Saita Publications.

Linck, Jared A., Meredith M. Hughes, Susan G. Campbell, Noah H. Silbert, Medha Tare, Scott R. Jackson, Benjamin K. Smith, Michael F. Bunting, and Catherine J. Doughty. 2013. "Hi-LAB: A New Measure of Aptitude for High-level Language Proficiency." *Language Learning* 63 (3): 530–66.

Macaro, Ernesto. 2006. "Strategies for Language Learning and for Language Use: Revising the Theoretical Framework." *Modern Language Journal* 90 (3): 320–37.

Mitits, Lydia, and Anna Sarafianou. 2015. "Activities for Minority Primary and Lower Secondary Schools." In *Foreign Language Learning Strategy Instruction: A Teacher's Guide*, edited by Angeliki Psaltou-Joycey, 175–211. Kavala: Saita Publications.

Nguyen, Le Thi Cam, and Peter Yongqi Gu. 2013. "Strategy-based Instruction: A Learner-focused Approach to Developing Learner Autonomy." *Language Teaching Research* 17 (1): 9–30.

O'Malley, J. Michael, and Anna Uhl Chamot. 1990. *Learning Strategies in Second Language Acquisition.* Cambridge: Cambridge University Press.

Oxford, Rebecca L. 1990. *Language Learning Strategies: What Every Teacher Should Know.* Boston: Heinle & Heinle.

——, ed. 1996. *Language Learning Strategies around the World: Cross-cultural Perspectives.* Second Language Teaching and Curriculum Centre: University of Hawaii at Manoa.

——. 1999. "Relationships between Second Language Learning Strategies and Language Proficiency in the Context of Learner Autonomy and Self-regulation." *Revista Canaria de Estudios Ingleses* 38: 108–26.

——. 2011. *Teaching and Researching Language Learning Strategies.* 1st edition. Harlow: Pearson Longman.

——. 2014. "What We Can Learn about Strategies, Language Learning, and Life from Two Extreme Cases: The Role of Well-being Theory." *Studies in Second Language Learning and Teaching* 4 (4): 593–615.

——. 2017. *Teaching and Researching Language Learning Strategies: Self-Regulation in Context.* 2nd edition. New York: Routledge.

Oxford, Rebecca L., Yunkyoung Cho, Santoi Leung, and Hae-Jin Kim. 2004. "Effect of the Presence and Difficulty of Task on Strategy Use: An Exploratory Study." *International Review of Applied Linguistics and Language Teaching* 42 (1): 1–47.

Panadero, Ernesto, and Jesús Alonso-Tapia. 2014. "How Do Students Self-regulate? Review of Zimmerman's Cyclical Model of Self-regulated Learning." *Anales de Psicología* 30 (2): 450–62

Plonsky, Luke. 2011. "The Effectiveness of Second Language Strategy Instruction: A Meta-analysis." *Language Learning* 61 (4): 993–1038.

Psaltou-Joycey, Angeliki, ed. 2015. *Foreign Language Learning Strategy Instruction: A Teacher's Guide.* Kavala: Saita Publications. Accessed May 30, 2015. http://www.saitabooks.eu/2015/05/ebook.162.html.

Rubin, Joan. 2001. "Language Learner Self-management." *Journal of Asian Pacific Communication* 11: 25–37.

Silva, Rita E., Lubna Alsagoff, and Christine C. M. Goh, eds. 2009. *Language Learning in New English Contexts.* London: Continuum.

Wenden, Anita. 1991. *Learner Strategies for Learner Autonomy.* Englewood Cliffs, NJ: Prentice Hall.

Winne, Philip H., and Nancy E. Perry. 2000. "Measuring Self-regulated Learning." In *Handbook of Self-regulation*, edited by Monique Boekaerts, Paul R. Pintrich, and Moshe Zeidner, 531–66. San Diego: Academic Press.

Zimmerman, Barry J., and Manuel Martinez-Pons. 1986. "Development of a Structured Interview for Assessing Student Use of Self-regulated Learning." *American Educational Research Journal* 23 (4): 614–28.

Zimmerman, Barry J., and Dale H. Schunk, eds. 2011. *Handbook of Self-regulation of Learning and Performance.* New York: Routledge.

3

How Individual Differences Relate to Successful Strategy Use

Self-Regulated Language Learners Around the World

Carol Griffiths
Auckland Institute of Studies, New Zealand

1. Literature review

In the years since Rubin's (1975) introduction of the good language learner to the language learning literature, strategies have been widely believed to be among the factors that contribute to successful language learning (Cohen 1998, 2011; Cohen and Macaro 2007; Griffiths 2013; O'Malley and Chamot 1990; Oxford 1990, 2011, 2017; Wenden 1991). So, what are language learning strategies? According to Rubin (1975, 43), strategies are actions: they are "what the good learner *does*" (emphasis added). These actions are *chosen* by the learners themselves (Cohen 1998), as distinct from being imposed by somebody else (e.g., the teacher). Language learning strategies are employed for a particular *purpose* in order to achieve a language learning goal (Cohen, Chapter 2 in this volume; Macaro 2006), and they are used to *learn or regulate* (Wenden 1991; Oxford 2011) the process of *learning* (as distinct, for instance, from communicating, which may or may not lead to learning). When combined, these elements suggest a concise definition of language learning strategies as *actions chosen by learners for the purpose of learning language* (Griffiths 2015). Strategies, however, do not exist in a vacuum. In fact, strategy use is mediated by a complex amalgamation of a vast and complicated network of other variables. These include contextual factors, the learning target, and the learner's own individual characteristics.

One of the first to acknowledge the key role of context in language learning was Oxford (1996) in her book on language learning strategies in various locations around the world. Norton and Toohey (2001) also stressed the need to view language learning as a situated experience in which the context plays a key role. Gao (2010) is another who examines context in relation to strategy use. Context includes the learning environment (e.g., classroom, distance, study abroad); whether students are studying in their own familiar first language or whether they must cope with a course taught in a CLIL (Content and Language Integrated Learning) or an EMI (English as a Medium of Instruction) situation; and all other factors in the background of the learner's life (e.g., family, job, classmates/ colleagues, culture). All of these diverse variables will impact on the strategies that a learner wishes or is able to employ in pursuit of a particular learning goal.

Clearly, strategies that might be effective for one learning goal may or may not be effective for a different goal (Oxford 2011). A student who effectively employs strategies to develop writing skills, for instance, may need to adapt and expand these strategies if the goal changes to pass an international language exam such as IELTS or TOEFL. Similarly, strategies that serve a learner well on a General English course may need adaptation if the goal changes to passing an ESP (English for Specific Purposes) course such as Business, Legal, or Medical English, English for pilots, tourism, or fashion, or any of the numerous other "perceived needs and imagined futures" (Belcher 2006, 133) for which such courses have been designed.

Ultimately, however, the success or otherwise of the learning endeavor is influenced not only by the situation or the target, but also by the characteristics of the individual learner him/herself (Pawlak 2012; Skehan 1989). The most important of these is perhaps motivation (Dörnyei and Ushioda 2011). Motivation is necessary if learners are to be prepared to invest the time and effort required to develop linguistic capital (Norton Peirce 1995). Investment may, in turn, depend on learners' beliefs, of which positive beliefs about themselves as language learners and about the language they are trying to learn seem to be essential (White 2008). In addition, good language learners seem to have the ability to autonomously take control of their own learning rather than waiting for someone else (e.g., the teacher) to make all their decisions (Cotterall 2008).

Although there is reasonably widespread agreement over the importance of motivation, investment, beliefs, and autonomy in language learning, there is less consensus over the role of various other individual differences such as age, gender, personality, learning style, and affect. When it comes to age, for instance, the belief that younger is better has been widespread, but recent research has suggested more optimism for older learners (Moyer 2014). When considering the role of gender, the belief that women are better language learners, and more strategic, than men is surprisingly common (Ellis 2008); however, many studies have shown no difference in the performance of men and women, and, where a female advantage has been shown, it is slight (Sunderland 2000). As for personality, Ehrman (2008, 70) concluded that "individuals can become good language learners whatever their personalities." Learning style has also been extensively researched but most research has not been able to demonstrate a consistent link between successful learning and any particular style (Griffiths and Inceçay 2016). And although the importance of affect has long been recognized (MacIntyre and Gregersen 2012), clear evidence of a relationship between any specific emotional state (such as anxiety, attitude, attribution, empathy, inhibition, or self-concept) and successful language learning or strategy use has proven elusive.

In sum, the literature suggests that good language learners are motivated and therefore invest considerable time and effort in their learning. They are autonomous and have positive beliefs about themselves and the target language. They frequently use and carefully orchestrate a large repertoire of language learning strategies chosen to suit their situation, their learning goals and their own individual characteristics. The question that therefore emerges from the literature is: which of these multiple variables, if any, is most salient in terms of successful language learning?

2. The study

Viewing language development holistically requires a re-thinking of traditional research methodologies, which tended to focus on discrete variables, or, at most, a limited number of variables. As noted above, however, each learner embodies a unique and complex synthesis of factors, which can be extremely challenging from a research point of view. At the same time, if we fail to address the complexities involved, we risk only ever seeing a narrow view of a multi-dimensional phenomenon. Or, as Larsen-Freeman (1997, 143) puts it, attempting "to under-stand the behavior of the whole by examining its parts piecemeal is inadequate."

2.1. Participants

The participants in this study were fourteen successful learners of English. They were personally known to the researcher and able to communicate effectively in English both orally and graphically using generally appropriate vocabulary and

Table 3.1 Participant details

No.	Name	Gender	Nationality
1	Liz	F	Turkish
2	Tina	F	Russian
3	Lana	F	Czech
4	Hanu	M	Indian
5	Lee	F	Korean
6	Hong	F	Chinese
7	Yasu	M	Japanese
8	Aziz	M	Iranian
9	Rose	F	Kyrgys
10	Ana	F	Pakistani
11	Kris	M	Polish
12	Hamed	M	Kenyan
13	Maria	F	Brazilian
14	Hana	F	Finnish

accurate grammar, though there may have been occasional slips. All participants were non-native speakers of English who were either working for or already holding post-graduate degrees. They were all either teaching English or teaching in English, the assumption being that those who are capable of performing at this level must be at least reasonably competent (i.e., "good") in English. Nine of the respondents were women and five were men. In order to minimize cultural bias they were deliberately chosen to represent diverse national backgrounds. The participants are listed in Table 3.1 with their names (changed for anonymity), genders, and nationalities.

2.2. Instrumentation

A Likert-scale questionnaire was constructed using the findings from the literature review regarding the importance of motivation, investment, beliefs, autonomy, and strategy use. Strategy use was further differentiated according to number, frequency, orchestration, target, context, and individual characteristics. Respondents were asked to respond on a scale of 5 (strongly agree) to 1 (strongly disagree) to a series of statements on which they were also asked to comment (see Table 3.2 for statements).

2.3. Data collection

The questionnaire was sent out by e-mail and returned by the respondents at their convenience. Interviews were considered for the qualitative data, but the participants were widely scattered geographically (and they were actually living and working in their countries of origin), so face-to-face interviews were not a practical option. Skype interviews were considered, but communicating across widely varying time zones and accommodating the schedules of busy academics was problematic. It was therefore decided to ask the participants to add their own comments to the questionnaire sheet. This had additional advantages. First, it eliminated tedious and time-consuming transcription. Second, it avoided the risk that the transcription process itself might distort what the respondents wanted to say, since transcribers themselves inevitably subjectively interpret the spoken data in the process of producing a written version (Dörnyei 2007). Third, asking the respondents to write comments gave them time to reflect because they could do it at their own convenience. Consequently, the qualitative data were transparently the respondents' own and readily available for checking, and they could be cut-and-pasted exactly as they were written. Some of the respondents produced only brief responses, while others provided rich, detailed, and insightful comments that added considerable depth to the quantitative ratings data.

2.4. Data analysis

The questionnaire data were analyzed for reliability (Cronbach's alpha) to determine whether the instrument was reliable for investigating the target construct (i.e., factors relating to successful language learning). Given that Likert-questionnaire ratings do not allow the use of means[1] (they are non-numerical), median ratings are quoted, which provides an indication of the overall agreement or disagreement with the given statements.

The comments were examined for clarification of the ratings and further insights. Comments were selected according to the extent to which they added insight to the discussion, and also in an attempt to give every participant an opportunity to have his or her voice heard at some stage. Since the participants themselves assigned their comments to the appropriate boxes, it was not necessary for the researcher to classify them, but an independent colleague checked the reported comments for accuracy.

2.5. Ratings results

The Cronbach's alpha co-efficient for reliability for the questionnaire was. 720. Given the relatively low numbers of respondents in the study, this was considered a good result and suggests that the instrument is reliable. Overall, median ratings in the "agree" (4) to "strongly agree" (5) range were given for all items of the questionnaire, with only one exception (Item 6, regarding strategy orchestration, see Table 3.2). In other words, the responses to eleven out of twelve items (92 percent) were on the positive side of the scale, while the remaining item was in the neutral range.

2.6. Participants' comments

Motivation (Item 1)

As can be seen from Table 3.2, motivation is rated very highly (median = 5) by these successful learners. In fact, not only is the median rating high, but thirteen of the fourteen respondents give motivation a rating of 5 (strongly agree). This is the highest rate of agreement of any of the items of the questionnaire. Reasons for the high ratings include:

> "If I learn a foreign language I will be able to communicate with others and understand the world better." (Liz)

> "Job, social status ... undertake higher studies, to maintain friendships etc." (Hanu)

> "I like English, especially the sound of English. Also, I wanted to use English well since I majored in English language and literature. (People expect English majors to use English at near-native level.)" (Lee)

> "I thought learning English will give me more opportunities, will open the door to the world." (Rose)

Yasu provides a lengthy and thoughtful comment regarding what motivated him, including some negative motivational factors:

> "My motivations include integrative, instrumental, achievement, carrot and stick, intrinsic, desire to feel self-efficacy, desire to have relationships with others and so forth. I did not have any inhibitions, either. Some people probably feared being proficient in English due to a self-defense mechanism (a fear of failure or a fear of losing one's identity); others are self-conscious ... Although I've experienced periods of English-related apathy, on average, I was highly motivated to learn English."

Table 3.2 Individual and median (M) ratings from the good language learner questionnaire

No	When learning English	Participants														Median
		1	2	3	4	5	6	7	8	9	10	11	12	13	14	
1	I was motivated	5	5	5	5	5	5	5	5	5	5	5	5	5	4	5
8	I chose strategies to suit my learning goal	5	5	4	5	5	5	4	4	5	4	5	5	3	2	5
10	I took charge of my own learning	4	4	4	5	4	5	3	5	5	5	4	5	5	5	5
12	I believe English is a good language to learn	5	5	5	5	5	5	4	4	5	5	5	5	5	5	5
2	I spent a lot of time working on my English	4	4	5	4	2	5	5	5	5	3	5	3	5	1	4.5
3	I put a lot of effort into my English studies	4	4	5	3	2	5	4	5	5	2	5	5	5	1	4.5
4	I used many strategies	5	5	3	4	5	5	5	4	4	3	4	3	4	2	4
5	I used strategies frequently	1	4	4	4	4	5	3	4	5	4	4	3	4	5	4
7	I chose strategies to suit my individual needs	4	4	3	5	5	2	3	4	5	3	5	5	3	1	4
9	I chose strategies to suit my situation	4	5	3	5	5	5	4	4	5	4	5	3	3	2	4
11	I believe I am a good language learner	5	4	4	5	5	3	4	5	4	5	4	3	5	4	4
6	I chose my strategies so they worked well together	4	3	3	4	2	4	2	4	5	3	3	3	3	2	3

Goal-orientation (Item 8)

Of the questionnaire items relating to strategies, the one that scores most highly (median = 5) is the one that relates strategy choice to goals, underlining the importance of goal-orientation in successful language learning. Goals mentioned include:

> "To communicate with others and be a member of a multicultural and multilingual world." (Liz)

> "To achieve accuracy and fluency ... and ... to sound like a native speaker." (Tina)

> "Higher studies, job, dating/social." (Hanu)

> "Acquiring a new/different language to understand a new/different culture in a better way." (Ana)

Hong's goal is somewhat tied to the realities of her exam-driven situation:

> "My learning goal on campus was to improve the four skills of English language so that I was confident in communicating with others and to pass the TEM-4 and TEM-8 exam."

Kris speaks of coming to terms with reality:

> "At first I was working towards being able to read without checking any vocabulary, but soon realized that it was a utopian scheme, probably impossible to achieve even for native speakers!"

Obviously, these goals are diverse, suggesting that the goal is not so important per se. It is the degree to which the learner is committed to it that would seem to be important.

Autonomy (Item 10)

Autonomy is also a feature of these successful learners, as demonstrated by the high positive response (median = 5) to the item regarding taking charge of one's own learning. The responses to this item indicated that

> "there was a certain degree of reliance on the teachers." (Tina)

There may also have been various significant others such as

> "my eldest sister." (Lee)

In general, however, this group did not wait for others to make their decisions. Hong, for instance, reports that:

"I had good self-control" and learnt "without teachers' urging."

Yasu comments that when he took charge of his own learning it

"made a tremendous difference."

Kris agrees that he took charge of his own learning

"with the proviso that I never questioned my teachers' decisions or balked at activities which they assigned me. I decided to work over and above what I was given, but also to do whatever was required of me."

Hana sums up her response in one word:

"Absolutely."

Ana is equally emphatic:

"Absolutely yes."

The belief that English is a good language to learn (Item 12)

This was also rated 5. Reasons vary from the largely practical to the affective achievement of personal pleasure. According to Hong, the grammar, pronunciation, and structure of English are easier than Chinese (her native language), while Hanu thinks English is good for employment, study, and social networks. According to Ana,

"It's a beautiful language to learn, to write in and to use in day to day routine."

Aziz puts his positive beliefs down to

"the status of English as an international language."

Hamed makes a similar point:

"It is, of course, now the dominant intellectual language of the era, just as Latin and Arabic had been, and ancient Greek had been in its time."

Kris is pragmatic:

"For better or worse, given the geopolitical situation, knowing English is necessary. But I also found a personal pleasure in learning it because so much of the culture I was exposed to was either British or American."

Hana's reasons also tend towards the practical:

> "English is a good language to learn, because it is "the" lingua franca, but also because it is an easy language for a beginner to learn."

Investment of time (Item 2)

The median ratings (= 4.5) given to Items 2 and 3 indicate that these successful learners were prepared to invest time and effort in their studies. For Item 2, relating to the investment of time, Aziz explains:

> "Yes, I consulted dictionaries, referred to grammar books, and spent a lot of time doing assignments and reading recommended and supplementary materials."

Hong gives quite a detailed answer:

> "Students at my time usually got up at 6 am and did morning readings and listened to [news in English] at 7 am every day. We spent our time mostly in the library for some self-study, by which I guess we learned more from the teachers in class. We also went to the English Corner on campus every Thursday evening to meet different people so as to improve our public speaking skills."

As examples of how he spent time working on his English, Hanu gives

> "Reading. Internet. Watching TV/DVDs. Listening to radio/CDs. Going to social gatherings etc."

Yasu explains:

> "In an EFL environment, becoming proficient in English is generally more time consuming."

A couple of the respondents, however, go against the trend. Hana gives Item 2 a rating of 1 (strongly disagree) and confesses:

> "I rarely studied at home for school."

Lee is another who gives the item a low rating (2 = disagree) and explains:

> "To be honest, I haven't spent much time nor made a great effort to improve my English."

Investment of effort (Item 3)

For Item 3, relating to the investment of effort, Hong explains:

> "I regarded learning English as my utmost goal and dedicated myself to it."

This investment of effort included paying careful attention, as Tina comments:

"I was diligent at what I was doing and gave much attention."

According to Hamed, his effort included

"reading extensively in different areas."

As with the investment of time, Lee disagrees (rating = 2) that she put a lot of effort into her study, although she does not give a reason, while according to Hana, who gave a rating of only 1 (strongly disagree):

"The only time I remember having been putting effort into studying was one afternoon when I practiced to memorize 4–5 pages of King Lear verbatim."

Number of strategies (Item 4)

Although there is disagreement in the literature regarding strategy quantity (Dörnyei and Ryan 2015), there is quite strong consensus (median = 4) among these successful learners regarding the use of many strategies, of which the respondents provide a number of examples:

"drilling; talking to a native speaker; reading English books; watching English films." (Lana)

"I revised, read, tried to talk to colleagues, did exercises, tried to risk and look for words and resources." (Maria)

"I planned what to study when and how long in detail, and monitored my progress. I also made a list of wrong answers after tests to reflect on the questions later." (Lee)

"I used memory and cognitive strategies in gaining knowledge of English as a student and as a teacher in high school. Metacognitive strategies were primarily used in preparing for entrance exams as well as tests required to study abroad. Communication strategies as well as affective and social strategies were primarily used in ESS activities." (Yasu)

"I used strategies suggested by an English magazine named English World which provided some suggestions and strategies from some successful English learners and university professors. I also developed my own strategies in the process of my learning." (Hong)

Rose reports that she studied early in the morning when she had a "clear mind" and provides a list of the strategies she used:

"1. For learning vocabulary, which is the most difficult area, I wrote down all the new words from every book I read and studied them in detail using dictionary.

I wrote down all of their meanings, collocations. Not just the translations, but its transcript, synonyms, antonyms etc. 2. I tried to learn as much synonymous words as possible. Because I believed they would enrich my speech. 3. I tried to watch movies in English or with English subtitles, even not very often. 4. Sometimes I and my close friend agreed on talking in English in our daily-life and we tried to keep speaking English."

Kris states:

"I read extracurricular materials (mostly books in English) and made up my own extensive vocabulary lists, supplying definitions from the dictionary. These I memorized afterwards, trying also to remember the context."

Strategy frequency (Item 5)

The item on frequency of strategy use (Item 5) is also rated highly (median = 4), although there are not as many responses as for the item on number of strategies (Item 4), and comments are generally not as detailed. Hana explains:

"I think trying out the language in my head was something I did continuously."

Yasu comments:

"I'm not certain the frequency was vast."

Lee provides some examples:

"I guess I used several other strategies when reading English often, like predicting, skimming, and summarizing."

And Hong adds:

"I tried to use strategies often and made reflections on how effective the strategies I used were on learning so that I could adjusted my strategies timely."

Individual characteristics (Item 7)

Also with a median rating of 4 is the item on choosing strategies to suit individual needs, although some of the respondents said they did not consider this important. Hong, for instance, says she

"only chose strategies that were useful for English learning without considering individual needs." In other words, the focus was on the goal rather than on the self.

Aziz makes a similar point:

"Yes, my learning strategies were based on my needs, motivation, and the nature of the task, but I suppose that I did not consider culture and gender to have much an effect on my learning."

Nevertheless, it might be possible to argue that individual needs are basically what determines choice of goal. As a consequence, individual needs are inescapably important whether the learner is actually aware of them or not. Of the participants, Kris was the only one to acknowledge this when he commented:

"Yes, that was the fun of it—the fact that I was able to combine my interest in music and literature with learning English, which was a pleasure all its own."

Lee considers her strategies in relation to her learning style:

"I guess I understood my learning styles when I was a high school student, so I used the strategies fit for my styles (e.g., step by step, detail oriented, auditory, and so on)."

Individual learning style is also considered by Yasu:

"Because I am a visual learner, I often use texts, tables and charts. I was not good at hands-on classroom activities, but I tried expanding my range."

Context (Item 9)

A variety of situations is noted by the participants, including precise locations such as

"Istanbul University." (Liz)

Others focus on characteristics of their situations such as

"Being taught by non-native English speakers." (Tina)

"I had to study in a studying room where many students study together." (Lee)

"My high school teacher never pronounced correctly, so that I went through a very hard time on correcting my own mispronunciations." (Hong)

"I was not exposed to authentic English." (Yasu)

"I started during the Communist regime. Therefore the learning situation was quite difficult, e.g. to talk to a native speaker or buy an English book." (Lana)

For many of these students the learning situation necessitated the development of management strategies. These included

"reading silently (without moving my lips)" in order not to disturb others in the overcrowded study room. (Lee)

Yasu recalls that he

"bought a bilingual TV in order to watch news in English," and he joined a conversation group in order to "create an English speaking environment even though my communication partners were non-native speakers."

Lana comments that although there were difficulties

"it made me even more eager to study English."

The belief in themselves as good language learners (Item 11)

This is rated somewhat lower (median = 4) than the belief that English is a good language to learn (median = 4.5), but still positive. For Lee, this belief was fostered

"because I got many rewards from English (e.g., high scores, teachers' praises etc.)."

Aziz also includes positive teacher feedback among the reasons for his positive beliefs. Tina, while agreeing that she believes herself to be a good learner (rating = 4) is also critical of her own performance. She reports:

"I suppose I could have done better if I had been more proactive, i.e., if I had taken more responsibility for my learning."

Kris is also positive (rating = 4) but self-critical. He explains:

"I used to be a better one when there was more time, but I certainly tried hard to learn. I'm not as pleased with my achievement as I thought I'd be, but that's probably due to realizing that there's always space for improvement."

Hamed gives Item 11 a neutral rating (3) and puts his ability down to environmental factors:

"Kenya is a multicultural society with 42 languages. The majority of the people are either trilingual, other even more."

Hong is uncertain but concludes by relating her ability to her skills in coping with everyday situations:

"what I believe is that I have no problem in communicating with foreigners and solving real-life problems in English."

Hanu, however, appears to have no self-doubts. Unashamedly he states that he considers himself to be

"as good as a native speaker."

Strategy orchestration (Item 6)

The item on combining strategies did not attract much comment and was given the lowest median rating (median = 3). Yasu, however, comments that in the beginning:

> "I did not pay attention to the effective combination of strategies. I could only hope that a relatively decent combination of strategies was chosen by Buddha ... After I became familiar with the strategies ... I may have tried more than was necessary."

This comment underlines that strategy orchestration does not always come easily but may require trial and error to get it right.

3. Discussion

With only one exception (respondent 14), all respondents strongly agreed that they were motivated. Also highly rated with medians of 5 were matching strategies to goals, taking charge of one's own learning, and the belief that English is a good language to learn. The investment of time and effort both received median ratings of 4.5, while the belief in self as a good language learner was rated 4 along with the frequent choice of many strategies to suit individual needs and situations. The choice of strategies so that they worked well together was rated lowest (median = 3). From these results we can infer that these good language learners were motivated, autonomous, goal-oriented, and had positive beliefs about what they were trying to learn. In general, they invested a lot of time and effort in their English study. In addition, overall they believed in their own ability and frequently used a large number of strategies appropriate for their contexts and their own individual characteristics. Although strategy orchestration received the lowest level of agreement, even for this item the rating was neutral rather than "disagree."

Since strategy use appears to be a common feature of good language learners, it would seem to make sense for teachers to encourage learners to expand their strategy repertoires and to use these repertoires frequently and appropriately. Although there are those who question the value of strategy instruction (for instance, Rees-Miller 1993), there are others (for instance, Chamot and Harris 2017; Cohen 2011; Gunning and Turner, Chapter 12 in this volume) who can point to successful efforts to teach strategies. Language learning strategies have the potential to be a "powerful learning tool" (O'Malley et al. 1985, 43), so it would seem to follow that learners should at least be exposed to strategy possibilities. Eventually they can make up their own minds about which ones are useful for their own individual characteristics, situations, and goals.

Since motivation is a major factor related to good language learning, it would seem obvious that teachers need to attend to the motivational levels of their learners so that they will be willing to invest the time and effort that is required for success. One way of promoting motivation may well be to respect learners' autonomy, which is another recurring theme as a characteristic of successful language learners. If students feel that they are able to take positive steps to control their own destinies, they are likely to feel more committed to the goal they are trying to achieve. Learner beliefs should also be reinforced, for example, the notion that what they are trying to do is worth doing and that they are able to do it.

Although this study has produced some interesting findings regarding the complex nature of the good language learner, caution is required with interpretation given the relatively small and selective sample. Further studies need to be carried out with larger numbers of randomly selected participants. The current study spread the net widely in order to obtain a broad picture. It would also be useful to take a more in-depth look at successful language learners in specific locations. Also, the criterion for "successful" in this study is relatively imprecise. A more exact definition of "good language learner" might be helpful, perhaps using standardized test results (such as *TOEFL*, *IELTS*, or *FCE*) or CEFR levels as a proficiency criterion.

4. Conclusions

Although it was originally hoped that knowledge of the strategies used by successful learners to manage their learning would be sufficient to enable everyone to become a good language learner (Rubin 1975), we now know that language development is an extremely complicated process where multiple variables interact in patterns of great complexity. A learner is not just an embodiment of various characteristics, a repertoire of strategies, a learner of some linguistic target, or an inhabitant of a particular environment. Every learner is the sum of all possible variables, the permutations of which are more or less infinite. As we can see, then, merely to ask "How many strategies did the learners use?" or "How often?" does not give a full answer to the complex question of what makes a good language learner. We also need to know the context in which the strategies are being used, the goal of the strategy use, the characteristics of the individual learner (especially their motivation, their beliefs, their level of investment and their ability to be autonomous), and how the strategies are used in combination. In other words, it is important that these multiple factors are viewed holistically and the complexities borne constantly in mind.

Note

1   For a very different discussion of this statistical issue, see Mizumoto and Takeuchi, Chapter 5 in this volume.

References

Belcher, Dianne. 2006. "English for Specific Purposes: Teaching to Perceived Needs and Imagined Futures in Worlds of Work, Study, and Everyday Life." *TESOL Quarterly* 40: 133–56.

Chamot, Anna Uhl, and Vee Harris, eds. 2017. *Learning Strategy Instruction in the Language Classroom: Issues and Implementation.* Bristol: Multilingual Matters.

Cohen, Andrew. 1998. *Strategies in Learning and Using a Second Language.* London: Longman.

——. 2011. *Strategies in Learning and Using a Second Language.* 2nd edition. London: Longman.

Cohen, Andrew, and Ernesto Macaro, eds. 2007. *Learner Strategies.* Oxford: Oxford University Press.

Cotterall, Sarah. 2008. "Autonomy and Good Language Learners." In *Lessons from Good Language Learners,* edited by Carol Griffiths, 110–20. Cambridge: Cambridge University Press.

Dörnyei, Zoltán. 2007. *Research Methods in Applied Linguistics.* Oxford: Oxford University Press.

Dörnyei, Zoltán, and Stephen Ryan. 2015. *The Psychology of the Language Learner Revisited.* New York: Routledge.

Dörnyei, Zoltán, and Ema Ushioda. 2011. *Teaching and Researching Motivation.* 2nd edition. Harlow: Pearson Longman.

Ehrman, Madeline E. 2008. "Personality and Good Language Learners." In *Lessons from Good Language Learners,* edited by Carol Griffiths, 61–72. Cambridge: Cambridge University Press.

Ellis, Rod. 2008. *The Study of Second Language Acquisition.* Oxford: Oxford University Press.

Gao, Xuesong Andy. 2010. *Strategic Language Learning: The Roles of Agency and Context.* Bristol: Multilingual Matters.

Griffiths, Carol 2013. *The Strategy Factor in Successful Language Learning.* Bristol: Multilingual Matters.

——. 2015. "What Have We Learnt from Good Language Learners?" *ELTJ* 69 (4): 425–33.

Griffiths, Carol, and Görsev Inceçay. 2016. "Styles and Style-Stretching: How Are They Related to Successful Learning." *Journal of Psycholinguistic Research* 45 (3): 599–613.

Larsen-Freeman, Diane. 1997. "Chaos/Complexity Science and Second Language Acquisition." *Applied Linguistics* 18 (2): 141–65.

Macaro, Ernesto. 2006. "Strategies for Language Learning and for Language Use: Revising the Theoretical Framework." *The Modern Language Journal* 90 (3): 320–37.

MacIntyre, Peter, and Tammy Gregersen. 2012. "Affect: The Role of Language Anxiety and Other Emotions in Language Learning." In *Psychology for Language Learning*, edited by Sarah Mercer, Stephen Ryan, and Marion Williams, 103–18. Houndsmills: Palgrave Macmillan.

Moyer, Alene. 2014. "Exceptional Outcomes in L2 Phonology: The Critical Factors of Learner Engagement and Self-Regulation." *Applied Linguistics* 35 (4): 418–40.

Norton, Bonny, and Kelleen Toohey. 2001. "Changing Perspectives on Good Language Learners." *TESOL Quarterly* 35 (2): 307–22.

Norton Peirce, Bonny. 1995. "Social Identity, Investment and Language Learning." *TESOL Quarterly* 29: 9–31.

O'Malley, J. Michael, and Anna Uhl Chamot. 1990. *Learning Strategies in Second Language Acquisition.* Cambridge: Cambridge University Press.

O'Malley, J. Michael, Anna Uhl Chamot, Gloria Stewner-Manzanares, Lisa Küpper, and Rocco P. Russo. 1985. "Learning Strategies Used by Beginning and Intermediate ESL Students." *Language Learning* 35 (1): 21–46.

Oxford, Rebecca L. 1990. *Language Learning Strategies: What Every Teacher Should Know.* Boston: Heinle & Heinle.

——, ed. 1996. *Language Learning Strategies around the World: Cross-cultural Perspectives.* Second Language Teaching and Curriculum Center: University of Hawai'i at Manoa.

——. 2011. *Teaching and Researching Language Learning Strategies.* Harlow: Pearson Longman.

——. 2017. *Teaching and Researching Language Learning Strategies: Self-Regulation in Context*, 2nd edition. New York: Routledge.

Pawlak, Mirosław, ed. 2012. *New Perspectives on Individual Differences in Language Learning and Teaching.* Berlin: Springer.

Rees-Miller, Janie. 1993. "A Critical Appraisal of Learner Training: Theoretical Bases and Teaching Implications." *TESOL Quarterly* 27 (4): 679–87.

Rubin, Joan. 1975. "What the 'Good Language Learner' Can Teach Us." *TESOL Quarterly* 9 (1): 41–51.

Skehan, Peter. 1989. *Individual Differences in Second-language Learning.* London: Edward Arnold.

Sunderland, Jane. 2000. "New Understandings of Gender and Language Classroom Research: Texts, Teacher Talk and Student Talk." *Language Teaching Research* 4 (2): 149–73.

Wenden, Anita. 1991. *Learner Strategies for Learner Autonomy.* Englewood Cliffs, NJ: Prentice Hall.

White, Cynthia. 2008. "Beliefs and Good Language Learners." In *Lessons from Good Language Learners*, edited by Carol Griffiths, 121–30. Cambridge: Cambridge University Press.

Part II

Research Methodologies for Exploring Learning Strategies and Individual Differences

Early studies about LLS aimed to explore the characteristics and practices of *good* language learners. Successful language learners were, for instance, found to create communicative learning situations in which they can use the target language actively with peers and native speakers, establish and maintain a positive attitude towards the target language, and develop a meta-awareness of the target language (Naiman et al. 1978).

Quantitative research using Likert-scale questionnaires has dominated the field with Oxford's (1990) *Strategy Inventory for Language Learning* (*SILL*) at the top of the popularity list of research instruments. In general, questionnaires that invite participants to anonymously indicate numbers on a scale in response to given statements have many advantages. They are easy to apply and can be handled without much knowledge of statistics. They generate large amounts of data in a cost-efficient manner and lead to objectively analyzable outcomes. As this volume shows, they can be translated in different languages (e.g., Psaltou-Joycey and Gavriilidou, Chapter 8; Amerstorfer, Chapter 6) and modified to suit specific target groups (e.g., the *Children's SILL* by Gunning 1997; Gunning and Turner, Chapter 12).

However, there are also negative aspects of questionnaires as tools for strategy research. Researchers have no way of knowing how honest and conscientious the responses to questionnaire items by individual participants are and whether the statements are understood in the same way as they were intended. Participants may skip items, have a hidden agenda when filling in a questionnaire, or tick responses at random. In large-scale studies there is virtually no possibility to eliminate or prevent such problems. What is more, Likert-scale inventories overemphasize categories, do not capture participants' emotional reactions, tend to ignore the context almost completely, and reveal nothing about the fluctuating, changeable, moment-by-moment use of LLSs. In other words, they can cover the numerical aspects of a group of participants but do not go into the depth and complexity of individual learners' strategy use.

Small-scale studies that use qualitative means to gather data, on the other hand, can capture more of the context in which a person studies an L2. Due to their potential to explore the richness and complexity of self-regulated and situated L2 learning, observations, interviews, and different forms of narratives (open-ended interviews, written or oral stories, diaries, journals, dialogue journals, and auto-ethnographies) have been used in LLS research. Other qualitative research techniques are also being used.

Despite the depth and richness offered by qualitative research methods, their limitations are usually at the hands of researchers. For instance, the researcher might incorrectly expect learners to remember details about their strategy use in a given week or for a series of tasks, without recognizing the fleeting, flexible, complex, and contextualized nature of LLS use. The researcher, as an interviewer, might not know how to ask questions skillfully enough to make learners comfortable. Diary instructions might imply that diary-keeping is a burden without any personal gains. In our experience, qualitative research takes time, creativity, intuition, organization, and compassion toward learners. The pros and cons of different approaches have motivated researchers to design studies that combine research methods to obtain the best of each method.

Part II of this volume presents three very different chapters revolving around research methodology in LLS research. The three studies included in this part were conducted in divergent educational settings in Greece, Austria, and Japan with participants who consequently spoke different first languages. In Chapter 4, Gkonou shares the qualitative part of a mixed-methods study that used two interrelated forms of narratives to gather information about foreign language learners' strategic actions to reduce learner anxiety. In Chapter 5, Mizumoto and Takeuchi review the use of questionnaires in the history of strategy research and share first-hand experience with a quantitative method that has never been used in strategy research before. Chapter 6 by Amerstorfer presents a mixed-methods study that focused on self-regulation in cooperative foreign language learning situations. In Amerstorfer's study, the *SILL*, observations, and different types of interviews were blended during data collection. Besides the varying methodological approaches in the three studies, in this part the chapters increase an awareness for contextual circumstances and individual learner characteristics in LLS research design and methodology.

References

Griffiths, Carol, and Rebecca L. Oxford. 2014. "The Twenty-first Century Landscape of Language Learning Strategies: Introduction to This Special Issue." *System* 43: 1–10.

Gunning, Pamela. 1997. "The Learning Strategies of Beginning ESL Learners at Primary Level." Master's thesis. Concordia University, Montreal. Accessed June 06, 2016. http://spectrum.library.concordia.ca/517/.

Naiman, Neil, Maria Fröhlich, Hans H. Stern, and Angie Todesco. 1978. *The Good Language Learner*. Toronto: Ontario Institute for Studies in Education.

Oxford, Rebecca L. 1990. *Language Learning Strategies: What Every Teacher Should Know*. Boston: Heinle & Heinle.

4

Listening to Highly Anxious EFL Learners through the Use of Narrative

Metacognitive and Affective Strategies for Learner Self-Regulation

Christina Gkonou
University of Essex, UK

There is no question that the problem of anxiety is a nodal point at which the most various and important questions converge, a riddle whose solution would be bound to throw a flood of light on our whole mental existence.

Sigmund Freud, Introductory Lectures on Psycho-Analysis

1. Introduction

This chapter is rooted in my firm belief that as educators who wish to improve our learners' learning experience, we should give them the opportunity to voice their thoughts and share with us their emotions, anxieties, and worries about classroom language learning; and of course we should be willing to listen to these carefully and respectfully! I begin this chapter by reviewing the literature on affect and one individual learner characteristic, language anxiety, which is a negative emotion. Next, I discuss the concept of *emotional* or *affective self-regulation* within education and Second Language Acquisition (SLA) research. I then report on a qualitative, narrative-based study, which aimed at exploring affective strategy use among highly anxious Greek EFL learners. The outcomes of the study revealed that affective, meta-affective, and metacognitive strategies played a crucial role in helping learners to mitigate their stress about learning English. Learners were further found to deploy a range of strategies from positive psychology in their attempt to minimize classroom anxiety levels. I conclude by discussing the implications of these findings for teaching practice and further research into affective strategies for language learning and language anxiety.

2. Literature review

2.1. Affect and language anxiety

Affect is "an abstract concept and an umbrella term" (Williams, Mercer, and Ryan 2015, 80) that encompasses the following interrelated psychological constructs: emotions, feelings, moods, and attitudes (Arnold 1999; Gabryś-Barker and Bielska 2013). Of the constructs that make up affect, emotions are particularly important as they are omnipresent, complex, powerful, and highly subjective. For example, a speaking activity is likely to make certain learners nervous, anxious, and self-conscious. At the same time, for other learners such an activity might be enjoyable, positive, and challenging to the degree that it alerts and motivates them to work on it. In addition, students' emotions and their affective reactions to an activity or to the language lesson in general are likely to influence teachers' emotions, and vice versa.

One emotion that has received considerable attention in the literature to date is anxiety. Within psychology-based and SLA research, anxiety is viewed as a negative emotion that impacts on individuals' behavior and actions. Specifically, Gregersen and MacIntyre (2014, 4) describe language anxiety as largely debilitating because it "interferes with acquisition, retention, and production of the TL [target language]." In their landmark publication on foreign language classroom anxiety, Horwitz, Horwitz, and Cope (1986, 128) defined anxiety as "a distinct complex of self-perceptions, beliefs, feelings, and behaviors related to classroom language learning, arising from the uniqueness of the language learning process." In early conceptualizations of this construct in SLA, two broad approaches were proposed: a) language anxiety could be viewed as a transfer of anxieties from other domains (e.g., stage fright and/or exam anxiety), and b) language anxiety could be seen as a unique emotional experience shaped by the specific characteristics of language learning that largely differs from learning other skills or studying other academic subjects (Horwitz and Young 1991).

Early SLA research has also attempted to position language anxiety within the well-established dichotomy in general psychology between trait and state anxiety (Spielberger 1983). Trait anxiety is a distinct personality trait, which remains stable over time and across different situations. State anxiety, in contrast, is "the moment-to-moment experience of anxiety; it is the transient emotional state of feeling nervous that can fluctuate over time and vary in intensity" (MacIntyre 1999, 28). This has raised the question of the extent to which language anxiety should be regarded as dynamic or stable. MacIntyre and Gardner (1989, 1991a, 1991b) argued that, at the initial stages of language learning, anxiety is an undifferentiated, stable personality trait, which learners do not yet associate with the language class due to their relatively limited experience as language learners. After repeated exposure to the foreign/second language (L2) environment and perhaps a series of negative experiences within it, learners are able to discriminate language anxiety from other anxiety types. Thus, their anxiety gradually becomes state or situation-specific.

More recent research (Dewaele 2002, 2013; Dewaele and Al-Saraj 2015) has revealed that personality traits such as neuroticism, introversion, and social initiative are significant predictors of language anxiety. In addition, the recent idiodynamic view of language anxiety and emotions has emphasized their tendency to fluctuate over time (Gregersen, MacIntyre, and Meza 2014; Gregersen, MacIntyre, and Olson 2017; MacIntyre and Gregersen 2012). These advances in research into language anxiety lead to the conclusion that language anxiety encompasses both aspects of the trait (i.e., stable) and state (i.e., dynamic) dichotomy in classrooms, thereby pointing to the complexity of the construct.

Research has shown that the fallout of language anxiety can be both diverse and immense. In particular, language anxiety can: increase competitiveness and peer pressure (Bailey 1983; Horwitz, Horwitz, and Cope 1986) thus causing tension among learners and posing a risk to interpersonal relationships; lead to fear of negative evaluation (Aida 1994; Gregersen and Horwitz 2002; Horwitz, Horwitz, and Cope 1986; Kitano 2001; Mak 2011) and weak self-concepts (Kitano 2001; MacIntyre, Noels, and Clément 1997); corrode learners' genuine interest and motivation to learn the language (Yan and Horwitz 2008); and, overall, have a deleterious effect on the process of language learning from a linguistic and a psychological perspective. Given the pervasive influence of anxiety on language learning and the learners, unsurprisingly, the search for ways of controlling it is deemed appropriate.

2.2. Emotional self-regulation in education and SLA

Self-regulation refers to individuals' ability to take certain actions in order to control their behavior in a range of settings. Within education, emotions and appraisals have a key role to play in self-regulation (Boekaerts 2007). The idea, however, is not new. Plato's view on emotions and that of his most famous student, Aristotle, suggested that emotions are largely controlled by our mind and are autonomous from physiology and the body. Aristotle in his treatise *On the Soul* introduced the notion of "catharsis," which highlights the importance of undermining negative and unpleasant emotions, a process that would lead to the purification of the human psyche. This Aristotelian perspective on emotions could be applied to classrooms, where it is vital for both learners and teachers to be able to turn their negative emotions into positive ones in order to create healthy relationships, positive group dynamics, and a positive classroom atmosphere.

There are different ways in which a specific emotion can be regulated (Jacobs and Gross 2014), and clearly some of these ways will work for certain students and not others, due to their individual learner characteristics. Research in general education has shown that cognitive appraisal can efficiently target the experience of negative emotions (Gross 1998, 2002; Hayes et al. 2010), thereby helping learners to control their current emotions, change them, and express positive ones. Thus, considering the type and nature of a negative emotion before actually expressing it might lead to enhanced social, behavioral, learning, and performance outcomes (Butler et al. 2003; Jacobs and Gross 2014; Srivastava et al. 2009).

Within SLA in particular, the term *affective strategies* has been used for the conceptualization and operationalization of emotion regulation. Specifically, in her seminal publication entitled *Language Learning Strategies: What Every Teacher Should Know*, Oxford (1990) listed the following strategy sets and specific strategies under her broader category of affective strategies: (a) lowering students' anxiety through progressive relaxation, deep breathing, meditation, music, and laughter; (b) encouraging oneself by making positive statements that are indicative of one's self-assurance, being eager to take risks, and rewarding oneself; and (c) taking one's emotional temperature by listening to the body, keeping a language learning diary, and discussing affect with others.

In her more recent and highly influential book entitled *Teaching and Researching Language Learning Strategies*, Oxford (2011) introduced the concept of *meta-affective strategies* to highlight the need for assigning a "meta-" level to affect in addition to meta levels of cognitive and sociocultural-interactive strategies. Oxford emphasized the importance of planning and evaluating for affect and specifically argued,

> Metastrategies, by virtue of their executive-control and management function, help the learner know whether and how to deploy a given strategy and aid in

determining whether the strategy is working or has worked as intended. Strategies and metastrategies in the model are highly dynamic, because they respond to changing needs of the learner for varying purposes in different sociocultural contexts.

Oxford (2011, 19)

Thus, under meta-affective strategies she listed the following strategy sets: paying attention to affect, planning for affect, obtaining and using resources for affect, organizing for affect, implementing plans for affect, orchestrating affective strategy use, monitoring affect, and evaluating affect.

Research into language anxiety in particular has primarily centered on how language teachers could mitigate their students' anxiety. To this end, a range of specific tips and teaching strategies has been suggested, which include among others: identifying those learners prone to becoming anxious (Gregersen 2007); lengthening the wait time after questions, reformulating questions, allowing students to write down their answers before sharing them with the rest of the class, encouraging team work in class, focusing on content rather than on form depending on the aims of the lesson, and establishing a good rapport with the students (Tsui 1996); boosting students' confidence, making the lesson aims clear, helping learners to set realistic goals, and allowing students to work at their own pace (Onwuegbuzie, Bailey, and Daley 1999; Williams and Burden 1997; Williams, Mercer, and Ryan 2015); enhancing learners' metacognitive awareness (Dörnyei 2005); encouraging risk-taking (Dewaele 2012; MacIntyre, Noels, and Clément 1997); and selecting appropriate error correction techniques with sensitivity to students' feelings (Aida 1994; Horwitz, Horwitz, and Cope 1986). Additionally, Gregersen and MacIntyre (2014) recently presented a series of fifteen anxiety-reducing activities that use systematic desensitization, discussion of positive and negative emotions, proverbs, favorable classroom experiences and memorable language learning moments, and stories, in an attempt to help students reflect on their anxiety, develop a sense of community, and realize that anxiety is a shared feeling among peers and thus requires mutual encouragement. In a very recent publication, Oxford (2017a) explains how anxious language learners can change their minds by presenting interventions from traditional psychology and positive psychology. In particular, she discusses how trait and state anxious learners can increase their calmness, positive emotions, emotional intelligence, flow, agency, hope, and optimism.

The range of types of pedagogical intervention presented so far highlights the urgent need for teachers to reduce their students' anxiety levels. However, indications of how learners—the actual bearers of anxiety—confront and manage anxiety has not received considerable empirical attention in the literature to date. Such empirical projects could help toward gaining situated understandings of individual learners and their anxieties and underlining the peculiarities of diverse learning and teaching contexts. To the best of my knowledge, the only exception is Kondo and Ying-Ling's (2004) investigation of the anxiety-coping strategies of 209 students enrolled in English language courses at two universities in central Japan. The researchers adopted a three-phase approach to collecting and analyzing data. In the first phase, they measured students' anxiety levels and explored their anxiety-reducing strategies. The second phase aimed at grouping similar coping strategies together. In the third phase, the correlations between students' anxiety levels and the types of strategies used were examined. The results revealed the following five strategy types: (a) preparation (the most frequently-cited strategy), referring to the development of study techniques in order to fully master English and diminish anxiety; (b) relaxation, including strategies to overcome a range of somatic symptoms, such as palpitations, sweating, and fidgeting; (c) positive thinking, where students attempted to shift their attention to pleasant situations and steer away from negative self-related cognition; (d) peer seeking, by looking for classmates who shared the same feelings of negative affect in class; and (e) resignation, when students refused to take any measures to allay their anxiety.

The present study will fill the gap in the field of emotional self-regulation in SLA from the perspective of the learner. It will look at EFL learners' anxiety-coping strategies and explore the importance for these learners to manage their negative emotions. An understanding of learner emotional self-regulation might help to tailor teaching strategies to highly anxious students' emotional needs in the language classroom. The study will therefore address the following research questions:

1. What strategies do EFL learners use to lower their anxiety?
2. What specific behaviors do they use in class in order to mitigate their stress?

3. Method

3.1. Research design

This chapter reports on the qualitative component of a larger, mixed-methods study on the language anxiety of EFL learners in private language schools in

Greece. A sequential explanatory design was employed for the present study (Creswell 2009; Tashakkori and Teddlie 2003). Specifically, in the first stage of the project, participants were administered a quantitative survey, the *Foreign Language Classroom Anxiety Scale* (*FLCAS*; Horwitz, Horwitz, and Cope 1986), which aimed at identifying the most highly anxious students in the cohort. The questionnaire data informed the process of recruiting participants and collecting data for the second, qualitative phase, which involved a diary study and semi-structured interviews with highly anxious students. This second step was intended to cast light on individual, highly anxious students' affective strategy use through narratives.

3.2. Participants

Seven adult Greek EFL learners, all L1 Greek speakers, who studied general English in two private language schools in Northern Greece participated in the qualitative part of the study. English was the first foreign language that these participants learned. Their level of proficiency ranged from B1 (i.e., pre-intermediate) to C1 (i.e., upper-intermediate) according to the Common European Framework of Reference for Languages (CEFR; Council of Europe 2001). The participants were classified as highly anxious on the basis of their total anxiety score on the *FLCAS*, which ranged from 93 to 147. All students gave their consent to participating in the study. Table 4.1 summarizes the information about the participating students.

Table 4.1 Information about the participants

Participant	Total language anxiety (LA) score (min. = 33, max. = 165)	Age	Proficiency level	Reasons for learning English
Student 1	147	26	C1	Job prospects
Student 2	144	19	B1	Importance of English as an international language
Student 3	126	30	B2	Job prospects
Student 4	113	35	C1	Job prospects
Student 5	112	27	B2	Academic goals abroad
Student 6	107	18	B1	Importance of English as an international language
Student 7	93	23	C1	Love for foreign languages

3.3. Instruments

Data were collected by using two interrelated forms of narratives (Barkhuizen, Benson, and Chik 2014; Kalaja, Menezes, and Barcelos 2008). Over a period of two months, the participants were first asked to complete one diary entry per week and to return it to the researcher electronically at the end of each week. The participants attended a training session prior to the commencement of diary keeping, where they were provided with a list of prompts of possible points that could be included in their entries. The prompts included questions such as "What is the most/least anxiety-provoking aspect of the lesson?" and "How do you reduce your anxiety about your English lessons?" among others. The participants could optionally write their entries in English or Greek, although the benefits of writing a diary in the target language were emphasized in order to encourage students to persist with the diary study. All diary data were composed in English. In terms of reciprocity and beneficence, at the end of the diary study, diarists were offered the opportunity to go through their writings with the researcher and discuss mistakes and inaccuracies.

An in-depth, follow-up, semi-structured interview was conducted with each diarist in Greek. An interview guide formed the basis of this phase of the study. At the same time flexibility was allowed to account for interesting points made by the interviewees that the researcher was keen to further inquire with specific, targeted questions. Additionally, the interview protocols were slightly modified for each participant to ensure that relevant aspects that were included in the diary entries were covered in the interviews, and to account for themes that were of particular significance to each student.

3.4. Data collection procedure

Once a group of highly anxious students was identified on the basis of their total *FLCAS* score, invitation emails to participate in the study were sent out. A training session was delivered by the researcher in both language schools. The training session aimed to present the diary study to the participants, to explain unclear points, to monitor and give feedback to the participants on their first diary entry, and to explain future steps such as the delivery of diary entries and the final part of the study. At the end of the diary study and once all diary data were coded, extra questions based on insights from the diary data were added to the interview protocols, and individual interviews were conducted with each diarist. All student interviews were audio-recorded.

3.5. Data analysis

The diary entries included a total of 60,697 words. All interview data were transcribed in full and digitally for coding using the data management software Atlas.ti. The interview data generated 79,850 words. Both diary and interview data were analyzed deductively and inductively (Lincoln and Guba 1985; Strauss 1987), by drawing on existing frameworks from the literature on language anxiety (for example, Horwitz, Horwitz, and Cope 1986) and taking into account the situated nature of the data and unique themes that were meaningful to the participants. The data were coded using first-level coding to create, define, and refine emerging themes, and then pattern (or second-level) coding to group the already identified codes into manageable sets (Miles and Huberman 1994; Saldaña 2013).

4. Findings

The analysis of the students' narratives suggested that, to minimize their language anxiety, students opted for a range of affective (relaxation and peer seeking), meta-affective and metacognitive (preparation and seeking practice opportunities), and positive psychology (positive thinking) strategies. Interestingly, one student reported no strategy use whatsoever during the language learning process. Table 4.2 presents the strategies for language anxiety reported by the participants. Additionally, it illustrates quotes in order to exemplify the participants' strategic activities with regard to each mentioned strategy.

The first strategy, *positive thinking*, includes learner action that steers away their attention from the anxiety-provoking situation to pleasant, and in most cases imaginary, conditions including scenarios of success in EFL learning. Participants reported the following:

"I try to think about something that makes me happy, such as a good mark on a test or a task, or think about times when I've studied hard. I try to think positively so I feel more relaxed." (Student 7, diary)

"When I am anxious, I try to think positively, to think about a success in the future, that I will do very well." (Student 2, diary)

"I try to think of why I get anxious. Then I consider all the possibilities, for example if this happens, it will result in this and that etc. I try to come up with a rational explanation to any result, and choose the result I like. To feel that I have found a solution to whatever might happen in the end. And I think I am not anxious this way." (Student 4, interview)

Table 4.2 Strategies for coping with language anxiety reported by learners

Strategy for language anxiety	Examples of strategic learner action
Positive thinking	I try to think of something that makes me happy. I think of times when I've studied hard. I try to think positively. I think of a success in the future. I try to think that I will do very well. I think of something else. I think of both success and failure possibilities, and I choose the one I like. I try not to think of my anxiety. I tell myself that I will do it. I tell myself that I am not anxious. I tell myself that there's still time to practice. I tell myself that there is no reason to be anxious. I tell myself that learning is more creative than being anxious. I try to convince myself that I will be able to find a solution.
Preparation	I review the material covered in class. I try to do my best. I aim to improve my grade. I study hard. Overviewing [i.e., revision] for the vocabulary test is for my own good. The more vocabulary I study, the easier these exercises become, and the less my anxiety is. I think carefully of my weaknesses and I try to work on them. The more I learn about the English language, the less anxious I am. I prepare myself better. I ask the teacher some questions. I ask my teacher to rephrase her question. I read the questions carefully. I try to guess the meaning of an unknown word. I peruse the material before I am called on by the teacher.
Relaxation	I close my eyes and I go to a place that calms me down. I try to relax. I try to calm down. I try to take it easy. I drink water. I take a deep breath.
Peer seeking	I ask other students if they understand the class. If possible, I try to compare my answers with other students' answers at the end of the task. Unless the teacher asks us to work individually, I work together with the person sitting next to me.
Seeking practice opportunities	I try to keep in touch with English. I listen to many English songs. I watch many English films.
No strategy use	I don't really believe that there exists a specific strategy you can use to reduce your anxiety, because as I said before, anxiety is a personality trait.

Students who reported using *positive thinking* also felt that suppressing stressful thoughts and focusing on the task at hand would help them to reduce their anxiety associated with the language class. Student 2, for example, said in the interview:

"When I am anxious, I avoid thinking about my anxiety and try to shift my focus on the task itself. For example, the teacher once asked us to do some writing in class. At that moment I was feeling that I couldn't write a word. But in the end I did very well. I tried to forget my anxiety."

Student 1 made a similar remark during the interview:

"I am trying not to focus on my anxiety. I know I want to learn English and I will do it. I am an optimist and I put effort in what I am doing. I also try to find a solution to overcome my anxiety rather than letting it interfere with my learning and performance in class."

The second strategy, *preparation*, refers to learner action that aims at improving study and learning skills, as well as performance. The diary account of Student 6 was illustrative of this point:

"I worry if I get a low mark. I then review the lessons to make sure I know what has been covered. Then I feel like I know everything, I feel more competent. And I aim for a higher mark next time."

Student 2 also commented in the interview:

"Vocabulary, and in particular synonyms, sometimes drive me crazy. However, I try to review this as often as possible and not only when we take a test. This way I am more confident about my knowledge and use of English."

The third strategy, *relaxation*, involves learner action that addresses how psychosomatic anxiety symptoms can be overcome. Examples are taking a deep breath, mental journeys to a place one likes, and dissuading oneself from taking the stressful situation seriously. Student 4 described this strategy expressively in the interview:

"The best way to reduce your anxiety is to close your eyes for two minutes and think of something irrelevant, something calm. Just go to a place that calms you down."

The fourth strategy, *peer seeking*, comprised learner action that helps students to realize that their peers also experience feelings of language anxiety. Student 7 explained this in the diary:

"If I know that someone else has the same problem as me, I am more relieved, I think."

Other students mentioned that they sought opportunities to work collaboratively in the classroom, for instance, by finding answers or discussing difficulties with peers. Student 1 made her point quite succinctly in the interview:

"If you panic because you don't have the answer or because you can't understand something and you may not feel at ease to ask the teacher, you can work with the person sitting next to you. I believe that this also reduces competitiveness among classmates, and you feel relaxed when you go to class."

The fifth strategy, *seeking practice opportunities*, referred to learners' active search for opportunities to practice English mainly outside of class. In the diary, Student 6 wrote:

"Exposure to English is getting easier and easier nowadays. I can listen to music, watch the news, talk with tourists. The more I practice the more proficient I am. And I think this decreases my anxiety."

A particularly interesting finding of the study is that Student 3, whose language anxiety is also high, reported *no strategy use* for coping with language anxiety. Student 3 views language anxiety as a stable personality trait, which was expressively argued in the interview:

"I don't really believe that there exists a specific strategy you can use to reduce your anxiety, because as I said before, anxiety is a personality trait. One of my friends suggested that we scream into a pillow. It helps to release your stress, she said. How can you do this in class? I did it at home, it doesn't work."

A final note concerns students' claims that they would rarely avoid activities in an attempt to minimize their language anxiety. For them, risk-taking was sometimes indispensable to help them overcome their stress. Accounts of how learners exercised their agency in an attempt to prioritize tasks and needs and how they evaluate the importance and usefulness of a task, surfaced in the interviews. Thus, the participants' sense and conscious exercise of their agency was a further sign of how they used their metacognition to alleviate their stress. The following extracts further support this point:

"If I am very anxious, and what I've been asked to do is something I really have to do and can't avoid, I will do it because I will have no other choice. You need to take risks at some point. I believe that anxiety is a kind of fear and something we have to get over. If there is no other way out, we will overcome our fears and whatever will be, will be." (Student 7, interview)

"Whether I would avoid an activity, that's a good question. It depends on the activity. If it is something that will not offer anything to me and there is no point doing it, I will avoid it, yes. If it is something that I have to expend effort on in order to succeed, I will not avoid it. I will try to overcome my anxiety instead." (Student 3, interview)

5. Discussion

The outcomes of this study point to a number of interesting implications of strategies to cope with language anxiety. First, the learner narratives revealed that the participants mainly opted for positive thinking and preparation. This finding partially supports Kondo and Ying-Ling's (2004) study about Japanese students' anxiety-reducing strategies, where preparation was the strategy most frequently used by participants, as opposed to positive thinking, which ranked third among students' strategy preference and use. Positive thinking, which could be facilitated through the use of pleasant images and hypothetical scenarios of success at learning English, could indeed be a key strategy for counteracting the negative effects of anxiety. Within SLA, vision and positive imagery have already been extensively discussed with reference to L2 motivation research (for example, Dörnyei 2009; Dörnyei and Kubanyiova 2014), but their application could also be extended to language anxiety. Clearly, this area still remains under-researched and in need of empirical investigation. In addition, the frequent use of positive thinking among highly anxious foreign language learners goes hand in hand with the recent upsurge of interest in the positive psychology movement within the field of SLA (for example, Dewaele and MacIntyre 2014; MacIntyre, Gregersen, and Mercer 2016; MacIntyre and Mercer 2014) and the recognition that looking at what learners do in order to thrive and flourish is a fruitful trajectory for research and teaching practice. Therefore, the research agenda on language learning strategies and language anxiety would need to be expanded to incorporate more interventions from positive psychology (Oxford 2017b).

The data further show that the highly anxious students who participated in the study consciously applied metacognitive strategies and in particular preparation and seeking practice opportunities. They also made use of their agentic resources in order to prioritize tasks and needs and decide on which tasks would actively promote their linguistic development. Thus, both metacognition and conscious exercise of agency were found to contribute toward mitigating language anxiety (for detailed information on the connection between learner agency and language anxiety see Gkonou 2014). This finding could perhaps add a further dimension to the existing literature in the field with regard to the complexity of avoidance behavior and how it might interact with language anxiety. Previous research has revealed that avoidance behavior was symptomatic of language anxiety (Bailey 1983; Bown 2009; Horwitz, Horwitz, and Cope 1986; Oxford 1999). However, the present study showed that highly anxious students would carefully consider whether they would avoid a challenging and hence potentially anxiety-provoking task, by examining whether language anxiety could be offset by the learning outcomes stemming from a specific task. Their decision to act or not to act, that is, to complete the task or deliberately avoid it, largely depended on where their priorities lay and on the significance of that particular task to them (see also Mercer 2011, 2012, 2015).

A further insight gained through the study is that highly anxious students do not experience exclusively negative emotions in class. The application of positive thinking and preparation specifically shows that they oscillate between positive and negative emotions and consciously endeavor to turn negative emotions into positive ones. Previous research has even shown that anxious learners might experience enjoyment about foreign language learning in the classroom (Dewaele and MacIntyre 2014, 2016; Şimşek and Dörnyei 2017). Within the framework of the flow theory, Csíkszentmihályi (1997) also suggested that learning can be pleasurable and exhilarating for certain learners. Therefore, in an effort to plan lessons that increase positive and eliminate negative emotions, language teachers should explore which aspects of language learning are particularly enjoyable for their learners (Williams, Mercer, and Ryan 2015) and which tasks, topics, and materials appeal to them.

Finally, the participants' attempts to change negative emotions into positive ones were indicative of their strong ability to assess their emotions and to self-regulate. The latter is a key component of emotional intelligence (Goleman 1995), and research has shown that emotionally intelligent individuals have lower levels of language anxiety (Dewaele, Petrides, and Furnham 2008). Hence, an ideal next step would be to raise teachers' awareness of this construct and make it an important component of teacher training programs (Mercer and Gkonou 2017) in order to equip teachers with the necessary skills for helping their students to control their emotions and to experience moments of positivity and low anxiety in the language classroom.

6. Conclusions

The present chapter has shown that emotional self-regulation plays a crucial role in mitigating anxiety about English language learning in the classroom. This could be achieved through a range of affective, meta-affective, and metacognitive strategies, which are all interconnected and work in tandem toward confronting anxiety and overcoming stressful situations. Emotional self-regulation, however, might not be as easy for every language learner because it depends on individual learner characteristics and differences as well as contextual influences on language learning. Thus, further research could empirically investigate the use of strategies to combat language anxiety among lower-level learners or learners in different language learning contexts such as an exam preparation course. The effectiveness of specific interventions employed or explicitly taught by the teacher could also be examined. In the absence of a longitudinal study, future research could center on the development of affective, meta-affective, and metacognitive strategies throughout a semester or a year, in order to focus on change, dynamicity, and complexity. Finally, exploring strategies while learners complete a task (and not retrospectively) through administering task-based or scenario-based questionnaires (Gkonou and Oxford 2016; Oxford 2017b) could broaden the scope of research into affective strategies for anxiety.

References

Aida, Yuki. 1994. "Examination of Horwitz, Horwitz, and Cope's Construct of Foreign Language Anxiety: The Case of Students of Japanese." *The Modern Language Journal* 78 (2): 155–68.

Arnold, Jane, ed. 1999. *Affect in Language Learning.* Cambridge: Cambridge University Press.

Bailey, Kathleen M. 1983. "Competitiveness and Anxiety in Adult Second Language Learning: Looking at and through Diary Studies." In *Classroom-oriented Research in Second Language Acquisition,* edited by Herbert W. Seliger and Michael H. Long, 67–103. Rowley: Newbury House.

Barkhuizen, Gary, Phil Benson, and Alice Chik. 2014. *Narrative Inquiry in Language Teaching and Learning Research.* London: Routledge.

Boekaerts, Monique. 2007. "Understanding Students' Affective Processes in the Classroom." In *Emotion in Education,* edited by Paul A. Schutz and Reinhard Pekrun, 37–56. Burlington: Academic Press.

Bown, Jennifer. 2009. "Self-regulatory Strategies and Agency in Self-instructed Language Learning: A Situated View." *The Modern Language Journal* 93 (4): 570–83.

Butler, Emily A., Boris Egloff, Fank H. Wilhelm, Nancy C. Smith, Elisabeth A. Erickson, and James J. Gross. 2003. "The Social Consequences of Expressive Suppression." *Emotion* 3: 48–67.

Council of Europe. 2001. *Common European Framework of Reference for Languages: Learning, Teaching, Assessment.* Cambridge: Cambridge University Press.

Creswell, John W. 2009. *Research Design: Qualitative, Quantitative, and Mixed Methods Approaches.* Thousand Oaks, CA: Sage.

Csíkszentmihályi, Mihály. 1997. *Finding Flow: The Psychology of Engagement with Everyday Life*. New York: Harper Collins.

Dewaele, Jean-Marc. 2002. "Psychological and Sociodemographic Correlates of Communicative Anxiety in L2 and L3 Production." *International Journal of Bilingualism* 6 (1): 23–38.

——. 2012. "Personality: Personality Traits and Independent and Dependent Variables." In *Psychology for Language Learning: Insights from Research, Theory and Practice*, edited by Sarah Mercer, Stephen Ryan, and Marion Williams, 42–58. Basingstoke: Palgrave Macmillan.

——. 2013. "The Link between Foreign Language Classroom Anxiety and Psychoticism, Extraversion, and Neuroticism among Adult Bi- and Multilinguals." *The Modern Language Journal* 97 (3): 670–84.

Dewaele, Jean-Marc, and Taghreed M. Al-Saraj. 2015. "Foreign Language Classroom Anxiety of Arab Learners of English: The Effect of Personality, Linguistic and Sociobiographical Variables." *Studies in Second Language Learning and Teaching* 5 (2): 205–28.

Dewaele, Jean-Marc, and Peter D. MacIntyre. 2014. "The Two Faces of Janus? Anxiety and Enjoyment in the Foreign Language Classroom." *Studies in Second Language Learning and Teaching* 4 (2): 237–74.

——. 2016. "Foreign Language Enjoyment and Foreign Language Classroom Anxiety: The Right and Left Feet of the Language Learner." In *Positive Psychology in SLA*, edited by Peter D. MacIntyre, Tammy Gregersen, and Sarah Mercer, 215–36. Bristol: Multilingual Matters.

Dewaele, Jean-Marc, K. V. Petrides, and Adrian Furnham. 2008. "The Effects of Trait Emotional Intelligence and Sociobiographical Variables on Communicative Anxiety and Foreign Language Anxiety among Adult Multilinguals: A Review and Empirical Investigation." *Language Learning* 58 (4): 911–60.

Dörnyei, Zoltán. 2005. *The Psychology of the Language Learner: Individual Differences in Second Language Acquisition*. Mahwah, NJ: Lawrence Erlbaum Associates.

——. 2009. "The L2 Motivational Self System." In *Motivation, Language Identity and the L2 Self*, edited by Zoltán Dörnyei and Ema Ushioda, 9–42. Bristol: Multilingual Matters.

Dörnyei, Zoltán, and Maggie Kubanyiova. 2014. *Motivating Learners, Motivating Teachers*. Cambridge: Cambridge University Press.

Freud, Sigmund. 1917. *Introductory Lectures on Psycho-Analysis*. Translated and edited by James Strachey. Reprinted in 1977. New York: Norton.

Gabryś-Barker, Danuta, and Joanna Bielska, eds. 2013. *The Affective Dimension in Second Language Acquisition*. Bristol: Multilingual Matters.

Gkonou, Christina. 2014. "Agency, Anxiety, and Activity: Understanding the Classroom Behavior of EFL Learners." In *Theorizing and Analyzing Agency in Second Language Learning: Interdisciplinary Approaches*, edited by Deters Ping, Xuesong Andy Gao, Elisabeth R. Miller, and Gergana Vitanova, 195–212. Bristol: Multilingual Matters.

Gkonou, Christina, and Rebecca L. Oxford. 2016. *Questionnaire: Managing Your Emotions for Language Learning Version 2.0*. University of Essex.

Goleman, Daniel. 1995. *Emotional Intelligence: Why It Can Matter More Than IQ*. New York: Bantam Books.

Gregersen, Tammy. 2007. "Breaking the Code of Silence: A Study of Teachers' Nonverbal Decoding Accuracy of Foreign Language Anxiety." *Language Teaching Research* 11 (2): 209–21,

Gregersen, Tammy, and Elaine K. Horwitz. 2002. "Language Learning and Perfectionism: Anxious and Non-anxious Language Learners' Reactions to Their Own Oral Performance." *The Modern Language Journal* 86 (3): 562–70.

Gregersen, Tammy, and Peter D. MacIntyre. 2014. *Capitalizing on Language Learner Individuality: From Premise to Practice*. Bristol: Multilingual Matters.

Gregersen, Tammy, Peter D. MacIntyre, and Mario Meza. 2014. "The Motion of Emotion: Idiodynamic Case Studies of Learners' Foreign Language Anxiety." *The Modern Language Journal* 98 (2): 574–88.

Gregersen, Tammy, Peter D. MacIntyre, and Tucker Olson. 2017. "Do You See What I Feel? An Idiodynamic Assessment of Expert and Peer's Reading of Nonverbal Language Anxiety Cues." In *New Insights into Language Anxiety: Theory, Research and Educational Implications*, edited by Christina Gkonou, Mark Daubney, and Jean-Marc Dewaele. Bristol: Multilingual Matters.

Gross, James J. 1998. "The Emerging Field of Emotional Regulation: An Integrative Review." *Review of General Psychology* 2: 271–99.

——. 2002. "Emotional Regulation: Affective, Cognitive, and Social Consequences." *Psychophysiology* 39: 281–91.

Hayes, Jasmeet P., Rajendra A. Morey, Christopher M. Petty, Srishti Seth, Moira J. Smoski, Gregory McCarthy, and Kevin S. LaBar. 2010. "Staying Cool When Things Get Hot: Emotion Regulation Modulates Neural Mechanisms of Memory Encoding." *Frontiers in Human Neuroscience* 4: 1–10.

Horwitz, Elaine K., Michael B. Horwitz, and Joann Cope. 1986. "Foreign Language Classroom Anxiety." *The Modern Language Journal* 70 (2): 125–32.

Horwitz, Elaine K., and Dolly J. Young, eds. 1991. *Language Anxiety: From Theory and Research to Classroom Implications.* Upper Saddle River, NJ: Prentice Hall.

Jacobs, Scott E., and James J. Gross. 2014. "Emotion Regulation in Education: Conceptual Foundations, Current Applications, and Future Directions." In *International Handbook of Emotions in Education*, edited by Reinhard Pekrun and Lisa Linnenbrink-Garcia, 183–201. New York: Routledge.

Kalaja, Paula, Vera Menezes, and Ana Maria F. Barcelos, eds. 2008. *Narratives of Learning and Teaching EFL*. Basingstoke: Palgrave.

Kitano, Kazu. 2001. "Anxiety in the College Japanese Language Classroom." *The Modern Language Journal* 85 (4): 549–66.

Kondo, David S., and Yang Ying-Ling. 2004. "Strategies for Coping with Language Anxiety: The Case of Students of English in Japan." *ELT Journal* 58 (3): 258–65.

Lincoln, Yvonna S., and Egon G. Guba. 1985. *Naturalistic Inquiry.* Beverly Hills, CA: Sage.

MacIntyre, Peter D. 1999. "Language Anxiety: A Review of the Research for Language Teachers." In *Affect in Foreign Language and Second Language Learning: A Practical Guide to Creating a Low-anxiety Classroom Atmosphere*, edited by Dolly J. Young, 24–45. Boston: McGraw-Hill.

MacIntyre, Peter D., and Robert C. Gardner. 1989. "Anxiety and Second Language Learning: Toward a Theoretical Classification." *Language Learning* 39 (2): 251–75.

——. 1991a. "Investigating Language Class Anxiety Using the Focused Essay Technique." *The Modern Language Journal* 75 (3): 296–304.

——. 1991b. "Language Anxiety: Its Relation to Other Anxieties and to Processing in Native and Second Languages." *Language Learning* 41 (4): 513–54.

MacIntyre, Peter D., and Tammy Gregersen. 2012. "Affect: The Role of Language Anxiety and Other Emotions in Language Learning." In *Psychology for Language Learning: Insights from Research, Theory and Practice*, edited by Sarah Mercer, Stephen Ryan, and Marion Williams, 103–18. Basingstoke: Palgrave Macmillan.

MacIntyre, Peter D., Tammy Gregersen, and Sarah Mercer, eds. 2016. *Positive Psychology in SLA.* Bristol: Multilingual Matters.

MacIntyre, Peter D., and Sarah Mercer. 2014. "Introducing Positive Psychology to SLA." *Studies in Second Language Learning and Teaching* 4 (2): 153–72.

MacIntyre, Peter D., Kimberly A. Noels, and Richard Clément. 1997. "Biases in Self-ratings of Second Language Proficiency: The Role of Language Anxiety." *Language Learning* 47 (2): 265–87.

Mak, Barley. 2011. "An Exploration of Speaking-in-class Anxiety with Chinese ESL Learners." *System* 39 (2): 202–14.

Mercer, Sarah. 2011. "Understanding Learner Agency as a Complex Dynamic System." *System* 39 (4): 427–36.

——. 2012. "The Complexity of Learner Agency." *Apples—Journal of Applied Language Studies* 6 (2): 41–59.

——. 2015. "Learner Agency and Engagement: Believing You Can, Wanting to and Knowing How to." *Humanising Language Teaching* 17 (4): 1–19.

Mercer, Sarah, and Christina Gkonou. 2017. "Teaching with Heart and Soul: Socio-emotional Learning in the Language Classroom." In *Innovative Practices in Language Teacher Education*, edited by Tammy Gregersen and Peter D. MacIntyre. Dordrecht: Springer.

Miles, Matthew B., and A. Michael Huberman. 1994. *Qualitative Data Analysis.* Thousand Oaks, CA: Sage.

Onwuegbuzie, Anthony J., Philipp Bailey, and Christine E. Daley. 1999. "Factors Associated with Foreign Language Anxiety." *Applied Psycholinguistics* 20 (2): 217–39.

Oxford, Rebecca L. 1990. *Language Learning Strategies: What Every Teacher Should Know.* Boston: Heinle & Heinle.

——. 1999. "Anxiety and the Language Learner: New Insights." In *Affect in Language Learning*, edited by Jane Arnold, 58–67. Cambridge: Cambridge University Press.

———. 2011. *Teaching and Researching Language Learning Strategies*. Harlow: Pearson Longman.

———. 2017a. "Anxious Language Learners Can Change Their Minds: Ideas and Strategies from Traditional Psychology and Positive Psychology." In *New Insights into Language Anxiety: Theory, Research and Educational Implications*, edited by Christina Gkonou, Mark Daubney, and Jean-Marc Dewaele. Bristol: Multilingual Matters.

———. 2017b. *Teaching and Researching Language Learning Strategies: Self Regulation in Context*. 2nd edition. New York: Routledge.

Saldaña, Jonny. 2013. *The Coding Manual for Qualitative Researchers*. Thousand Oaks, CA: Sage.

Şimşek, Erdi, and Zoltán Dörnyei. 2017. "Anxiety and L2 Self-Images: The 'Anxious Self.'" In *New Insights into Language Anxiety: Theory, Research and Educational Implications*, edited by Christina Gkonou, Mark Daubney, and Jean-Marc Dewaele. Bristol: Multilingual Matters.

Spielberger, Charles D. 1983. *Manual for the State-Trait Anxiety Inventory (STAI)*. Palo Alto, CA: Consulting Psychologists Press.

Srivastava, Sanjay, Maya Tamir, Kelly M. McGonigal, Oliver P. John, and James J. Gross. 2009. "The Social Costs of Emotional Suppression: A Prospective Study of the Transition to College." *Journal of Personality and Social Psychology* 96: 883–97.

Strauss, Anselm L. 1987. *Qualitative Analysis for Social Scientists*. Cambridge: Cambridge University Press.

Tashakkori, Abbas, and Charles Teddlie. 2003. *Handbook of Mixed Methods in Social and Behavioral Research*. Thousand Oaks, CA: Sage.

Tsui, Amy B. M. 1996. "Reticence and Anxiety in Second Language Learning." In *Voices from the Language Classroom*, edited by Kathleen M. Bailey and David Nunan, 145–67. Cambridge: Cambridge University Press.

Williams, Marion, and Robert L. Burden. 1997. *Psychology for Language Teachers: A Social Constructivist Approach*. Cambridge: Cambridge University Press.

Williams, Marion, Sarah Mercer, and Stephen Ryan. 2015. *Exploring Psychology in Language Learning and Teaching*. Oxford: Oxford University Press.

Yan, Jackie X., and Elaine K. Horwitz. 2008. "Learners' Perceptions of How Anxiety Interacts with Personal and Instructional Factors to Influence Their Achievement in English: A Qualitative Analysis of EFL Learners in China." *Language Learning* 58 (1): 151–83.

5

Modeling a Prototypical Use of Language Learning Strategies

Decision Tree-Based Methods in Multiple Contexts

Atsushi Mizumoto
Osamu Takeuchi
Kansai University, Japan

It is well documented that "questionnaires have formed the 'backbone' of strategy research methodology" (Griffiths and Oxford 2014, 3). This chapter reviews the issues of questionnaire use, construction, and analysis for the research and practice of language learning strategies (LLS). We also propose decision tree-based methods, a flexible alternative to conventional approaches, to model essential features of strategies and situate strategies into specific contexts.

1. Questionnaire use in strategy research

This section provides a historical view of strategy questionnaire use, followed by issues in strategy questionnaire construction.

1.1. Historical view

To provide an overview of the number of questionnaires used in LLS research or mentioned in LLS literature, a database search was conducted in December, 2016. The search was conducted using four databases and included only reviewed journal articles (PhD theses and books were excluded). These databases were: *ERIC (Education Resources Information Center)*, *Library and Information Science Abstracts (LISA)*, *Linguistics and Language Behavior Abstracts (LLBA)*, and *MLA International Bibliography*. The research term used was "language learning

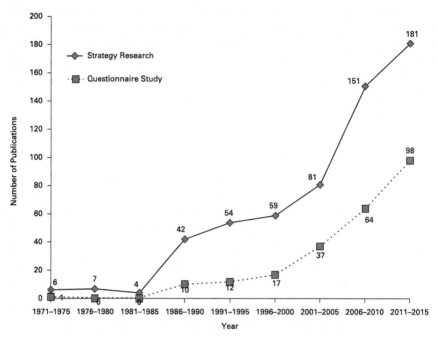

Figure 5.1 A database search of language learning strategies research and questionnaire use during the period 1971 to 2015

Note: The search was conducted with five databases on December 9, 2016

(learner) strategy (strategies)." The number of publications concerning LLS and questionnaire use from 1971 to 2015 in which this term was included in the title or abstract is shown in Figure 5.1. This is a rough estimate because there may be relevant LLS studies that do not include those words in the title or abstract. The number of studies using questionnaires was determined by searching for words such as index, instrument, inventory, item, Likert, measure, questionnaire, respondent, response, scale, subscale, and survey. These words were selected by referring to a small corpus of articles and books (e.g., Dörnyei and Taguchi 2010), the topic of which was survey questionnaires.

A few authors have argued that scholarly interest in LLS, which was once referred to as the "Robin Hood in SLA" (Gu 1996), has been "waning" (Dörnyei and Ryan 2015, 148) or has reached "an all-time low" (Gu 2012, 330) in recent years. However, our multi-database search contradicts this view. The number of research publications on LLS has consistently risen globally. LLS research is obviously alive and kicking, given that the databases mentioned above and reflected in Figure 5.1 included LLS research articles not only in applied linguistics but also in other fields, such as educational psychology.[1] To reiterate, all of Figure 5.1's research, drawn from four respected databases, consisted of LLS studies, no matter which fields they came from. Note the tremendous rise in LLS studies over the years, without any waning or all-time lows.

Paralleling this increase in LLS research publications, questionnaire use in strategy LLS research is also increasing, as shown in Figure 5.1. This trend indicates that much of the long-term development of LLS research was built on the use of questionnaires. Although mixed-methods research, which combines quantitative and qualitative approaches, has been increasingly employed in recent years (Amerstorfer, Chapter 6 in this volume; Oxford 2011), as Griffiths and Oxford (2014, 4) put it, "[o]ver the years, probably the most common method used in strategy research has been the Likert-scale type questionnaire" (Figure 5.1). One reason why questionnaire use is so prevalent in LLS research is due to the user-friendliness of the *Strategy Inventory for Language Learning* (*SILL*) (Oxford 1990), which undoubtedly pushed the field of LLS research forward despite statistical issues. At the same time, over-dependence on questionnaires has been problematized in LLS research because a questionnaire is just one of the possible alternatives in data collection methods, considering the nature of LLS (see Gao 2004 and Oxford 1990, 2011 for many non-questionnaire strategy assessment tools).

Just as language tests and their constructs reflect the current views and theories of second or foreign language learning and SLA, the refined definitions of LLS in the post-*SILL* era are reflected in the constructs of LLS questionnaires, with much emphasis placed on specific skill areas, situations, and contexts or metacognitive aspects (e.g., Vandergrift et al. 2006). Oxford (1999) first introduced the theme of self-regulation to the language field and contrasted it with learner autonomy, with further recommendations for in-depth strategy assessment using the self-regulation construct (Oxford 1999, 2011, 2017). Research reporting the development of LLS questionnaires has now been expanded to include the notion of self-regulation (Tseng, Dörnyei, and Schmitt 2006).

1.2. Issues in questionnaire construction

It is possible to have strategy questionnaires that include both quantitative items and qualitative items (the latter being open-ended responses in learners' own words). Fully qualitative questionnaires are also possible. Both kinds of questionnaires, partially and fully qualitative, can be used for exploring orchestration of personalized strategies in detail. However, this chapter deals only with quantitative questionnaires because the use of other questionnaires is rare in the strategy field.

Likert scales ask respondents to mark their attitudes toward certain issues (i.e., strategy use) that are expressed in the given items. While several variations on Likert scales exist, the assumption is that the options expressed along a continuum from least to most (for example, "strongly disagree" to "strongly agree") indicate the intensity of the respondents' answers to the criteria being measured.

There are two types of measurement scales for Likert-type questionnaires: (a) single-item scales and (b) multi-item scales. With a single-item scale, only one item supposedly taps into the target construct. On the other hand, a multi-item scale measures each construct based on more than two items. The scale score, which can be gained from averaging (or adding up) item scores for similar questions, represents an underlying trait in the same category or subscale. Because a multi-item scale is designed to be a psychometric instrument, a reliability coefficient such as Cronbach's alpha is calculated for each subscale. If a single-item scale is used to measure one construct, a learner's response to a specific item may be unreliable due to measurement error. As measurement error (e.g., resulting from mood, fatigue, or wording of the items) is inevitable in any measurement instrument, for more accurate measurement, a psychometric "scale" consisting of more than three items is required, rather than just one. However, in a questionnaire study, researchers and practitioners often fail to deal with measurement error. As Dörnyei and Taguchi (2010, 23) argue, "the notion of multi-item scales is the central component in scientific questionnaire design, yet this concept is surprisingly little known in the L2 profession." They also note that "because of the fallibility of single items, there is a general consensus among survey specialists that more than one item is needed to address each identified content area" (2010, 25). Furthermore, it has been demonstrated that "multi-item scales clearly outperform single items in terms of predictive validity" (Diamantopoulos et al. 2012, 434).

Despite its superiority as a measurement instrument, a multi-item scale (questionnaire) can be problematic when it is used to measure a strategic "behavior," because frequency of strategy use alone (i.e., how often) is not a sign of successful learning. An orchestration of a contextualized, personalized set of strategies is a more apt measure of successful learning (i.e., how well). For this reason, Dörnyei (2005) suggests using Cohen, Oxford, and Chi's (2002) *Language Strategy Use Inventory and Index* (*LSUII*) for pedagogical and practical purposes but not for research. The *LSUII* is a single-item scale invented as a classroom tool with no intention of summating items under each subscale (category). Therefore, it provides a list of strategic behaviors under the six categories of listening, speaking, reading, writing, vocabulary learning, and translation skills, with each item measuring only one specific behavior.

Considering the above, is it then inappropriate and impossible to create a questionnaire on strategy use using multi-item scales? The answer is no. The key to doing so relates to the scope and range of the construct to be measured with a subscale in the questionnaire. For example, Gu and Johnson (1996) created the *Vocabulary Learning Questionnaire*, composed of multi-item scales to assess the use of vocabulary learning strategies. The items below are included in the subscale of "Using Word-Structure," which comprises three items to be averaged as an indicator of word structure use in vocabulary learning (Gu and Johnson 1996).

1. I analyze words in terms of prefixes, stems, and suffixes.
2. I deliberately study word-formation rules to remember more words.
3. I memorize the commonly used stems and prefixes.

Obviously, summing or averaging the responses to these items as a means of investigating the use of word structure in vocabulary learning makes sense because the scope and range to be measured with these items are very limited, and the task is straightforward (i.e., remembering vocabulary). In this case, the multi-item scale is thus tenable and cumulative. In contrast, if the construct to be measured with these items is "cognitive strategies," that would be too wide a concept to cover, and could not possibly be assessed using these three items that are so limited in range and scope. As a result, summing or averaging the responses of these items in this specific subscale does not reflect the use of strategy as a cumulative scale (see Dörnyei and Ryan 2015 for a detailed discussion). It should be noted that the strategy "Using Word-Structure" in Gu and Johnson's (1996) study falls under the category of "encoding strategies," which is further placed under a higher dimension of "cognitive strategies." By using a hierarchical structure in their questionnaire (i.e., dimensions, categories, and strategies), which includes ninety-one items in total, Gu and Johnson successfully operationalized the constructs of vocabulary learning strategies with multi-scale items by focusing on a certain aspect in a target skill area.

We began this section with a study of LLS questionnaire use from 1971 to 2015 and then discussed questionnaire construction issues. The next section concentrates on analysis.

2. Statistical analyses used in questionnaire studies of LLS

The definitional concepts and assessment instruments of LLS have evolved as the field has advanced over the years. However, those advances have not been fully reflected in the statistical analyses used in LLS questionnaire studies. Rather, conventional analysis methods such as *t*-test, ANOVA, and correlation-based analysis have been used predominantly in LLS studies. This is in line with the general trend in L2 research, which falls under the domain of applied linguistics (Plonsky 2013).

2.1. A reform movement

Quantitative methods in L2 research have recently been at the center of a statistical reform movement (Plonsky 2015), in which appropriate statistical analyses and better reporting practices are encouraged in order to improve the overall quality of research papers in the field, especially to promote replication and reproducibility (see Larson-Hall and Plonsky 2015 for recommended reporting practices). LLS researchers must also seek methodological rigor, as LLS is an established research field in applied linguistics.

2.2. Data levels and parametric/nonparametric statistics

When analyzing questionnaire data, the levels of measurement (i.e., nominal, ordinal, interval, and ratio) should be considered, whether involving a single-item or multi-item scale, in order to apply an appropriate analytical method. Questionnaire responses comprise ordinal data, so it is inappropriate to add, subtract, multiply, or divide the numbers, which are basic numerical operations in any parametric statistical analysis. With three or four categories (points) in the scale, the data will probably not be distributed normally, thus violating a key assumption for using parametric procedures (Plonsky 2015). Thus, nonparametric techniques based on rank order (i.e., ordinal scale) or counting and percentages (i.e., nominal scale) are often recommended in LLS measurements that use questionnaires (e.g., Griffiths and Oxford 2014; Oxford 2011). Nonparametric procedures will gradually be replaced by modern statistical techniques such as bootstrapping and resampling (e.g., Larson-Hall and Herrington 2010; Plonsky, Egbert, and LaFlair 2014), but nonparametrics are here to stay until those novel techniques spread to the end users.

Although the level of measurement for questionnaire data is regarded as ordinal, if there are five or more categories (points) on the scale, as in five-point

Likert scales, it is generally accepted that the data should be treated as interval scales because the wider range of these scales would yield data resembling an interval scale (Hatch and Lazaraton 1991). Therefore, parametric statistics are actually acceptable for strategy questionnaires, provided that the data is normally distributed.[2] Converting the data obtained from a questionnaire into interval scales using the Rasch model (Bond and Fox 2015) or Item Response Theory (IRT) is another possible solution to the criticisms that have been directed at the levels of measurement of questionnaire data (e.g., Mizumoto and Takeuchi 2009a).

The whole issue of which statistics (parametric or nonparametric) to use for strategy questionnaires, which are ordinal-scale in nature, boils down to the distribution of data. If the data is normally distributed, we can justify the use of numerical summaries of the data such as the means and the standard deviations, and those values are used for making assumptions about a population's parameters (hence the name "parametric" statistics).

Suppose we administer a five-point Likert scale strategy questionnaire to 100 participants, and obtain a mean (*M*) of 3.20 and a standard deviation (*SD*) of 0.80 as the result. Because it is a five-point Likert scale, the minimum score is 1 and the maximum score is 5. If the distribution of the data is normal, we can imagine a distribution such as the one seen in the left panel of Figure 5.2. We can

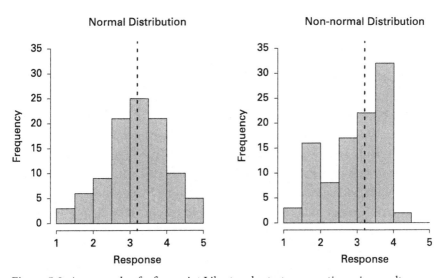

Figure 5.2 An example of a five-point Likert scale strategy questionnaire result

Note: The means (*M* = 3.20) and the standard deviations (*SD* = 0.80) are the same for both the normal distribution (*left*) and the non-normal distribution (*right*). Vertical lines in the figures show the means

even say that about 68 percent of the participants' responses could be found between 2.40 (M—1SD: 3.20 – 1 × 0.80) and 4.00 (M + 1SD: 3.20 + 1 × 0.80), and about 95 percent; between 1.60 (M—2SD: 3.20 – 2 × 0.80) and 4.80 (M + 2SD: 3.20 + 2 × 0.80) because that is the property of normal distribution, and we use it as the "model" in statistical analyses. In fact, only the sample size (i.e., the number of participants: n), means (M), and standard deviations (SD) are necessary for computing statistics such as t-values in the t-test and F-values in ANOVA (and their corresponding p-values), and as such, even the original data would not be necessary to reproduce the statistical results. That is why reporting these values (n, M, and SD) is compulsory in the results section of the study (e.g., Larson-Hall and Plonsky 2015).

However, problems arise if the distribution of the data is non-normal (Figure 5.2, *right*). Figure 5.2 shows that we can obtain the exact means (M = 3.20) and standard deviations (SD = 0.80) whether the data is normally distributed or not. When we apply parametric statistics, the assumption of data distribution is the left panel of Figure 5.2 (i.e., a normal distribution) or one that is close to normal distribution, and again, that is why we only need to know the mean and the standard deviation to imagine this model distribution of the data. It is thus unsurprising that we would obtain statistically inaccurate results if we apply parametric statistics to non-normal data, as the model distribution is not reflected in the actual data at all. In this case, obviously, we should use nonparametric statistics. From this example, it is clear that we should always check the distribution of the data graphically, as reporting means and standard deviations alone, of course, does not guarantee the normal distribution of data.

The debate over whether it is appropriate to treat the ordinal, Likert-type measurement scale as the interval scale has continued to this day. It is thus conceivable that this practice is "frowned upon" by hardline fundamentalists. However, the predominant view held by researchers across a wide range of scientific fields, after decades of debate, is that "it is perfectly appropriate to use parametric techniques" (Carifio and Perla 2008, 1151). If the assumption of normal distribution is met, therefore, we can apply parametric statistics to Likert-type strategy questionnaires. For this reason, it is simply wrong to condemn a strategy questionnaire like the *SILL* solely based on its use of parametric statistics.

It should also be noted here that some parametric tests, such as t-test and ANOVA, are known to be robust to non-normality (i.e., the statistical results will be the same in parametric and nonparametric procedures). Consequently, in many studies utilizing Likert-scale instruments, the parametric and nonparametric results turn out to be almost identical on a consistent basis (Oxford 2011). When in doubt, therefore, it is best to try both parametric and nonparametric procedures and compare the results.

2.3. Specific parametric analyses

With respect to the statistical analyses used in questionnaire studies, means-based analyses (e.g., *t*-test, ANOVA) are often conducted to investigate group comparisons of LLS use and the gains before and after strategy instruction. Focusing on the effectiveness of strategy instruction for L2 students, Plonsky (2011) conducted a meta-analysis, an established statistical method for integrating the quantitative results from primary studies, and reported that, overall, a small to medium effect size ($d = 0.49$) can be expected from strategy instruction.[3] Plonsky's study (2011) demonstrates just how prevalent means-based analyses are in LLS research (because a large number of studies are required in order to conduct a meta-analysis). At the same time, his study demonstrated that a certain number of studies lacked the appropriate information necessary for meta-analysis, which underscores the importance of improving reporting practices among LLS researchers.

Correlation-based analyses (e.g., correlation analysis, multiple regression analysis, and exploratory and confirmatory factor analyses) are also often used to examine the relationship between variables in LLS questionnaire studies. Multivariate analyses, which can deal with multiple variables simultaneously, are often employed, especially since the interest of LLS researchers is often focused on several variables, including individual difference factors. For questionnaire development, exploratory factor analysis has traditionally been employed in the LLS literature (e.g., Tragant, Thompson, and Victori 2013).

Of all the multivariate techniques, multiple regression analysis is most widely used in LLS research (e.g., Nisbet, Tindall, and Arroyo 2005). Nevertheless, it should be emphasized that the use of standardized regression coefficients (β) to determine the importance of predictor (independent) variables is often misleading and misinterpreted both in LLS research specifically and in L2 studies generally. Researchers often make claims regarding what the best predictor variables among many variables are by conducting stepwise multiple regression analyses, implying that those variables with larger standardized regression coefficients are more important than other variables with smaller standardized regression coefficients. Whereas the regression formula using the best predictor variables is useful for predicting the value of the dependent (outcome) variable in future studies, the relative importance among predictor variables against an outcome variable cannot be determined by a multiple regression analysis. As Jaccard and Daniloski (2012, 185) explain, "[r]eliance on standardized coefficients requires the assumption that the variance of a predictor is constant at each combination of the other predictors. This assumption is often unrealistic." Unfortunately, the misuse of standardized regression coefficients to determine important predictors has continued to this day. Thus, LLS researchers should be aware of this misuse, and they should not use multiple regression analysis if their research purpose is to determine which predictor variables are more important than others.

Another multivariate technique, Structural Equation Modeling (SEM), has notably contributed to the advancement of LLS research. SEM encompasses numerous other analysis methods, such as multiple regression analysis and exploratory or confirmatory factor analysis. Because SEM can simultaneously handle a set of observed variables (i.e., individual questionnaire items), latent variables (i.e., underlying traits that can be represented with the subscales or categories of the questionnaire), and measurement errors, researchers who investigate the relationship among constructs using questionnaires have utilized SEM as a more sophisticated approach in LLS research (e.g., Gardner, Tremblay, and Masgoret 1997; Hsiao and Oxford 2002; Tseng, Dörnyei, and Schmitt 2006; Tseng and Schmitt 2008; Woodrow 2005).

However, all the statistical methods mentioned above only examine means and correlations as a group. In LLS research, another multivariate analysis, cluster analysis, has been used extensively to reflect individual learner differences, including strategy use (e.g., Gu and Johnson 1996; Kojic-Sabo and Lightbown 1999; Mizumoto and Takeuchi 2009b; Yamamori et al. 2003). Cluster analysis is an exploratory statistical technique used to identify homogeneous subgroups within the whole group. Learners in the same cluster (i.e., the subgroup) are more similar than those in other clusters in terms of their patterns in the target variables. Figure 5.3 is a profile plot of a group of 244 Japanese EFL learners arising from cluster analysis (Mizumoto and Takeuchi 2008), which shows their outcome measures (listening and reading), vocabulary learning strategies (self-managing, input-seeking, imagery, writing rehearsal, oral rehearsal, and association), motivation (extrinsic and intrinsic), and study time, according to the clusters (subgroups) into which they have been categorized. As is clear from the figure, strategy use and its relationship with other variables can be examined in a fine-grained manner at each cluster level by using cluster analysis.

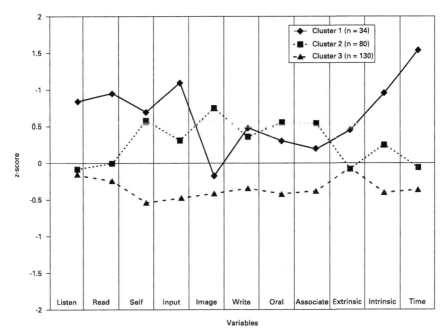

Figure 5.3 A profile plot in cluster analysis (Mizumoto and Takeuchi 2008)

While cluster analysis can illustrate both individual differences and the orchestration of strategy use, it remains the case that only the patterns (means) of the subgroups can be highlighted. Thus, it remains unclear how individual learners make sequential choices among strategies (i.e., strategy chains). In strategy use, the element of choice (Cohen 1998; see also Chapter 2 of this volume) is crucial in that learners themselves, for some reason, select the most appropriate strategies from their available repertoire for a specific task in a specific context (i.e., situating strategies into contexts). If such a series of decisions on strategy use could be modeled, it would provide researchers and practitioners with new and more detailed perspectives on the interplay between strategy use and other situational and individual factors.

Above we introduced statistical analyses used in LLS questionnaire studies. We touched on a statistical reform movement in the L2 field, discussed data levels and the use of parametric/nonparametric statistics, explained circumstances under which ordinal data can be treated as interval data, and described specific multivariate techniques widely used in LLS research. The next section presents an innovative way of analyzing contextualized strategy questionnaire data.

3. Proposing decision tree-based methods for LLS research and practice

Decision tree analysis, also known as decision tree-based analysis, is a predictive modeling approach often used in marketing research, in which consumer behavior is analyzed and future courses of action decided on. A decision tree, which is a flowchart-like display for recommending appropriate behaviors, has traditionally been used, but in recent years, this method has also attracted attention in computer-assisted data mining and machine learning. Machine learning is a type of artificial intelligence with which computers are equipped to learn and improve automatically with experience without being explicitly programed.

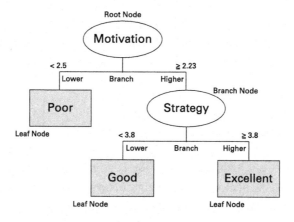

Figure 5.4 The concept of decision trees

Decision tree analysis, also known as decision tree-base, is similar to multiple regression analysis in that it uses multiple predictor (or independent) variables to predict the values of the target (dependent, outcome, or criterion) variable. The biggest advantage of decision tree analysis is that it can flexibly deal with categorical and continuous data in both independent and dependent variables. Decision tree analysis is therefore a nonparametric, nonlinear method for predicting or explaining a phenomenon. Nonlinearity is one of the hallmarks of complexity, which itself is a characteristic of language learning (see Oxford, Lavine, and Amerstorfer, Chapter 1 in this volume).

3.1. Uses of decision tree analysis

The results of decision tree analysis are normally presented in the simple form of IF-THEN classification rules (statements) associated with each predictor variable in a tree-like graph (Figure 5.4). If the target variable is categorical (Figure 5.4, *left*), the trees are called *classification trees*, and if the target variable is continuous (Figure 5.4, *right*), the trees are called *regression trees*. Note that the difference of names signifies the difference of parametric and nonparametric procedures. The methods of using these trees are thus sometimes called classification and regression trees (CART). The optimal cut point, where the trees branch out, is defined using statistical tests, Gini's impurity index, or information gain (see Kotsiantis 2013; McArdle 2012 for algorithms). Figure 5.4 shows that the trees can be used to predict the category (the left panel) or value (the right panel) of the target variable. Decision trees are therefore very intuitive and easy to interpret, and have a variety of applications in quantitative investigations across many disciplines.

Advances in machine learning techniques have made computationally intensive algorithms possible (Hastie, Tibshirani, and Friedman 2009). Random Forest (Breiman 2001) is one such machine learning technique; it is an advanced method of decision tree analysis. As its name suggests, Random Forest creates more than one decision tree by repeating the random sampling of the predictor variables, and then aggregating the result (Tono 2013), in a procedure known as the ensemble learning method. The idea behind this technique is similar to bootstrapping, a computer-intensive technique by which repetitive resamples are taken from the observed sample data to estimate the population data (Larson-Hall and Herrington 2010; Plonsky, Egbert, and LaFlair 2014). As it uses aggregations of data, the Random Forest method is known to outperform decision tree analysis (McArdle 2012).

These decision tree-based methods have been used in other fields, but in applied linguistics, their use has been limited to corpus studies, especially automatic text analysis (e.g., Jarvis 2012; Tono 2013; Wang, Waple, and Kawahara 2009). We assume that decision tree-based methods are also applicable to LLS research that uses questionnaires because they can: (a) model the element of choice in strategy use; (b) demonstrate the prototypical use of LLS in a given context (i.e., situating strategy use into contexts); (c) provide more diagnostic feedback on strategy use for teachers and learners using IF-THEN classification statements; and (d) be used for any quantitative LLS measures (e.g., a practical classroom single-item scale and a multi-item scale) or any categorical variables (e.g., "yes–no" or "success–failure"). These features enable strategy researchers and practitioners to investigate the situated strategy use of language learners in a more detailed way than has been previously possible.

3.2. Example of decision tree analysis with an EFL strategy study

As an illustration, we report here a questionnaire study with a group of 711 EFL (English as a foreign language) learners from universities in Japan. The participants responded to a questionnaire (a six-point Likert scale) on cognitive aspects of vocabulary learning strategies (Mizumoto 2010). Because the items used were based on and similar to those in Gu and Johnson (1996), the scope and range to be measured with these items were limited, and thus averaging the items in each subscale proved to be psychometrically justifiable in a previous study (Mizumoto 2010). In addition, the participants answered a six-point Likert scale questionnaire on their metacognitive control of strategy use (or strategic vocabulary learning involvement, as Tseng and Schmitt 2008 might say), which was composed of four items (Mizumoto 2013). These items were also averaged as a multi-item scale and included the following: "I have my own way of learning and reviewing when learning vocabulary" and "I devise various methods to memorize vocabulary." A measure of metacognitive control of strategy use was included because its effect on strategic behaviors has previously been established in numerous LLS studies (e.g., Gu 2005; Mizumoto 2010; Tseng and Schmitt 2008). The Cronbach's alpha coefficients, descriptive statistics, and correlations of all measures are presented in Table 5.1. Decision tree analysis and Random Forest were performed using vocabulary learning strategies (Imagery, Writing Rehearsal, Oral Rehearsal, and Association) as predictor variables and Metacognitive Control of Strategy Use (MCSU, a continuous variable) as a target variable. R version 3.2.3 was used for all the analyses described in this chapter. R is a free programming language that is primarily used for statistical computing and graphics.[4]

Table 5.1 Cronbach's alpha coefficients, descriptive statistics, and correlations of measures ($n = 711$)

Measure	No. of Items	α	M	SD	Skewness	Kurtosis	Correlations				
							1	2	3	4	5
1. Imagery	5	0.76	3.75	1.07	-0.16	-0.31	—				
2. Writing Rehearsal	3	0.78	3.84	1.33	-0.09	-0.84	0.28	—			
3. Oral Rehearsal	3	0.84	3.59	1.28	-0.14	-0.72	0.42	0.29	—		
4. Association	3	0.89	3.44	1.26	-0.02	-0.77	0.57	0.23	0.43	—	
5. Metacognitive Control	4	0.87	3.47	1.14	-0.11	-0.44	0.54	0.31	0.51	0.55	—

Note. Range for the means (1–6)

Figure 5.5 is a regression tree obtained from the result of decision tree analysis. The nodes at the bottom of the tree show the predicted values of the target variable, MCSU. The root node, which is the most important in predicting the values of the target variable, is Association. Depending on the values of other predictor variables, combinations of strategies result in different values in the target variable. For example, learners who are categorized in Node 3 (n = 93) use Association and Oral Rehearsal less, and their expected values in MCSU are much lower than those of other learners. From this result, we can learn that it is these learners who require support in strategy use through instruction.

At the same time, the result of this decision tree analysis underscores the importance of Imagery and Oral Rehearsal because these strategies play a role as the nodes from which branches diverge. Moreover, as decision tree analysis is a non-linear method, an effective combination of strategies, previously undetected using conventional linear methods, can be identified. Specifically, Writing Rehearsal has been reported to have a low correlation with outcome measures such as the *TOEIC* test (Mizumoto 2010), but learners in Node 14 (n = 26) had relatively high levels of metacognitive control. This may be because those learners simultaneously employed the strategies of Writing Rehearsal, Oral Rehearsal, and others, which requires a higher level of metacognition (Macaro 2006). A problem arises when learners use only Writing Rehearsal, which is likely to lead to unsuccessful strategy use. This argument is supported by the results of Gu and Johnson's study (1996), in which Visual Repetition was negatively correlated with outcome measures.

Figure 5.6 shows the estimate error rate and number of trees grown (left) and the plot of importance of predictor variables (right) obtained from the results of Random Forest. The left panel of Figure 5.6 indicates that 500 (decision) trees were grown, and the corresponding error rate decreases as the number of trees increases. In the right panel, the importance of predictor variables is similar to the regression coefficients obtained from multiple regression analysis (because it was a regression tree), but they are more accurate, since they were extracted as a result of the ensemble learning method of Random Forest. While a more accurate estimate of variable importance is of great value, too much emphasis should not be placed on this index when used in LLS research because, as we have seen above and as the definition of LLS suggests, the important features of manifested strategic behaviors are not single strategy use, but rather the mixture of strategies used to meet the needs and individual differences of learners (Amerstorfer, Chapter 6 in this volume).

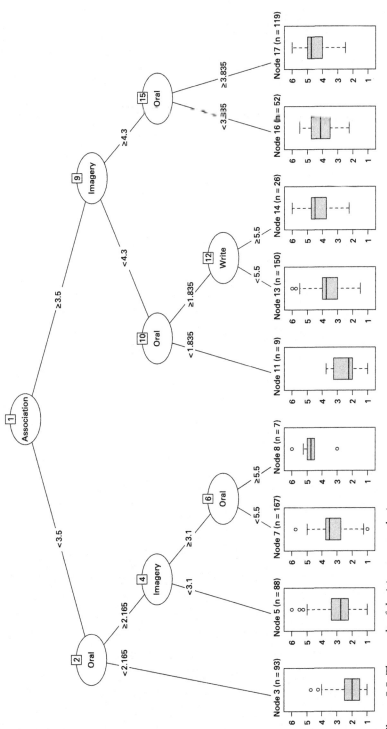

Figure 5.5 The result of decision tree analysis

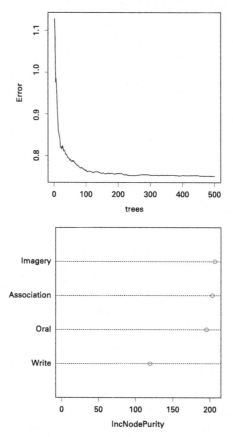

Figure 5.6 Error rate and the number of grown trees (*top*); variable importance plot (*bottom*)

3.3. Value of decision tree-based methods for LLS researchers and practitioners

As illustrated, decision tree based methods can provide LLS researchers and practitioners with an interesting alternative to conventional methods. The visual output of decision tree analysis is very powerful and appealing to anyone interested in investigating the LLS use of learners in a specific context using a quantitative approach. To use decision tree-based methods in research, however, one needs to know about the more technical aspects of data mining, such as pruning, in order to avoid over-learning of algorithm and cross-validation (Witten, Frank, and Hall 2011). As machine learning can be intimidating for those with statistics phobia, we have prepared a web application for the purpose of developing the reader's initial understanding of tree-based models (http://

langtest.jp/shiny/trees/). All the decision tree-based procedures introduced in this chapter can be experienced through this application, and users can even supply their own datasets. All that is required is to copy and paste the data from a spreadsheet (see Mizumoto and Plonsky 2016 for an introduction to this web application called *langtest*); users can then see the results within seconds. For practical purposes, such as an initial investigation of the use of a set of strategies before strategy instruction, this web application can empower users and provide them with a rich source of insightful information on learners' strategic behaviors.

In sum, we proposed decision tree-based methods as an alternative quantitative approach to LLS questionnaire analysis. Advantages of such methods include modeling the element of choice in strategy use and the contextualizing of strategy use. We applied decision tree-based methods to a strategy study and introduced a user-friendly web application to show the value of decision tree-based methods for LLS research and practice.

4. Summary and final comments

In this chapter, after reviewing the questionnaire use and various quantitative methods used so far in LLS research, we proposed using decision tree-based methods for quantitative LLS research.[5] We proposed this innovative analysis framework because questionnaires remain the prevalent instrument in LLS research and practice, despite the common understanding among many LLS researchers that strategic behaviors are highly complex phenomena unanalyzable by quantitative instruments alone.

By using decision tree-based methods, we demonstrated that it is possible to model a prototypical use of strategic behaviors by learners in a given learning context. Such modeling could change the expectations of strategy researchers and practitioners because it allows them to observe the intricate, multifaceted mix of strategic behaviors from a different, more revealing angle. At the same time, decision tree-based methods can provide users and learners with clearer diagnosis and feedback on LLS use in a specific context, especially in contrast with the conventional data analysis methods used in strategy research.

One caveat is that decision tree-based methods are simply a data analysis approach and, as such, they do not change the constructs that are measured using questionnaires. In other words, what we can learn from a given questionnaire is limited to what that questionnaire can measure. Thus, researchers and practitioners should be aware of the limitations and constraints of questionnaires and quantitative approaches in general.

If we use them judiciously, tree-based methods could constitute, with their flexibility and applicability, an alternative LLS data analysis tool for researchers and practitioners who are greatly interested in the ingenious, situated strategic behaviors that reflect individual differences at the dawn of the new era of LLS research and practice.

Notes

1   Editors' note: LLS research reviews (e.g., in Oxford 2011, 2017), LLS-themed special issues of journals (Oxford and Griffiths 2014, Oxford and Pawlak 2018), and an LLS instruction meta-analysis (Plonsky 2011) support key findings of the database search, namely that LLS research and interest in such research has not waned and has, in fact, continued briskly, most often using questionnaires. Another investigation (Donker et al. 2014) meta-analyzes nearly five dozen strategy instruction studies across multiple subject areas, underscoring the fact that strategy research has not slowed down.

2   Editors' note: This chapter employs the common phraseology of "data is," rather than the more formal "data are."

3   Donker et al. (2014) showed a larger effect size for strategy instruction across a range of subject areas.

4   For transparent sharing of data and results, the data and R codes used in this chapter are available online (http://mizumot.com/files/trees.html). This access will enable our readers to trace the results and explore decision tree-based methods in a hands-on manner.

5   A recent special issue (Hodis and Hancock 2016) is devoted to still other advances in quantitative research methods for education and educational psychology. Some of these methods, in addition to decision tree-based methods, might be useful to consider for LLS research.

References

Bond, Trevor, and Christine M. Fox. 2015. *Applying the Rasch Model: Fundamental Measurement in the Human Sciences.* 3rd edition. New York: Routledge.

Breiman, Leo. 2001. "Random Forests." *Machine Learning* 45: 5–32.

Carifio, James, and Rocco Perla. 2008. "Resolving the 50-year Debate around Using and Misusing Likert Scales." *Medical Education* 42 (12): 1150–52.

Cohen, Andrew D. 1998. *Strategies in Learning and Using a Second Language.* London: Longman.

Cohen, Andrew D., Rebecca L. Oxford, and Julie C. Chi. 2002. *Language Strategy Use Survey.* Minneapolis, MN: Center for Advanced Research on Language Acquisition, University of Minnesota.

Diamantopoulos, Adamantios, Marko Sarstedt, Christoph Fuchs, Petra Wilczynski, and Sebastian Kaiser. 2012. "Guidelines for Choosing between Multi-item and Single-item Scales for Construct Measurement: A Predictive Validity Perspective." *Journal of the Academy of Marketing Science* 40 (3): 434–49.

Donker, Anouk S., Hester de Boer, Danny Kostons, Charlotte Dignath-van Ewijk, and Margaretha P. C. van der Werf. 2014. "Effectiveness of Learning Strategy Instruction on Academic Performance: A Meta-Analysis." *Educational Research Review* 11: 1–26. http://dx.doi.org/10.1016/j.edurev.2013.11.002

Dörnyei, Zoltán. 2005. *The Psychology of the Language Learner: Individual Differences in Second Language Acquisition.* Mahwah, NJ: Lawrence Erlbaum Associates.

Dörnyei, Zoltán, and Stephen Ryan. 2015. *The Psychology of the Language Learner Revisited.* New York: Routledge.

Dörnyei, Zoltán, and Tatsuya Taguchi. 2010. *Questionnaires in Second Language Research: Construction, Administration, and Processing.* 2nd edition. New York: Routledge.

Gao, Xuesong Andy. 2004. "A Critical Review of Questionnaire Use in Learner Strategy Research." *Prospect: An Australian Journal of TESOL* 19: 3–14.

Gardner, R. C., Paul F. Tremblay, and Anne-Marie Masgoret. 1997. "Towards a Full Model of Second Language Learning: An Empirical Investigation." *The Modern Language Journal* 81: 344–62.

Griffiths, Carol, and Rebecca L. Oxford. 2014. "The Twenty-first Century Landscape of Language Learning Strategies: Introduction to this Special Issue." *System* 43 (1): 1–10.

Gu, Peter Yongqi. 1996. "Robin Hood in SLA: What Has the Learning Strategy Researcher Taught Us." *Asian Journal of English Language Teaching* 6: 1–29.

———. 2005. *Vocabulary Learning Strategies in the Chinese EFL Context.* Singapore: Marshall Cavendish Academic.

———. 2012. "Learning Strategies: Prototypical Core and Dimensions of Variation." *Studies in Self-Access Learning Journal* 3: 330–56.

Gu, Peter Yongqi, and Robert K. Johnson. 1996. "Vocabulary Learning Strategies and Language Learning Outcomes." *Language Learning* 46 (4): 643–79.

Hastie, Trevor, Robert Tibshirani, and Jerome Friedman. 2009. *The Elements of Statistical Learning: Data Mining, Inference, and Prediction.* 2nd edition. New York: Springer.

Hatch, Evelyn, and Anne Lazaraton. 1991. *The Research Manual: Design and Statistics for Applied Linguistics.* Boston: Heinle & Heinle.

Hodis, Flaviu A. and Gregory R. Hancock, eds. 2016. *Advances in Quantitative Research Methods to Further Research in Education and Educational Psychology.* Special issue, *Educational Psychologist* 51 (3–4).

Hsiao, Tsung-Yuan, and Rebecca L. Oxford. 2002. "Comparing Theories of Language Learning Strategies: A Confirmatory Factor Analysis." *The Modern Language Journal* 86: 368–83.

Jaccard, James, and Kim Daniloski. 2012. "Analysis of Variance and the General Linear Model." In *APA Handbook of Research Methods in Psychology: Vol 3: Data Analysis and Research Publication*, edited by Harris Cooper, Paul M. Camic, Debra L. Long, A. T. Panter, David Rindskopf, and Kenneth J. Sher, 163–90. Washington, DC: American Psychological Association.

Jarvis, Scott. 2012. "The Detection-Based Approach: An Overview." In *Approaching Language Transfer through Text Classification: Explorations in the Detection-Based Approach*, edited by Scott Jarvis and Scott A. Crossley, 1–33. Bristol: Multilingual Matters.

Kojic-Sabo, Izabella, and Patsy M. Lightbown. 1999. "Students' Approaches to Vocabulary Learning and Their Relationship to Success." *The Modern Language Journal* 83: 176–92.

Kotsiantis, S. B. 2013. "Decision Trees: A Recent Overview." *Artificial Intelligence Review* 39: 261–83.

Larson-Hall, Jenifer, and Richard Herrington. 2010. "Improving Data Analysis in Second Language Acquisition by Utilizing Modern Developments in Applied Statistics." *Applied Linguistics* 31 (3): 368–90.

Larson-Hall, Jenifer, and Luke Plonsky. 2015. "Reporting and Interpreting Quantitative Research Findings: What Gets Reported and Recommendations for the Field." *Language Learning* 65 (Suppl. 1): 127–59.

Macaro, Ernesto. 2006. "Strategies for Language Learning and for Language Use: Revising the Theoretical Framework." *The Modern Language Journal* 90 (3): 320–37.

McArdle, John J. 2012. "Exploratory Data Mining Using CART in the Behavioral Sciences." In *APA Handbook of Research Methods in Psychology: Vol 3: Data Analysis and Research Publication*, edited by Harris Cooper, Paul M. Camic, Debra L. Long, A. T. Panter, David Rindskopf, and Kenneth J. Sher, 405–21. Washington, DC: American Psychological Association.

Mizumoto, Atsushi. 2010. *Exploring the Art of Vocabulary Learning Strategies: A Closer Look at Japanese* EFL *University Students.* Tokyo: Kinseido.

———. 2013. "Effects of Self-Regulated Vocabulary Learning Process on Self-Efficacy." *Innovation in Language Learning and Teaching* 7 (3): 253–65.

Mizumoto, Atsushi, and Luke Plonsky. 2016. "R as a Lingua Franca: Advantages of Using R for Quantitative Research in Applied Linguistics." *Applied Linguistics* 37 (2): 284–91.

Mizumoto, Atsushi, and Osamu Takeuchi. 2008. "Exploring the Driving Forces behind TOEIC Scores: Focusing on Vocabulary Learning Strategies, Motivation, and Study Time". *JACET Journal* 46: 17–32.

———. 2009a. "Comparing Frequency and Trueness Scale Descriptors in a Likert Scale Questionnaire on Language Learning Strategies." *JLTA (Japanese Language Testing Association) Journal* 12 (116–136).

———. 2009b. "Examining the Effectiveness of Explicit Instruction of Vocabulary Learning Strategies with Japanese EFL University Students." *Language Teaching Research* 13: 425–49.

Nisbet, Deanna L., Evie R. Tindall, and Alan A. Arroyo. 2005. "Language Learning Strategies and English Proficiency of Chinese University Students." *Foreign Language Annals* 38: 100–107.

Oxford, Rebecca L. 1990. *Language Learning Strategies: What Every Teacher Should Know.* Boston: Heinle & Heinle.

———. 1999. "Relationships between Second Language Learning Strategies and Language Proficiency in the Context of Learner Autonomy and Self-Regulation." *Revista Canaria de Estudios Ingleses* 38: 108–26.

———. 2011. *Teaching and Researching Language Learning Strategies.* Harlow: Pearson Longman.

———. 2017. *Teaching and Researching Language Learning Strategies: Self-Regulation in Context.* 2nd edition. New York: Routledge.

Oxford, Rebecca L. and Carol Griffiths, eds. 2014. "Language Learning Strategy Research in the Twenty-first Century." Special issue, *System* 43.

Oxford, Rebecca L. and Mirosław Pawlak, eds. 2018. *Language Learning Strategies: International Perspectives and Possibilities.* Special issue, *Studies in Second Language Learning and Teaching* 7.

Plonsky, Luke. 2011. "The Effectiveness of Second Language Strategy Instruction: A Meta-analysis." *Language Learning* 61: 993–1038.

———. 2013. "Study Quality in SLA: An Assessment of Designs, Analyses, and Reporting Practices in Quantitative L2 Research." *Studies in Second Language Acquisition* 35 (4): 655–87.

———, ed. 2015. *Advancing Quantitative Methods in Second Language Research.* New York: Routledge.

Plonsky, Luke, Jesse Egbert, and Geoffrey T. LaFlair. 2014. "Bootstrapping in Applied Linguistics: Assessing Its Potential Using Shared Data." *Applied Linguistics* 36 (5): 591–610.

Tono, Yukio. 2013. "Critical Feature Extraction Using Parallel Learner Corpus Data." In *Automatic Treatment and Analysis of Learner Corpus Data*, edited by Ana Díaz-Negrillo, Nicolas Ballier, and Paul Thompson, 169–203. Amsterdam: John Benjamins.

Tragant, Elsa, Marilyn S. Thompson, and Mia Victori. 2013. "Understanding Foreign Language Learning Strategies: A Validation Study." *System* 41: 95–108.

Tseng, Wen-Ta, and Norbert Schmitt. 2008. "Toward a Model of Motivated Vocabulary Learning: A Structural Equation Modeling Approach." *Language Learning* 58: 357–400.

Tseng, Wen-Ta, Zoltán Dörnyei, and Norbert Schmitt. 2006. "A New Approach to Assessing Strategic Learning: The Case of Self-regulation in Vocabulary Acquisition." *Applied Linguistics* 27 (1): 78–102.

Vandergrift, Larry, Christine C. M. Goh, Catherine J. Mareschal, and Marzieh H. Tafaghodtari. 2006. "The Metacognitive Awareness Listening Questionnaire: Development and Validation." *Language Learning* 56 (3): 431–62.

Wang, Hongcui, Christopher J. Waple, and Tatsuya Kawahara. 2009. "Computer Assisted Language Learning System Based on Dynamic Question Generation and Error Prediction for Automatic Speech Recognition." *Speech Communication* 51: 995–1005.

Witten, Ian, Eibe Frank, and Mark Hall. 2011. *Data Mining: Practical Machine Learning Tools and Techniques.* 3rd edition. Burlington, MA: Kaufmann.

Woodrow, Lindy. 2005. "The Challenge of Measuring Language Learning Strategies." *Foreign Language Annals* 38: 90–98.

Yamamori, Koyo, Takamichi Isoda, Tomohito Hiromori, and Rebecca L. Oxford. 2003. "Using Cluster Analysis to Uncover L2 Learner Differences in Strategy Use, Will to Learn, and Achievement over Time." *International Review of Applied Linguistics in Language Teaching* 41: 381–409.

6

Mixing Methods

Investigating Self-Regulated Strategies in a Cooperative EFL Learning Environment

Carmen M. Amerstorfer
Alpen-Adria-Universität Klagenfurt, Austria

1. Introduction

Paula is pacing up and down in her room like a tiger in a cage. Sometimes she looks up at the ceiling or closes her eyes while whispering words and phrases to herself. Once in a while she looks at the notebook in her hand or sits down at her desk to scribble something in the notebook. It does not take long before she gets up again and continues walking and whispering. The way in which Paula studies vocabulary looks like a well-practiced routine that she has repeated many times since she started learning English as a foreign language (EFL) nine years ago.

Earlier on the same day, Paula received a new reading assignment during an EFL lesson at school. The assignment consisted of a text and a set of questions to be answered as preparation for a group discussion in a follow-up lesson. Paula first skimmed the questions to focus her mind on the information that should be elicited from the text. Then she read the whole text and underlined all words and phrases that she did not understand. She searched the unknown items in an online dictionary and wrote German equivalents in the margin. The assignment encouraged learner cooperation, so Paula and the pupil sitting next to her complemented each other's translations. Then Paula transferred all new expressions and the German translations into her notebook, which she uses to memorize the new English vocabulary in her idiosyncratic manner.

Paula is one of five participants in case study that was conducted at an Austrian school (Amerstorfer 2016). The study was an in-depth investigation of self-regulated language learning strategies applied during cooperative EFL lessons. The purpose of the study was to gain a holistic understanding of individual learners' self-regulated, strategic language learning activities. This chapter aims to exemplify how a mix of research methods can lead to exciting insights about strategic language learning in context. This chapter will first present a basic understanding of situated, self-regulated language learning strategies. Then the specific aims of the study and the research questions will be presented. The learning environment in which the case study was conducted will be described in much detail because it is important to understand contextual influences. A report of the study, which will highlight how the research methods were combined, will lead to the presentation of the results. Finally, the conclusions that were gained from the study will bring the chapter to an end.

2. Self-regulated language learning strategies in context

What learners do to support foreign language learning processes has fascinated language teachers and researchers for many years. During the past four decades, typologies of language learning strategies have been developed (for example, Naiman et al. 1978; O'Malley et al. 1985; Oxford 1990; Rubin 1981), practical applications of strategies have been highlighted (for example, Gregersen and MacIntyre 2014; Gunning and Oxford 2014; Psaltou-Joycey 2015), and terminological ambiguities have been discussed (Oxford 2017). Strategies have been classified according to certain criteria (Cohen, Chapter 2 in this volume) and have been found to be rarely used in isolation. In fact, the occurrence of strategic actions in chains and clusters is characteristic of effective language learning strategies (Amerstorfer 2016; Cohen 2007; Oxford and Schramm 2007).

Single strategies as well as strategy chains and clusters are connected to thought processes that cannot be easily identified by teachers and researchers. Sometimes even learners struggle when explaining how they completed a task or solved a problem. Although learners consciously select and apply strategies (Oxford 2011), they sometimes find it difficult to remember the steps taken in a particular learning activity and to identify single or conjoined strategies involved in a process. Learners often register strategic actions as "something I always do." This lack of full awareness creates challenges for research about language learning strategies. It demands a careful selection of a suitable research environment and a thoroughly (strategically) planned research design.

Observations have been a popular method to detect strategies in foreign language classes. However, the degree to which strategic activity is observable varies. In contrast to obvious learner actions, like physically searching a word in a dictionary, other strategies are applied covertly and cannot be revealed because they happen in the learner's brain. For instance, the creation of thought-linkages between already existing knowledge and newly acquired information, thoughts about planning ahead, and the evaluation of learning progress remain hidden from an observer's senses. Hence, the problematic issue of strategy observability should be considered as it may influence the choice of research environment and the design of a study.

Once strategy groups and their individual components have been detected and identified, the analysis of the relationships between strategies and the reasons for their application present another major challenge. For instance, why does Paula whisper the new English words to herself when she tries to memorize them? Does she do it to practice pronunciation, or does she say the words in order to hear them? Are several reasons true? What role do the almost unnoticeable movements of Paula's lips play? And how are the comparatively large movements in the room related to the memorization process? The list of questions seems endless and Paula's self-regulated study of the new words incredibly complex.

Complexity has become a central interest in research related to foreign language learning (for example, Larsen-Freeman and Cameron 2008; Mercer 2014; Oxford, Lavine, and Amerstorfer, Chapter 1 in this volume). To get an idea of the extent of complexity in Paula's situation, we need to rewind a few hours to the English lesson when Paula first encountered the new text. Paula's strategic vocabulary revision in the afternoon is connected to the situation in school because during the revision of the new words and phrases at home, Paula remembers the words' location in the text. Paula also recalls who was sitting next to her in class, how hungry, tired, and warm she felt, what a beautiful necklace the teacher was wearing, and much more. In Paula's memory, the new vocabulary items do not exist in isolation but are embedded in a network of details related to the learning situation in school. During the self-study in the afternoon, Paula creates new links between the vocabulary and the situation at home. For example, she notices a bird that is chirping outside her window, and she can smell the dinner her mother is preparing in the kitchen. The web of connections related to studying the vocabulary continues to grow in size and complexity.

The simplified description of Paula's self-regulated vocabulary learning only scratches the surface of what is happening in actual fact. The complexity becomes mindboggling if we take into account that Paula already has associations with some of the words on her list. For instance, Paula might associate new words with already existing phrases in her English vocabulary. She might notice similarities between the spelling and sounds of the new English words and expressions in her first language or other foreign languages. Paula may recall situations where she encountered certain phrases before she knew their meaning, for instance, in a TV commercial or in a song.

Needless to say, complex constructs as in Paula's example of self-regulated, strategic language learning are not restricted to vocabulary learning. They exist for all areas of foreign language learning, for example, studying and applying grammar rules, the improvement of reading, writing, speaking, and listening skills, as well as memorizing factual knowledge about the target language, the geographical region where it is spoken, and cultural aspects. Since strategies are usually related to other strategies, and their selection is influenced by situational circumstances and learners' personal preferences, it was essential for the study reported in this chapter to investigate strategic language learning in context. In other words, situated strategies require situated research conditions.

3. The study

3.1. Purpose of the study

The purpose of the study was an in-depth examination of self-regulated language learning strategies applied by five EFL learners. Initiated by a long-lasting general curiosity about strategy choice and inspired by personal experiences as a learner of foreign languages and EFL teacher, the study aimed to develop explanatory theories about the strategic actions individual learners select to support foreign language learning. The intention was to develop holistic portraits of each participant with much detail about personal preferences and situational circumstances. All of this was to be blended into the general context of EFL instruction in Austria and the school where the study was conducted.

3.2. Research questions

To meet the objectives of the study, the following set of research questions was developed:

- Why do pupils prefer certain strategies and neglect others?
- What are individual purposes of strategy application?
- Would it be possible to classify strategy types according to their purposes?

- Would purpose-related strategy types overlap? If yes, how would they overlap?
- What themes emerge from the data?

A research environment that would provide suitable framework conditions was needed to answer the research questions.

3.3. Research environment

A suitable research environment for a study on self-regulated, strategic foreign language learning must provide opportunities to collect authentic and recordable information. Lesson observations are one way of data collection although they may not capture all strategic activity, as was mentioned before. A research environment that promotes the observability of language learning strategies was found in an innovative teaching approach called CoOperative Open Learning (COOL).

COOL was initiated by a small team of teachers at an Austrian vocational school twenty years ago (Wittwer n.d.). On the one hand, it developed as a reaction to increasingly heterogeneous classrooms in Austria. On the other hand, there was a rising request for "soft skills" to be taught at schools in order to prepare young people for future employment. The term "soft skills" summarizes social competences such as communication skills and other personal qualities like self-regulation, integration, and creativity that are usually expected from job applicants besides the relevant qualifications for a particular position. The philosophy of the state-funded teaching concept COOL is to enable learners to discover their own resources and expand their soft skills.

The pedagogical roots of COOL are grounded in the Dalton Plan (Parkhurst 1922), a humanistic teaching approach that is based on three central ideas: freedom, cooperation, and self-reliance. According to Parkhurst, freedom is a basic requirement for an individual to grow within a community. The Dalton Plan promotes children's development in a free but structured manner. Pupils are involved in decision-making processes and learn to deal with the consequences of their actions. Parkhurst believed that social consciousness develops through learner cooperation, for instance, when pupils pursue a joint goal and achieve a commonly agreed outcome. Self-reliance in a COOL context means that pupils take responsibility for their actions and abide by the terms and conditions of the COOL assignments, for instance, to submit an expected outcome by a certain date.

COOL assignments are written learning agreements designed by a single teacher or by a group of teachers. The assignments can integrate different subjects and are usually task-based. COOL EFL assignments integrate features of communicative language teaching. For example, they promote a learning-by-doing approach where language is understood as "a tool for communication" (Nunan 2004, 7). Communicative language teaching suits a COOL setup well because language learning is believed to happen through interaction with others. Pupils use their social environment and opportunities to communicate with others to learn the foreign language. Following Vygotsky's (1978) perception for foreign language learning, more proficient learners are expected to help less advanced learners to grow within their zones of proximal development, which is the "distance between the present level of ability [and knowledge] and a higher potential level" (Williams, Mercer, and Ryan 2015, 16).

In COOL schools, about a third to half of all lessons on the timetable are so-called "COOL lessons" during which pupils work self-directedly and independently of a teacher. The pupils decide autonomously when, where, and with whom they will work on current COOL assignments. During COOL lessons, the teacher functions as facilitator and supervisor and provides encouragement and support on demand. In comparison with teacher-centered classrooms, COOL requires pupils to speak to each other when they complete assignments together, which has a positive effect on the observability of strategies. Many thoughts that would remain unnoticed during individual study are verbalized in cooperative learning, for example, when pupils evaluate their progress, divide tasks amongst team members, and plan ahead. In this sense, the COOL methodology and the participants' learning environment nurtured favorable conditions for the study.

3.4. Research design

Generally speaking, a researcher's worldview and beliefs determine the type of research he or she prefers. Oxford (2011; following Grotjahn 1987) describes different forms of research that exist on a continuum between two extremes. On one side are experimental studies with quantitative data and statistical analysis. On the other side are exploratory studies with qualitative data and interpretative analysis. The criteria that define the actual form of a study are related to the design of a research project, the kind of data collected, and the analysis type applied. The design of a project in strategy research depends on the research questions posed, which are fundamentally influenced by the researcher's methodological beliefs about foreign language learning and teaching. Other factors that shape strategy research, in particular *situated* strategy research, are a suitable research environment, the type of analysis conducted to make sense of the obtained data, and the methods used to collect data.

The choice of quantitative and qualitative research methods is usually based on the strengths of a method; however, its weaknesses must be considered, too. For example, quantitative research is capable of delivering large amounts of data, but it pays little attention to contextual influences and individual learners. Qualitative research, on the other hand, studies small numbers of participants in detail, but it relies heavily on the researcher's personal interpretations. By mixing methods researchers counterbalance the strengths and weaknesses of individual methods and in doing so maximize the quality of the outcomes. Mixing methods enables a broader and deeper understanding of a specific research problem than it would be possible with a single approach (Creswell and Plano Clark 2011). The study reported in this chapter combined quantitative and qualitative methods in a way beyond known practices as qualitative and quantitative methods were merged rather than applied parallel to each other. The precise approach will be described in detail below but first, the participants will be briefly introduced.

3.5. Sample

Five female volunteers whose first language (L1) is German took part in the study. They were between 14 and 18 years of age, and their proficiency levels in EFL ranged from A2 to B2 according to the Common European Framework of Reference for Languages (CEFR; Council of Europe 2001). The participants were suggested by their English teachers for their outgoing personality types, which implied that the pupils were likely to speak about themselves in interview situations and would not be easily intimidated by technical devices to record data. At the time of data collection, three participants (Lisa, Paula, and Stella[1]) had the highest possible pass grade in the school subject English, while the other two (Christina and Sabrina) had the lowest possible pass grade. The sample selection tried to avoid a focus on a specific performance group and gender differences in foreign language learning.

3.6. Instrumentation

As was indicated above, the study combined quantitative and qualitative methods for data collection in a particular manner. The instrument used to collect quantitative data was the *Strategy Inventory for Language Learning* (*SILL*; Oxford 1990). The *SILL* contains fifty statements about learning English as a foreign language that are rated from 1 (never or almost never true of me) to 5 (always or almost always true of me). Based on Oxford's (1990) typology, the fifty statements are grouped in six categories: remembering more effectively (memory strategies; nine items), using all your mental processes (cognitive strategies; fourteen items), compensating for missing knowledge (compensation strategies; six items), organizing and evaluating your learning (metacognitive strategies; nine items), managing your emotions (affective strategies; six items), and learning with others (social strategies; six items).

The *SILL* is a useful tool to identify how frequently pupils apply language learning strategies. However, the responses to individual *SILL* statements are based on the participants' self-perception and memory, which can weaken the reliability of a study (White, Schramm, and Chamot 2007). Furthermore, more than 25 years after its publication and many technological innovations later, the original *SILL* is somewhat outdated. Current aspects of foreign language teaching and learning are not included, particularly those related to the Internet and modern technologies. Regardless, the *SILL* was used in the current study in its original form albeit translated into the participants' L1. It was one of several components and served four purposes. First, it was used as an ice-breaker at the beginning of the data collection. Second, it focused the participants' minds on the topic. Third, it fulfilled its original intention to generate quantitative data about the participants' language learning strategy use. Fourth, it supported the acquisition of complementary qualitative information and hence merged with the methods of qualitative data collection (see the exact procedures below).

Despite past criticism (Dörnyei 2005; LoCastro 1994), the *SILL* is the most frequently used research tool to collect measurable data about language learning strategies (Mizumoto and Takeuchi, Chapter 5 in this volume). Countless projects have been based on the *SILL* or were supported by the *SILL*—a trend that can be expected to continue in the future. A reason for the popularity of Oxford's (1990) inventory is that it can be handled by virtually everybody. It does not require any previous knowledge about data collection or statistics, and no software is needed to generate results. Another major advantage of the *SILL* is that it can be adapted for specific purposes, target groups, and situations. It can be translated into other languages and modified to suit different sociocultural settings. In fact, its author recommends modification to meet local needs and goals. Last but not least, the *SILL* is not restricted to quantitative research but can be used in a mixed-methods project and for multiple purposes, as the current study shows.

In order to gain qualitative information about the participants and their self-regulated language learning strategies, lesson observations and two types of semi-structured interviews were conducted. The first meeting with the participants included an initial interview with questions about the participants' bio data, about their families and social lives, about learning English as a foreign language, and about cooperative learning. The final part of the interview protocol concerned the *SILL* statements that were rated highest and lowest. The aim was to elicit reasons for the frequent application or avoidance of particular strategies.

In addition to the initial interviews, which were audio recorded and transcribed, further qualitative data were collected through lesson observations in combination with retrospective interviews. The observations of the individual participants in COOL EFL lessons were video recorded. The recordings were watched together with the respective pupils shortly after the observed lessons. The stimulated recall interviews followed a semi-structured protocol and consisted of three phases. First, a fixed set of questions was asked about the learning environment, cooperation partner(s), and learning resources used during the observed lesson. Second, targeted questions were asked while watching the video of the respective lesson. Third, at the end of the interview, each participant was asked to reflect on the observed lesson and on the strategies used. All stimulated recall interviews were audio recorded and transcribed. Finally, the EFL assignments that had been completed throughout the duration of the research project were collected in order to gain a comprehensive understanding of the learning situations observed.

3.7. Data collection procedures

The data were collected over a period of four weeks. In the first week, an initial interview with each individual participant was conducted.[2] At the beginning of the interview, every participant was given a German translation of the *SILL* (Oxford 1990). The participants had unlimited time to read each statement carefully and to tick one response per statement. They were reminded that there were no right or wrong answers and that they should only think about themselves rather than what others might do or expect them to do. The researcher stayed in the room while the inventory was filled in, which provided constant opportunity to ask questions of clarification. After that, each participant was interviewed according to the semi-structured protocol described above. The interview ended with questions why certain statements on the *SILL* were rated highest (5) or lowest (1). These questions added a qualitative component to the *SILL* and revealed some interesting insights. The rest of the first week was used to familiarize the participants with the procedures involved in the lesson observations and stimulated recall interviews. Beside a standard audio recording device, a small-scale camera was used. The latter was operated via a mobile phone app and wireless Internet connection to minimize distraction.

For the duration of a further three weeks, each participant was observed and video-recorded during one COOL lesson per week. During these lessons, the participants were working on the completion of cooperative EFL assignments together with one or multiple cooperation partners. The observer took notes and formulated follow-up questions, which were used in the stimulated recall interviews that succeeded each observation. The video footage of the respective lesson was watched during those interview sessions. The recordings were stopped, fast forwarded, and rewound as required, and the participants were encouraged to narrate the videotaped classroom situations while watching. Additionally, the interviewer elicited explanations about what had happened during the lessons.

The overlapping combination of different means for data collection yielded a mix of quantitative and qualitative information about each of the five participants:

- quantitative data that demonstrated the participants' self-evaluation of their preferences regarding language learning strategy use,
- qualitative data in relation to the *SILL* statements that were rated highest and lowest, and
- qualitative data about self-regulated strategy use in authentic cooperative EFL learning situations.

The following section will explain how the collected information was analyzed.

3.8. Data analysis procedures

The quantitative data obtained through the *SILL* were analyzed according to Oxford's (1990) guidelines. Oxford nominated high, medium, and low frequency of strategy use as demonstrated in Table 6.1.

In addition to the calculation of the participants' *SILL* profiles, computer-assisted qualitative data analysis (atlas.ti) brought to light the participants' personal motives for using and avoiding certain strategies and how individual strategies may relate to each other. Furthermore, general information about the participants' lives in and outside of school, about studying English, and about the COOL approach in EFL instruction was gained from the transcripts of the initial interviews.

Table 6.1 Key to determine high, medium, and low frequency of LLS use

High	Always or almost always used	4.5 to 5.0
	Usually used	3.5 to 4.4
Medium	Sometimes used	2.5 to 3.4
Low	Generally not used	1.5 to 2.4
	Never or almost never used	1.0 to 1.4

Source: Adapted from Oxford 1990, 300

The analysis of the stimulated recall interviews was targeted at self-regulated learning strategies applied during cooperative EFL lessons. By coding strategic learner action (including talk) from the interview material, four main purposes of self-regulated strategic learning in cooperative EFL lessons were identified:

- to improve knowledge about and skills in the foreign language (lang), for example, to look up a word in an online dictionary,
- to support learner cooperation or to cooperate with peers (coop), for example, to share a set of earphones in a listening comprehension task,
- to complete a task or assignment (task), for example, to read silently in order to answer content-related questions,
- to motivate each other or to increase one's own motivation (mot), for example, to take short breaks.

The combination of quantitative data from the *SILL* and qualitative data from interviews, led to some interesting findings about self-regulated strategies in the context of cooperative language learning. It showed how individual learners' preferences influence strategy selection, how strategic actions are related to each other, and that learning strategies are contextualized.

4. Results

The quantitative information and the qualitative information collected in the study are strongly related to each other. A summary of the participants' *SILL* profiles is illustrated in Table 6.2. The numbers represent the participants' self-perceived frequency of strategy use per strategy type in sum and on average. It also includes a total number, which shows the participants' self-rated overall frequency of strategy use. Paula, whose complex strategies for vocabulary memorization have been described above, gave low ratings to the memory

Table 6.2 Overview of the participants' *SILL* profiles

Strategy type	Number of items	Christina		Lisa		Paula		Sabrina		Stella	
		Sum	Av.	Sum	Av.	Sum	Av.	Sum	Av.	Sum	Av.
Memory	9	29	3.22	17	1.89	17	1.89	20	2.22	28	3.11
Cognitive	14	49	3.50	45	3.21	43	3.07	37	2.64	53	3.79
Compensation	6	19	3.17	18	3.00	19	3.17	17	2.83	24	4.00
Metacognitive	9	39	4.33	25	2.78	25	2.78	27	3.00	29	3.22
Affective	6	17	2.83	10	1.67	15	2.50	18	3.00	18	3.00
Social	6	19	3.17	16	2.67	20	3.33	16	2.67	19	3.17
Total	50	172	3.44	131	2.62	139	2.78	135	2.70	171	3.42

strategies in the *SILL*. Her self-perception of strategy use in this area is quite different from the information that was revealed during observations and interviews. A possible reason for Paula's low rating of memory strategies may be a lack of awareness, a topic that is related to strategy instruction and discussed in Part IV of this book.

In addition to the quantitative data, the *SILL* was used to go beyond explanations like "because I *always* do it like this" and to elicit detailed supplementary information regarding the participants' strategy use. Christina, for example, declared that she always plans *a minimum of four hours a week* to study English.[3] Stella explained that making flashcards is *too much work* and *not worth the time and effort* because studying English vocabulary is easy for her.[4] The participants further explained relationships between individual strategies, for instance, how strategies are connected by sequence ("Strategy X is only meaningful if strategy Y was used before.") or how strategies sometimes exclude each other ("I don't use strategy X because I do Y instead."). Stella, for example, explained a link between *SILL* statements 22 ("I try not to translate word-for-word.") and 24 ("To understand unfamiliar English words, I make guesses."). She said that she avoids word-for-word explanations and *instead* guesses from the context.

In an interview, Paula explained that her idiosyncratic manner to study vocabulary happens in stages and leads to a reward in the end. At the beginning, Paula clusters the new words and phrases in her notebook in groups of five. She tries to memorize each group while walking back and forth in her room. Then she sits down and reorganizes the vocabulary items to form new groups to be studied while walking around. Paula said that when she makes a mistake, she gets a little angry at herself, stomps her foot, or kicks the wastepaper basket. Then she tries again and does not stop until she knows every new English item on the list and its German translation. Once Paula has achieved her self-defined goal, she treats herself to some social media time.

The results of the study confirm that strategies are often connected to other strategies. Furthermore, the results show that self-regulated strategic language learning is complex and influenced by many factors. Other important findings of the study are related to the reasons why strategies are used. Strategies can have a single purpose or multiple purposes, which may vary due to situational circumstances. Single-purpose strategies sometimes fulfil the same purpose in different learning situations, but sometimes the purposes are not identical. Table 6.3 demonstrates two learning situations in which Lisa and her cooperation partner applied the same strategy (divide the work load). In both cases the strategy fulfilled the purpose of cooperation.

Table 6.3 Example of a strategy with identical purposes in two situations

Situation 1	Situation 2
Lisa and her cooperation partner divide the work load.	
One pupil will write sentences, while the other one will look up unknown words. **(Cooperation)**	Each pupil will answer half of the questions from a given list. **(Cooperation)**

Depending on situational influences, a strategic action can, however, be applied for different reasons in two situations. Table 6.4 illustrates that Paula and her cooperation partner used an online dictionary to translate a word from English into German in situation 3. In situation 4, they used a dictionary too, but the second time the purpose was to inquire about the existence of an unfamiliar word in order to detect the odd one out in a task. Paula and her partner applied the same strategy (using an online dictionary) in both situations, but the objectives were different (language improvement; task completion).

In light of the original aim of the study to investigate *language* learning strategies, language improvement could be understood as a purpose of higher order in comparison to task achievement, cooperation, and motivation. Using a dictionary to complete a task, for instance, could be viewed as a strategic move towards the extended purpose of language improvement. However, the study focused on the *immediate* purposes of strategic learner actions in contextualized learning situations. It showed that not all strategies applied during the observed lessons were generally targeted at the overall aim of language improvement.

The illustrations above exemplify situations in which learning strategies fulfil the same single purpose (Table 6.3) and different single purposes (Table 6.4). The examples have been simplified to demonstrate reasons for strategy application and do not represent the full complexity of self-regulated strategic learning. The analysis became increasingly complicated with situations in which one strategy

Table 6.4 Example of a strategy with different purposes in two situations

Situation 3	Situation 4
Paula and her cooperation partner use an online dictionary ...	
for a translation. **(Language improvement)**	to see if a word exists. **(Task completion)**

fulfilled multiple purposes. During one observed lesson, for instance, Sabrina sent her absent cooperation partner a text message to ask about a text that they had prepared together. Sabrina's strategic act of contacting her partner had the joint purposes of "coop" (i.e., to cooperate with peers) and "task" (to complete a task or assignment). Many strategies registered in the study had two purposes. Some were applied for three, and a few even for all four identified reasons.

One important outcome of the study underlies all factual results about strategies and their purposes: Research about self-regulated, strategic language learning requires a wide perspective that captures a broad and deep image. Such a three-dimensional view must allow room for much complexity and deal with a general notion of *strategic learning* rather than a narrow focus on individual *learning strategies*.

5. Conclusions

An important outcome of this study mirrors what others have found before: Strategies are often applied in combination with one or several other strategies. The results that this study added to previous findings concern the manner in which strategies relate to each other and how strategies and strategy combinations function. Strategies can cause, support, and restrict each other. The study showed that the participants took into account influencing factors from the learning environment and personal preferences when they selected strategies for specific purposes. The study further demonstrated that single strategies can fulfil one or multiple situation-dependent purposes and that strategies are almost always combined with other strategies in self-regulated language learning. Based on the summarized findings, two important conclusions can be drawn from the study.

First, a mix of research methods is appropriate and advisable for a study about contextualized, self-regulated language learning strategies. This chapter demonstrated how a combination of research methods increased the effectiveness of the study. Without Paula's explanations during interviews, the observations would only have delivered a partial picture that is quite different from Paula's self-perception (*SILL*). The combination of methods put together individual puzzle pieces and contributed to a holistic perception of Paula's and the other participants' strategic learning. What is extraordinary about the study's design is that the quantitative and qualitative methods were not applied independently of each other. The quantitative tool was used, amongst other reasons, to generate qualitative data. The quantitative and qualitative methods were not simply combined with each other but merged, which resulted in findings that could not have been achieved with either method alone or two methods used parallel to each other.

Second, language learning strategies should not be considered in isolation. This chapter demonstrated that strategic language learning is complex and flexible. It involves the learner as the agent of self-regulated strategy use and a multitude of interrelated factors. Some factors concern the learner (for example, Paula's preferences in strategy choice; her general level of motivation to learn EFL; her level of awareness of strategies), others concern the learner's immediate surrounding in a particular learning situation (for example, the temperature in the room; the availability of technology, study materials, and cooperation partners), and yet others concern the learner's wider learning environment (for example, the methodology of EFL instruction and the school's policy). The learner's relationships with other people (for example, cooperation partners, the EFL teacher, and family members) and the learner's personal life also play important roles in strategic language learning (for example, previous experiences in foreign language learning, the learner's own future expectations and expectations of others). Finally, the whole construct of strategic, self-regulated language learning is integrated in the learner's culture and influenced by cultural values and beliefs. It is necessary to acquire a holistic perspective to understand self-regulated, strategic foreign language learning, which can be achieved by combining research methods.

Notes

1   Pseudonyms were used to protect anonymity.
2   The language of all interviews was the participants' first language, German.
3   In response to *SILL* statement 43: "I plan my schedule so I will have enough time to study English."
4   In response to *SILL* statement 6: "I use flashcards to remember new English words."

References

Amerstorfer, Carmen M. 2016. "Situated Strategy Use in Cooperative Learning: A Descriptive Case Study of Five Learners of English as a Foreign Language." Unpublished PhD dissertation, Alpen-Adria-Universität Klagenfurt.

Cohen, Andrew D. 2007. "Coming to Terms with Language Learning Strategies: Surveying the Experts." In *Language Learner Strategies: Thirty Years of Research and Practice*, edited by Andrew D. Cohen and Ernesto Macaro, 29–45. Oxford: Oxford University Press.

Council of Europe. 2001. *Common European Framework of Reference for Languages: Learning, Teaching, Assessment.* Cambridge: Cambridge University Press.

Creswell, John W., and Vicki L. Plano Clark. 2011. *Designing and Conducting Mixed Methods Research.* 2nd edition. Thousand Oaks, CA: Sage.

Dörnyei, Zoltán. 2005. *The Psychology of the Language Learner: Individual Differences in Second Language Acquisition.* Mahwah, NJ: Lawrence Erlbaum.

Gregersen, Tammy, and Peter D. MacIntyre. 2014. *Capitalizing on Language Learners' Individuality: From Premise to Practice.* Bristol: Multilingual Matters.

Grotjahn, Rüdiger. 1987. "On the Methodological Basis of Introspective Methods." In *Introspection in Second Language Research*, edited by Claus Faerch and Gabriele Kasper, 54–81. Clevedon: Multilingual Matters.

Gunning, Pamela, and Rebecca L. Oxford. 2014. "Children's Learning Strategy Use and the Effects of Strategy Instruction on Success in Learning ESL in Canada." *System* 43: 82–100.

Larsen-Freeman, Diane, and Lynne Cameron. 2008. *Complex Systems and Applied Linguistics.* Oxford: Oxford University Press.

LoCastro, Virginia. 1994. "Learning Strategies and Learning Environments." *TESOL Quarterly* 28 (2): 409–14.

Mercer, Sarah. 2014. "The Self from a Complexity Perspective." In *Multiple Perspectives on the Self in SLA*, edited by Sarah Mercer and Marion Williams, 160–76. Clevedon: Channel View Publications.

Naiman, Neil, Fröhlich Maria, Hans H. Stern, and Angie Todesco. 1978. *The Good Language Learner.* Toronto: Ontario Institute for Studies in Education.

Nunan, David. 2004. *Task-Based Language Teaching.* Cambridge: Cambridge University Press.

O'Malley, J. Michael, Anna Uhl Chamot, Gloria Stewner-Manzanares, Rocco P. Russo, and Lisa Küpper. 1985. "Learning Strategies Used by Beginner and Intermediate ESL Students." *Language Learning* 35 (1): 21–46.

Oxford, Rebecca L. 1990. *Language Learning Strategies: What Every Teacher Should Know.* Boston: Heinle & Heinle.

———. 2011. *Teaching and Researching Language Learning Strategies.* Harlow: Pearson/ Longman.

———. 2017. *Teaching and Researching Language Learning Strategies: Self-Regulation in Context.* 2nd edition. New York: Routledge.

Oxford, Rebecca L., and Karen Schramm. 2007. "Bridging the Gap between Psychological and Sociocultural Perspectives on L2 Learner Strategies." In *Language Learner Strategies: Thirty Years of Research and Practice*, edited by Andrew D. Cohen and Ernesto Macaro, 47–68. Oxford: Oxford University Press.

Parkhurst, Helen. 1922. *Education on the Dalton Plan.* New York: E.P. Dutton & Company.

Psaltou-Joycey, Angeliki, ed. 2015. *Foreign Language Learning Strategy Instruction: A Teacher's Guide.* Kavala, Greece: Saita Publications.

Rubin, Joan. 1981. "The Study of Cognitive Processes in Second Language Learning." *Applied Linguistics* 11 (2): 117–31.

Vygotsky, Lev S. 1978. *Mind in Society: The Development of Higher Psychological Processes.* Cambridge, MA: Harvard University Press.

White, Cynthia, Karen Schramm, and Anna Uhl Chamot. 2007. "Research Methods in Strategy Research: Re-Examining the Toolbox." In *Language Learner Strategies: Thirty Years of Research and Practice,* edited by Andrew D. Cohen and Ernesto Macaro, 93–116. Oxford: Oxford University Press.

Williams, Marion, Sarah Mercer, and Stephen Ryan. 2015. *Exploring Psychology in Language Learning and Teaching.* Oxford: Oxford University Press.

Wittwer, Helga. n.d. "Cooltrainers." Accessed December 29, 2015. www.cooltrainers.at.

Part III

Studies of Learning Strategies Emphasizing Diverse Contexts and Individual Difference Factors

As one of the first researchers in the strategy field, Hosenfeld (1976, 118) referred to L2 learners as "extraordinarily complex, thinking, and feeling" people, who can express their thoughts and describe their actions. In contrast to traditional approaches to L2 teaching that emphasized the imitation of role models, choral repetition, and memorization, modern-day L2 teaching in the western world usually takes a communicative approach, which involves a social setting and interaction between learners and other speakers of the target language. The countless components involved in L2 learning situations (see Part I) make research about strategic L2 learning very complex because "we need to grasp not only interpersonal differences (differences among a group of people) but also intrapersonal dynamics (how the phenomena actually operate inside someone)" (Gregersen and MacIntyre 2014, x).

Due to the complexity and the flexible nature of strategic L2 learning (see Chapter 1), Williams, Mercer, and Ryan (2015, 142) argue that it is to some degree "inevitable that we have to generalize or simplify reality to make it manageable and comprehensible." Nevertheless, researchers must stay clear of black-and-white thinking and should not reduce "the complexity of the interrelatedness between the diverse elements of an individual's psychology and the context they act within" (ibid.). Part II provided three examples of methodologies and research design that may help researchers in handling the complexity of LLS research.

By respecting the complexity of strategic L2 learning, researchers avoid thinking in boxes and nurturing stereotypes (e.g., "Strategies A and B are only useful to memorize vocabulary" or "Learners who frequently apply strategy C will become good at reading"). Although generalizable results from large-scale studies are conceivably convenient for researchers and L2 teachers, individual learner characteristics must be acknowledged because "groups are rarely homogeneous" and "usually full of unique individuals, who may vary from whatever is considered to be the group norm" (Williams, Mercer, and Ryan 2015, 144). Mercer (2014, 160) describes the self as "the hub at the center of [every individual person's] lived experiences." A learner's self is characterized by "a range of self-related cognitions, beliefs, emotions, motives, roles, relationships, memories, dreams and goals" (ibid.). With this in mind, researchers in the LLS field and L2 teachers have been asking how much sense it makes to measure all L2 learners with the same yardstick.

Similar to the diversity of individual L2 learners, the contexts in which foreign and second languages are studied are diverse. Contextual diversity is reflected in the three chapters of Part III. Gu (Chapter 7) takes stock of L2 strategy research in China and how it has influenced L2 teaching in a country that deals with massive numbers of learners. It is challenging for an immense, collectivist country such as China to take individual learner differences into account. Gu's plea to make strategy research accessible, understandable, and useful for practical implications is an important step in that direction. With Gu's efforts in China at its roots, Chapter 7 provides important insights for effective L2 education in the rest of the world.

In Chapter 8, Psaltou-Joycey and Gavriilidou present a nation-wide study about EFL learners in Greek primary and secondary schools. The study reports how individual learner characteristics influence strategic L2 learning and focuses specifically on four aspects, namely, gender, education level, proficiency level, and region of residence. The impact of contextual variables and individual learner differences are also central to Pawlak's Chapter 9.

The author investigated the under-researched topic of pronunciation learning strategies in L2 learning. In Pawlak's empirical study of a group of English majors in a BA program in Poland, the influence of EFL proficiency, gender, and learning styles on the application of self-regulated strategies to enhance pronunciation learning were analyzed. The three chapters included in Part III allow valuable and thought-provoking perceptions of different EFL teaching and learning situations in Europe and Asia. It is up to the readers of this chapter to draw parallels to their own L2 teaching, learning, and research situations, which will hopefully lead to more studies about situated strategies in L2 learning.

References

Gregersen, Tammy, and Peter D. MacIntyre. 2014. *Capitalizing on Language Learners' Individuality: From Premise to Practice.* Bristol: Multilingual Matters.

Hosenfeld, Carol. 1976. "Learning About Learning: Discovering Our Students' Strategies." *Foreign Language Annals* 9 (2). 117–29.

Mercer, Sarah. 2014. "The Self from a Complexity Perspective." In *Multiple Perspectives on the Self in SLA*, edited by Sarah Mercer and Marion Williams, 160–76. Clevedon: Channel View Publications.

Williams, Marion, Sarah Mercer, and Stephen Ryan. 2015. *Exploring Psychology in Language Learning and Teaching.* Oxford: Oxford University Press.

7

Making Language Learning Strategies Research Useful

Insights from China

Peter Yongqi Gu
Victoria University of Wellington, New Zealand

1. Introduction

Research on language learning strategies (LLS) has come of age. Forty years of dedicated efforts around the word have produced many insights into learner agency and the strategic learning of languages (Oxford 2017). In this chapter, I ask two fundamental questions: (a) What is LLS research for? (b) To what extent has LLS research achieved its purposes? In answering these questions, I focus on LLS research done in China, although the rest of the world can also benefit. I will briefly introduce the large quantity of research on the topic published in China that is less known outside the Chinese readership, and bring to the readers' attention a major gap between research on the one hand and policy and practice on the other.

2. The issue

At least 240-million Chinese students at various levels are learning English as a foreign language (EFL) in China (MOE China 2010). Only a tiny proportion of these learners can achieve a level of proficiency good enough for communication in English. The Herculean task of learning means that finding effective and efficient ways of learning will be among the most popular research interests. Indeed, learning strategies (LS) for EFL learning in China have received a lot of research attention.

This article is not meant to be a comprehensive and systematic review of language learning strategy research published in China. In fact, I will be deliberately brief about achievements over the decades. Focus will be placed upon the application of research findings. That said, many insights do come from my analysis of journal publications on the topic included in the China National Knowledge Infrastructure (CNKI), a large database that has digitized almost all formal publications in China since its establishment in 1999. A search of "English language learning strategies," "foreign language learning strategies," and "learning strategies" in CNKI shows that the number of publications on the topic rapidly increased over the years and peaked around 2006 to 2009 (see Table 7.1).

My observations in this chapter are mainly based on the 67 most cited articles with a minimum of one-hundred citations each centrally related to EFL learning strategies and autonomous learning, ranging from 1,737 citations (Wen 2001) to 107 citations (Yao 2000). Drawing on forty years of research on the topic throughout the world, as well as the list of most cited articles and other publications in China—e.g., the national curriculum standards and a widely used textbook series (Q. Wang and Editorial Team 2009a), I will first present a general summary of the research and then provide my own judgement as to the areas of research that have been well applied, not well applied, or over applied.

3. Strategic language learning: What is it and what is it for?

Strategic learning refers to a learner's active, intentional engagement in the learning process by selectively attending to a learning problem, mobilizing available resources, deciding on the best available plan for action, carrying out the plan, monitoring the performance, and evaluating the results for future action. Strategic learning is triggered and defined by task demands and is tied to a purpose. The purpose of strategic learning is to solve a learning problem, perform a novel task, accelerate the learning rate, or achieve overall learning success.

The above definition focuses on the individual learner's active engagement with the learning task. This focus on the learner and his/her own desires, aspirations, and efforts for success in language learning come from the cognitive tradition of learning theories. Therefore, it has been seen as promoting a marginalized, decontextualized, individualized, and psychologized form of learner autonomy (Pennycook 1997). For many scholars (e.g., Canagarajah 2006,

Table 7.1 Number of publications by year (1997–2012)

	1997	1998	1999	2000	2001	2002	2003	2004	2005	2006	2007	2008	2009	2010	2011	2012
Foreign LLS	2	1	6	4	5	16	23	25	20	25	34	34	34	31	24	21
English LLS	2	5	9	8	16	26	44	71	77	138	182	217	202	205	206	211
LS	77	129	149	216	296	451	633	777	851	1105	1,451	1,686	1,844	1,861	1,855	1,865

20), the term *learner strategy* is "defined at the most micro level of consideration in somewhat individualistic and psychological terms," and may therefore "lack direction without a larger set of pedagogical principles." Indeed, researchers now believe that LLS do not have to be confined to the "individualistic" and "psychologized" focus on language learning outcomes. Getting students engaged in their own process of learning and reflecting on how they can learn better is to ensure that learners obtain a sense of control, eventually establish their own voice in the target language, and be able to author their own lives (Pennycook 1997). Similarly, Brown (1991, 256) is upbeat about a "transformative" role of LLS as early as 1991, and views learner strategy training as "the strategic investment of learners in their own linguistic destinies."

Another way of broadening the strategic learning concept is the widely accepted integration of learning strategies and learner autonomy (Oxford 1990, 1999, 2017; Wen and L. Wang 2004b). In other words, successful use of learning strategies should not only lead to higher proficiency in language, but also more learner autonomy. This also entails a more balanced perspective of strategic learning, between the individual and the social side of learning, in that the strategic and autonomous learner not only actively self-regulates his/her own learning process, but is also keenly aware of the situatedness and the social nature of the learning task. Littlewood (1996) postulates three aims of autonomous learning: the autonomous learner, the autonomous communicator, and the autonomous person. In other words, teachers can help their students become self-regulated learners, strategic communicators and users of the language, and proactive, self-reflective members of society who are keenly aware of the balance between the self and others around them. By the same token, LLS research should eventually aim to empower learners as learners, communicators, and socially responsible problem solvers as well.

All of this may sound a tall order, but the idea is simple. Teaching students to use a strategy for a particular learning task is simple, and often effective, in completing that learning task (e.g., Gu 2007). But our main purpose is to empower learners so that they can become strategic in making learning decisions on their own, out of class and after school, in task analysis, self-diagnosis, and strategy choice and use, while at the same time being aware of environmental support or constraints. In this sense, there is nothing new in the idea. In fact, it coincides with traditional expectations of teachers in the Chinese context, in that teachers are expected to play two roles, in both instructing (*jiao shu*) and educating (*yu ren*) (Jin and Cortazzi 1998).

4. What have we learned about strategic language learning?

Academic interest in the strategic learning of a second/foreign language started with Rubin's (1975) and Stern's (1975) lists of "good" language learning behaviors (e.g., guessing, risk-taking, and actively using what has been learned) that were thought to be precursory qualities for the successful learning of a second language. The lists were substantially expanded during the 1980s and 1990s when researchers went to the classrooms and learners to collect the naturally occurring strategies for language learning. LLS research was introduced to China at the beginning of the 1990s, especially with the publication of Wen's landmark study in *Foreign Language Teaching and Research* (Wen 1995). Today, LLS research in China has gone a long way in understanding the nature of strategic language learning, from initial exploratory examinations of "language learning strategies" to a much more detailed look at strategies for different aspects of language learning, as well as reflective summaries of learner strategy research.

Many of these studies employed exploratory approaches and investigated the strategy use of Chinese students in performing various aspects of English language learning. For example, Zhang (2005) used a survey and correlated five types of metacognitive strategies with general proficiency grades. S. Yang (2002) used a writing strategies questionnaire and a think-aloud approach to discover that successful and unsuccessful writers used different writing strategies at different stages of writing. He and R. Liu (2004) combined a survey with a corpus-based approach and discovered that communication strategies were employed more by low oral proficiency students than by their high oral proficiency counterparts, and that the low oral proficiency group mainly used L1-based strategies, time-gaining strategies, and reduction strategies while the high oral proficiency group mainly used L2-based strategies.

While many studies (e.g., X. Wang and Yin 2003; Wen and L. Wang 2004b) attempted to put learner strategies in an overall framework of interrelated factors, Wen and Wang's (2004a) insightful reflections and critiques added considerable depth in current thinking on learner strategies. They first reviewed findings on three common research threads: strategic differences between top and bottom scoring students, predictive power of strategies, and effects of strategy training. Next they pointed out some of the fallacies in a few underlying assumptions. For example, current research has focused much attention on the strategies that the top students use exclusively at the expense of those strategies that are used by both top and bottom students. When both groups use the same strategies or a substantial proportion of students in each group use the same strategies, the effects of these strategies will be cancelled out and their predictive power will not be shown in a statistical analysis. This, however, should not be taken as meaning that these shared strategies between top scorers and low scorers are not useful in learning. Wen and Wang also rightly maintained that the ultimate purpose of strategy training is learner autonomy which is not something that is achievable within a short period. In sum, they argued that the relationship between learner strategies and learning results is much more complex than a linear model can offer. For many strategies, e.g., guessing, excessive use beyond the appropriate level will not result in positive learning results. Many strategies arise out of learning difficulties. In some circumstances, good learners will have fewer problems and therefore many problem-solving strategies will not need to be activated.

One study (Lu 2002) is worth mentioning in that it tried to explore the relationship between metacognitive and cognitive strategies in meticulous detail. It focused on the effects of metacognitive judgment of learning aim, task difficulty, time pressure, and perceived interest on the cognitive strategy of time allocation. Three experiments were used to manipulate the conditions of metacognitive judgment. Results showed that in free reading, the subjects allocated more time to materials that were judged to be easy; while in a reading for test condition, the subjects allocated more time to difficult materials. When under high time pressure, the subjects allocated more time to easy materials; while under less time pressure, the subjects allocated more time to difficult materials. Under all conditions, materials that were judged to be more interesting were given more time. While I believe that learner strategies research should continue to explore patterns of strategy choice and use and their relationship to learning results, studies like this that explore aspects of strategy choice and use should receive more attention.

To sum up, LLS research in China has answered some major exploratory questions such as "What strategies do Chinese EFL learners use?" "How are these strategies related to learning results?" and "Do successful learners and unsuccessful learners use different strategies?" Like LLS research elsewhere, a large repertoire of strategies for the learning of the four skills and vocabulary has been identified, and is found to be correlated with learning outcomes. The relationship between strategy choice, use, and effectiveness has been found to be complicated, and mediated by various learner-, task-, and context-related factors. While this is quite an achievement, research on LLS has generally failed to produce the practical impact on teaching and learning many had hoped for at the beginning of our field (e.g., Rubin 1975).

5. Has LLS research made a difference to EFL classrooms?

Most LLS studies in China have focused on exploring and establishing a relationship between LS and some measures of learning outcomes. These findings have exerted limited influence on the ways students learn and the ways teachers teach. In fact, most research findings hardly reach the classroom at all. Even if they do, teachers and learners have little idea as to how these findings can be applied to teaching and learning tasks. Excepting a few, e.g., Gu et al. (2011), which provides detailed rationale, materials, and procedures for strategy-based instruction in the classroom, most publications are directed at the academic community, and their research findings are normally not packaged in ways that are accessible to teachers and learners in the classroom.

One type of research, strategy intervention, has reached the classroom, albeit mostly for research purposes. For example, J. Yang (2003) trained a group of freshman students on their use of metacognitive strategies for listening and reported some positive results on both listening improvement and strategy use. L. Wang (2002) trained a group of second year English majors on three communication strategies (topic avoidance/replacement, circumlocution, and stalling devices) over a 20-week period and found that the training was useful in increasing the frequency of strategy use. In particular, increasing the use of fillers improved the fluency of these students. Yue Meng's (2004) intervention involved two classes of university non-English majors (n = 84). The experimental class was taught four reading strategies (skimming, scanning, making global inferences, and making lexical inferences) for twelve weeks. At the end of the training, the experimental class outperformed the control class on a reading comprehension test and on a test of reading speed. Interestingly, Meng also compared the training effect on the four types of comprehension questions involved in the reading test. Strategy training was found useful in questions that focused on the main idea, global inferencing and new word guessing, but not on finding detailed information in the text. It should be noted that a number of these studies do not include details as to what exactly was trained, why, how the training took place, and how effectiveness was exactly measured. As such, teachers will find it hard to make use of the research findings.

Indeed, while these studies reveal some useful findings about the importance of strategy training, it has been hard to find articles that describe how classroom teachers have incorporated some of these findings successfully. One apparent reason is that these articles normally do not reach teachers. And even if they do, teachers do not get enough information as to what exactly each strategy is, and how exactly it is used to obtain the beneficial effect described in the published reports. Most Chinese journals publish very short articles that cannot accommodate a detailed methodology section. Sometimes even the findings section can also be very short and sketchy. For most of the intervention studies, readers are normally not given the instruction materials and the step-by-step procedures for strategy intervention, making it very hard for teachers to apply the research results in their classrooms. For example, in a report on the development of LLS among early primary school pupils published by a flagship journal for school teachers (Institute of Foreign Language Teaching and Teacher Education, Beijing Normal University, Beijing Institute of Curriculum Studies, and The Primary School Integrated Curriculum Reform Experiment Project Team 2008), strategy training details were totally removed from the report. Instead, nine tables of statistics were presented. Research reports like this will not be helpful in guiding teachers on incorporating strategy training inside their classrooms.

The problem is especially serious at the primary or secondary school levels. There is enough evidence suggesting that when classroom teachers talk about LLS, they mean their own perceived methods of language learning, perceptions from their own experiences as learners and from their informal observations as teachers (experience-based) rather than from research findings (research-informed). In a survey of "strategy guidance" by junior secondary school teachers of English, F. Wang (2011) asked 62 teachers to report on their LS guidance in teaching. Although these teachers reported a moderate level of strategy guidance on the questionnaire (with frequency averages between 3.38 and 4.04 on a 5-point Likert scale), follow-up interviews indicated that the teachers basically understood strategy guidance as experience-based general ways of helping students learn, e.g., memorizing words, categorizing rules, planning revision, and encouraging students to participate in class. The only article I have found that gave some detailed guidance on how teachers should incorporate strategy training into their regular teaching practices, talked about strategies of analysis, revision, induction, planning, and making use of resources (Xiang 2010). There is no indication that these suggestions were based on insights from previous research on LLS. To my knowledge, practical textbooks such as Ellis and Sinclair (1989) and Chamot et al. (1999) providing research-based advice on LLS are not available in China. Chinese researchers have in general not bothered to compile such practical texts for classroom teachers either.

For tertiary level teachers of English who should be more informed than school teachers in terms of access to LLS research findings, many articles introduce the idea of LLS instruction (e.g., Hou and Dai 2011; D. Liu and Fu 2003). Numerous studies report the effect of strategy training (e.g., Cheng 2006). There is, however, little evidence suggesting that LLS research has been widely drawn upon in the teaching and learning of English at the tertiary level. In a comparison between teachers' (N = 35) teaching and students' (N = 174) learning of listening strategies at a top university in Shanghai, Ji and He (2004) found that the teachers reported a moderate level of frequency in teaching metacognitive strategies (Mean = 3.18), cognitive strategies (Mean = 3.17), and social/affective strategies (Mean = 3.14) on a 5-point Likert scale. Their students' reported frequency of strategy use was found to be lower (Mean = 2.93, 3.04, and 2.69 respectively). The report did not include details about the teachers' and the students' understanding of LS and exactly how the strategy training was done. Since no qualitative descriptions of how LS were taught or used could be found, the self-report data could hardly form convincing evidence for anything.

Out of the 67 most cited articles in the CNKI related to LLS, fourteen focused on an aspect of learner autonomy. Some studies (e.g., Xu, Peng, and Wu 2004) explored the status quo of learner autonomy among Chinese students, but the majority presumed the usefulness in fostering learner autonomy. On the one hand, the popularity of the topic is encouraging, especially in fostering independent learning habits. On the other hand, most of these publications stopped short of seeing the relevance of learner autonomy and LLS as tools for the establishment of a voice in a foreign language at individual and social levels. In other words, almost all LS and learner autonomy studies have taken a weak (Smith 2003) or narrow (Kumaravadivelu 2003) approach to the concepts, seeing them as "learning to learn," and not "learning to communicate," not to mention "learning to be" (Littlewood 1996). Rarely can we see research aimed at the nurturing of proactive, self-reflective, and self-regulated, responsible members of society. Not much can be found about teachers making use of research findings on fostering learner autonomy either.

One reason why LLS research in China has in general not reached its target consumers, as it were, must be that people doing the research are mostly academics in tertiary institutions, and their audience is in fact their peers in academia. Only one (Ge 2006) of the most cited publications on LLS focused on secondary school learners; another (Si, Zhao, and He 2005) focused on students at the vocational level; and the remaining either focused on LLS at the tertiary level, or talked about LLS in general. China's examination culture must have also played a part in preventing LLS research from reaching the classroom. Even if classroom teachers are informed about research findings, the pressure from high-stakes examinations would mean that most strategies may well become irrelevant in real learning situations where students are mostly interested in getting high scores in exams rather than learning and using the language, not to mention becoming independent learners, or thinking and responsible members of society. If these above reasons are generally out of the researcher's control, the following reason is very much at the heart of the researcher's own choice. For many researchers, the ultimate goal of research is publication and not application. In this sense, improving the usefulness of LLS research must start from researchers, in becoming more aware of our social and educational responsibilities, and in a re-orientation of research criteria from publishability to usefulness.

It should be fair to point out at this juncture that LLS researchers in China are not alone in their inability to close the gap between research and practice. In fact, the lack of research impact is a perennial problem not just for educational research (Levin 2004), but also for the social sciences in general (Wittrock 1991). Schneider (2014, 34) outlined four characteristics of "boundary-crossing scholarship:" perceived significance (visible), philosophical compatibility (believable), occupational realism (practicable), and transportability (sharable). Looking back at LLS research in China, it seems that we have been weak in all four aspects. There is a long way ahead of us in strengthening the research-to-practice pathway.

6. Praiseworthy application efforts

Despite the general pattern above, certain aspects of LLS research have been well applied. Researchers now know much more about how Chinese learners learn English than we did 20 years ago. In fact, this knowledge has become so deeply rooted that strategies have become one of the five curriculum targets in China since 2001, along with language skills, knowledge about language, affect and attitudes, and cultural awareness (MOE China 2001; MOE China 2003; MOE China 2011). Textbooks designed after 2001 incorporate LLS. In addition, a few researchers have integrated LLS research findings into an online learner support system.

6.1. Curriculum integration

One area where LLS research has been well applied is curriculum integration. In fact, I am not aware of any other national curriculum that explicitly spells out

LLS as a major curricular target. Starting from 2001, China's national curriculum standards have included not only a mention of LLS, but also explicit strategy standards for levels 2, 5, and 8, which correspond to the end targets at Grade 6 for primary school, Grade 9 for junior secondary school, and Grade 12 for senior secondary school respectively (MOE China 2001; MOE China 2003; MOE China 2011)

In the latest curriculum standards for compulsory education (which ends at Grade 9 or the end of junior secondary school) (MOE China 2011), five types of LLS are listed as the curriculum targets for strategies. At the end of primary school (level 2), students should be able to obtain eleven "basic strategies," including, for example, "being able to make simple plans for English learning." By the end of junior secondary school (level 5), students should be able to make use of ten "cognitive strategies," eight "regulation strategies," six "communication strategies," and four "resource strategies." Table 7.2 includes examples taken and translated from the 2011 curriculum standards.

Table 7.2 Learning strategy standards by level

Level	Description of LLS standard
2 (Age = 12)	Basic strategies (11 strategies)
	• be able to make simple plans for English learning
	• attempt to read stories and other extracurricular materials in English
	• actively use the English learned to express themselves
	• can learn independently by making use of dictionaries and other tools
5 (Age = 15)	Cognitive strategies (10 strategies)
	• can focus attention on learning English
	• know what's important in learning
	• be able to use associations to learn and remember words
	• can be aware of their own errors and be able to correct the errors
	Regulation strategies (8 strategies)
	• know their targets of learning
	• be able to make feasible learning plans
	• know what's important and what's difficult in learning
	• be able to be aware and reflect upon their own improvements and difficulties
	• be able to explore methods of learning appropriate to themselves

(Continued)

Table 7.2 (Continued)

Level	Description of LLS standard
	Communication strategies (6 strategies)
	• be good at finding opportunities for using English to communicate with others
	• be able to focus on meaning during communication
	• be able to use body language such as gestures and facial expressions
	• be aware of custom differences in communication between China and foreign countries
	Resource strategies (4 strategies)
	• make use of multimedia resources to support their own learning
	• pay attention to what's available in English in the media and in everyday lives
	• be able to make use of simple library skills and internet resources

Source: Adapted from MOE China 2011, 22–23

Of course, explicitly including LLS standards in the national curriculum does not necessarily lead to classroom implementation. In a classroom observation study not designed to study LLS (Gu 2014), a senior secondary school teacher simply ignored the references to LLS in the curriculum and the textbook (see next section). Teachers should not be blamed for the lack of implementation, because they are not given information as to what it means to have reached the curricular target for each strategy; nor do they know how exactly strategy performances should be promoted and evaluated. There is also a lack of transparency as to why these strategies and not others were chosen in the first place. Despite all these problems, having some concrete targets in the curriculum standards is arguably one of the best ways of making teachers and learners aware of the importance of strategic learning.

6.2. Textbook integration of LLS

Some new textbooks published with the express purpose of implementing the curriculum standards (e.g., Q. Wang and Editorial Team 2009a) have included LLS. In *Senior High English*, for example, there is a *Learning to Learn* section at the beginning of each compulsory module of the Learner's Book, which aims to foster learner independence by informing learners what the module covers, how

Table 7.3 Strategy boxes in Unit 11 of *Senior High English*

LISTENING STRATEGIES: Listening for specific information

- Before you listen, read the questions. Try to guess possible answers (e.g. dates, places, names, numbers, objects, actions, reasons).
- While you are listening, listen for words from the questions or synonyms of them (e.g. star/celebrity).
- Don't worry if you don't understand everything. Concentrate on the important words.
- Write down your answers in note form. Don't use full sentences.

Source: Wang and Editorial Team 2009a, 24

READING STRATEGIES: Dealing with cultural references

- Look out for names and expressions related to British or American culture.
- Use the context to guess what the names represent, or what the expressions mean. If there is not enough information to guess, use an atlas, dictionary or encyclopaedia.

Source: Wang and Editorial Team 2009a, 29

SPEAKING STRATEGIES: Interacting in discussions

- Don't try to control the discussion. Listen to what the other person says.
- When you want to say something, wait for the other person to pause.
- If you have to interrupt, use the polite expressions above.
- Involve the other person, asking his/her opinions (e.g. What do you think about...?)

Source: Wang and Editorial Team 2009a, 31

---

to make use of dictionaries, how to organize vocabulary books and make grammar notes (Q. Wang and Editorial Team 2009b). In each theme-based unit of teaching, there are strategy boxes that contain a few strategy tips for a particular task (see Table 7.3).

This is definitely an encouraging sign. However, to what extent are these strategies related to the strategies listed in the curriculum standards? To what extent are they applications of research findings? A quick look at the list does not give me a very positive answer. For example, the listening strategies look more like test-taking strategies than strategies for an authentic listening task. Further questions that arise immediately would have to include "Are teachers teaching these strategies?" and "Are students able to make use of these strategies?" Again, answers are not that encouraging. The strategies for reading suggest that learners guess what an expression means, and if they are not able to guess, look it up in a dictionary, an atlas or an encyclopedia. The point is: learners are not taught how to guess, or how to look up an expression in a dictionary. In the teacher's book (Q. Wang and Editorial Team 2009b, 44), the guide reads:

- Read the strategies with the class.
- Have students look at the newspapers you have brought in and find cultural references that would not be familiar to a British or American reader.
- In pairs, students underline names in the texts and classify them into the given categories.

Previous research informs us that teachers need to show how a task is done before students can be expected to perform the task strategically (Crabbe 1993). This means that simply reading the strategies to the class will not be useful. In fact, video recordings of a senior teacher teaching this unit in a key school in Beijing (Gu 2014) showed that the strategies part of the teaching and learning aims were completely ignored in the classroom. This shows the importance of teacher education in the integration of LLS (see Chamot, Chapter 10 in this volume). Despite the good practice of listing LLS in the curriculum and including LLS in the textbook, more concrete research findings such as what strategies Chinese EFL learners need to learn at which level, and how best they should be learned and taught should be taken into consideration before classroom integration of LLS can become a fruitful reality.

6.3. Learning strategies in learner guidance

Another area where research on LLS has been applied is exemplified by one group of scholars' work on integrating LLS into a "Personalized Online System for Diagnosis and Advice in English Learning Strategies" (Ma and Yaru Meng 2008; Ma Xiaomei Research Team 2008; also see Ma's system in Oxford 2017). This is a web-based system where students can log on and get diagnostic information and then advice for learning, plus customized exercises in language skills, personality, learning style, and LS. Conceptualization of the whole system was based on an analysis of theoretical and empirical research on learner variables, learning styles, language learning theories and LS. The system comprises four modules: (a) a self-diagnosis module which elicits a learner's personality type, learning style, motivation and LS; (b) a dynamic diagnosis module that tries to establish a student's current ways of learning, e.g., reading behaviors; (c) an "autonomous learning and strategic guidance" module that provides customized guidance based on the information obtained from (a) and (b) above; and (d) an independent module that provides narratives from successful learners about how they have achieved success. This is a very innovative system that makes integrated use of not just research results on LLS but also how LS work in relation to task demands and personal preferences. Despite a lack of research findings in terms of its effectiveness, the system has reportedly received very encouraging feedback from users.

7. A few more worries

The whole idea of strategic learning assumes intentional and deliberate learning of certain targeted aspects of language competence. While an emphasis on strategic learning does not rule out the intentional use of appropriate strategies for the incidental learning of implicit skills, there is a potential danger of overlooking the incidental aspects of learning that are necessary for the building of skills, and for the contextualized, intuitive, and implicit competence of language in use. This is especially true in an input-poor EFL environment such as China, where textbooks and classrooms are practically the only resources for language input, and high-stakes examinations are the main tools for the evaluation of learning results. Indeed, of the sixty-seven most cited articles in CNKI, none of the empirical studies has focused on the strategic learning of implicit knowledge. My point is, in a learning culture that stresses intentional efforts in learning, there is a need for special attention to be paid to the strategic deployment of efforts on not just the explicit knowledge aspect of language (e.g., the meaning, the grammar rules), but also the implicit aspect of language competence. In other words, deliberate, intentional deployment of strategies such as reading for pleasure should be encouraged in order to pick up implicit knowledge, such as processing automaticity, contextual nuances in meaning, and depth of vocabulary knowledge.

A related area is in the excessive attention paid to certain aspects of language learning, e.g., vocabulary size (or breadth), that are believed to be both difficult and important. A central core of strategic learning begins with task analysis (Gu 2012). Deployment of the right strategies comes only after the learner has come to a temporary conclusion that the chosen strategies will help in solving the immediate learning problem and in improving learning outcomes, given the contextual support or constraints, and given the learner's own strengths, weaknesses, and repertoire of available strategies for similar tasks. Implementation success will be evaluated against the criteria of task completion and problem solution. Wrong conclusions in task analysis will lead to the deployment of strategies that do not help with the solution of problems in learning.

A case in point is the widespread overuse of memory strategies in China for the vocabulary learning. This overuse is based on (a) a common misconception of language competence being words plus grammar, and (b) a frequent misperception that a vocabulary learning task is mainly a memory task. Neither researchers nor teachers have paid enough attention to the strategic learning of productive vocabulary. For example, vocabulary learning strategies have received much attention. Out of the sixty-seven most cited articles, nine focused on vocabulary learning strategies. Apart from J. Liu's (1999) study, which compared the spontaneous use of guessing strategies in both English and Chinese and concluded that the ability to guess is related to both English proficiency and ability to guess in Chinese, all other studies were exploratory surveys, and the dependent variable normally involved a passive vocabulary-size measure. Given the gravity of the perceived vocabulary-learning difficulty and the research emphasis on passive vocabulary size, teachers and learners are unsurprisingly overusing memory strategies which help increase the number of words learners know.

Another example is the overemphasis on mnemonic devices. Research on mnemonics (e.g., Hulstijn 1997) has in general shown the usefulness of mnemonic devices in vocabulary learning. However, book-length volumes (e.g., Song 1989) and TV programs and multimedia packages (J. Zhang and M. Wang 2007), which provide learners with a bizarre associative link between the English spelling of each word and a Chinese sound-alike word (e.g., DELAY: Landmines /dilei/ delayed the enemy's attack), reveal that the research result is being strangely overapplied. Another strategy that is widely researched in vocabulary learning is using word lists and the use of repetition in learning the lists. Common sense tells us that repetition is useful in committing a word to memory. However, when we see bookstores full of books that contain nothing but lists of words for memorization, and notice learners doing everything to memorize decontextualized word lists, we know it is overkill, at the expense of other useful strategies for not just the memory but also the depth and automaticity of the words memorized.

8. Summary and conclusions

The topic of LLS is now a mature research focus in China, as reflected in the huge number of publications in Chinese journals, as well as the number of citations these articles receive. For example, an early article (Wen 1995) has been cited almost two thousand times, suggesting both the popularity and the maturity of the research. The overwhelming majority of this research has remained exploratory and correlational, finding patterns of strategy use and charting relationships among variables. Strategy training studies are gaining momentum, but most of these studies cater to research rather than practical needs. Most strategy training studies do not go beyond a language learning framework, without making the leap from the autonomous learner to the autonomous communicator and finally to the autonomous person (Littlewood 1996). In general, it is sad to see most LLS research findings not applied or not well applied to language learning. It is perhaps even sadder to see researchers not being aware of the necessity of making their findings applicable in the first place. The same points could likely be made concerning LLS research and researchers in some other parts of the world.

Researchers on LLS should do more teacher/learner-friendly research. This involves making research results more readable to classroom teachers and learners. More practical textbooks should be published aiming at integrating LLS research findings into real teaching and learning situations. Teacher-friendly research also involves teachers being encouraged to do their own action research by trying out different ways of LLS intervention. Another way to make research useful is to create simple toolkits (Popham 2010) for the diagnostic and formative use of strategies. So far, strategy elicitation tools have been created mainly for research purposes. It is hard for teachers and learners to make use of these tools to catch and solve learning problems. Much more needs to be done in the creation and validation of classroom-friendly tools such as questionnaires, observation sheets, and task-specific diagnostic instruments, so that teachers can make use of research findings more easily, and learners can be taught how to use specific strategies to self-diagnose learning problems. Perhaps a fundamental way of moving this forward is to build LLS into teacher training programs, so that pre-service and in-service teachers begin to rely more on research findings and less on their own teaching and learning experiences only.

Not all research findings have been shelved. In fact, a few have received too much attention, so much so that there is a real danger that learners and teachers can be misguided as to how a foreign language should be learned. One such example is the overuse of memory strategies. A related issue is the overuse of strategies for explicit knowledge, at the expense of those for implicit aspects of language competence. This is mainly an issue of selected use of research findings on the part of learners and teachers, but as researchers we cannot shrug off our responsibility of informing those who need our research. As researchers we cannot be collectively silent in the face of market-hungry profiteers who selectively oversell a few learning gimmicks that may or may not be related to our research findings.

On a more positive note, we now know much more than before in terms of both a whole repertoire of LLS Chinese students use and the relationship between strategy use and EFL learning results. Strategic learning as an important phenomenon in language learning has received so much attention in China that it has become an important part of the national curriculum and has been included in textbooks. Despite a lack of clarity and transparency in the selection of LLS and in the guidance for implementation and evaluation, a concrete set of curriculum standards in strategic learning provides at least a basis for teachers and learners to take strategic learning seriously. Given the problem of curriculum implementation, which to a certain extent can be remedied by teacher education, raising the awareness of LLS among teachers and learners and showing some examples of use are certainly a good start. With this level of emphasis and guidance at the top, and the ubiquitous need of learning how to learn at the classroom level, what is left is a re-orientation of research focus from basic research to applied research, from an aim for the advancement of knowledge about strategic language learning only to the ultimate aim of improving language learning results, and empowering language learners.

References

Brown, H. Douglas. 1991. "TESOL at Twenty-five: What Are the Issues?" *TESOL Quarterly* 25 (2): 245–60. doi:10.2307/3587462.

Canagarajah, Suresh. 2006. "TESOL at Forty: What Are the Issues?" *TESOL Quarterly* 40: 9–34.

Chamot, Anna Uhl, Sarah Barnhardt, Pamela Beard El-Dinary, and Jill Robbins. 1999. *The Learning Strategies Handbook*. White Plains, NY: Longman.

Cheng, Bing. 2006. "Daxue Yingyu Xuexi Celue Peixun Shijian Yu Xiaoguo Fenxi [Effects of Learning Strategy Instruction on College English Proficiency]." *Journal of Xi'an International Studies University* 14 (3): 48–50.

Crabbe, David. 1993. "Fostering Autonomy from within the Classroom: The Teacher's Responsibility." *System* 21 (4): 443–52.

Ellis, Gail, and Barbara Sinclair. 1989. *Learning to Learn English: Learner's Book*. Cambridge: Cambridge University Press.

Ge, Bingfang. 2006. "Guanyu Zhongxuesheng Yingyu Xuexi Dongji Guannian Celue Guanxi de Yixiang Shizheng Yanjiu [An Empirical Study of Motivation, Beliefs, and

Learning Strategies among Secondary School Students]." *Foreign Language Teaching Abroad* 1: 14–23.

Gu, Peter Yongqi. 2007. "Strategy-Based Instruction." In *Proceedings of the International Symposium on English Education in Japan: Exploring New Frontiers*, edited by Tomoko Yashima and Toshiyo Nabei, 21–38. Osaka: Yubunsha.

———. 2012. "Learning Strategies: Prototypical Core and Dimensions of Variation." *Studies in Self-Access Learning Journal* 3 (4): 330–56.

———. 2014. "The Unbearable Lightness of the Curriculum: What Drives the Assessment Practices of a Teacher of English as a Foreign Language in a Chinese Secondary School?" *Assessment in Education: Principles, Policy & Practice* 21 (3): 286–305.

Gu, Peter Yongqi, Guangwei Hu, Jun Zhang, and Rui Bai. 2011. *Strategy-based Instruction: Focusing on Reading and Writing Strategies.* Beijing: Foreign Language Teaching and Research Press.

He, Lianzhen, and Rongjun Liu. 2004. "Jiyu Yuliaoku de Daxuesheng Jiaoji Celue Yanjiu [A Corpus-Based Study of Communication Strategies among University Students]." *Foreign Language Research* 83: 60–65.

Hou, Yali, and Zhongxin Dai. 2011. "Daxue Yingyu Jiaoxue Zhong de Xuexi Celue Zhidao: Xunlian Fangshi Yu Jiaoshi Jiaose [Learning Strategy Guidance in College English Teaching: Modes of Training and the Teacher's Role]." *Technology Information* 20: 452–53.

Hulstijn, Jan H. 1997. "Mnemonic Methods in Foreign Language Vocabulary Learning." In *Second Language Vocabulary Acquisition*, edited by James Coady and Thomas Huckin, 203–24. Cambridge: Cambridge University Press.

Institute of Foreign Language Teaching and Teacher Education, Beijing Normal University, Beijing Institute of Curriculum Studies, and The Primary School Integrated Curriculum Reform Experiment Project Team. 2008. "Xiaoxue Yi Zhi San Nianji Xuesheng Yingyu Xuexi Celue Fazhan Yanjiu [A Study of the Development of English Learning Strategies among Primary 1 to 3 Learners]." *Foreign Language Teaching in Schools* 8: 1–6.

Ji, Peiying, and Mengyi He. 2004. "Daxue Yingyu Shisheng Tingli Celue Yanjiu [A Survey of Listening Strategies among College English Teachers and Learners]." *Foreign Language World* 103 (5): 40–46.

Jin, Lixian, and Martin Cortazzi. 1998. "The Culture the Learner Brings: A Bridge or a Barrier." In *Language Learning in Intercultural Perspective: Approaches through Drama and Ethnography*, edited by Michael Byram and Michael Fleming, 98–118. Cambridge: Cambridge University Press.

Kumaravadivelu, B. 2003. *Beyond Methods: Macrostrategies for Language Learning.* New Haven, CT: Yale University Press.

Levin, Ben. 2004. "Making Research Matter More." *Education Policy Analysis Archives* 12 (56). http://dx.doi.org/10.14507/epaa.v12n56.2004.

Littlewood, William. 1996. "'Autonomy': An Anatomy and a Framework." *System* 24 (4): 427–35.

Liu, Dianzhi, and Yurong Fu. 2003. "Ketang Jiaoxue Zhong de Xuexi Celue Zhidao [Learning Strategy Guidance in Classroom Teaching]." *Journal of Southwest China Normal University (Humanities and Social Sciences Edition)* 29 (6): 36–39.

Liu, Jinkai. 1999. "Waiyu Xuexi Celue Yanjiu: Cai Ci Nengli Yu Waiyu Shuiping [Foreign Language Learning Strategies: Vocabulary Guessing and Foreign Language Competence]." *Foreign Language Education* 20 (3): 31–35.

Lu, Zhi. 2002. "Yingyu Xuesheng de Yuanrenzhi Yu Xuexi Shijian Fenpei Celue [English Learners' Metacognitive Strategies for Time Management]." *Modern Foreign Languages* 25: 396–407.

Ma Xiaomei Research Team. 2008. "Gexinghua Yingyu Xuexi Zhenduan Yu Zhidao Xitong Shizheng Yanjiu Yu Xitong Jiagou Gaiyao [A Framework and Empirical Research for the Personalized English Learning Diagnosis and Advice System]." *Foreign Language Teaching and Research* 40 (3): 184–87.

Ma, Xiaomei, and Yaru Meng. 2008. "Jiyu Xuexizhe Kekong Yinsu de Gexinghua Yingyu Xuexi Celue Zhenduan Yu Zhidao Xitong Yanfa [Developing a Diagnostic and Counseling System for Personalized English Learning Strategies Based on EFL Learners' Controllable Factors]." *Journal of PLA University of Foreign Languages* 31 (4): 38–42.

Meng, Yue. 2004. "Daxue Yingyu Yuedu Celue Xunlian de Shiyan Yanjiu [An Experimental Study of Reading Strategies Training at the Tertiary Level]." *Foreign Languages and Their Teaching* 179: 24–27.

MOE China. 2001. *English Language Curriculum Standards for Full-Time Compulsory Education and Senior Secondary Schools (Trial Version).* Beijing: Beijing Normal University Press.

———. 2003. *English Language Curriculum Standards for Senior Secondary Schools (Experimental).* Beijing: People's Education Press.

———. 2010. "2009 Nian Jiaoyu Tongji Shuju [Education Statistics 2009]." Accessed August 16, 2016. http://www.moe.edu.cn/publicfiles/business/htmlfiles/moe/s4959/index.html

———. 2011. *English Curriculum Standards for Compulsory Education, Version 2011.* Beijing: Beijing Normal University Publishing Group.

Oxford, Rebecca L. 1990. *Language Learning Strategies: What Every Teacher Should Know.* Boston: Heinle & Heinle.

———. 1999. "Relationships between Second Language Learning Strategies and Language Proficiency in the Context of Learner Autonomy and Self-Regulation". *Revista Canaria de Estudios Ingleses. [Canary Islands Journal of English Studies].* 38: 108–126.

———. 2017. *Teaching and Researching Language Learning Strategies: Self-Regulation in Context.* 2nd edition. New York: Routledge.

Pennycook, Alastair. 1997. "Cultural Alternatives and Autonomy." In *Autonomy and Independence in Language Learning*, edited by Phil Benson and Peter Voller, 35–53. New York: Longman.

Popham, W. James. 2010. "Wanted: A Formative Assessment Starter Kit." *Assessment Matters* 2: 182–90.

Rubin, Joan. 1975. "What the 'Good Language Learner' Can Teach Us." *TESOL Quarterly* 9 (1): 41–51.

Schneider, Jack. 2014. "Closing the Gap . . . between the University and Schoolhouse." *Phi Delta Kappan* 96 (1): 30–35. doi:10.1177/0031721714547859.

Si, Jianguo, Jizheng Zhao, and Mengyi He. 2005. "Zhongguo Gaozhi Xuesheng Yingyu Xuexi Celue Diaocha [A Survey of English Language Learning Strategies among Vocational School Students]." *Foreign Language Teaching Abroad* 1: 23–27.

Smith, Richard C. 2003. "Pedagogy for Autonomy as (Becoming-) Appropriate Methodology." In *Learner Autonomy across Cultures: Language Education Perspectives*, edited by D. Palfreyman and Richard Smith, 129–46. New York: Palgrave Macmillan.

Song, Yichang. 1989. *Fengbao Mi Shi Yingyu Danci Sujifa [The Storm Puzzle Method of Accelerated English Vocabulary Learning]*. Beijing: Popular Science Press.

Stern, Hans H. 1975. "What Can We Learn from the Good Language Learner?" *Canadian Modern Language Review* 31: 304–18.

Wang, Fang. 2011. "Chuzhong Yingyu Jiaoshi Xuexi Celue Zhidao de Xianzhuang Diaocha [A Survey of Middle School English Teachers' Learning Strategy Guidance]." *Collected Papers in Science and Technology* 5: 154–55.

Wang, Lifei. 2002. "Daxuesheng Yingyu Kouyuke Jiaoji Celue Jiaoxue de Shiyan Baogao [Teaching Communication Strategies in Spoken English Classes at the Tertiary Level]." *Foreign Language Teaching and Research* 34: 426–30.

Wang, Qiang, and Editorial Team, eds. 2009a. *Senior High English—Module 4: Student Book*. Beijing: Beijing Normal University Press; Pearson Education.

———, eds. 2009b. *Senior High English—Module 4: Teacher's Book*. Beijing: Beijing Normal University Press; Pearson Education.

Wang, Xiaowei, and Tiechao Yin. 2003. "Yingyu Xuexi Celue Xitong Juedingxing Yinsu de Shizheng Yanjiu [An Empirical Study of the Factors Affecting English Language Learning Strategies]." *Foreign Language Research* 115: 99–102.

Wen, Qiufang. 1995. "Dui Waiyu Xuexi Celue Youxiaoxing Yanjiu de Zhiyi [On the Effectiveness of Foreign Language Learning Strategies]." *Foreign Language Teaching and Research* 92 (3): 61–66.

———. 2001. "Yingyu Xuexizhe Dongji Guannian Celue de Bianhua Guilu Ye Dedian [Developmental Patterns in Motivation, Beliefs and Strategies of English Learners in China]." *Foreign Language Teaching and Research* 33 (2): 105–10.

Wen, Qiufang, and Lifei Wang. 2004a. "Dui Waiyu Xuexi Celue Youxiaoxing Yanjiu de Zhiyi [On the Effectiveness of Foreign Language Learning Strategies]." *Foreign Language World* 100: 2–7.

———. 2004b. "Yingxiang Waiyu Xuexi Celue Xitong Yunxing de Gezhong Yinsu Pingshu [Factors in the Effective Use of Foreign Language Learning Strategies]." *Foreign Languages and Their Teaching* 186: 28–32.

Wittrock, Björn. 1991. "Social Knowledge and Public Policy: Eight Models of Interaction." In *Social Sciences and Modern States*, edited by Peter Wagner, Carol

Hirschon Weiss, Björn Wittrock, and Hellmut Wollman, 333–54. Cambridge: Cambridge University Press.

Xiang, Juping. 2010. "Chuzhong Yingyu Jiaoxue Shentou Xuexi Celue Zhidao de Tansuo [Strategy-Based Instruction in the Teaching of English in Junior Secondary Schools]." *Examination, Teaching and Research* 12: 58–60.

Xu, Jinfen, Renzhong Peng, and Weiping Wu. 2004. "Fei Yingyu Zhuanye Daxuesheng Zizhuxing Yingyu Xuexi Nengli Diaocha Yu Fenxi [A Survey of Learner Autonomy among Non-English Majors]." *Foreign Language Teaching and Research* 36: 64–68.

Yang, Jianding. 2003. "Tingli Jiaoxue Zhong de Yuanrenzhi Celue Peixun [Metacognitive Strategy Training in the Teaching of Listening]." *Foreign Language Education* 24 (4): 65–69.

Yang, Shuxian. 2002. "Yingyu Xiezuo Chenggongzhe Yu Bu Chenggongzhe Zai Celue Shiyong Shang de Chayi [Successful and Non-Successful Writers and Their Use of Writing Strategies]." *Foreign Language World* 89: 57–64.

Yao, Meilin. 2000. "Dangqian Waiyu Cihui Xuexi Celue de Jiaoxue Yanjiu Quxiang [Teaching and Research Trends on Vocabulary Learning Strategies]." *Journal of Beijing Normal University (Humanities and Social Sciences)* 161 (5): 123–29.

Zhang, Jie, and Maohua Wang. 2007. *Danci Buyong Ji 3.0 [Words Don't Need to Be Memorized, Ver. 3]*. Multimedia. Guangong, China: Sun Yat-sen University Press.

Zhang, Xuan. 2005. "Jichu Jieduan Yingyu Zhuanye Xuesheng Yuanrenzhi Celue Diaocha [A Survey of Metacognitive Strategies among English Majors at the Foundation Stage]." *Journal of PLA University of Foreign Languages* 28 (3): 59–62.

8

Language Learning Strategies in Greek Primary and Secondary School Learners

How Individual Characteristics Affect Strategy Use

Angeliki Psaltou-Joycey
Aristotle University of Thessaloniki, Greece

Zoe Gavriilidou
Democritus University of Thrace, Greece

1. Introduction

Language learning strategies (LLSs) have to do with learners' decisions and behaviors regarding the processes they adopt to maximize learning outcomes, the significance of which is prominent in foreign language (FL) learning contexts. Individual, group, and situational learner needs justify the study of variables such as age, gender, proficiency level, socio-geographical status, motivation, learning style, culture, language skill development, and the nature of the language learning task. Especially with young learners, who are at their initial stages of developing their learning practices, offering them opportunities to identify suitable LLSs is an important step towards helping them acquire language learning awareness and cope with the demands of a language situation (i.e., learning and communicating) (Macaro 2001).

1.1. The present study

The present study investigated the strategic profile of mainstream primary and secondary school children learning English as a foreign language (EFL) in Greece. Particularly, it examined the variables of gender, proficiency level, education level, and region of residence within a specific educational and sociocultural context, in order to determine how these variables affect learners' self-reported selection and use of LLSs. The motivation for a detailed examination of learners' profiles was twofold. First, international studies on LLSs inspired our study: they relied on data selected from small numbers of foreign/second language learners having either the same first language (L1) or a multilingual background and attending a school (or a small number of schools)/college/university department(s), in a town/city (but see Cheng's 2011 study in Hong Kong) but not from a sample population covering a whole nation and being more or less homogeneous, like our own. Second, despite the fact that the current Greek National Curriculum and FL course books identify strategies as an important component of the syllabus, little research has been produced nationwide towards mapping the strategies Greek state school learners employ.

1.2. Cooperating universities and aims

The study materialized within the Greek THALES project from 2012 to 2015 as part of the National Strategic Reference Frame and was co-funded by the European Social Fund and national resources. The project involved four Greek universities, namely, Democritus University of Thrace as the coordinating university, Aristotle University of Thessaloniki, the University of Macedonia of Thessaloniki, and Hellenic Open University, under the leadership of Professor Zoe Gavriilidou. Its aims were:

(a) to shorten, translate, simplify and culturally adapt Oxford's (1990) *Strategy Inventory for Language Learning (SILL)*, version 7.0 (ESL/EFL) in Greek and Turkish and to administer the resulting inventory to school-aged learners (the three upper grades of primary and the three grades of lower secondary schools),

(b) to profile the LLS use of the population attending Greek state mainstream and minority primary and secondary schools when learning English as a FL,

(c) to identify the factors related to learners' choice of language learning strategies,

(d) to construct and validate an instrument based on the *SILL* for profiling EFL teachers' LLS promotion in class,

(e) to draw the teachers' strategic profile, and

(f) to provide language teachers and education policy makers with a guide containing activities that promote strategic teaching.

As we can deduce from the above, the aims and design of the project link well with the central theme of this volume: they are concerned with a variety of learners' individual characteristics in relation to language learning strategy use, situated in the Greek educational and cultural context.

2. Research background

2.1. Self-regulated learning

Self-regulation learning theory integrates cognitive, affective, motivational, and behavioral components trying to explain how individuals adjust their actions and goals to achieve desired ends under variable conditions (Pintrich 2000; Ryan and Deci 2000). The theory involves the "whole self" as each individual component constitutes an indispensable factor of learning achievement. "Learners personally activate and sustain cognitions, affects and behaviors that are systematically oriented toward attainment of learning goals" (Schunk and Zimmerman 2008, preface). Subscribing to this theory for L2 learning, Oxford (2011, 7) promotes her *Strategic Self-Regulation Model* of language learning and argues that "learners actively and constructively use strategies to manage their own learning."

2.2. Complexity of language learning

Language learning is a complex process requiring the employment of particular categories and combinations of LLSs in different learning and cultural situations. In most cases, and especially when L2 learning takes place in classroom contexts, several parameters regarding strategic, self-regulated L2 learners have to be considered. These parameters are related to learners' individual or group characteristics and influence their cognition, affect, motivation, and behavior. Learners' gender, level of education, proficiency level, and region of residence in which the L2 is learned are some variables that may differentiate the frequency of strategy use, and may lead to variations of self-regulation in L2 learning. As these issues are central to our study, relevant research is briefly presented below.

Much LLS research investigates and reports on the overall strategic profiles of various learner groups all over the world. The significance of these profiles is that such information allows researchers, educationalists, and classroom practitioners to make comparisons, work out possible reasons for apparent differences among learner groups, produce materials to reinforce or promote strategy categories according to individual learner preferences or the cultural/educational context, and implement strategy instruction accordingly.

2.2.1 Gender

Studies on *gender* in mainstream psychology and social interaction theory have shown that males and females follow different paths to process information and acquire knowledge (Lakoff 1975; Nyikos 1990; Tannen 1986), both capable of reaching high levels of language proficiency (Green and Oxford 1995; Nyikos 2008). With regard to LLSs, most gender studies have reported overwhelming female superiority on the frequency of self-reported overall strategy use (Gavriilidou and Papanis 2009; Gu 2002; Hong-Nam and Leavell 2006; Kazamia 2003; Lan and Oxford 2003; Peacock and Ho 2003; Psaltou-Joycey and Kantaridou 2009; Vrettou 2009, 2011). Fewer studies pointed at strategy-item-specific male superiority (Wharton 2000), a finding that corroborates the statement about different ways of processing similar information by the two genders (Nyikos 1990), whereas some studies did not show any statistically significant differences between men and women (Griffiths 2003; Nisbet, Tindall, and Arroyo 2005; Psaltou-Joycey 2008). Conclusively, we should not look at gender differences in strategy use in a single, oversimplified way but instead we should account for them in relation to other influencing factors such as social beliefs, personality type, culture, or educational context (Psaltou-Joycey 2010).

2.2.2 Level of education

Learners' *level of education* and LLS use has been extensively researched in relation to the interrelated *age* factor. Due to maturational changes, learners of various age groups, reflecting different educational levels and cultural contexts, have diverse needs and, consequently, employ different learning strategies (Gavriilidou and Psaltou-Joycey 2009; Griffiths 2008; Lan and Oxford 2003; Peacock and Ho 2003; Psaltou-Joycey and Kantaridou 2009; Tragant and Victori 2012). The effect of age and level of education on LLSs interrelates with further factors in a rather complex manner. Besides the obvious level of L2 language proficiency, it involves culture, motivation, and attitudes as well as beliefs about language learning (Psaltou-Joycey 2010). Learners' age and level of education are therefore rather important individual characteristics that invite further elaboration.

Using a cross-sectional and a longitudinal study, Victori and Tragant (2003) reported a wider range of strategy use by older EFL learners although the linear pattern was not confirmed for all strategy categories. In their 2006 study, Tragant and Victori found that as learners grow older, they show a preference for more sophisticated strategies. Similarly, in a comparative cross-sectional study of 6th primary and 3rd secondary school grades of EFL learners in Greece, Psaltou-Joycey and Sougari (2010) found qualitative differences in the selection of individual strategies between the two groups. Also Psaltou-Joycey et al. (2014)

concluded that age was the most important factor regarding EFL strategies employed by primary school learners of different grades.

There is lack of consensus regarding preference of strategy categories by young learners and adolescents across cultures and contexts, suggesting a strong influence of these two variables on strategy preferences. For instance, Greek primary and lower secondary school EFL learners in Vrettou (2009, 2011) and secondary school learners in Mitits (2014) reported favouring metacognitive strategies and not using memory and compensation strategies much. In their comparative study of upper primary and lower secondary learners, Platsidou and Sipitanou (2014) also found that the learners most preferred metacognitive strategies. On the other hand, Lan and Oxford (2003) found that primary school learners in Taiwan reported using compensation and affective strategies most frequently, whereas Ardasheva and Tretter (2013) discovered that school-aged learners in the USA reported a higher use of metacognitive strategies, and the lowest preference for affective strategies.

2.2.3 Language proficiency level

Ever since the "good language learner" studies of the 1970s, a high language *proficiency level* has been found to correlate positively with frequency of strategy use. A linear relationship between the two was attested in many L2 learning strategy use studies (Green and Oxford 1995; Griffiths 2003; Peacock and Ho 2003; Psaltou-Joycey and Kantaridou 2009; Vrettou 2009, 2011; Wharton 2000; Yang 2007). Although the majority of published studies have focused on the upper grades of secondary school, college or university levels, and adults, here we report only on studies that have examined young and adolescent learners as the present study concerns such populations.

Chamot and El-Dinary (1999) examined the reading strategies of two immersion groups (high and low achievers respectively), of primary school children enrolled in French, Japanese, and Spanish classrooms and found qualitative differences between the two groups in the categories of strategies employed. Lan and Oxford (2003) found that Taiwanese primary learners who were highly proficient in English tended to use strategies from the cognitive, compensation, metacognitive, and affective categories more frequently than did their lower level counterparts. In Lee's (2003) study, Korean secondary school learners of high proficiency were found to use significantly more memory, cognitive, metacognitive, and social strategies than did low proficiency learners. In her study of 3rd grade lower secondary EFL learners, Vrettou (2009) found a linear frequency of use with beginners and elementary learners employing fewer strategies than lower, upper intermediate, and advanced learners. Mitits (2014) also observed a correlation between secondary school learners who reported higher EFL achievement and frequency of strategy use in most strategy categories. All in all, more and less proficient learners have been found to differ in relation to the number and range of strategies they employ, the strategies they apply to given tasks, and whether the selected strategies are appropriate for a task (Chamot 2004).

2.2.4 *Contextual factors based on region of residence*

With regard to the *region of residence* where the L2 is learnt (in the same school/ country or diverse schools/countries, with L1 homogeneous/heterogeneous groups) attested differences in strategy use are attributed to differences in culture, teaching methods, and educational priorities (Griffiths 2013; Psaltou-Joycey 2010). Oxford and Schramm (2007, 48) argue that "in a critically sociocultural framework, issues of power, oppression, imperialism, and resistance are applied to the teaching and learning of L2 learner strategies," thus accepting the importance of sociocultural factors besides psychological factors in L2 learning strategy research.

However, to the best of our knowledge, few studies (Butler 2014; Grenfell and Harris 2012) have investigated the effect of socioeconomic or sociocultural factors on foreign language learning, strategy use, performance, and motivation of L2 involving large numbers of learners of an entire country. An exception within Greece is the study by Mitits, Psaltou-Joycey, and Sougari (2016) which reports on results of the exploratory study that preceded the present, main one. Some small-scale studies (Frangoudaki 1985; Katsikas and Kavvadias 2000; Mattheoudakis and Alexiou 2009) have investigated socioeconomic and geographical differences among learners within the boundaries of a single city and found that learners' academic progress is affected by different economic strata. However, socioeconomic dimensions are largely missing in current major theories of second or foreign language acquisition. We consider it important to integrate socioeconomic dimensions in theorizing second or foreign language acquisition especially with regard to learning prestigious and powerful languages such as English (Butler 2014).

In response to this lack of data concerning the influence of sociocultural or socioeconomic factors on strategy use, and to address the importance of these factors in LLS research, we included the *region of residence* (Eurostat 2007; Willenborg and de Waal 1996) in our study. Gross domestic product (GDP) per capita in different regions, cultural practices, and purchasing power may affect learners' attitudes. From a sociological perspective, socioeconomic structure and culture may shape individual behavior and provide a context that restricts how individuals live and act in everyday life. Part of the explanation for regional differences is attributable to the extent to which regions differ in their rural/ urban composition and the subsequent proximity to main centers, educational attainment, GDP per capita, unemployment rate, cultural values towards language learning, travelling, and working abroad. From that point of view, the region of residence may be an important factor that influences language learners' behavior.

For the study of the *region of residence* in this research, we adopted the most current administrative division of Greece, named *Callicrate*,[1] which includes thirteen peripheries[2] (see Figure 8.1). Table 8.1 lists the GDP and the unemployment

Figure 8.1 Greece's current administrative areas according to Law 3852/2010

Table 8.1 Unemployment rate and GDP in Greek peripheries

Administrative peripheries	Work Force 2013				GDP 2013 per capita in €
	Total	Employed	Unemployed	% Unemployment	
East Macedonia & Thrace	252.9	186.4	66.6	26.3	12,270
Central Macedonia	833.7	587.2	246.5	29.6	13,645
West Macedonia	119.4	80.9	38.5	32.3	13,946[3]
Epirus	154.1	112.3	41.9	27.2	12,207
Thessaly	318.5	237.1	81.4	25.6	12,757
Ionian Islands	102.6	78.8	23.8	23.2	16,100
West Greece	317.1	231.6	85.5	27.0	13,431
Central Greece	234.8	169.1	65.7	28.0	15,075
Attica	1,872.0	1,344.5	527.5	28.2	24,099
Peloponnese	258.9	204.2	54.7	21.1	13,870
North Aegean	83.4	63.7	19.6	23.5	13,394
South Aegean	131.0	99.2	31.8	24.3	18,064
Crete	272.7	201.1	71.7	26.3	1,2854

rate in each periphery according to data from the Hellenic National Statistical Authority (ELSTAT 2016).

3. Purpose of the study

Taking into account the shortcomings and gaps in relevant published studies, the purpose of the present study was to investigate the self-perceived use of LLSs of mainstream[4] primary and secondary school EFL learners in Greece. Specifically, it aimed to inquire how the frequency of strategy use is influenced by the learners' gender, education and proficiency levels, as well as by the region of residence in which learners receive EFL instruction. For these reasons we posed the following research questions:

RQ 1: What is the strategic profile of learners of English as a FL in mainstream primary and secondary schools in Greece overall?

RQ 2: Are there any differences in the self-perceived frequency of strategy use between boys and girls of the school population?

RQ 3: Are there any differences in the self-perceived frequency of strategy use between primary and secondary school EFL learners?

RQ 4: Are there any differences in the perceived frequency of strategy use according to their self-perceived proficiency level?

RQ 5: Are there any differences in the self-perceived frequency of strategy use by the school population according to their region of residence?

4. Methodology

4.1. Participants

The research was conducted in the spring of 2014 and data were collected from 1,676 primary school learners ranging from 10–12 years of age and 1,680 lower secondary learners between 13–15 years of age. The learners came from 42 schools in 21 cities of 18 prefectures and all 13 regions of the Greek territory (see Table 8.1).

4.2. Instrumentation

The final instrument used was an adapted Greek version (Gavriilidou and Mitits 2016; Petrogiannis and Gavriilidou 2015) of the *SILL* Version 7.0 (ESL/EFL) (Oxford 1990), piloted during the exploratory phase of the THALES project. It had three parts: Part A consisted of 29 items designed to capture the learners' strategy use for FL learning. They described a wide range of strategies learners are expected to use in the Greek educational context: (a) memory (4 items); (b) cognitive (7 items); (c) compensation (3 items); (d) metacognitive (7 items); (e) affective (3 items); and (f) social (5 items). Respondents were asked to indicate how often they use each of the strategies listed, using a five-point Likert-type scale ranging from 1 (never or almost never) to 5 (always or almost always). Part B included eight questions concerning demographic information. Part C contained six questions about the English language.

4.3. Procedure

In the exploratory study necessary preparations were made and actions were taken in order to fulfill the required aim (a) of the project (see introduction). The results of this study are reported in Gavriilidou and Mitits (2016), Mitits, Psaltou-Joycey, and Sougari (2016), and Petrogiannis and Gavriilidou (2015).

For the main study, the adapted Greek and Turkish versions of the *SILL* were administered by the EFL class teachers during regular instruction time. Previous to administration, approval was granted by the Institutional Review Board (National Pedagogical Institute) and written consent was obtained from the legal guardians where necessary. The collected data responded to aims (b) and (c) of the THALES project (see introduction). In this chapter we present only data concerning the strategic profile of the learners attending mainstream upper primary and lower secondary schools in Greece, corresponding to the numbers of participants presented above.

Independent samples *t*-tests were used in the study of the independent variables of *gender* and *level of education*. Kruskal-Wallis was used for all non-normal distributed variables. One-way analysis of variance (ANOVA) with the criterion Brown Forsythe was used to check the effects of *region of residence* and *language proficiency* on strategy use. "Within-variable" differences were checked using the Tukey post-hoc test. In addition, descriptive statistics (means and standard deviations) were also used. Results were considered statistically significant at the 0.001 level. A mean score over 3.5 on all the *SILL* items was considered to reflect "high use" of a given strategy, 2.5 to 3.4 indicates "medium use," and below 2.4 indicates "low use" of a strategy (Oxford 1990).

5. Results

The mean frequency of overall strategy use for the whole sample was found to reflect the "medium frequency range" (m = 3.18, s.d. = 0.87). The means for the six language learning strategy categories also fell within the same range with *metacognitive* strategies exhibiting the highest mean frequency (m = 3.28, s.d. = 0.85), followed by *compensation* (m = 3.15, s.d. = 0.97), *affective* (m = 3.10, s.d. = 0.88), *cognitive* (m = 3.02, s.d. = 0.92) and *memory* strategies (m = 2.96, s.d. = 0.81). *Social* strategies revealed a mean of 2.95 (s.d. = 0.84) and were the least used strategies.

With regard to gender (Table 8.2), girls demonstrated higher mean scores (representing frequencies of use) in all six LLS categories. The mean differences were statistically significant in all cases.

As far as the level of education was concerned (Table 8.3), primary school learners demonstrated higher mean scores in all LLS categories except the compensation strategies. The mean differences were statistically significant in all cases.

Table 8.2 Descriptive data and *t*-test comparisons by LLS and gender

LLS	Gender		t	p
	Boys Mean (s.d.)	Girls Mean (s.d.)		
Memory	2.90 (0.78)	3.01 (0.74)	−3.75	0.000
Cognitive	2.86 (0.82)	3.13 (0.81)	−8.87	0.000
Compensation	3.03 (0.84)	3.26 (0.82)	−7.5	0.000
Metacognitive	3.11 (0.83)	3.41 (0.79)	−9.76	0.000
Affective	3.00 (0.95)	3.19 (0.94)	−5.53	0.000
Social	2.78 (0.87)	3.09 (0.86)	−9.37	0.000

Table 8.3 Descriptive data and *t*-test comparisons by LLS and level of education

LLS	Level of education		t	p
	Primary Mean (s.d.)	Secondary Mean (s.d.)		
Memory	3.13 (0.78)	2.81 (0.71)	11.78	0.000
Cognitive	3.14 (0.81)	2.88 (0.87)	8.56	0.000
Compensation	3.08 (0.87)	3.23 (0.81)	−4.69	0.000
Metacognitive	3.44 (0.80)	3.12 (0.83)	10.60	0.000
Affective	3.26 (0.95)	2.95 (0.93)	9.05	0.000
Social	3.17 (0.86)	2.74 (0.86)	13.51	0.000

One-way analysis of variance (ANOVA) with the criterion Brown Forsythe showed that mean scores in all six categories of strategies present statistically significant differences according to proficiency level (memory: $F = 84.73$; $p < 0.001$, cognitive: $F = 143.11$, $p < 0.001$; compensation: $F = 35.09$ $p < 0.001$; metacognitive: $F = 116.31$ $p < 0.001$; affective: $F = 53.67$ $p < 0.001$; social: $F = 49.48$ $p < 0.001$). The Tukey post-hoc test showed that the higher proficiency level learners believe they have, the higher their strategy use is ($p < 0.001$) (Table 8.4).

The Kruskal-Wallis non-parametric test showed that "region of residence" had a significant effect in all six categories of strategies (memory: $x^2 = 70.75$; $p < 0.001$; cognitive: $x^2 = 36.01$, $p < 0.001$; compensation: $x^2 = 41.49$ $p < 0.001$; metacognitive: $x^2 = 44.00$ $p < 0.001$; affective: $x^2 = 39.43$ $p < 0.005$; social:

Table 8.4 Descriptive statistics of the LLS use according to proficiency level

LLS	Mean (s.d.)				
	Low	I could do better	Satisfactory	Good	Very good
Memory	2.11 (0.94)	2.39 (0.74)	2.73 (0.72)	2.97 (0.67)	3.20 (0.74)
Cognitive	1.94 (0.84)	2.30 (0.81)	2.65 (0.72)	2.99 (0.72)	3.35 (0.78)
Compensation	2.47 (1.01)	2.73 (0.86)	2.98 (0.78)	3.20 (0.80)	3.30 (0.84)
Metacognitive	2.28 (0.97)	2.52 (0.80)	2.99 (0.75)	3.27 (0.72)	3.58 (0.77)
Affective	2.04 (0.99)	2.60 (1.02)	2.85 (0.91)	3.15 (0.87)	3.30 (0.94)
Social	2.09 (1.11)	2.44 (0.85)	2.75 (0.83)	2.95 (0.81)	3.16 (0.88)

$x^2 = 27.90$ p < 0.005) (Table 8.5). One-way analysis of variance (ANOVA) with the criterion Brown Forsythe showed that this variable had a significant effect on language learning strategy use (F = 4.26, p < 0.001). Children attending schools in Eastern Macedonia and Thrace used fewer strategies than those attending schools in Attica (MD = –0.203, p < 0.005), Thessaly (MD = –0.236, p < 0.001), and Peloponnese (MD = –0.154, p < 0.001). Furthermore, children attending schools in Western Macedonia used fewer strategies than those attending schools in Thessaly (MD = –0.417, p < 0.05) and Peloponnese (MD = –0.450, p < 0.05).

Table 8.5 Descriptive statistics of the LLS use according to region of residence

Region of residence	Mean (s.d.)
Eastern Macedonia & Thrace	2.98 (0.74)
Central Macedonia	3.05 (0.66)
Western Macedonia	2.76 (0.53)
Epirus	3.15 (0.56)
Thessaly	3.18 (0.70)
Ionian Islands	3.09 (0.53)
Central Greece	3.09 (0.61)
Peloponnese	3.21 (0.55)
Northern Aegean	3.09 (0.70)
Southern Aegean	3.02 (0.54)
Attica	3.13 (0.61)
Crete	3.19 (0.68)

6. Discussion

The purpose of the study reported in this chapter was to investigate the frequency of self-reported strategy use by EFL learners attending mainstream primary and secondary schools in Greece. Its focus was on the effect gender, level of education, proficiency in English, and region of residence had on the participants' LLS use.

With regard to the participants' LLS profiles, it was found that the total sample made overall medium use of all strategy categories. Such results have been attested in most studies in Greece and other countries, concerning different age groups (Green and Oxford 1995; Kazamia 2003; Lan and Oxford 2003; Mitits 2014; Mitits, Psaltou-Joycey, and Sougari 2016; Psaltou-Joycey and Kantaridou 2009; Vrettou 2009, 2011; Wharton 2000; Yang 2007). In our case, given that the Revised Curriculum for TEFL in primary and lower secondary schools follows a *holistic* approach to knowledge and places particular emphasis on the cultivation of the "learning how to learn" skill within a multilingual and multicultural world, one should expect higher overall strategy use. It seems that despite such educational policies to promote learner autonomy and to incorporate language learning strategies in curricula and EFL textbooks (Psaltou-Joycey 2014), learners' selection and use of strategies is neither self-evident nor automatic. Young learners and adolescents need instruction and this may be applied only by their teachers once they are shown how to employ strategic teaching (Psaltou-Joycey 2015; see also Bielak and Mystkowska-Wiertelak, Chapter 11; Chamot, Chapter 10; Gunning and Turner, Chapter 12 in this volume).

Another important overall result was that the use of metacognitive strategies exhibited the highest mean of all the other strategy categories. The same category ranked first in the reported strategy use of the participants in Ardasheva and Tretter (2013), Hong-Nam and Leavell (2006), and Lee (2003), but also in studies conducted in Greece (Kazamia 2003; Mitits, Psaltou-Joycey, and Sougari 2016; Psaltou-Joycey and Sougari 2010; Vrettou 2009, 2011). This indicates that metacognitive awareness starts at an early age (primary school) and continues through to adolescence and adulthood.

With regard to gender, girls were found to outperform boys in reported use of all strategy categories. Similar results have been reported in a large number of studies in Greek and non-Greek contexts for all age groups (Kazamia 2003; Mitits 2014; Mitits, Psaltou-Joycey, and Sougari 2016; Platsidou and Sipitanou 2014; Psaltou-Joycey and Kantaridou 2009; Vrettou 2009, 2011). This pattern could be attributed to differences in biological, affective, and social aspects characterizing males and females, and that may lead to differentiated learning processes (Beal 1994; Nyikos 2008). Girls generally mature cognitively earlier, exhibit higher degrees of socialization, and seem to be more emotionally sensitive than boys. They are thus better disposed towards self-managing their learning, finding ways to practice, organizing their study time, and discussing their concerns about their progress (Mitits 2014; Oxford and Nyikos 1989; Psaltou-Joycey and Kantaridou 2009).

Regarding differences between primary and secondary school learners in their selection and use of strategies, primary learners outperformed secondary learners in the frequency of use of most strategy categories except the compensation one. These results agree with similar studies in Greece (Gavriilidou and Petrogiannis 2016; Mitits 2014; Platsidou and Sipitanou 2014; Mitits, Psaltou-Joycey, and Sougari 2016; Vrettou 2011) and in other contexts (Chen 2009; Magno 2010). The outcomes indicate that differences such as age (maturational changes), degree of motivation (changes in priorities and interests), and proficiency level (ability to handle language problems) may become determinant factors for results regarding education levels. The findings provide evidence that primary learners are willing to experiment with FL learning in order to achieve better learning outcomes. In comparison, lower secondary learners make use of certain strategies but to a lesser degree. Presumably, as learners grow older and become more proficient in the foreign language, they can cope better with uncertainty by using compensation strategies such as synonyms, or guessing meanings from context. In addition, secondary learners may look for fluency and natural communication rather than accuracy in the FL, hence they are less afraid to make mistakes and can handle their FL anxiety better.

Our results may also reflect differences in FL instruction, as tutoring in primary education is generally more experiential and relaxed whereas it becomes more exam-oriented and academic in secondary education. Also, as learners become more experienced in the mechanisms and techniques that underlie language learning, they may integrate the use of strategies in a non-conscious way, which is not recorded in self-reported accounts but is noted as a decline in use. These two latter suggestions need further support through research with classroom observations and student interviews.

As for the question about differences in perceived proficiency level and strategy use, the results also confirmed previous studies that showed a high degree of positive correlation between proficiency and strategy employment. There was a linear relationship between frequency of use with all categories of strategies and perceived proficiency scores, ascending from "low" to "very good," verifying Green and Oxford's (1995, 288) argument about a causal relationship between strategy use and proficiency level of an ascending spiral nature: "Active use strategies help learners attain higher proficiency, which in turn makes it more likely that learners will select these active use strategies."

The highest linear indices were noted with metacognitive strategies in the three upper levels and the lowest with cognitive strategies in the two lowest levels. These findings reinforce previous studies which showed that learners who make higher use of metacognitive strategies also demonstrate higher EFL competence (Nunan 1991). Furthermore, a shortage of use of cognitive strategies is indicative of low proficiency (Ehrman and Oxford 1995; Psaltou-Joycey 2010) as the two constructs help learners not only self-regulate their general learning but also accomplish specific language learning tasks effectively (Chamot 2004).

Finally, the region of residence was found to have a profound influence on the strategy use of the sample. Children attending schools in East Macedonia and Thrace (EMTh) used fewer strategies than those attending schools in Attica, Thessaly, and Peloponnese (Figure 8.1). As illustrated above, this region, situated at the frontier with Turkey, is the most distanced periphery from Athens, the country's capital (800 km). The information in Table 8.1 indicates that it is also one of the peripheries with the lowest GDP, in any case lower than in Athens, Thessaly, and Peloponnese. Also the unemployment rate is higher in comparison. Similarly, children attending schools in West Macedonia (WM) used fewer strategies than those in Thessaly and Peloponnese. WM is situated at the other extreme frontier of Greece with Albania and the Former Yugoslav Republic of Macedonia. Although it is considered to be the energy pylon of Greece, it demonstrates the highest unemployment rate. Consequently, both regions are considered to be deprived compared with Attica, Thessaly, or Peloponnese.

In analogy to the fact that children of poorer socioeconomic families demonstrate lower academic achievements (Hakuta, Butler, and Witt 2000), one could suggest that children from poorer socioeconomic regions of residence, like EMTh and WM, tend to use fewer strategies than children living in richer areas. This may be the case because in schools with higher concentrations of lower socioeconomic status, learners tend to have limited educational resources and fewer educational opportunities that would promote LLS use. In addition, children from poorer regions of residence may lack cultural capital such as certain types of "expected" parental involvement in school life and activities or education at home (Butler 2014).

It should also be noted that compared with Attica, Peloponnese, and Thessaly, which are considered to be respectively famous tourist destinations and rich agricultural regions, EMTh and WM are not at all touristic or agriculturally affluent. Tourism may be an important motive for children of Attica or Peloponnese to learn a foreign language but not so for children in EMTh and WM. Finally, learners' shared or different direct and indirect behaviors, beliefs, and stances, which can be identified as sub-cultures within a given cultural context (i.e., Greece), may account for differences in LLS use of learners living in specific regions of residence.

7. Conclusions

This study was internationally the first large-scale attempt to shift the focus from adult learners and, instead, examine young learners' and early adolescents' language learning strategy use. Data were collected from the whole territorial area of Greece. The study was one of the very few projects that investigate the influence of socioeconomic or sociocultural factors on language learning strategy use by using a large sample. It reported the overall strategic profile of EFL learners in mainstream primary and secondary schools in Greece, and examined how this profile is affected by gender, level of education, perceived level of proficiency in English, and region of residence.

The results showed that these four factors affect the selection and use of LLSs confirming earlier research. Girls reported using all types of strategies more than boys; primary learners outperformed secondary learners in the use of most strategy categories; learner-perceived higher proficiency level correlated positively with more frequent strategy use; and children from poorer socioeconomic regions of residence were found to use fewer strategies than children living in richer and more touristic areas. We suggested that complex mechanisms, affecting motivation and beliefs about the role of FLs or individual characteristics may underlie the effect of gender, level of education, perceived level of proficiency, and region of residence on strategy application.

This large-scale investigation also yielded a number of substantive findings with important implications for foreign language teaching and strategy instruction. It showed that it is not sufficient to incorporate LLSs in curricula and EFL textbooks. Further strategic instruction is needed to promote the use of strategies for foreign language learning. This chapter presented the results of a THALES project on LLS. Given the scope of the THALES project, the amount of data collected and the number of important issues addressed, many insights about variables affecting LLS use and the complexity of FL learning will be taken up in future publications.

Acknowledgments

This study is part of the THALES project MIS 379335, run under the National Strategic Reference Frame (NSRF) and co-funded by the European Social Fund.

Notes

1 Greek Law 3852/2010. http://www.kedke.gr/uploads2010/N38522010_KALLIKRA TIS_FEKA87_07062010.pdf

2 Attica, Thessaly, Central Greece, Epirus, Central Macedonia, West Macedonia, Peloponnese, West Greece, Ionian Islands, North Aegean, South Aegean, Crete, East Macedonia, and Thrace.

3 This number should be viewed with caution as it is based on records of the Public Power Corporation in the area.

4 In this chapter, the term "mainstream" schools is used to describe all state primary and secondary schools as opposed to "minority" schools which only children of the Muslim minority population in Thrace can attend, if they wish so. Actually, according to the 1923 Treaty of Lausanne, the Greek state must provide segregated primary education for the Muslim minority citizens living in Thrace (Greece), which is a region situated at the North-Eastern part of Greece (see Figure 8.1).

References

Ardasheva, Yuliya, and Thomas R. Tretter. 2013. "Strategy Inventory for Language Learning—ELL Student Form: Testing for Factorial Validity." *Modern Language Journal* 97 (2): 472–87.

Beal, Carole R. 1994. *Boys and Girls: The Development of Gender Roles.* New York: McGraw-Hill.

Butler, Yuko Goto. 2014. "Parental Factors and Early English Education as Foreign Language: A Case Study in Mainland China." *Research Papers in Education* 29 (4): 410–37.

Chamot, Anna Uhl. 2004. "Issues in Language Learning Strategy Research and Teaching." *Electronic Journal of Foreign Language Teaching* 1 (1): 14–26.

Chamot, Anna Uhl, and Pamela Beard El-Dinary. 1999. "Children's Learning Strategies in Language Immersion Classrooms." *Modern Language Journal* 83 (3): 319–38.

Chen, Mei-Lin. 2009. "Influence of Grade Level on Perceptual Learning Style Preferences and Language Learning Strategies of Taiwanese English as a Foreign Language Learners." *Learning and Individual Differences* 19 (2): 304–8.

Cheng, Eric C. K. 2011. "Management Strategies for Promoting Teacher Collective Learning." *US-China Education Review* 8 (1): 33–45.

Ehrman, Madeline E., and Rebecca L. Oxford. 1995. "Cognition Plus: Correlates of Language Learning Success." *Modern Language Journal* 79 (1): 67–89.

Eurostat Methodologies and Working Papers. 2007. "Task Force on Core Social Variables Final Report." Accessed November 28, 2015. http://ec.europa.eu/eurostat/ramon/statmanuals/files/KS-RA-07-006-EN.pdf.

Frangoudaki, Anna. 1985. *Koinoniologia tis Ekpaidefsis [Sociology of Education]*. Athens: Papazizi.

Gavriilidou, Zoe, and Lydia Mitits. 2016. "Adaptation of the Strategy Inventory for Language Learning (*SILL*) for Students Aged 12–15 into Greek: Developing an Adaptation Protocol. In *Selected Papers of the 21st International Symposium on Theoretical and Applied Linguistics,* edited by Marina Mattheoudakis and Katerina Nikolaidou, 588–601. Thessaloniki: Aristotle University. https://ejournals.lib.auth.gr/thal/article/view/5256/5144

Gavriilidou, Zoe, and Alexandros Papanis. 2009. "The Effect of Strategy Instruction on Strategy Use by Muslim Pupils Learning English as a Foreign Language." *Journal of Applied Linguistics* 25: 47–63.

Gavriilidou, Zoe, and Konstantinos Petrogiannis. 2016. "Language Learning Strategy Use of English FL Learners in Greek Schools: The Role of School Type and Educational Level." *International Journal of Research Studies in Language Learning* 5 (4):67–71.

Gavriilidou, Zoe, and Angeliki Psaltou-Joycey. 2009. "Language Learning Strategies: An Overview." *Journal of Applied Linguistics* 25: 11–25.

Green, John M., and Rebecca L. Oxford. 1995. "A Closer Look at Learning Strategies, L2 Proficiency and Gender." *TESOL Quarterly* 29 (2): 261–97.

Grenfell, Michael, and Vee Harris. 2012. "Making a Difference in Language Learning: The Role of Socio-cultural Factors in Learner Strategy Instruction." *Curriculum Journal* 24 (1): 121–52.

Griffiths, Carol. 2003. "Patterns of Language Learning Strategy Use." *System* 31: 367–83.
——. 2008. "Strategies and Good Language Learners." In *Lessons from Good Language Learners*, edited by Carol Griffiths, 83–98. Cambridge: Cambridge University Press.
——. 2013. *The Strategy Factor in Successful Language Learning*. Bristol: Multilingual Matters.

Gu, Peter Yongqi. 2002. "Gender, Academic Major, and Vocabulary Learning Strategies of Chinese EFL Learners." *RELC Journal* 33 (1): 35–53.

Hakuta, Kenji, Yuko Goto Butler, and Daria Witt. 2000. "How Long Does It Take English Learners to Attain Proficiency?" University of California Linguistic Minority Research Institute. Accessed January 6, 2016. http://escholarship.org/uc/item/13w7m06g#page-1.

Hellenic Statistical Authority (ELSTAT). 2016. *Greece in Figures*. Accessed November 15, 2016. http://www.statistics.gr/greece-in-figures

Hong-Nam, Kyunsim, and Alexandra G. Leavell. 2006. "Language Learning Strategy Use of ESL Students in an Intensive English Learning Context." *System* 34: 399–425.

Katsikas, Christos, and Georgios K. Kavvadias. 2000. *H Anisotita stin Elliniki Ekpaidefsi [Inequality in Greek Education]*. Athens: Gutenberg.

Kazamia, Vassilia. 2003. "Language Learning Strategies of Greek Adult Learners of English: Vol. I and II." Unpublished PhD dissertation, University of Leeds.

Lakoff, Robin. 1975. "Language and Woman's Place." *Language in Society* 2 (1): 45–80.

Lan, Rae, and Rebecca L. Oxford. 2003. "Language Learning Strategy Profiles of Elementary School Students in Taiwan." *IRAL* 41 (4): 339–79.

Law 3852/2010, in *Governments' Gazette* 87, vol. 1, 7-6-2010. Accessed November 15, 2016. http://www.kedke.gr/uploads2010/N38522010_KALLIKRATIS_FEKA87_07062010.pdf

Lee, Kyung O. 2003. "The Relationship of School Year, Sex and Proficiency on the Use of Learning Strategies in Learning English of Korean Junior High Students." *Asian EFL Journal* 5 (3): 1–36.

Macaro, Ernesto. 2001. *Learning Strategies in Foreign and Second Language Classes*. London: Continuum.

Magno, Carlo. 2010. "Korean Students' Language Learning Strategies and Years of Studying English as Predictors of Proficiency in English." *TESOL Journal* 2: 39–61.

Mattheoudakis, Marina, and Thomaï Alexiou. 2009. "Early Foreign Language Instruction in Greece: Socioeconomic Factors and their Effect on Young Learners' Language Development." In *Contextualising the Age Factor: Issues in Early Foreign Language Learning and Teaching*, edited by Marianne Nikolov, 227–51. Berlin: Mouton de Gruyter.

Mitits, Lydia. 2014. "Language Learning Strategy Use by Early Adolescent Monolingual EFL and Multilingual EFL/L2 Greek Learners in the Greek Educational Context." PhD dissertation, Democritus University of Thrace. Accessed January 6, 2016. http://www.saitabooks.eu/2015/03/ebook.147.html.

Mitits, Lydia, Angeliki Psaltou-Joycey, and Areti-Maria Sougari. 2016. "Language Learning Strategy Profiling of Greek Primary/Secondary School Learners of English as a FL." In *Language Learning Strategies in the Greek Context*, edited by Zoe Gavriilidou and Konstantinos Petrogiannis, 26–41. Kavala: Saita Publications.

Nisbet, Neanna, L., Evie R. Tindall, and Alan A. Arroyo. 2005. "Language Learning Strategies and English Proficiency of Chinese University Students." *Foreign Language Annals* 38: 100–107.

Nunan, David. 1991. "Methods in Second Language Classroom Research: A Critical Review." *Studies in Second Language Acquisition* 13 (2): 249–74.

Nyikos, Martha. 1990. "Sex-related Differences in Adult Language Learning: Socialization and Memory Factors." *The Modern Language Journal* 74 (3): 273–87.

——. 2008. "Gender and Good Language Learners." In *Lessons from Good Language Learners,* edited by Carol Griffiths, 73–82. Cambridge: Cambridge University Press.

Oxford, Rebecca L. 1990. *Language Learning Strategies: What Every Teacher Should Know.* Boston: Heinle & Heinle.

——. 2011. *Teaching and Researching Language Learning Strategies.* Harlow: Pearson Education.

Oxford, Rebecca L., and Martha Nyikos. 1989. "Variables Affecting Choice of Language Learning Strategies by University Students." *The Modern Language Journal* 73 (3): 291–300.

Oxford, Rebecca L., and Karen Schramm. 2007. "Bridging the Gap Between Psychological and Sociocultural Perspectives on L2 Learner Strategies." In *Language Learner Strategies: Thirty Years of Research and Practice,* edited by Andrew D. Cohen and Ernesto Macaro, 47–68. Oxford: Oxford University Press.

Peacock, Matthew, and Belinda Ho. 2003. "Student Language Learning Strategies Across Eight Disciplines." *International Journal of Applied Linguistics* 13 (2): 179–200.

Petrogiannis, Konstantinos, and Zoe Gavriilidou. 2015. "Strategy Inventory for Language Learning: Findings of a Validation Study in Greece." In *Education Applications and Developments,* edited by Mafalda Carmo, 223–36. Lisbon: inScience Press.

Pintrich, Paul R. 2000. "The Role of Goal Orientation in Self-regulated Learning." In *Handbook of Self-regulation,* edited by Monique Boekaerts, Paul R. Pintrich, and Moshe Zeidner, 451–502. San Diego, CA: Academic Press.

Platsidou, Maria, and Athena Sipitanou. 2014. "Exploring Relationships with Grade Level, Gender and Language Proficiency in the Foreign Language Learning Strategy Use of Children and Early Adolescents." *International Journal of Research Studies in Language Learning* 4 (1): 83–96.

Psaltou-Joycey, Angeliki. 2008. "Cross-cultural Differences in the Use of Learning Strategies by Students of Greek as a Second Language." *Journal of Multilingual and Multicultural Development* 29 (4): 310–24.

——. 2010. *Language Learning Strategies in the Foreign Language Classroom.* Thessaloniki: University Studio Press.

——. 2014. "Language Learning Strategy Instruction: The English Language Coursebooks in Greek State Schools." *Journal of Applied Linguistics* 29: 6–23.

——. ed. 2015. *Foreign Language Learning Strategy Instruction: A Teacher's Guide.* Kavala: Saita Publications. Accessed May 30, 2015. http://www.saitabooks. eu/2015/05/ebook.162.html.

Psaltou-Joycey, Angeliki, and Zoe Kantaridou. 2009. "Foreign Language Learning Strategy Profiles of University Students in Greece." *Journal of Applied Linguistics* 25: 107–27.

Psaltou-Joycey, Angeliki, and Areti-Maria Sougari. 2010. "Greek Young Learners' Perceptions about Foreign Language Learning and Teaching." In *Advances in Research on Language Acquisition and Teaching: Selected Papers*, edited by Angeliki Psaltou-Joycey and Marina Mattheoudakis, 387–401. Thessaloniki: Greek Applied Linguistics Association.

Psaltou-Joycey, Angeliki, Areti-Maria Sougari, Eleni Agathopoulou, and Thomaï Alexiou. 2014. "The Role of Age, Gender and L1 Strategies in the L2 Strategies of Primary School Children in Greece." In *Selected Papers of the 11th International Conference on Greek Linguistics*, edited by George Kotzoglou, Kalomoira Nikolou, Eleni Karantzola, Katerina Frantzi, Ioannis Galantomos, Marianthi Georgalidou, Vasilia Kourti-Kazoullis, Chrysoula Papadopoulou, and Evangelia Vlachou, 1436–48. Rhodes: University of the Aegean, Faculty of Humanities, Department of Mediterranean Studies.

Ryan, Richard M., and Edward L. Deci. 2000. "Intrinsic and Extrinsic Motivations: Classic Definitions and New Directions." *Contemporary Educational Psychology* 25: 54–67.

Schunk, Dale H., and Barry J. Zimmerman. 2008. *Motivation and Self-regulated Learning: Theory, Research and Applications.* New York: Routledge.

Tannen, Deborah. 1986. *That's Not What I Mean!* New York: Morrow.

Tragant, Elsa, and Mia Victori. 2006. "Reported Strategy Use and Age." In *Age and the Rate of Foreign Language Learning*, edited by Carmen Muñoz, 208–36. Clevedon: Multilingual Matters.

——. 2012. "Language Learning Strategies, Course Grades and Age in EFL Secondary School Learners." *Language Awareness* 21(3): 293–308.

Victori, Mia, and Elsa Tragant. 2003. "Learner Strategies: A Cross-sectional and Longitudinal Study of Primary and High-school EFL Learners." In *Age and the Acquisition of English as a Foreign Language*, edited by Maria del Pilar Garcia Mayo and Maria Luisa Garcia Lecumberri, 182–209. Clevedon: Multilingual Matters.

Vrettou, Athina. 2009. "Language Learning Strategy Employment of EFL Greek-Speaking Learners in Junior High School." *Journal of Applied Linguistics* 25: 85–106.

——. 2011. "Patterns of Language Learning Strategy Use by Greek-speaking Young Learners of English." Unpublished PhD dissertation, Aristotle University of Thessaloniki.

Wharton, Glenn. 2000. "Language Learning Strategy Use of Bilingual Foreign Language Learners in Singapore." *Language Learning* 50 (2): 203–43.

Willenborg, Leon, and Ton de Waal. 1996. *Statistical Disclosure Control in Practice.* New York: Springer Verlag.

Yang, Ming-Nuan. 2007. "Language Learning Strategies for Junior College Students in Taiwan: Investigating Ethnicity and Proficiency." *Asian EFL Journal* 9 (2): 35–57.

9

Contextual and Individual Difference Variables

Pronunciation Learning Strategies in Form-Focused and Meaning-Focused Activities

Mirosław Pawlak

Adam Mickiewicz University and
State University of Applied Sciences, Poland

1. Introduction

In spite of advances that have been made in research of language learning strategies (LLS) in the last three decades (e.g., Anderson 2005; Cohen 2011, 2014; Cohen and Macaro 2007; Griffiths and Oxford 2014; Oxford 2011; Pawlak 2011a), there are some areas that have been surprisingly neglected, good examples being strategies used for learning grammar or pronunciation. However, while the former have at least received a mention in state-of-the-art papers, and appeals have been made for empirical investigations in this area (e.g., Anderson 2005; Cohen 2011; Oxford 2011; Oxford and Lee 2007; Pawlak 2011b, 2013a), finding even a passing reference to the latter is usually a futile effort, one notable exception being the book-length treatment by Berkil (2009). A similar comment applies to publications dealing with pronunciation instruction, including the latest ones (e.g., Derwing and Munro 2015; Szpyra-Kozłowska 2015), where much is said about teaching priorities or selecting appropriate techniques, but nothing about the use of strategic devices. Such a situation is disconcerting because, as emphasized by Pawlak (2006a), autonomy plays a key role in learning this target language (TL) subsystem and adept use of strategies is a major way in which this autonomy can be exercised.

This scant attention to pronunciation learning strategies (PLS) in the fields of LLS and pronunciation instruction has not precluded researchers from making attempts to investigate such strategic devices. However, there is admittedly a striking paucity of research in this area, valid and reliable data collection tools have yet to be developed, and most of the relevant studies have relied on questionnaires completed by respondents with respect to general strategic actions and thoughts rather than the application of PLS in performing specific tasks. Moreover, the main emphasis has thus far been placed on the identification and description of strategies for learning pronunciation, with the effect that little is known about the extent to which the employment of PLS is related to attainment or mediated by Individual Difference (ID) variables. The present chapter seeks to fill this gap by reporting the results of a study that examined the use of PLS by Polish university students majoring in English as they were engaged in the completion of two activities, one with a focus on form and the other on meaning. At the outset, a brief overview of previous empirical investigations into PLS is provided, which is followed by the description of research procedures and the presentation and discussion of findings. The chapter closes with a consideration of possible pedagogical implications and suggestions for future research on PLS, particularly with respect to their use in pronunciation learning tasks.

2. Previous research on pronunciation learning strategies

Before embarking on an overview of studies that have investigated the use of pronunciation learning strategies, it is warranted to explain how these strategic devices are understood in the present chapter. Extrapolating from the definitions of grammar learning strategies offered by Oxford and Lee (2007), and Cohen and Pinilla-Herrera (2009), PLS could be described as actions and thoughts, typically used in a logical sequence, that learners consciously fall back upon to learn and gain greater control of different aspects of TL pronunciation with the purpose of making the process easier, more effective, efficient, and enjoyable (see Pawlak 2010). Adopting such a definition recognizes the fact that, as is the case with grammar, learners need to develop both explicit, declarative knowledge of pronunciation features and implicit, procedural knowledge of such features, or at the least automatize the former to such an extent that it can be accessed in spontaneous communication (cf. DeKeyser 2010; Ellis 2007). In other words, it is not enough, for example, to become aware of specific sound contrasts and to develop the ability to produce these contrasts accurately in controlled pronunciation exercises (e.g., minimal pairs practice). Rather, learners also need to be capable of articulating these sounds correctly in ongoing conversation, when their scant attentional resources are allocated to other priorities (e.g., appraising the situation, taking into account pragmatic considerations, planning messages, monitoring). After all, as any pronunciation teacher would attest, it is one thing to read a text with good pronunciation, particularly if learners have ample time to prepare, and quite another to get the segmental and suprasegmental features right in real-life interaction. This is the reason why learners who seem to have mastered aspects of pronunciation in class often make basic errors on oral interviews. A definition of pronunciation learning strategies must take account of this fact, and it is this recognition that provided an inspiration for the study reported in this chapter, which made a clear distinction between the use of PLS in a form-focused and meaning-focused task.

As mentioned in the introduction, the bulk of the available research has specified as its main purpose identification and description of PLS, usually taking as a point of reference existing, general classifications of LLS. By contrast, little attention has been given to factors impacting PLS use, few insights have been obtained into the link between the application of such strategic devices and mastery of this TL subsystem, few specific taxonomies have been proposed, little is known about the effects of strategies-based instruction (SBI) in this area, and virtually no empirical evidence has been forthcoming on the employment of PLS in specific learning tasks (Berkil 2009; Szyszka 2016; Pawlak 2010). Some preliminary information about the use of PLS can be obtained from the findings of the so-called good language learner studies (e.g., Naiman 1978; Rubin 1975), with the caveat that such data are sketchy, they were collected primarily through observation, and the analysis was not based on any specific taxonomy. PLS also constituted just one of many foci of investigation of LLS applied by Polish secondary school students conducted by Dróździał-Szelest (1997), who, using open-ended questions and taking as a point of reference O'Malley and Chamot's (1990) taxonomy, identified a number of specific PLS representing metacognitive and cognitive strategies.

To the best knowledge of the present author, the first study that focused specifically on the use of PLS was undertaken by Peterson (2000). With the help of diary and interview data, she identified 21 entirely new tactics employed by American university students in learning Spanish pronunciation (e.g., trying to recall how the teacher pronounced a word, practicing saying words slowly and then faster, deciding to focus on particular sounds), which she classified into twelve strategies on the basis of Oxford's (1990) taxonomy. In the years that followed, further attempts at identification and description of PLS have been made. Vitanova and Miller (2002), for example, used open-ended prompts to gather opinions from ESL students about their perceived utility of PLS, demonstrating potential value of metacognitive and socio-affective strategies. Osburne (2003) employed interviews and think-aloud protocols to gather information about the use of PLS by advanced second language learners and identified eight distinct strategic devices (e.g., individual syllables, prosody, individual words, paralanguage, or memory and imitation). Pawlak (2006b, 2008, 2011c) carried out three studies among high school learners and university students in Poland, including English majors, providing evidence for a predominance of traditional cognitive strategies, such as repetition or rule application, infrequent reliance on strategy chains, little appreciation of naturalistic practice, and the existence of a close link between PLS use and teachers' instructional practices. In a later publication, Pawlak (2010) proposed a division of PLS into metacognitive, cognitive, affective, and social, as well as developing and piloting a data collection tool on this basis.

An attempt to categorize strategies for learning pronunciation was also made by Eckstein (2007), who assigned different types of PLS to four stages of language acquisition (e.g., Ellis 2004), that is input/practice (e.g., eagerly listening to new sounds), noticing/feedback (e.g., listening and inferring key sounds), hypothesis formation (e.g., finding out about pronunciation), and hypothesis testing (e.g., using proximal articulations). Also worth mentioning are two research projects undertaken by Szyszka (2014, 2015), which involved in-service and prospective teachers of English. In the first (Szyszka 2014), qualitative analysis of data collected by means of diaries and interviews yielded evidence for the use of strategy chains suited to specific learning tasks. In the second, Szyszka (2015) compared the PLS employed by good and average pronunciation users, concluding that the former relied on a wider repertoire of individualized strategies and were convinced of the positive contribution of appropriately chosen PLS.

There are also empirical investigations that have aimed to establish a link between the use of PLS and attainment, tap the mediating effects of ID variables or establish the effects of SBI, with the caveat that they have been conducted in different contexts and used diverse designs, research tools, and analytical procedures, which precludes valid generalizations. As regards the relationship between PLS application and achievement, Samalieva (2000) concluded on the basis of interviews with twenty Bulgarian university-level learners of English that more proficient students opted for metacognitive strategies, such as monitoring and self-correction, while less proficient ones favored social strategies, particularly those involving correction. It must be emphasized, however, that no concrete measures of attainment were employed in this study. A more systematic approach was adopted by Eckstein (2007) who constructed a tool for eliciting PLS, called a *Strategic Pronunciation Learning Scale* (*SPLS*), and correlated the use of 28 strategic devices reported by 183 international students with their spontaneous oral performance. He found significant relationships for five PLS, three of which were positive (i.e., noticing pronunciation errors, adjusting facial muscles, and requesting assistance) and two negative (i.e., silent repetition and modulation of speech volume).

A similar research design was employed by Berkil (2009), who investigated the application of PLS by forty Turkish students representing three levels of proficiency. She collected the relevant data with the help of the *Strategy Inventory for Learning Pronunciation* (*SILP*), drawing on Oxford's (1990) classification and including 52 PLS-related items, as well as two tasks, eliciting controlled (i.e., a reading passage) and spontaneous (i.e., expressing opinions) oral performance. Although no link was detected between overall reported PLS use and attainment, two of the PLS turned out to be the most frequently used in the moderate group (i.e., purposeful listening to sounds and using listening resources) and one the least frequently (i.e., using phonetic symbols or own codes). Of relevance is also the study of 63 English majors in Poland conducted by Rokoszewska (2012), who, using a tool including 65 Likert-scale items and a battery of perception and production tasks, found that while the use of PLS did not correlate with the perception of TL vowels, there existed a significant, albeit weak, relationship for production. When it comes to the role of ID factors, the only study that investigated it systematically was undertaken by Szyszka (2016) and involved 94 English majors at different levels of a three-year BA program. Using an adapted version of Berkil's (2009) *SILP*, the *Foreign Language Classroom Anxiety Scale* (Horwitz, Horwitz, and Cope 1986), an instrument tapping into anxiety at different language processing stages (MacIntyre and Gardner 1994) and several qualitative tools, she demonstrated that there were differences in PLS use between high and low anxiety participants, with the latter placing a premium on memory and compensation strategies. There is also a virtual lack of research that would examine the contribution of SBI, one exception being the study by Varasarin (2007), who showed that PLS training leads to increased confidence and intelligibility.

As can be seen from this overview, despite the fact that some attempts have been made to investigate PLS, these have mainly been confined to identification, description, or categorization, with researchers involving quite different populations, using diverse designs and relying on a diversity of data collection tools, which makes generalizations extremely difficult, if not impossible. The situation is even less optimistic in the case of the relationship between the application of PLS and attainment, the importance of ID variables or the effect of SBI. Most importantly, thus far there have been no studies that would have tapped into the use of PLS with respect to the completion of different types of tasks, let alone such that would have attempted to simultaneously provide insights into the role of ID factors. This means that the research conducted so far has embraced what can be labeled a macro-perspective which, while undeniably valuable, largely ignores the qualitative, contextual, and situated character of PLS use (cf. Macaro 2006). Thus, there is an urgent need to adopt a finer-grained view of such strategies, one that would consider the contribution of different types of tasks, learner characteristics, the degree of clustering, or the strategy chains that PLS form (see Ehrman, Leaver, and Oxford 2003; McDonough 1999; White, Schramm, and Chamot 2007). In constituting an attempt to shed light on these issues, the study reported in this chapter can be considered to fill a conspicuous gap in the literature.

3. The study

3.1. Aims and research questions

The study aimed to investigate the use of PLS in the performance of two activities focused on pronunciation, a form-focused and a meaning-focused one, which differed in the amount of attentional resources that the participants were able to allocate to this TL subsystem, as well as the mediating role of ID factors in this respect. More specifically, the following research questions were addressed:

- What PLS do students use when preparing for, performing, and after completing the two tasks?
- What is the effect of task type on the use of PLS?
- What is the impact of ID variables, such as gender, proficiency, and learning style, on the use of PLS?

3.2. Participants

The participants were 54 advanced learners of English, 42 females and 12 males, English majors enrolled in the last year of a three-year BA program. Their average experience in learning English equaled 11.36 years and there was limited individual variation in this respect as the SD amounted to 3.07. Nominally, their level of proficiency fell between B2 and C1 in terms of the Common European Framework of Reference (Council of Europe 2001), with the qualification that the sample was mixed, with some of the students manifesting a lower or higher level and differences also being noticeable in specific TL skills and subsystems. When filling out the questionnaires used for the purpose of data collection (see below), the participants were requested to self evaluate their mastery of English on a scale of 1 (lowest) to 6 (highest), both in general and with respect to pronunciation, speaking, and listening, as it was felt that oral skills were the most germane to the focus of the study.

The results were as follows: overall TL mastery—4.07, pronunciation—4.14, speaking—4.01, and listening—4.24, which indicates that the students were equally confident about their command of English, both in general and in the domains under investigation. Apart from that, they were to a large extent representative of other Polish university students majoring in English, having the benefit of an intensive English course including separate practical phonetics classes, attending courses in linguistics, literature, and culture taught through the medium of the TL, and receiving training in foreign language methodology. As regards contact with the TL outside the course of study, it primarily occurred through the media (e.g., songs, movies), books, the Internet or computer-mediated communication, and seldom involved face-to-face interaction with native speakers or other proficient users of English. However, there also were students who did not conform to this pattern (e.g., those who participated in international exchanges, interacted with Erasmus students in Poland or worked abroad).

3.3. Data collection and analysis

The data were collected by means of immediate reports in the form of two questionnaires that the participants filled out immediately after completion of activities focusing on pronunciation. More precisely, the students were instructed to perform two tasks, a form-focused and meaning-focused one, which were based on the same text. The text was constructed by the present author for the purpose of an earlier study on the effects of explicit and implicit corrective feedback (CF), and, in line with the recommendation concerning pronunciation instruction targets made by Szpyra-Kozłowska (2015), it contained a number of words that were problematic for English majors in Poland (e.g., *colonel, society, beard, photographic, accuracy, opponents*; see Pawlak 2013b, for an explanation of how such items were identified).

The form-focused activity involved reading a text aloud, with the following procedure being applied: (1) the students were given about four minutes to prepare for reading, (2) they were told they were expected to focus on pronunciation, (3) they took turns reading the text aloud in pairs, four minutes each, while their partners were expected just to listen but in some cases also providing CF, and (4) on completion of the task, several students were asked to read the text aloud, but no feedback was provided on pronunciation errors, both in general and with respect to the targeted lexical items, a phase that lasted about six minutes. The inclusion of this follow-up provided the students with a tangible product of their efforts and ensured that they remained focused on pronunciation. Immediately afterwards, participants were asked to fill out a questionnaire, which, apart from items concerning their profiles, included the following open-ended questions:

- What strategies did you use to prepare for reading?
- What strategies did you use when reading?
- What did you pay attention to when reading?
- What did you try to do when you were listening to your friends in pairs?
- What helped you the most when you were reading?
- What strategies did you use after performing the task (when others were reading to the whole class)?

This was immediately followed by the meaning-focused task, which involved retelling the text, with the following procedure being applied: (a) the students were given about ten minutes to prepare for the task, which entailed going over the text, remembering its contents, and jotting down crucial ideas; (b) they were sensitized to the need to focus on pronunciation; (c) without access to the original text, they took turns retelling the text in pairs, with each of them taking about ten minutes to complete the task; although no error correction was expected, some students did provide feedback, perceiving it as assistance to their peers; and (d) once the task had been completed, several students were asked to retell the text to the rest of the class but, as was the case before, no CF was offered, with this phase taking about six minutes. Similarly to the first task, immediately after this, the participants were requested to fill out a questionnaire composed of queries similar to the previous ones, but modified to reflect the different character of the second activity:

- What strategies did you use to prepare for the retelling task?
- What strategies did you use when retelling the text?
- What did you pay attention to when retelling the text?

- What did you do when you were listening to your friends?
- What helped you the most when you were retelling the task?
- What strategies did you use after performing the retelling task (when others were telling their versions to the class)?

Both of the questionnaires were worded in English, but it was made clear to the participants that they could respond in the TL or the mother tongue, as they saw fit. Interestingly, all students decided to answer in English, even if it was sometimes imperfect, which can perhaps be related to their overall high proficiency.

After the two tasks had been completed, the participants were asked to fill out the *Learning Style Survey* (LSS; Cohen, Oxford, and Chi 2001), an instrument that taps eleven facets of learning styles, which are: (a) reliance on physical senses (i.e., visual, auditory, and hands-on); (b) dealing with other people (i.e., extroversion vs. introversion); (c) handling possibilities (i.e., intuitive-random vs. concrete-sequential); (d) dealing with ambiguity or deadlines (i.e., closure-oriented vs. open); (e) receiving information (i.e., global vs. particular); (f) further processing of information (i.e., synthesizing vs. analytic); (g) committing material to memory (i.e., sharpener vs. leveler); (h) dealing with language rules (i.e., deductive vs. inductive); (i) handling multiple inputs (i.e., field-independent vs. field-dependent); (j) dealing with response time (i.e., impulsive vs. reflective); and (k) the extent to which reality is taken literally (i.e., metaphoric vs. literal). The data were subjected to qualitative analysis, which took as points of reference the taxonomy of PLS proposed by Pawlak (2010), the items included in the two questionnaires, and the responses to the LLS.

4. Findings

For the sake of clarity, the insights obtained from the analysis will first be discussed separately for the two tasks, then comments about the impact of individual differences will be made, and all of these themes will be brought together in the discussion section. As regards the form-focused activity, when preparing for the reading, participants most frequently mentioned paying attention to the words that they thought were the most difficult to pronounce (a metacognitive PLS), practicing subvocally the pronunciation of longer and difficult words (a cognitive PLS), using a dictionary, mostly online, to check how lexical items were pronounced (a cognitive PLS), and, less frequently, trying to stay calm and focused (an affective PLS) or consulting the partner about how a given word should be pronounced (a social PLS). These tendencies are illustrated in such excerpts as: "Firstly, I read the text silently and paid attention to the most difficult words (...)," "I repeated difficult words," "I checked the words that seemed to be the most difficult," "I asked for pronunciation of a few words that I was not sure how to pronounce," or "I took a glance at the text—it made me feel more comfortable." Interestingly, some students made comments that were irrelevant to the task (e.g., predicting what would happen, trying to link the content to prior experiences), stated that they did not use any strategies, or left blank spaces.

With respect to the process of reading aloud, the students most often reported paying a lot of attention to pronunciation, guessing how some words should be pronounced, trying to control emotions, or pausing to get help from their peers, PLS that can be classified as metacognitive, compensation, affective, and social. One of the participants made the following comment: "I tried to keep the right pace, not too slow and not too fast, in order to keep a good flow of reading and to achieve good pronunciation." Another explained: "I wanted to find out the correct pronunciation. If I could not or did not know how to pronounce, I tried to make the pronunciation of some of the words up." Truly baffling was the large number of strategies that simply could not have been used in performing the task, such as creating mental images, scanning and skimming, trying to identify the purpose of the text, or making a word list. As for the main focus of attention when reading aloud, participants most often pointed to efforts to avoid pronunciation errors, stress and intonation, specific sounds, suffixes, suprasegmental features, or linguistic context. This is evident in the following comments: "I tried to read fluently and not to make mistakes in pronunciation" or "I concentrated on difficult and unknown words, on words with 'r' after vowels and on the '-s' ending."

When asked what they were doing when listening to their peers, most of the participants stated that they were making comparisons (a cognitive PLS), focusing in particular on the words that they did not know how to pronounce or had had difficulty in pronouncing (a metacognitive PLS), correcting the pronunciation errors they noticed, either doing it in private speech, interrupting their partner, or providing CF once he or she had finished reading. The following comments illustrate these points: "I focused on words that I had problems with and repeated after my friend. I followed the text and read it quietly" or "I tried to check whether she was pronouncing particular words correctly and I kept them in my mind. After she finished, we checked these words in a dictionary and learned the correct pronunciation."

In response to the query concerning the things that helped them the most in reading, the respondents most often mentioned familiarity with difficult words (a metacognitive PLS), attempts to ignore the presence of the listener (an affective PLS), sufficient planning time (a metacognitive PLS), assistance from their peer (a social PLS), and the fact that they were the second person to read the text, which enabled them to verify their pronunciation (a metacognitive PLS). This is evident in the following excerpts: "The most helpful was that I read the paper earlier, before reading out loud and knowing the text," "I was trying to forget about the other person listening to me and speak fluently," or "I had a chance to correct my mistakes while listening to my friend and I could read the text alone before reading it aloud." Irrelevant strategies were reported as well, such as highlighting key information or trying to have one's own opinion. Finally, when it comes to the strategies that the students reported employing after reading, they largely mirrored those in earlier stages and included comparing pronunciation with that of other students, trying to remember how difficult words are pronounced through repetition or transcription, or looking up the pronunciation of some items (cognitive PLS in all cases). One of the students wrote: "I tried to listen to others carefully and focused on particular words that I was not sure about how to pronounce. I tried to hear their pronunciation."

Moving on to the strategies employed in preparation for the meaning-oriented task, the participants most often mentioned trying to remember the main points and events, which was accompanied by reading the text several times, identifying keywords, and sometimes note-taking. For example, one of the students wrote: "I wanted to focus on the main points of the story and remember them. I imagined the person described in the story and it helped me a lot later." Another commented: "I tried to remember as many facts as I could. Sometimes I just created some kind of 'map of thoughts' in my mind using the key words from the text." Even though such strategies are not related to pronunciation, their preponderance was to be expected given the students' awareness that access to such information would be denied during the retelling. With respect to actions and thoughts directly linked to pronunciation, just a handful were mentioned, similar to those used in the form-focused activity. These included checking the pronunciation of problematic lexical items (a cognitive PLS), requesting assistance (a social PLS), or practicing the pronunciation of difficult words (a cognitive PLS). Examples can be seen in such excerpts as "I asked the teacher to correct my pronunciation (...)" or "I asked for some words, checked them in the dictionary (...)."

The focus on conveying the content as precisely as possible and very limited concern with pronunciation was also evident in the actual performance of the task, which, again, was reflective of its nature. Accordingly, the most weight was given to including crucial facts, relating events in the right order, creating a mental image of the individual being described, or resorting to communication strategies when problems arose with getting the message across. The following responses illustrate these points: "I combined images in my mind, such as 'a bald, bearded man with a moustache, dirty one,' and I described a picture of a real man (...)" or "I was trying to associate the part of the text with a particular place in the text. It helped me remember more details." At this stage, pronunciation turned out to be of relevance only to several students who mostly reported reliance on the metacognitive strategy of monitoring, evident from the following comment: "I was trying to focus on the way I pronounce difficult words, so I was speaking slowly."

When they became cognizant that they were not sure how to articulate a particular item, some students would use words that were easier to pronounce, which represents application of a compensatory PLS. Such trends are reflected only to some extent in the reported focus of attention manifested in the process of retelling. While many participants still reported placing a premium on content, meaning, or fluency, many others indicated their concern with correct pronunciation, which testifies to their awareness that aspects of this subsystem were targeted by the task. The PLS reported most often was that of monitoring one's articulation, as in the following excerpts: "I paid attention to telling a story with a British accent" or "I tried to be accurate and understandable and pronounce the words correctly." Some participants emphasized the challenge involved in striking a balance between a focus on content and pronunciation, indicating that the latter might have to take the backseat in some cases. One of them wrote: "While retelling the text, I focused on the most important facts but not so much on proper pronunciation. I am sure I made some mistakes." As suggested by some of the students, what aggravated the situation was the fact that pronunciation sometimes had to compete for limited attentional resources with grammar, a subsystem that can be viewed as more important in constructing spoken utterances, particularly when it is not sufficiently automatized.

When it comes to the strategic behaviors in which the students engaged when listening to others, they involved, in the order of frequency of mention, checking the accuracy of events their interlocutors reported, which is a clear manifestation of a focus on meaning rather than form, paying attention to TL forms, mainly pronunciation but also grammar (a metacognitive PLS of monitoring), making comparisons concerning the articulation of lexical items, either before or after one's own retelling (a cognitive PLS), and providing CF (a social PLS). The following examples illustrate these trends: "Because I was first, when I listened to my partner, I was checking if I had said everything" or "I tried to correct pronunciation and grammar mistakes."

Aspects that proved to be most conducive to the performance of the task included ample planning time (a metacognitive PLS), note-taking, monitoring the pronunciation of difficult words (a metacognitive PLS), talking to someone familiar (a social PLS), displaying a positive attitude (an affective PLS), and assistance from the listener (a social PLS). The students offered comments such as: "Reading the text a few times before I started retelling it," "The notes that I prepared before reading helped me a lot," or "My partner's support was something that helped me the most and the fact that I knew him." Such responses indicate once again that the students were struggling to maintain a balance between a focus on content and pronunciation. The strategies reported on completion of the activity were not very inventive, often constituting replicas of those used in earlier stages or applied in the form-focused task, with the qualification that a focus on pronunciation was more marked here. The participants most often compared their pronunciation with that of other students, repeated words in their minds, looked up the pronunciation of difficult words, or read the text again (cognitive PLS). A comment representative of this stage was: "I checked if I was right and I compared what I had said with what others were saying," with a dual focus on meaning and form being evident here.

The data collected through the two questionnaires and the information obtained about the participants also enabled insights into the relationship between PLS use and such ID variables as gender, proficiency, and learning style. What has to be stressed at the very start, however, is that these insights are severely limited due to a conspicuous lack of clear-cut patterns, which suggests that the contribution of such factors may have been overridden by contextual considerations reflective of the task performed. As for gender, the analysis indicated, much in line with previous research (see e.g., Oxford 2011; Pawlak 2011a; Takeuchi, Griffiths, and Coyle 2007), that females employed PLS more frequently than males, and they also appeared to be more concerned with accuracy in both the form-focused and meaning-oriented activity (see Psaltou-Joycey and Gavriilidou, Chapter 8 in this volume). It should be recalled at this juncture, though, that females constituted a vast majority of participants (ca. 78 percent), which dictates that any interpretations can only be viewed with great circumspection. With regard to proficiency, operationalized in terms of self-assessment, no evident patterns emerged in the self-report data. By contrast, there were some indications of the impact of learning styles, since the students who were field-independent, particular, and analytic were more likely to attend to form (i.e., pronunciation features) and engage in practice (e.g., reading the text several times or repeating difficult words). However, such findings should be viewed only as tendencies in need of further empirical verification, all the more so that a considerable interplay of various contextual and individual factors was visible, also such that were not explored in the present study.

5. Discussion

In general, on the one hand, mainly due to its innovative design, the study offered valuable insights into the use of PLS in a form-focused and meaning-oriented task, providing evidence of a combined effect of both contextual and individual variables, but, on the other, few definitive patterns were pinpointed, mainly owing to design issues. As regards the first research question, which concerned PLS that the students fell back on in different phases of task performance, it should first be emphasized that the range of the reported strategies was narrow. Additionally, many of the strategic behaviors were similar across the stages of the task as well as between the two activities, although, as will be explained below, different foci were manifested as well. When it comes to PLS proper, preparation for the two activities involved attending to words that were difficult to pronounce, practicing pronunciation, often in private speech, using resources, especially online ones, asking for assistance and, much more rarely, controlling emotions. As the tasks were being completed, the students resorted to attending to the targeted pronunciation features and making comparisons with their own output, either that intended, if they came first, or that already executed, if they came second. They also relied on the assistance of their peers, often through CF or actively sought such assistance, with the caveat that such instances were more frequent and feasible in the form-focused task. What they regarded as the most beneficial was ample time to prepare, assistance from others, familiarity with the interlocutors, and overall knowledge of phonetics. On completion of the task, they would engage again in making comparisons between their own output and that of others, try to repeat problematic words to themselves and fall back on resources. As to the second research question, dealing with the differences between the activities, while many of the PLS employed may have been identical, different foci were clearly evident, as dictated by the nature of the challenge posed. Predictably, since the reading task was less demanding on working memory, the students were able to focus more on form and accuracy of their pronunciation. By contrast, even though the retelling task was facilitated by familiarity with the text, it placed heavy demands on participants' attentional resources, which resulted in concerns with content, fluency, and meaning. This led to efforts to strike a balance between a focus on meaning and form, with the situation being exacerbated by the fact that attention also needed to be directed to other TL subsystems, such as grammar. Nevertheless, as illustrated by the excerpts, a dual focus on form and meaning was feasible, which bodes well for getting students to use pronunciation features in communication. Finally, as for the third research question, there was tentative evidence suggesting that females were more likely to fall back on PLS than males and that they were more concerned with accuracy. Additionally, quite expectedly, field-independent, particular, and analytical styles could be associated with a focus on form with respect to pronunciation. This said, it must be emphasized that such evidence is tenuous, other ID variables, such as goals or beliefs, could have played a part, and the impact of ID factors was intricately intertwined with the nature of the task.

Despite its undeniable contributions to the field, the research project suffers from some weaknesses that may account for the difficulty in identifying definite patterns and teasing out the influence of moderating variables. First, somewhat paradoxically perhaps, the main culprit could be the large number of participants, which might be a liability rather than an asset in qualitative research because it was idiosyncrasies rather than commonalities that appeared to come to the fore in responses to the open-ended items. Had the study involved, say sixteen participants, matched for gender, proficiency, learning style but perhaps also beliefs, motivations and learning strategies, the analysis might have yielded more concrete patterns of PLS use and shed more light on the impact of mediating variables. Moreover, it would seem that a mixed-methods approach should have been applied, with qualitative data being augmented by quantitative information, which could have been attained through the inclusion of task-related Likert-scale items adopted from existing taxonomies. This would have allowed insights into PLS that the students applied but were not fully aware of or simply did not consider to be worth reporting. Finally, the use of additional data collection instruments, such as post-task interviews with selected participants would have enabled the researcher to probe deeper and obtain information about whether, when and why specific PLS were employed.

6. Conclusions, implications, and directions for future research

As accentuated on several occasions throughout this chapter, the value of the study can hardly be overestimated on account of the fact that it addresses an evident gap in the existing research and, although its findings may be preliminary and inconclusive, it constitutes the first attempt to tap the application of PLS in the performance of form-focused and meaning-focused tasks, also taking account of the role of contextual and individual variables. While the results are far too tentative to serve as a basis for concrete pedagogical implications, it seems clear that effective application of PLS may be of special relevance for English majors who, in theory at least, should strive to attain near-native pronunciation and who need to be autonomous to accomplish this goal. In particular, they might benefit from being made cognizant of how to monitor their pronunciation as they are engaged in spontaneous TL production, a situation that places heavy demands on their attentional resources. Obviously, for such pedagogic proposals to be concrete, context-sensitive, and practicable, further research is necessary into how PLS can be applied in the completion of pronunciation learning tasks. Such research could target other types of activities (e.g., different types of form- and meaning-focused tasks), ID factors (e.g., beliefs, motivation), and context-related variables (e.g., planning time). With respect to methodology, studies of this kind should be more structured, combine quantitative and qualitative paradigms and draw on different data collection tools, including post-hoc interviews, stimulated recall (see Amerstorfer, Chapter 6 in this volume) or recordings of oral production. Also, as the present author has emphasized with respect to grammar learning strategies (Pawlak, 2013a), a complete picture of use of PLS is only possible when the micro-perspective, as it was applied in the present study, is complemented with a macro-perspective, where general patterns can be established with the aid of valid and reliable tools administered to large populations manifesting various characteristics.

References

Anderson, Neil J. 2005. "L2 Learning Strategies." In *Handbook of Research in Second Language Teaching and Learning*, edited by Eli Hinkel, 757–71. Mahwah, NJ: Lawrence Erlbaum.

Berkil, Gulcin. 2009. *A Closer Look at Pronunciation Learning Strategies.* Saarbrücken: VDM Publishing.

Cohen, Andrew D. 2011. "Second Language Learner Strategies." In *Handbook of Research in Second Language Teaching and Learning,* edited by Eli Hinkel. Volume II, 681–98. Mahwah, NJ: Lawrence Erlbaum.

——. 2014. *Strategies in Learning and Using a Second Language.* 2nd edition. London: Routledge.

Cohen, Andrew D., and Ernesto Macaro, eds. 2007. *Language Learner Strategies: Thirty Years of Research and Practice.* Oxford: Oxford University Press.

Cohen, Andrew D., Rebecca L. Oxford, and Julie C. Chi. 2001. "Learning Style Survey." Accessed November 18, 2016. http://carla.umn.edu/maxsa/documents/LearningStyle Survey_MAXSA_IG.pdf

Cohen, Andrew D., and Angela Pinilla-Herrera. 2009. "Communicating Grammatically: Constructing a Learner Strategies Website for Spanish." In *Teaching and Testing: English as Subject and Vehicle,* edited by Tien-En Kao and Yaofu Lin, 63–83. Taipei, Taiwan: The Language Testing and Training Center.

Council of Europe. 2001. *Common European Framework of Reference for Languages: Learning, Teaching, Assessment.* Cambridge: Cambridge University Press.

DeKeyser, Robert M. 2010. "Cognitive-psychological Processes in Second Language Learning." In *The Handbook of Language Teaching,* edited by Michael H. Long and Catherine J. Doughty, 119–38. Oxford: Blackwell.

Derwing, Tracy M., and Murray J. Munro. 2015. *Pronunciation Fundamentals: Evidence-based Perspectives for L2 Teaching and Research.* Amsterdam: John Benjamins.

Droździał-Szelest, Krystyna. 1997. *Language Learning Strategies in the Process of Acquiring a Foreign Language.* Poznań: Motivex.

Eckstein, Grant T. 2007. "A Correlation of Pronunciation Learning Strategies with Spontaneous English Pronunciation of Adult ESL Learners." Unpublished MA thesis. Brigham Young University, Provo, UT, USA

Ehrman, Madeline E., Betty Lou Leaver, and Rebecca L. Oxford. 2003. "A Brief Overview of Individual Differences in Second Language Learning." *System* 31: 313–30.

Ellis, Rod. 2004. *The Study of Second Language Acquisition.* 2nd edition. Oxford: Oxford University Press.

——. 2007. "Implicit and Explicit Learning, Knowledge, and Instruction." In *Implicit and Explicit Knowledge in Second Language Learning, Testing and Teaching,* edited by Rod Ellis, Shawn Loewen, Catherine Elder, Rosemary Erlam, Jenefer Philip, and Hayo Reinders, 3–25. Bristol: Multilingual Matters.

Griffiths, Carol, and Rebecca L. Oxford. 2014. "The Twenty-first Century Landscape of Language Learning Strategies: Introduction to This Special Issue." *System* 43: 1–10.

Horwitz, Elaine K., Michael B. Horwitz, and Joann Cope. 1986. "Foreign Language Classroom Anxiety." *Modern Language Journal* 70: 125–32.

Macaro, Ernesto. 2006. "Strategies for Language Learning and for Language Use: Revising the Theoretical Framework." *Modern Language Journal* 90: 320–37.

MacIntyre, Peter D., and Robert C. Gardner. 1994. "The Subtle Effects of Language Anxiety on Cognitive Processing in the Second Language." *Language Learning* 44: 283–305.

McDonough, Stephen H. 1999. "Learner Strategies." *Language Teaching* 32: 1–18.

Naiman, Neil. 1978. *The Good Language Learner.* Clevedon: Multilingual Matters.

O'Malley, J. Michael, and Anna Uhl Chamot. 1990. *Learning Strategies in Second Language Acquisition.* Cambridge: Cambridge University Press.

Osburne, Andrea G. 2003. "Pronunciation Strategies of Advanced ESOL Learners." *International Journal of Applied Linguistics in Language Teaching* 41: 131–43.

Oxford, Rebecca L. 1990. *Language Learning Strategies: What Every Teacher Should Know.* Boston: Heinle & Heinle.

——. 2011. *Teaching and Researching Language Learning Strategies.* Harlow: Longman.

Oxford, Rebecca L., and Kyoung Rang Lee. 2007. "L2 Grammar Learning Strategies: The Second Cinderella and Beyond." In *Language Learner Strategies: Thirty Years of Research and Practice*, edited by Andrew D. Cohen and Ernesto Macaro, 117–39. Oxford: Oxford University Press.

Pawlak, Mirosław. 2006a. "The Place of Learner Autonomy in Pronunciation Instruction." In *Dydaktyka Fonetyki Języka Obcego. Zeszyty Naukowe Państwowej Wyższej Szkoły Zawodowej w Płocku. Tom VIII*, edited by Włodzimierz Sobkowiak and Ewa Waniek-Klimczak, 131–43. Płock: Wydawnictwo Państwowej Wyższej Szkoły Zawodowej w Płocku.

——. 2006b. "On the Use of Pronunciation Learning Strategies by Polish Foreign Language Learners." In *Dydaktyka Fonetyki Języka Obcego. Zeszyty Naukowe Państwowej Wyższej Szkoły Zawodowej w Płocku. Tom VIII*, edited by Włodzimierz Sobkowiak and Ewa Waniek-Klimczak, 121–35. Konin: Wydawnictwo Państwowej Wyższej Szkoły Zawodowej w Koninie.

——. 2008. "Another Look at the Use of Pronunciation Learning Strategies: An Advanced Learner's Perspective." In *Issues in Accents of English*, edited by Ewa Waniek-Klimczak, 304–22. Newcastle upon Tyne: Cambridge Scholars Publishing.

——. 2010. "Designing and Piloting a Tool for the Measurement of the Use of Pronunciation Learning Strategies." *Research in Language* 8: 189–202.

——. 2011a. "Research into Language Learning Strategies: Taking Stock and Looking Ahead." In *Individual Differences in SLA*, edited by Janusz Arabski and Adam Wojtaszek, 17–37. Bristol: Multilingual Matters.

——. 2011b. "Grammar Learning Strategies: State of the Art." In *Learning and Teaching English: Insights from Research*, edited by Luciana Pedrazzini and Andrea Nava, 69–90. Monza-Milano: Polimetrica.

——. 2011c. "Students' Successes and Failures in Learning Foreign Language Pronunciation: Insights from Diary Data." In *The Acquisition of L2 Phonology*, edited by Janusz Arabski and Adam Wojtaszek, 164–181. Bristol: Multilingual Matters.

——. 2013a. "Researching Grammar Learning Strategies: Combining the Macro- and Micro-perspective." In *Perspectives on Foreign Language Learning*, edited by Łukasz

Salski, Weronika Szubko-Sitarek, and Jan Majer, 191–210. Łódź: University of Łódź Press.

———. 2013b. "The Effects of Explicit and Implicit Corrective Feedback on Eliminating Pronunciation Errors." In *Teaching and Researching English Accents in Native and Non-native Speakers*, edited by Ewa Waniek-Klimczak and Linda R. Schockey, 85–101. Heidelberg: Springer.

Peterson, Susan S. 2000. "Pronunciation Learning Strategies: A First Look." Accessed November 18, 2016. http://files.eric.ed.gov/fulltext/ED450599.pdf.

Rokoszewska, Katarzyna. 2012. "The Influence of Pronunciation Learning Strategies on Mastering English Vowels." *Studies in Second Language Learning and Teaching* 2: 391–413.

Rubin, Joan. 1975. "What the 'Good Language Learner' Can Teach Us." *TESOL Quarterly* 9: 41–51.

Samalieva, Marina. 2000. "Strategies in Foreign Language Pronunciation: A Qualitative Investigation." Accessed November 18, 2016. http://www.beta-iatefl.org/697/blog-publications/strategies-in-foreign-language-pronunciation-qualitative-investigation/.

Szpyra-Kozłowska, Jolanta. 2015. *Pronunciation in EFL Instruction: A Research-Based Approach.* Bristol: Multilingual Matters.

Szyszka, Magdalena. 2014. "Pronunciation Learning Strategy Chains: A Qualitative Approach." In *Studying Second Language Acquisition from a Qualitative Perspective*, edited by Danuta Gabryś-Barker and Adam Wojtaszek, 35–47. Heidelberg: Springer.

———. 2015. "Good English Pronunciation Users and Their Pronunciation Learning Strategies." *Research in Language* 13: 93–106.

———. 2016. "The Interplay of Language Anxiety and Pronunciation Learning Strategies Among English Teacher Trainees." Unpublished PhD dissertation, Opole University, Poland.

Takeuchi, Osamu, Carol Griffiths, and Do Coyle. 2007. "Applying Strategies to Context: The Role of Individual, Situational, and Group Differences." In *Language Learner Strategies: Thirty Years of Research and Practice*, edited by Andrew D. Cohen and Ernesto Macaro, 69–92. Oxford: Oxford University Press.

Varasarin, Patchara. 2007. "An Action Research Study of Pronunciation Training, Language Learning Strategies and Speaking Confidence." Unpublished PhD dissertation, Victoria University, Melbourne. Accessed November 18, 2016. http://wallaby.vu.edu.au/adt-VVUT/uploads/approved/adtVVUT20070911.162030/public/01front.pdf.

Vitanova, Gergana, and Ann Miller. 2002. "Reflective Practice in Pronunciation Learning." *The Internet TESL Journal* 8. Accessed November 18, 2016. http://iteslj.org/Articles/Vitanova-Pronunciation.html.

White, Cynthia, Karen Schramm, and Anna Uhl Chamot. 2007. "Research Methods in Strategy: Re-examining the Toolbox." In *Language Learner Strategies: Thirty Years of Research and Practice*, edited by Andrew D. Cohen and Ernesto Macaro, 93–116. Oxford: Oxford University Press.

Part IV

Preparing Teachers and Presenting Strategy Instruction to Learners

Educational, social, and positive psychology books written for in-service teachers and prospective teachers often provide useful tips on how L2 teachers can take into account contextual influences while respecting individual learner needs and characteristics. Williams, Mercer, and Ryan (2015), for instance, list eight principles that aim to support L2 teachers in their teaching practice. Examples are: "Principle 2: Learners' lives beyond the classroom are central to who they are" and "Principle 5: Provide opportunities for and encourage self-regulation" (see Williams, Mercer, and Ryan 2015, 144–147 for details). As editors of this volume, we emphasize that teachers should, as a matter of principle, assist L2 learners in developing their strategic abilities. We believe that "[t]he central goal in language strategy instruction is to transform learners into self-managers and self-regulators so they can select strategies that will accomplish a defined task, skill, or goal and ultimately become more self-directed in their learning" (Gregersen and MacIntyre 2014, 152).

At the end of their chapter on LLS, Gregersen and MacIntyre (2014) provide some strategy activities, which can be integrated in L2 classes by the teacher without much effort. Two sets of seven tasks each are designed to be completed in consecutive order to generate unique results for each individual learner. Learners who engage in the individual and peer tasks take full control over the strategy-generating processes involved, which are "(1) raising learners' awareness; (2) deepening awareness-raising; (3) presentation and modeling; (4) practice; (5) self-evaluation; (6) transfer; and (7) evaluation" (see Gregersen and MacIntyre 2014, 156-173 for details).

L2 teachers and researchers have recognized for decades the importance of strategy instruction, as reflected in the creation of numerous (and sometimes similar) models for strategy instruction. In recent years, strategy instruction has not ceased to be acknowledged as a very valuable ingredient of formal L2 education (Chamot and Harris 2017; Gu 2007; Gunning and Oxford 2014; Harris 2007; Oxford 2017; Plonsky 2011; Psaltou-Joycey and Gavriilidou 2015). In the current volume, Part IV is specifically dedicated to this important topic.

This final section of the book is a gold mine for L2 teachers who want to help support their learners in becoming better at self-regulated, strategic language learning and for researchers interested in strategy instruction. Chamot's Chapter 10 shows how strategy instruction is integrated in a teacher education program at a U.S. university. Three of the mandatory courses in the university's master's program contain parts about strategies instruction. Chamot summarizes some of the experiences she has made with the program and shares materials that can be used and adapted by L2 teacher educators around the globe.

Chapter 11 by Bielak and Mystkowska-Wiertelak deals with the anxiety-provoking exam culture of an EFL program at a Polish university. The authors' empathy with exam takers has over the years led them to develop specific exercises to increase the application of affective strategies that reduce test anxiety. In Chapter 11, Bielak and Mystkowska-Wiertelak present the results of a study that investigated the different effects of affective strategy instruction on low-anxiety, medium-anxiety, and high-anxiety students.

In the final Chapter 12 of this volume, Gunning and Turner address a young age-group of EFL learners in Canada. The authors provide an invaluable contribution to the under-researched field of classroom-based strategy assessment with young language learners. They share tools that were specifically designed for researchers and L2 teachers to assess young language learners' strategy use in an age-appropriate fashion. The authors further report their own experience with young language learners' strategy assessment and provide guidance for teachers who want to investigate such issues in their own classrooms.

References

Chamot, Anna Uhl, and Vee Harris, eds. 2017. *Learning Strategy Instruction in the Language Classroom: Issues and Implementation.* Bristol: Multilingual Matters.

Gregersen, Tammy, and Peter D. MacIntyre. 2014. *Capitalizing on Language Learners' Individuality: From Premise to Practice.* Bristol: Multilingual Matters.

Gu, Peter Yongqi. 2007. "Strategy-based Instruction." In *Proceedings of the International Symposium on English Education in Japan: Exploring New Frontiers,* edited by Tomoko Yashima and Toshiyo Nabei, 21–38. Osaka, Japan: Yubunsha.

Gunning, Pamela, and Rebecca L. Oxford. 2014. "Children's Learning Strategy Use and the Effects of Strategy Instruction on Success in Learning ESL in Canada." *System* 43: 82–100.

Harris, Vee. 2007. "Exploring Progression: Reading and Listening Strategy Instruction with Near Beginner Learners of French." *Language Learning Journal* 35 (2): 189–204.

Oxford, Rebecca L. 2011. *Teaching and Researching Language Learning Strategies.* Harlow: Pearson/Longman.

—— 2017. *Teaching and Researching Language Learning Strategies: Self-regulation in Context.* 2nd edition. New York: Routledge.

Plonsky, Luke. 2011. "The Effectiveness of Second Language Strategy Instruction: A Meta-analysis." *Language Learning* 61 (4): 993–1038.

Psaltou-Joycey, Angeliki, and Zoe Gavriilidou, eds. 2015. *Foreign Language Learning Strategy Instruction: A Teacher's Guide.* Kavala, Greece: Saita Publications.

Williams, Marion, Sarah Mercer, and Stephen Ryan. 2015. *Exploring Psychology in Language Learning and Teaching.* Oxford: Oxford University Press.

10

Preparing Language Teachers

New Teachers Become Ready to Teach Learning Strategies in Diverse Classrooms

Anna Uhl Chamot
The George Washington University, USA

1. Introduction

Teaching second and foreign language learners to use strategies appropriate to the language tasks they undertake is intended to improve their success in learning. A substantial amount of research has shown that language learners who can choose and use appropriate learning techniques, or strategies, are more successful and self-confident learners (Chamot 2005, 2009; Cohen 2011; Grenfell and Harris 1999; Gu 2007; Macaro 2010; O'Malley and Chamot 1990; Oxford 2011; Rubin et al. 2007; Vandergrift and Goh 2012). However, teaching language learning strategies in second and foreign language classrooms is not yet featured in most language programs. For language learning strategies to become an integral part of second and foreign language curricula, teachers need to develop expertise in effective language learning strategy instruction (LLSI). How do teachers acquire such expertise? Some may acquire it through a process of autonomous learning, in which a teacher might develop an interest in language learning strategies, explore the research, use resource guides on LLSI[1], use the learning strategy suggestions in many recent language textbooks to try out learning strategy activities with students, and/or seek information from more knowledgeable colleagues and researchers in this field. Most teachers, however, do not have the time for such extensive self-education efforts.

Another way to develop expertise could be through in-service professional development, in which teachers attend workshops, seminars, conference presentations and other short-term activities on LLSI, then go on to try out some of the ideas gleaned in their classrooms. Without follow-up, mentoring, and collaboration with other teachers engaged in similar activities, short-term professional development of one day or less is rarely successful in effecting teaching change. However, success has been reported for longer, five-day summer institutes on styles and strategies-based instruction for language teachers conducted at the University of Minnesota for more than twenty years (Cohen 2011).

A third way in which language teachers can learn to teach strategies is through collaboration in a classroom-based research project. In this approach, teachers work directly with researchers to plan, implement, and evaluate LLSI in their own classrooms. A number of studies have reported success with this approach, though numerous problems can arise that need to be resolved (Chamot 1993; Chamot and El-Dinary 1999; Chamot and Küpper 1989; Chamot et al. 2000; Grenfell and Harris 1999; Gu 2007; Gunning and Oxford 2014; Harris 2007; O'Malley and Chamot 1990).

Finally, a fourth approach to developing teachers' skill in LLSI is in pre-service preparation programs in which learning how to teach strategies is part of the required curriculum. In this way, teachers are exposed to the theory and practice of language learning strategies simultaneously with their first exposure to language pedagogy. This chapter describes one such teacher preparation program, providing examples of activities and assignments to familiarize teacher candidates with both a rationale for teaching language learning strategies, awareness of their own learning strategies, and practical techniques for teaching their future students to choose and use appropriate learning strategies for various language learning tasks. The rationale for the activities and assignments described is that teacher candidates need to participate in activities that mirror actual classroom teaching if they are to translate theoretical knowledge into pedagogical actions (Bartels 2009). A guiding principle is that teachers who incorporate LLSI in their language classroom need to engage in learner-centered teaching (Rubin 2010).

2. Program background

The Graduate School of Education and Human Development at the George Washington University offers a Master's level program for Kindergarten to Grade 12 teacher preparation. Students (henceforth teacher candidates) must already have a Bachelor of Arts four-year degree with a major in a discipline that qualifies them for teaching a specific school subject. For example, the B.A. degree can be in history or government (for teacher candidates who aspire to teach history/social studies), a science such as biology, chemistry, or physics (for those planning to teach science), mathematics or engineering (for those who wish to teach math), English literature (for students who would like to teach English), and a language such as Arabic, Chinese, French, German, Italian, Russian, or Spanish (for teacher candidates who want to teach a world/foreign language). However, in the case of future teachers of English as a foreign or second language, a specific undergraduate major is not required. Instead, applicants must have had the experience of being a foreign language learner, as demonstrated by a minimum of twelve credit hours (four university courses) in a language other than English. Upon completion of the program, teacher candidates attain a Master's degree in Education and also earn a license to teach their subject(s) not only locally but in 36 additional states with which the licensing authority has a reciprocal agreement.

The university's admission policy requires applicants to not only have the required credit hours in the subject they will teach, but also a grade point average (GPA) of at least 2.9 (out of a possible 4.0). Until recently, applicants also had to have a satisfactory score on the Graduate Record Exam (GRE). As a final part of the selection process, applicants write a response to an educational issue (under supervision) and also participate in an interview with the faculty member specializing in the candidate's teaching subject. This rigorous selection process ensures that teacher candidates are not only knowledgeable in their field and have some understanding of current issues in education in general, but also have an awareness of and empathy for learners' strengths and challenges.

Because of the careful selection process, teacher candidates in the Master's program in Education are not only intelligent and well-versed in their teaching area, but also have well-defined life goals. In fact, many of these future teachers have already had careers in professions such as business, politics, law, and the like; they have made conscious decisions to change their career path to education, usually because they believe that as teachers they can effect more good than they could have in their previous profession. Thus, the teacher candidates in this Master's program are highly qualified in their school subject areas, mature in their thinking, and dedicated to making a difference to their world by providing the best possible education to K-12 students. In fact, these graduate students are highly motivated, inquisitive, challenging, and a joy to teach.

The curriculum for all teacher candidates includes a combination of general education courses and subject specialization courses, each of which is a semester-long three-credit graduate course meeting weekly for two and a half hours. For example, all teacher candidates complete courses in learning theories, instructional models and classroom management, development and diversity, assessment, and courses specific to teaching each subject area. In language education, both English as a Second Language (ESL) and Foreign Language (FL) teacher candidates take specialization courses in *Second Language Acquisition, Second Language Instruction,* and *Teaching Second Language Reading and Writing.* ESL teacher candidates also take courses in *Linguistic Applications for ESL* and *Psychosocial and Academic Assessment for Culturally and Linguistically Diverse Students.*

In order to obtain licensure to teach, students must not only complete the coursework identified above, but also pass teacher licensure examinations (*PRAXIS*) in both content knowledge and pedagogy. FL teacher candidates also take the American Council on the Teaching of Foreign Languages (ACTFL) Oral Proficiency Interview (*OPI*) and achieve a minimum level of Advanced Low. Thus, graduates of this Master's program are not only proficient in the language they will teach, but also knowledgeable about how to teach it.

3. Integrating LLSI into the language teacher preparation program

As an active researcher in the field of language learning strategies, I added a language learning strategy component to the language teacher preparation program when I joined the GWU faculty in 1996. Over time, the learning strategies component was continually updated and expanded. This section provides descriptions of the approach taken in the three courses addressing language learning strategies. The topics included in the three courses address both knowledge about language, and procedures for teaching a second language, as suggested by the research (Ellis 2009; Graves 2009; Griffiths 2013). In addition, all courses in the teacher preparation program emphasize the importance of teacher reflection as a means of effecting change in teaching practices (Borg 2006; Johnson 2009).

3.1. Second Language Acquisition course

This is a foundation course for Master's students specializing in ESL or FL education. Topics addressed in its fourteen sessions include: overview of first language acquisition, comparison of first and second language acquisition (SLA), general learning and language learning theoretical perspectives, learning styles, language learning strategies, affective factors in SLA, motivation, sociocultural aspects of SLA, communicative competence, analyzing learner language and understanding errors, and instructional applications of SLA theories. Weekly reading assignments are designed to help students gain an understanding of the nature and complexity of second language acquisition processes and how they affect student learning. In addition, students read, discuss, and report on both recent and seminal SLA research.

An important objective in *Second Language Acquisition* is to develop teacher candidates' thoughtful reflection about the process of learning a new language. This begins with their own language learning autobiography. The purpose of this initial assignment is for teacher candidates to think through their own life experiences in learning one or more second or foreign languages. This personal reflection lays the foundation for understanding the second language acquisition process. After thinking through relevant life experiences in learning languages, they write a journal-style reflection that can include recollections about effective and non-effective teachers, learning techniques (i.e., strategies) that worked for them, their own motivation and willingness to learn the language, self-efficacy, classroom experiences, traveling or living abroad, affective considerations, interactions with native speakers, and use of media/Internet. This assignment is followed by a classroom discussion in which students are asked to share some of their comments about their own language learning experiences.

Another opportunity for teacher candidates to reflect on their own learning is provided in a class activity in which they work in pairs to identify a recent learning problem or challenge and describe to their partner how they have solved it. They take notes on their partner's problem and solution, then share it with the class. In this way, teacher candidates not only reflect on how they have approached a learning problem but also gain insight into how a classmate has solved their problem.

This class discusses a relatively short list of language learning strategies (Chamot 2009). The list of language and content learning strategies was extracted from the various research-oriented classification systems (Chamot and O'Malley 1994; Cohen 1998; Grenfell and Harris 1999; O'Malley and Chamot 1990; Oxford 1990; Wenden 1991). The adopted teacher-friendly list is intended to be practical and usable by both teachers and their students. Thus, instead of multiple categories of learning strategies, only two are suggested: metacognitive strategies that represent executive processes usable with any learning or problem-solving task (planning, monitoring, evaluating, and managing one's own learning), and task-based strategies that are related to specific types of tasks. The task-based strategies are subdivided into four categories: Use What You Know (tapping into prior knowledge), Use Your Senses (applying visual, auditory, and kinesthetic aids to learning), Use Your Organizational Skills (familiar study skills), and Use a Variety of Resources (including technology, social resources, and one's own affective regulation). Each strategy is accompanied by a representative icon and several task-based examples of how the learner might use the strategy. The intention is to make the strategies as concrete as possible.

After the first reading assignment on language learning strategy research and discussion in class, teacher candidates complete a short self-evaluation questionnaire about their initial understanding of learning strategies. Examples of questions are: What are the major differences between metacognitive and task-based strategies? What is the difference between a learning strategy and a teaching strategy? What learning strategy or strategies are you using to complete this questionnaire? At the end of the questionnaire, teacher candidates are asked to rate themselves as having a good understanding of learning strategies, a basic understanding, or being confused about strategies. The responses have proven useful as springboards to further discussions and as diagnostic information for the course instructor.

Teacher candidates are asked to keep a learning strategies diary during part of the semester. The purpose of this assignment is for them to reflect on and identify their own learning strategies and thus increase personal understanding of how each individual learns and the techniques he or she uses to solve learning challenges. Writing about events and examining them introspectively is a valuable tool in revealing a teacher's mental processes (Borg 2006). By self-reflection, it is hoped that future teachers will be better prepared to model and teach learning strategies to their students (Johnson 2009). The directions for the learning strategies diary are as follows:

1. Choose a class (either academic or other) or a self-study program you are taking. It should be a class that is challenging and one in which you encounter some problems or difficulties.
2. Keep a diary for at least a week and record your learning experiences, including assignments and preparation for the class. Describe the tasks, tell why they were a challenge, and describe the actions and also the mental processes you used to overcome the challenges or solve the problems.
3. After you have written your descriptions, read them over carefully. Then identify the learning strategies you used by underlining what you did or thought and writing the name of the strategy in the right margin.
4. Please use one of the learning strategy classification schemes we have examined in class or others that you find. Be sure to identify which one you use.

5. Finally, please write one or two paragraphs about what you have learned by doing this exercise.

To summarize the language learning strategy goals for *Second Language Acquisition*, future teachers should have an understanding of major research studies on this topic, develop an awareness of their own approach to learning a new language, identify their own personal language learning strategies, become familiar with a classification scheme for language and content learning strategies that was designed for classroom applications, reflect in a written journal about their own use of learning strategies, and complete a self-evaluation of their own understanding of language learning strategies.

3.2. Second Language Instruction course

This required course for teacher candidates specializing in ESL and/or FL education addresses instructional methodology for teaching a new language to K-12 students. Topics include TESOL and/or ACTFL Standards, a brief history of language teaching methods and the theories underlying them, current approaches such as communicative language teaching, content-based language instruction, task-based instruction, language learning strategies instruction (LLSI), teaching of listening, reading, speaking, and writing in a second/foreign language, immersion approaches, and assessment of language proficiency and language achievement. The learning strategies components of this course are described below.

Ways to teach learning strategies in the language classroom are explored through reading articles and chapters on this subject, class discussions, various assignments, and a comparison of different instructional models (Chamot 2005, 2009; Chamot and O'Malley 1994; Cohen 1998, 2011; Grenfell and Harris 1999; Manchón 2008; Oxford 1990, 2011; Rubin et al. 2007). To begin, teacher candidates engage in a brief review activity to match names of strategies and their descriptions and are then referred to the previously distributed list of content and language learning strategies (Chamot 2009).

The main assignment in this course (25% of final grade) is a content-based thematic unit for the language and level(s) teacher candidates plan to teach. They are introduced to the conceptual framework of Understanding by Design (UbD) as a basis for their unit planning (Wiggins and McTighe 2006) and use the Cognitive Academic Language Learning Approach (CALLA) instructional framework to plan their lessons (Chamot 2009). The template for this unit plan includes UbD features such as Big Ideas, Essential Questions, and the development of assessment tasks and rubrics before planning teaching and learning activities. It also includes the CALLA components of content, language, and learning strategies as well as the sequence of lesson phases of Preparation, Presentation, Practice, Self-Evaluation, and Expansion. This planning template and a checklist/scoring sheet for unit components are provided in Appendix A.

The unit plan is due in mid-semester rather than as a final project for the course so that teacher candidates can revise it as many times as they wish in order to receive full credit for the assignment. Typically, the first iterations of the units show that most students do not easily grasp the idea of *explicit* learning strategy instruction. That is, although they might indicate that students will guess at the meanings of new words by using context clues, they do not mention how the teacher will identify what strategies students already use, model the new strategy, encourage practice with specific activities, or self-evaluate how well the strategy worked. After specific feedback, students may elect to revise their unit until they are satisfied with their grade. For most, one revision is necessary for the learning strategy component and any other weaknesses; however, occasionally a third revision is necessary. This procedure is intended to provide structured feedback and to help teacher candidates understand that learning is a process (Rubin 2010).

Another assignment in the methodology course is microteaching in which teacher candidates individually teach a short language activity to their peers. They prepare a class handout of a complete lesson plan, including learning strategy instruction, and then choose one of the five phases in the lesson for microteaching. Depending on whether they are specializing in ESL or FL, teacher candidates are given a choice in emphasis for the microteaching activity with their peers. These choices include topics such as cooperative learning, vocabulary, grammar, interpersonal communication, interpretive communication, presentational communication, and learning strategies. Teacher candidates are further asked to review textbooks and complete a critical evaluation form, including whether learning strategy instruction is provided in the student book and/or in the teacher's guide.

In addition to class attendance and assignments, all candidates for ESL or FL licensure participate in a thirty-hour field experience in a school. This observation experience takes place in the semester before teacher candidates engage in a semester-long internship (student teaching) experience. The purpose of this field experience is to observe and reflect on practicing language teachers and classrooms over an extended period of time. Teacher candidates observe a variety of classes and levels, and interact with teachers and their students as suggested by the host teacher. They keep a detailed record of their observations and use it to write a reflective journal about the experience, addressing the topics stated below:

1. A chart describing the school's ESL or foreign language program, type of instruction (e.g., language-based, content-based, immersion, or other), use of TESOL or ACTFL Standards, levels, and the like.
2. A critical description of one language teacher's approach, including methodology, use of standards, beliefs, effectiveness, and any learning strategy instruction.
3. An in-depth observation and interview of a language learner's cultural background, motivation, personal learning strategies, proficiency level, and self-efficacy.
4. For ESL specialization, an interview with a content subject teacher who has some of the students from the ESL class being observed in his or her content class. The purpose is to gain insight into the content teacher's attitudes and approaches (including learning strategies) towards helping linguistically and culturally diverse students achieve success in a content subject class.
5. A chart describing assessment and placement procedures in the ESL or FL program.
6. A description of critical moments during the thirty hours of classroom observation that have influenced the teacher candidate's philosophy of teaching.

Thus, the goals of *Second Language Instruction* are meant to provide teacher candidates with both understanding and skills—understanding of what and how to teach and skillful practice in planning, teaching, and assessment.

3.3. Teaching Second Language Reading and Writing course

The purposes of this course are to provide teacher candidates with an understanding of the literacy needs of ESL and/or FL students, a theoretical background on second language reading and writing processes, and practice with instructional approaches that assist ESL/FL students in becoming skilled and motivated readers and writers. The recommended scheduling of this course is during the same semester that teacher candidates are engaged in their school internships, as this provides them with opportunities to practice what is discussed in class with students in their student teaching classroom.

In order to review the concepts about language learning strategies developed in the previous two courses (*Second Language Acquisition* and *Second Language*

Instruction), teacher candidates engage in an activity in which they apply learning strategies to reading a story. They practice using three learning strategies with a story such as *Ooka and the Stolen Smell* (Edmonds 1961, in Chamot and O'Malley 1994) or, for foreign language specialization, a Spanish story such as *Una carta a Dios* (López y Fuentes 1984, in Walqui-van Lier and Barraza 1994) or a similar short story in the language they intend to teach. Teacher candidates work in small groups to read the story and apply the strategies *Use Imagery, Make Inferences,* and *Use Selective Attention.* Instructions are as follows:

1. Work in a group of three. Each of you will choose one of the learning strategies described below. Your goal is to be able to retell the story as accurately as possible, using only the notes you take for one of the learning strategies.
2. The three learning strategies are:
   (a) *Use Imagery*: Draw a picture or comic strip that illustrates the story.
   (b) *Make Inferences*: List words new to your students and write down your inferences about possible meanings.
   (c) *Use Selective Attention*: Decide on the 10 most important words in the story and write them in the order that will help you retell the story.
3. Read the story. Then discuss and record the strategy you have selected.

Upon completing the reading, discussion, and recording of learning strategies, teacher candidates are called on to retell the story as completely as possible using only the notes recorded on the strategy sheets. This leads to a discussion of how well the strategies worked for individuals, which strategies are preferred, and why. Teacher candidates are asked to adapt this activity to their own student teaching classroom and try it out with their students, reporting the results back to the class.

Another early assignment for teacher candidates is to identify the learning strategies already used by their students for various learning tasks, including both first and second language reading and writing. Teacher candidates observe their students and ask them to describe how they approach a learning task. One way to identify language learners' current strategies is to provide them with a task and ask them to describe how they plan to work on it. Then, after completing the task, teachers can ask students how they carried out their plan and if they changed it-and why. The following suggestions are provided to give teacher candidates some ideas for possible tasks:

1. Learning new vocabulary—What special techniques do your students have for learning the meanings and uses of new words, phrases, idioms, and collocations?

2. Listening for information—What do your students do to help them understand information that is presented orally, such as a teacher's presentation, or a story read aloud?

3. Following Directions—Do your students have strategies for carrying out a procedure such as a science experiment, math problem, or multi-step assignment?

4. Reading for comprehension—What strategies do your students use to understand the main ideas, events, or points of an informational or literary text?

5. Viewing—How do your students go about understanding and remembering information presented in a video, film, DVD, Internet, or television program?

6. Writing—How do your students engage in the writing process? Do they plan, draft, share, revise, edit? How? What else do they do?

7. Understanding Graphic Information—How do your students get meaning from maps, charts, graphic organizers, tables, etc.? How do they remember this information?

This assignment provides teacher candidates with an opportunity to learn about their students' thinking processes and to reflect on how these should inform their teaching. It also helps them choose which new strategies to teach and how to differentiate their strategy instruction so that their students have some choice in the strategies to practice.

In this reading and writing course teacher candidates develop a portfolio of three different lessons, teaching one of them to their classmates in the microteaching assignment. Particular lessons should focus on the following:

Part 1. Literature and Writing

This lesson must be based on a piece of literature and must incorporate writing. You can choose the level of student language proficiency (i.e., beginning, intermediate, or advanced).

Part 2. Literacy

This lesson must assume low-literacy ESL students (the equivalent of first grade reading level for native speakers) OR beginning level FL students, including low-literacy heritage speakers of the language (such as Arabic or Spanish). You must include some sort of word attack instruction as well as reading and writing.

Part 3. Content Area

> This lesson must show that you can teach lessons that incorporate reading and writing in other content areas (math, science, and/or history/social studies), or culture for foreign language lessons.

These lessons follow the same format as the units developed in the methodology course the previous semester and each must contain learning strategy instruction. A typical rubric provided to students includes the following:

1. Objectives and assessments are stated for content, language, and learning strategies.
2. Activities develop reading and writing.
3. One (or two) learning strategies are *explicitly* taught and practiced.
4. **Preparation Phase.** Students' prior knowledge about the reading and writing topics is elicited.
5. **Presentation Phase.** Skills and new information are made accessible to students through techniques like demonstration, modeling, visual support, etc. Learning strategy is modeled and explained.
6. **Practice Phase.** Students use the information and skills learned in the Presentation Phase in a variety of activities such as collaboration, problem solving, inquiry, etc.
7. **Self-Evaluation Phase**. Opportunity for *student self-evaluation* of how well they mastered content, language, and/or strategy is included.
8. **Expansion Phase.** Activities and/or discussion addresses real-life application of content.
9. Contributions of students' own culture(s) related to the topic are identified/discussed.
10. For the literacy lesson only: Word Attack strategies or patterns are directly taught and practiced.
11. For the content or culture-based lesson only: Language and learning strategies are presented in the context of **culture, science, math, and/or history/social studies.**

The final exam for this course on Teaching Second Language Reading and Writing is a performance assessment. Two weeks before the final exam, teacher candidates are given a list of seven questions, each of which addresses a major topic in the course. They decide whether the questions accurately cover the course topics and may suggest changes. One of the seven questions is: *Discuss the role metacognition plays in learning to read and write in a second language and how learning strategy instruction can develop both metacognitive awareness and reading and writing proficiency.* On the day of the exam, teacher candidates are divided into groups of three or four, and each group has a turn sitting in front of the class, drawing one of the questions, planning their response as a group, then responding to the question they have randomly selected, with each person answering at least one part of the question. Teacher candidates are graded on this final exam according to a rubric that is provided to them at the same time as the list of questions. They are assessed by the instructor, by their peers, and also complete a self-evaluation of their performance. This reading and writing course is offered in the spring semester and is the final one in the sequence of courses containing language learning strategies components. For most it is the final course for licensure and the Master of Education degree.

4. Evaluation of the program's language learning strategies instruction (LLSI) component

The most reliable evaluation of this Master's level teacher preparation program's component of language learning strategy instruction (LLSI) would be follow-up observation of graduates' practices in their subsequent teaching assignments. Unfortunately, this has not been an option. Therefore, the evaluation takes place during teacher candidates' last course addressing language learning strategies, *Teaching Second Language Reading and Writing.* Towards the end of the final course, teacher candidates complete a self-evaluation questionnaire about their own perceptions of their readiness and ability to teach language learning strategies in their future classrooms. This questionnaire is provided in Appendix B. Five years (2008–2012) of questionnaire data are available for a total of 61 teacher candidates specializing in ESL and/or foreign language education in the Master's licensure program described above.

The first question asks teacher candidates to provide their personal definition of a learning strategy. Almost all respondents were able to provide satisfactory and often thoughtful responses. Some examples of these definitions are:

> "To me, learning strategies are what 'smart' kids have been doing unconsciously all along, but most students need to be taught explicitly how to be more deliberate and efficient in their learning."
> "To enable the students to become independent learners."
> "Strategy is a mental technique/method to help you out with difficulties while learning, and become [a] more effective learner."

"It's a helpful tool that helps me learn easier/better."

"Consciously, actively doing something to achieve success in learning."

"A specific method of study, memory, or organization that will aid a student in improving academic success."

"A technique that aids one's effectiveness in learning."

"Learning strategies are ways that each individual person can best learn new information."

"A learning strategy is a method that students use to attack and acquire the material that is being taught."

"A 'tool' that one can use in order to 'fix' a problem that occurs while reading, writing, or listening."

The second question asks teacher candidates to rate the frequency with which they incorporate (or plan to incorporate) learning strategy instruction into their teaching. There were 39% who said they teach or will teach strategies occasionally, while 61% indicated that they do/will do so frequently. No one chose the option of *rarely*. Responses on the third question revealed that 54% of the teacher candidates felt somewhat confident in their ability to teach language learning strategies, while 46% felt very confident about teaching strategies. No one indicated feeling not at all confident on this question.

The fourth question asked teacher candidates to rate the effectiveness of thirteen different class activities and assignments on language learning strategies and how to teach them during the three courses they had completed. This was accomplished by rank-ordering the activities from 1 to 13, with instructions to rank two or more activities the same if they were of equal usefulness. In addition to ranking some activities as of equal value, some teacher candidates did not rank every item in Question 4, but chose to mark only the higher-ranking items. The rankings were tabulated, then collapsed into three levels: High (ranked 1–4), Mid (ranked 5–9), and Low (ranked 10–13). Table 10.1 shows the results of the rankings at each of the three levels for the thirteen activities and assignments.

As can be seen in Table 10.1, 50% of the activities and assignments were ranked high, 32% were ranked at the mid-level, and 18% were ranked low. The most highly ranked activity was observing a teacher when teaching learning strategies (79%), followed by trying out strategies with their own students (62%), reading about how to teach learning strategies (57%), watching a video of a language teacher teaching learning strategies (49%), and watching a demonstration of strategy instruction (44%).

Mid-level ranked activities and assignments had a different emphasis. The highest mid-ranking was for planning lessons that include language learning

Table 10.1 Question 4: High-, mid-, and low-level rankings of learning strategy activities/assignments (2008–2012; N = 61)

Activity description	High- ranked 1–4		Mid- ranked 5–9		Low- ranked 10–13		TOTALS	
	No.	%	No.	%	No.	%	No.	%
Read LLS research studies	23	38	20	33	18	30	61	7.9
Keep LS diary	23	38	15	25	22	36	60	7.8
Read about LLSI	35	57	20	33	10	16	65	8.5
Listen to lectures on LLS, LLSI	27	44	17	28	19	31	63	8.2
Discuss LS and LLSI in class	26	43	28	46	4	7	58	7.5
Watch live demo of LLSI	35	57	17	28	4	7	56	7.3
Watch video of LLSI	30	49	18	30	8	13	56	7.3
Observe teacher's LLSI	48	79	8	13	3	5	59	7.7
Role play as LS student	24	39	21	34	12	20	57	7.4
Plan lessons that include LLSI	25	41	29	48	6	10	60	7.8
Micro teach LLS to classmates	24	39	22	36	14	23	60	7.8
Teach LLS to own students	38	62	13	21	6	10	57	7.4
Get own students feedback on LLSI	27	44	18	30	12	20	57	7.4
TOTALS	385	50	246	32	138	18	769	100

LLS = Language Learning Strategies; LLSI = Language Learning Strategy Instruction

Note: Some activities were ranked equally by some of the teacher candidates, and not all activities were marked by all teacher candidates

strategies instruction (48%), discussing language learning strategies and their instruction during class (46%), micro teaching language learning strategies to classmates (36%), and role-playing in class as a student being instructed in using learning strategies (34%).

The lowest ranked activity for learning how to teach learning strategies was writing a learning strategies diary (36%), followed by listening to lectures on language learning strategies (31%), reading about research on language learning strategies (30%), role-playing language learners in a demonstration of LLSI (20%), and obtaining feedback from students taught language learning strategies (20%).

However, when comparing the percentage of teacher candidates ranking a particular activity as high to those ranking it low, a more complex picture emerges. For example, keeping a learning strategies diary was ranked high by 38% of the participants and ranked low by 36%, reading about language learning strategy research was ranked at the mid-level by 33% of respondents and at the low-level by 30%, participating in class discussions about language learning strategies was rated high by 43% of teacher candidates and at the mid-level by 46%, micro teaching a learning strategies activity to classmates was ranked high by 39% of participants and at the mid-level by 36%, and role-playing the part of a student learning about strategies was ranked high by 39% of respondents and at the mid-level by 34%. This shows variation in how well the language learning strategies activities and assignments worked for different members of the classes. The highest negative rating (for the learning strategies diary) was at 36% compared to 38% of teacher candidates who rated the same assignment as positive. Reading about research on language learning strategies was rated at a similar level by all three groups of respondents: 38% high, 33% mid, and 30% low.

Finally, the fifth question on the self-evaluation learning strategies questionnaire asked teacher candidates to identify challenges in teaching language learning strategies and possible steps to overcoming these challenges. Since this was an open-ended question, the answers varied greatly, but could be divided into challenges attributed to student learning and those attributed to teaching issues. Table 10.2 shows a summary of the challenges and solutions described by respondents.

Descriptions of student learning challenges focused on two general areas: student resistance to learning strategy instruction and diversity of numerous student characteristics. For solutions to student issues, teacher candidates consistently identified what they could do as teachers to overcome these challenges. None indicated that a challenge was insoluble or that the blame lay with students.

Four areas were identified in teaching challenges: the language of instruction, time constraints, the teacher's self-efficacy or confidence in their own ability to teach language learning strategies, and negativism from colleagues in their teaching context. The main problem with the language of instruction was because of difficulties in teaching strategies in the target language to beginning level students, reflecting challenges described by a number of researchers (Chamot 2011, 2016; Grenfell and Harris 1999; Oxford 2011; Rubin et al. 2007). Three major solutions were suggested: teaching the strategies in the learners' first

Table 10.2 Question 5: LLSI challenges and solutions (2008–2012; N = 61)

Learning Challenges	Examples of Student Issues	Solutions
Student resistance to LLSI	Students don't: Use strategies taught; see value of strategies; accept new strategies; transfer strategies; understand the purpose of strategies. Students lose interest if they already know strategy; feel they don't need them; can't describe their strategies even after teacher modeling; high school students find LS childish.	Explain contexts for strategy use; make personally relevant; provide frequent practice; model step by step; use rubrics; try to motivate- be persistent; let students choose strategy; keep it short students who get it can teach to peers; need more research on this; make sure strategy is appropriate; demonstrate usefulness of LS in college and beyond.
Student diversity	Students have different needs, interests, language levels, cultural background; L1 skills; metacognitive levels; learning styles; ability to understand directions; prior knowledge about LS.	Get to know students' difficulties and motivation; provide choices in learning strategies; scaffold and differentiate LLSI; teach strategies explicitly; use visuals and realia; make certain strategies a routine in class.
Teaching Challenges	**Examples of Teaching Issues**	**Solutions**
Language of instruction, especially for beginners	The language barrier; very hard to teach learning strategies in a foreign language to beginners; beginning ESOL students do not understand you; opportunities to teach LS go un-seized because of students' limited language proficiency; English vocabulary used to even explain the strategy; language needed to explain is too advanced.	Teach strategies in L1; find out L1 strategies; give examples; provide peer help; use visuals; simplify my language without "talking down;" model and give positive reinforcement; teach vocabulary for each strategy; a lot of patience and optimism; have students learn one word in target language to remember a strategy; speak slowly and clearly; use manipulatives; break it down to simplified steps.

(*Continued*)

Table 10.2 Continued

Learning Challenges	Examples of Student Issues	Solutions
Time constraints	Finding time in crowded curriculum, especially to get student feedback; balancing LLSI with language/content instruction; pressure of preparing for tests; state standards; to save time, teachers tell students what to think instead of having them figure it out; too much to teach!	No solution! Set goals for myself to incorporate learning strategies more; limit to 1–2 strategies per unit.
Teacher's self-efficacy level/ability to teach LLS	Difficult to articulate and explain the metacognitive strategies; need to make it more systematic by including in lesson plan; remembering to reinforce the strategy constantly without making it a burden for students; hard to focus on strategies and content at same time; difficulty being explicit; hard to teach strategies I don't find useful myself; knowing which strategies to use and when; really struggled with grasping learning strategies; knowing how to scaffold; being consistent; hard to understand students' difficulties; difficult to model L.S. I can teach LLS, but have trouble getting students to consciously practice LLS. Not much of a problem—as long as I understand strategies I can teach them.	Think of simple language to explain strategies; learn how to fit most important strategies into a lesson; incorporate LLS into lessons seamlessly; need more time in class on this topic; familiarize myself more with strategies to become more comfortable teaching them; get feedback from students; post lists and reminders around the room; include strategies in my lesson plans; ask students about their difficulties and ask successful learners what they do.
Colleagues' resistance/negative approach	Many experienced teachers called learning strategies a waste of time. Difficulty in getting my co-teacher to use LLS. My student teaching classroom not conducive to LLSI.	Plan to be more explicit with LLSI when I have my own classroom.

Note: These examples are illustrative of the range of comments. Many respondents addressed the same challenges and/or solutions. Some identified a challenge but did not provide a solution

language (L1), adapting the teacher's instructional language, and using a variety of teaching techniques to model and illustrate the strategies.

A number of respondents identified time constraints as a major problem in teaching language learning strategies, given prescribed curricula, mandated testing, and the demands of teaching a content-based language program. Solutions were few; many did not offer any, and one even stated that there was no solution.

There were many examples of teacher candidates' self-efficacy related to their perceived ability to teach language learning strategies successfully. Although one indicated that this was not much of a problem, others articulated personal difficulties that included teaching explicitly, choosing appropriate strategies to teach, consistency and scaffolding, understanding student difficulties, and modeling the strategies. Many of these difficulties echo questions raised in LLSI research (Chamot and Keatley 2003; Harris 2007, 2008; Oxford 2011). Solutions offered were changes to teaching behavior such as modifying language of explanation, lesson planning, seeking student feedback, and posting strategy lists and reminders in the classroom. These are also the solutions suggested by LLSI researchers (Chamot 2011; Grenfell and Harris 1999; Oxford 2011). One respondent felt that more time spent on LLSI in the teacher preparation program would have been helpful. Interestingly, no teacher candidate suggested using technology to assist in LLSI.

A few of the teacher candidates commented on negative reactions to language learning strategies from other teachers in their school settings and how this impeded their own ability to try out LLSI, especially for those engaged in student teaching. Similar macro-structures impeding teachers' ability to implement learner-centered teaching were identified by Rubin (2010). The only solution offered was to postpone the teaching of language learning strategies until teacher candidates had their own classroom and more freedom to try out different approaches to language teaching.

To sum up, the LLSI Questionnaire was extremely valuable for program evaluation and improvement. Responses to Questions 4 and 5 provided useful ranges of information. By ranking the language learning strategy activities and assignments in the three courses described, teacher candidates revealed that they are as diverse as their students in their approaches and preferences for learning. The most frequent high-ranked activities should continue to be included in the program. The mid-ranked activities could be improved or modified according to teacher candidate feedback. The activities ranked low by a sizeable percentage of teacher candidates could become optional, while those ranked low by a very small percentage of teacher candidates could be modified to make them more acceptable. In general, teacher candidates should have more choice in the activities and assignments undertaken to help them learn about language learning strategies and ways to teach them. As for the challenges perceived by teacher candidates, these could be addressed during class sessions to generate an awareness of potential difficulties and could lead to concrete plans on how to address them, including the use of technology such as the flipped instruction model in which the strategy instruction is delivered through online materials (in the L1 if possible), outside of class (Chamot 2016; National Capital Language Resource Center 2004a, Appendix A).

5. Conclusions

This chapter has described the learning strategies component of a graduate level teacher preparation program for teaching second and foreign languages. Activities and assignments in each of the three courses addressing language learning strategies (*Second Language Acquisition, Second Language Instruction,* and *Teaching Second Language Reading and Writing*) were described. Finally, the self-evaluation of the whole learning strategy component was completed by teacher candidates by means of a questionnaire at the end of the third course. The results of the questionnaire provided diagnostic information useful for improving this component of the program.

Many questions remain about the most effective way to integrate language learning strategies into second and foreign language teacher preparation programs. For example, should the topic of language learning strategies be addressed in a separate course, perhaps a shorter one-credit course, instead of being added to three existing courses? How much choice should teacher candidates be given in learning strategy activities and assignments? Should those who dislike reading about research be allowed to choose a different assignment and what might that assignment be? Or can foundational research information be provided through a more palatable means? These and other questions await further research and descriptions of language learning strategy components in teacher preparation programs in diverse contexts.

Note

1   Teacher guides for teaching language learning strategies at different levels include: Cohen and Weaver 2006; National Capital Language Resource Center 2003, 2004a,

2004b; Nyikos 1991; Psaltou-Joycey 2015; Vrettou 2015. Student guides for using language learning strategies include: National Capital Language Resource Center 2004a, Appendix A; Paige et al. 2006; Rubin and Thompson 1994. Additional language learning strategy guides can be found in Oxford 2011.

References

Bartels, Nat. 2009. "Knowledge about Language." In *The Cambridge Guide to Second Language Teacher Education*, edited by Anne Burns and Jack C. Richards, 125–34. New York: Cambridge University Press.

Borg, Simon. 2006. *Teacher Cognition and Language Education: Research and Practice.* London: Continuum.

Chamot, Anna Uhl. 1993. "Student Responses to Learning Strategy Instruction in the Foreign Language Classroom." *Foreign Language Annals* 26 (3): 308–21.

——. 2005. "Language Learning Strategy Instruction: Current Issues and Research." *Annual Review of Applied Linguistics* 25: 112–30.

——. 2009. *The CALLA Handbook: Implementing the Cognitive Academic Language Learning Approach.* 2nd edition. White Plains, NY: Pearson Education/Longman.

——. 2011. "Preparing Language Teachers to Teach Learning Strategies." In *Foreign Language Teaching in Asia and Beyond: Current Perspectives and Future Directions*, edited by Wai Meng Chan, Kwee Nyet Chin, and Titima Suthiwan, 29–44. Boston: De Gruyter Mouton.

——. 2016. "Teaching Learning Strategies in a Flipped Instruction Model." In *IATEFL 2015: Manchester Conference Selections*, edited by Tania Pattison, 73–74. Faversham: IATEFL.

Chamot, Anna Uhl, and Pamela Beard El-Dinary. 1999. "Children's Learning Strategies in Language Immersion Classrooms." *Modern Language Journal* 83 (iii): 319–41.

Chamot, Anna Uhl, and Catharine W. Keatley. 2003. *Learning Strategies of Adolescent Low-literacy Hispanic ESL Students.* Paper presented at the Annual Meeting of the American Educational Research Association, Chicago, IL, April 2003.

Chamot, Anna Uhl, and Lisa Küpper. 1989. "Learning Strategies in Foreign Language Instruction." *Foreign Language Annals* 22: 13–24.

Chamot, Anna Uhl, and J. Michael O'Malley. 1994. *The CALLA Handbook: Implementing the Cognitive Academic Language Learning Approach.* White Plains, NY: Addison Wesley Longman.

Chamot, Anna Uhl, Catharine W. Keatley, Amy Mazur, Kristina Anstrom, Xiomena Márquez, and Mary Adonis. 2000. *Literacy Development in Adolescent English Language Learners.* Final report submitted to Office of Educational Research and Improvement, U. S. Department of Education.

Cohen, Andrew D. 1998. *Strategies in Learning and Using a Second Language.* 1st edition. New York: Addison Wesley Longman.

——. 2011. *Strategies in Learning and Using a Second Language.* Harlow, UK: Pearson Education.

Cohen, Andrew D., and Susan J. Weaver. 2006. "Styles- and Strategies-based Instruction: A Teachers' Guide." Accessed February 15, 2016. www.carla.umn.edu/strategies/resources/SBIimpact.pdf.

Edmonds, I. G. 1961. "Ooka and the Stolen Smell." In Anna Uhl Chamot and J. Michael O'Malley. 1994. *The CALLA Handbook: Implementing the Cognitive Academic Language Learning Approach,* 307–10. White Plains, NY: Addison Wesley Longman.

Ellis, Rod. 2009. "SLA and Teacher Education." In *The Cambridge Guide to Second Language Teacher Education,* edited by Anne Burns and Jack C. Richards, 135–43. New York: Cambridge University Press.

Graves, Kathleen. 2009. "The Curriculum of Second Language Teacher Education." In *The Cambridge Guide to Second Language Teacher Education,* edited by Anne Burns and Jack C. Richards, 115–24. New York: Cambridge University Press.

Grenfell, Michael, and Vee Harris. 1999. *Modern Languages and Learning Strategies: In Theory and Practice.* London: Routledge.

Griffiths, Carol. 2013. *The Strategy Factor in Successful Language Learning.* Bristol: Multilingual Matters.

Gu, Peter Yongqi. 2007. "Strategy Based Instruction." In *Proceedings of the International Symposium on English Education in Japan: Exploring New Frontiers,* edited by Tomoko Yashima and Toshiyo Nabei, 21–38. Osaka: Yubunsha.

Gunning, Pamela, and Rebecca L. Oxford 2014. "Children's Learning Strategy Use and the Effects of Strategy Instruction on Success in Learning ESL in Canada." *System* 43: 82–100.

Harris, Vee. 2007. "Exploring Progression: Reading and Listening Strategy Instruction with Near-beginner Learners of French." *Language Learning Journal* 35 (2): 189–204.

Johnson, Karen E. 2009. "Trends in Second Language Teacher Education." In *The Cambridge Guide to Second Language Teacher Education,* edited by Anne Burns and Jack C. Richards, 20–29. New York: Cambridge University Press.

López y Fuentes. 1984. "Una Carta a Dios." In *Sendas Literarias,* edited by Aida Walqui-van Lier and Ruth A. Barraza.1994, 96–101. Boston: Heinle & Heinle.

Macaro, Ernesto. 2010. "The Relationship between Strategic Behavior and Language Learning Success." In *Continuum Companion to Second Language Acquisition,* edited by Ernesto Macaro, 268–99. London: Continuum.

Manchón, Rosa M. 2008. "Taking Strategies to the Foreign Language Classroom: Where Are We Now in Theory and Research?" *International Review of Applied Linguistics* 46 (4): 221–43.

National Capital Language Resource Center. 2003. "Elementary Immersion Learning Strategies Resource Guide." 2nd edition. Accessed February 16, 2016. www.nclrc.org.

——. 2004a. "Sailing the 5 Cs with Learning Strategies: A Resource Guide for Secondary Foreign Language Educators." Appendix A: Using Strategies for a Purpose: A

Resource Guide for Secondary Foreign Language Learners. Accessed February 16, 2016. www.nclrc.org.

——. 2004b. "Developing Autonomy in Language Learners: Learning Strategy Instruction in Higher Education." Accessed February 16, 2016. www.nclrc.org.

Nyikos, Martha. 1991. "Prioritizing Student Learning: A Guide for Teachers." In *Focus on the Foreign Language Learner: Priorities and Strategies*, edited by Lorraine Strasheim, 25–39. Lincolnwood, IL: National Textbook Company.

O'Malley, J. Michael, and Anna Uhl Chamot. 1990. *Learning Strategies in Second Language Acquisition*. Cambridge: Cambridge University Press.

Oxford, Rebecca L. 1990. *Language Learning Strategies: What Every Teacher Should Know*. Boston: Heinle & Heinle.

——. 2011. *Teaching and Researching Language Learning Strategies*. Harlow: Longman.

Paige, R. Michael, Andrew D. Cohen, Barbara Kappler, Julie C. Chi, and James P. Lassegard. 2006. *Maximizing Studying Abroad: A Student's Guide to Strategies for Language and Culture Learning and Use*. 2nd edition. Minneapolis, MN: Center for Advanced Research on Language Acquisition, University of Minnesota.

Psaltou-Joycey, Angeliki, ed. 2015. *Foreign Language Learning Strategy Instruction: A Teacher's Guide*. Kavala, Greece: Saita Publications.

Rubin, Joan. 2010. "Language Teacher Education: Challenges in Promoting a Learner-centered Perspective." *Revista Canaria de Estudios Ingleses* 61: 29–42.

Rubin, Joan, and Irene Thompson. 1994. *How to Be a More Successful Language Learner*. Boston: Heinle & Heinle.

Rubin, Joan, Anna Uhl Chamot, Vee Harris, and Neil J. Anderson. 2007. "Intervening in the Use of Strategies." In *Language Learner Strategies: Thirty Years of Research and Practice*, edited by Andrew D. Cohen and Ernesto Macaro, 141–60. Oxford: Oxford University Press.

Vandergrift, Larry, and Christine C. M. Goh. 2012. *Teaching and Learning Second Language Listening: Metacognition in Action*. New York: Routledge.

Vrettou, Athina. 2015. "Language Learning Strategy Instruction." In *Foreign Language Learning Strategy Instruction: A Teacher's Guide*, edited by Angeliki Psaltou-Joycey, 32–48. Kavala, Greece: Saita Publications.

Walqui-van Lier, Aida, and Ruth A. Barraza, eds. 1994. *Sendas Literarias*. Boston: Heinle & Heinle.

Wenden, Anita. 1991. *Learner Strategies for Learner Autonomy*. Hemel Hempstead, UK: Prentice Hall International.

Wiggins, Grant, and Jay McTighe. 2006. *Understanding by Design*. Expanded 2nd edition. Upper Saddle River, NJ: Pearson Education.

11

Investigating English Majors' Affective Strategy Use, Test Anxiety, and Strategy Instruction

Contextual Influences

Jakub Bielak
Anna Mystkowska-Wiertelak
Adam Mickiewicz University and
State University of Applied Sciences, Poland

1. Introduction

Research on language learning strategies (LLSs) began in the mid-1970s as an offshoot of interest in "good language learners" (e.g., Rubin 1975; Stern 1975) and has not lost momentum. Recent years have witnessed many important advances. First, general classifications of LLSs (O'Malley and Chamot 1990; Oxford 1990) are being complemented by those pertaining to language skills, such as reading and speaking, and subsystems, such as grammar and vocabulary (e.g., Oxford 1990, 2017; Pawlak 2010; Schmitt 1997; Sheorey and Mokhtari 2001; Takač 2008). Second, definitions of LLSs and related notions such as *tactics* are being debated and refined (cf., Dörnyei and Skehan 2003; Oxford 2011, 2017). Third, tools for measuring LLS use and/or self-regulation are being developed (Cohen, Oxford, and Chi 2002; Gkonou and Oxford 2016; Tseng, Dörnyei, and Schmitt 2006). Fourth, procedures for and effects of strategy instruction (SI) to learners are being considered (e.g., Chamot, Chapter 10 in this volume; Cohen 2014; Cohen and Weaver 2006; Grenfell and Harris 1999; O'Malley and Chamot 1990; Oxford 1990, 2011). Finally, the interaction of strategy use, SI, individual differences, and contexts is being highlighted by Takeuchi, Griffiths, and Coyle (2007) and by contributors to the current book (Chamot, Chapter 10; Gunning and Turner, Chapter 12; Oxford, Lavine, and Amerstorfer, Chapter 1; Psaltou-Joycey and Gavriilidou, Chapter 8; and others).

This chapter directly reflects several of these advances. In an English as a foreign language (EFL) context, specifically a small university in central Poland, we address relationships between affective (emotion regulation) LLS use and affective SI. We identify how these factors relate to learners' emotions caused by an anxiety-provoking, sometimes traumatic, final EFL exam. As casual observers in the corridor and sometimes as exam managers, we witnessed the exam's negative emotional effects. Polish educational reform has fostered extensive standardized testing in schools, "studying to the test," and test anxiety in the absence of SI to help students "learn how to learn" or take tests effectively.

2. Research review

This research review covers language anxiety (LA), test anxiety (TA), LLSs, and SI.

2.1. Language anxiety and test anxiety

LA is "a distinct complex of self-perceptions, beliefs, feelings and behaviors related to classroom language learning arising from the uniqueness of the language learning process" (Horwitz, Horwitz, and Cope 1986, 128). Research indicates a relationship between higher LA and lower language achievement (e.g., Dewaele 2007; Gardner and MacIntyre 1993; Horwitz, Horwitz, and Cope 1986; Woodrow 2006). LA probably interferes with cognitive processing at the input, processing, and output stages (MacIntyre and Gardner 1994). Correlates of LA are communication apprehension, fear of negative evaluation, and TA (Horwitz 2010). TA is a performance anxiety related to fear of failure (Zeidner 1998) and can be a trait (a rather permanent characteristic) and/or a state (anxiety experienced in the moment). Its manifestations are excessive worry, tension, irrelevant and chaotic thinking, and physiological reactions, such as fast heartbeat or excessive perspiration (Spielberger, Anton, and Bedell 1976; Spielberger and Vagg 1995).

2.2. Anxiety, LLSs, and SI

Relationships between affective (emotional) factors, especially anxiety, and LLS use have been researched to a limited extent and sometimes with conflicting results. LA correlates negatively with the use of social, cognitive, and metacognitive strategies, meaning that LA is lower among learners who use such strategies (MacIntyre and Noels 1996). Pawlak (2011) discovered LA to be weakly negatively related to the same three strategy types, i.e., somewhat lower LA is linked to these strategies, though causality cannot be assumed. Mihaljević Djigunović (2001) found that LA correlates negatively with communication strategies but, paradoxically, is positively linked with socioaffective strategies. Kondo and Ying-Ling's (2004) research showed another paradox: affective strategies for anxiety reduction are not related to LA.

Research has pointed to possible relationships between SI on the one hand and (a) improved performance with respect to certain skills (e.g., Cohen 2014; Graham and Macaro 2008; Iwai 2006; Vandergrift and Tafaghodtari 2010) and (b) increased rapidity of language learning (Leaver 2003). These studies suggest that SI might improve language skill performance and might speed up language learning. Most of these studies allow the researchers to claim causality because of their quasi-experimental nature and statistical significance. Plonsky (2011) conducted a meta-analysis of sixty-one experimental or quasi-experimental studies of effects of SI for language learners. These designs allowed causality (effects of SI) to be assessed. A small to medium effect size ($d = 0.49$) arose, meaning that SI had a discernible but mild effect. Plonsky correctly lamented that SI studies do not adequately assess socioaffective strategies, so we have no meta-analysis concerning effects of SI on those strategies.

This chapter presents a study addressing this relatively neglected research area. The study investigated the interplay of strategy use and TA, as well as the effects of affective SI on strategy use of a group of intermediate learners of English. We chose to study TA instead of the more often researched LA because the anxiety reactions investigated occurred in a strictly evaluative situation involving a high-stakes EFL university exam.

3. Research questions

The present study aimed to address the following research questions (RQs):

RQ 1   Is there a relationship between strategy use (general and affective) and TA (both trait and state)? If so, is that relationship positive or negative?

RQ 2   Does affective SI relate to more frequent strategy use?

RQ 3   Are high-, medium- and low-TA learners equally responsive to affective SI in terms of strategy use?

4. Methodology

4.1. Sample

The sample included 41 year-2 English majors (six males, 39 females) studying at a small university in central Poland. Their mean age was 21.6, with most being between 20 and 22. They had experienced an average of 11.6 years of instruction in English. Their general self-assessed proficiency in English on a scale from 2 to 5 (following the Polish grading system) equaled 3.78, and their self-rating of the skill of speaking was 3.57.

Participation in the study was entirely voluntary; however, the participants received bonus points contributing to their grade in a university course for taking part. Participation did not influence EFL exam scores or course grades.

4.2. The exam

At the end of every academic year these students take a final EFL exam with a very important speaking component, which is an oral proficiency exam and has the form of a 10-minute interview with two or three examiners during which topics covered throughout the year are discussed. This exam is relatively high-stakes for this population, as failure may exclude promotion to the next year of university study or postpone graduation. Examiners use analytic scoring and focus on pronunciation, grammar, vocabulary, and communicative efficiency/fluency.

4.3. The treatment: Affective SI

Affective SI was used in the present study as the treatment condition and was delivered in Polish. It was based mostly on several activities included in Gregersen and MacIntyre (2014). It also involved a TED talk (online video) by Cuddy (2012), with the video's language being English but the discussion done in Polish. The instruction was emotion-focused and cognition-focused (Zeidner 1998) and included elements of behavioral and cognitive therapy/interventions called systematic desensitization, relaxation, and cognitive restructuring.

In the treatment we also taught meta-affective strategies (i.e., paying attention to, planning for, organizing and obtaining resources for, and monitoring and evaluating for affect; Oxford 2011) to a certain extent. However, it was done as a sideline (we simply encouraged participants to pay attention to, plan, etc. their affect) and only complemented the teaching of affective strategies proper. Henceforth, when we discuss affective SI, the term also covers a limited amount of meta-affective SI. This is legitimate given Oxford's (2017) protest against rigid strategy classifications and her claim that it is better to talk about the flexible roles that strategies play in particular circumstances and settings. Table 11.1 indicates the components of the affective SI.

Table 11.1 Three components of the treatment (affective SI)

COMPONENT 1

The *first major component* of instruction induced *systematic desensitization* (Wolpe 1958), or "unlearning" anxiety, aimed at reducing the intensity of anxious reactions to oral language tests. Each participant created six detailed and vivid descriptions of situations related to speaking tests and exams that trigger his/her anxiety, but not with the same force; they were supposed to be situations inducing anxiety of different levels of intensity, and the participants arranged them into hierarchies from the least to the most anxiety-provoking. During the treatment, systematic desensitization was intertwined with relaxation training. Therefore, the participants were trained in the use of autogenic relaxation, that is, relaxation of the mind and body induced by imagining peaceful environments, repetition of soothing words, and trying to slow down breathing and the heart rate; progressive muscle relaxation, that is, relaxation achieved by tensing subsequent muscle groups for several seconds and then relaxing them for about thirty seconds; and visualization accompanied by activation of other senses, that is, vividly imagining being in a peaceful setting and "switching on" other senses in order to imagine hearing, smelling, and touching various stimuli in this environment. After practicing relaxation in these ways, the participants were told that desensitization is achieved when one can realistically and vividly imagine one's stressors without experiencing anxiety. Therefore, they relaxed using a technique of their choice out of the three introduced earlier, and directly after this they read each of the vivid descriptions of anxiety triggers they had created, each at least twice, beginning with the least anxiety-inducing one. While reading, they imagined themselves experiencing a given situation, and after finishing they noted the level of anxiety they had experienced on a scale from 1 to 10; if on the second reading the imaginary level of anxiety was lower than on the first, they moved on to reading the next anxiety-inducing scene, and the whole procedure kept being repeated up until the greatest anxiety trigger was dealt with.

COMPONENT 2

The *second component* of affective SI focused not only on emotions but also on the cognitive dimension of this reaction. First, in groups of five or six, the participants brainstormed anxiety triggers related to oral language tests as well as ways of coping with anxiety provoked by such exams. The groups then shared their ideas with other groups to see that they were not alone in being prone to TA as well as to learn about new ways of coping. Another activity was performed in groups of ten students. Each participant first imagined that the other participants were members of the examination committee during an oral exam and that they, associating the examiners

(Continued)

Table 11.1 (Continued)

COMPONENT 2

with members of a stern institution such as the Inquisition, were experiencing great stress, anxiety, and tension. They were then asked to express these negative feelings by means of body language including facial expressions and body posture. While they were doing this, the instructors asked them to freeze as if they were statues and said: "We are now in the museum of speaking exam anxiety." The participants first looked at one another, and then only one student still maintained the anxious expression and posture while the others, "visitors in the museum of anxiety," jointly described the "statue of exam anxiety" and tried to establish how this kind of body language may influence examiners. Subsequently, the whole procedure was repeated, but this time the participants imagined that the examiners were the opposite of Inquisitors, that is, they were friendly and considerate teachers who were as interested as the test takers in assigning high scores and grades to their students, with the result that the participants were feeling relaxed and confident, also because of previous good preparation for the exam. Obviously, this time the "museum of anxiety" gave way to something like the "museum of examination calm and composition." All the activities so far described were always closed by debriefing in which the merits of the tactics were summarized and some possible ways of planning their use were considered.

COMPONENT 3

The *last component* of affective SI in relation to oral language tests consisted in watching and briefly discussing Cuddy's (2012) talk in which she presents some evidence for the influence of one's nonverbals on one's emotions, and, through this, on outcomes of evaluative situations. In brief, "acting out" power and confidence by open poses such as stretching out one's arms and raising one's chin for as little time as 2 minutes, for example in the restroom directly before an oral exam, may reduce anxiety and thus significantly improve the outcome of an evaluative situation such as an exam.

4.4. Instruments

Several instruments were used to collect data for the study. Except for the *SILL* (see below), the language of which was assumed not to pose a challenge to the participants, instruments were translated into or written in Polish to reduce cognitive load and possible misunderstanding. Similarly, all the answers were provided in Polish, which was hoped to generate more insightful comments not constrained by insufficient knowledge of English. See Table 11.2 for the instruments.

4.5. Data collection procedures

The schedule of data collection and of the final EFL exam is presented in Table 11.3. Seven weeks before the final EFL exam, at Time 1, the *SILL* and *RTT* were administered. As discussed in the results section, the *SILL* and the open-ended

Table 11.2 The instruments

Strategy Inventory for Language Learning (SILL, Oxford 1990)	The 5-point Likert scale *Strategy Inventory for Language Learning (SILL,* Oxford 1990) focuses on memory, cognitive, compensation, metacognitive, affective, and social strategies. The 50-item version that was used was slightly modified to refer to English rather than any foreign or second language. Internal consistency was highly satisfactory for the whole SILL (Cronbach's alphas = 0.91 and 0.93 for the first and second administration, respectively). However, the reliabilities of the parts of the *SILL* dealing with the strategy categories were occasionally less satisfactory. Therefore, in addition to all the strategies in total, we report our results only for affective strategies, which were especially important for this study (Cronbach's alphas = 0.44 and 0.67 for the first and second administration, respectively), and two more categories with the best reliabilities: cognitive (Cronbach's alphas = 0.78 and 0.79 for the first and second administration, respectively) and metacognitive (Cronbach's alphas = 0.86 and 0.85 for the first and second administration, respectively). In addition to the *SILL*'s affective strategies, participants were also asked (in Polish) to list other strategies they used to increase positive emotions and reduce stress or anxiety related to speaking English.
Survey of Exam-Related EFL Affective Strategies (SEREAS, Bielak and Mystkowska-Wiertelak 2015)	This strategy survey contains seven four-point Likert scale items concerning affective and meta-affective strategy use in relation to the final EFL exam, namely sometime before, immediately before, during, and immediately after it. Survey items were designed to capture the strategies/ tactics the participants were encouraged to use in the instructional intervention. The anchors were 1 (*not at all true of me*) and 4 (*very true of me*). Reliability was acceptable, with Cronbach's alpha = 0.68. In addition to the closed-ended items, there was one open-ended question requesting the listing of additional strategies employed before, during and after the EFL exam "in order to experience favorable emotions (low level of stress/ anxiety, self-confidence, self-efficacy, etc.)." (See English translation in Appendix C.)
Reactions to Tests (RTT, Sarason 1984)	This is a standard TA scale used in psychology, stated Zeidner (1989), which views TA as being composed of tension, worry, test-irrelevant thinking and bodily reactions. It is a 40-item four-point Likert scale with 10 items for each component; the anchors are 1 (*not at all typical of me*) and 4 (*very typical of me*). The original scale was slightly modified to focus on oral language tests rather than tests in general. Reliability in our study was highly satisfactory, with Cronbach's alpha = 0.95.

(Continued)

Table 11.2 (Continued)

Anxometers (MacIntyre and Gardner 1991)	The final measures were three *anxometers* ("anxiety thermometers"), i.e., 1-item visual analog instruments used for measuring state anxiety. They were used to record participants' self-ratings of anxiety experienced immediately before, during and immediately after the EFL exam. As the results indicated, the state anxiety thus recorded, experienced during the EFL exam, showed the same patterns of relationships with the use of LLSs as trait TA, and it is therefore referred to as state TA. Supporting this interpretation is the fact that the *anxometers* were completed by the participants immediately after the EFL exam and that the instruction asked them to indicate the levels of their anxiety in relation to the exam. However, it is impossible to be certain of the nature of this state anxiety, which may have been also partly contributed to by such other factors as LA (which is related to TA), anxiety about life circumstances, and so on. This is, however, true of any measure of state anxiety. (See English translation in Appendix D.)

Table 11.3 Data collection procedures

Time	Event
Time 1 (7 weeks before the final EFL exam)	*SILL* (first administration), *RTT*
6 weeks between Time 1 and Time 2	Affective SI
Time 2 (the day of the final EFL exam, 7 weeks after Time 1)	Final EFL exam (interview)
	Anxometers, SEREAS, SILL (second administration)
	Final EFL exam (announcement of grade and scores)

question appended to it revealed that the participants were not using affective strategies very often at the beginning of the study. The affective SI intervention was conducted during the six weeks between Time 1 and the day of the final EFL exam, Time 2. We administered SI during five university lectures, with all participants receiving SI at the same time in a lecture hall, and during one class, which was repeated three times, for the three groups into which the participants were divided for the purposes of university classes. The possibility cannot be excluded (though it is unlikely) that the participants got acquainted with or were exposed to some form of SI during other classes they were attending between Times 1 and 2.

Following the 6-week treatment the participants took the final EFL exam, for which they entered the examination room one by one. After being interviewed for several minutes by three examiners, they left the examination room to give the examiners some time for discussing their performance and calculating the final score and grade. During this time, they filled in the instruments included in Appendices C and D, that is the *anxometers*, *SEREAS* and *SILL* (for the second time). The list in the previous sentence follows the recommended order of filling in the tools; the *anxometers* were the first to be completed to prevent the memory of the levels of anxiety experienced immediately before, during, and just after the exam from fading away. Subsequently, every participant entered the examination room again, submitted the questionnaire form, and was informed about his or her scores and grade and given customary after-exam feedback.

4.6. Data analysis procedures

The quantitative data were first converted into descriptive statistics to reveal general trends. Subsequently, to answer RQ 1, Pearson correlations were used to determine the possible relations between the variables of TA and strategy use. Inferential statistics were also used in the form of dependent-samples *t*-tests and one-way and repeated measures analyses of variance (RM ANOVAs).

- To answer RQ 2, *t*-tests were used to determine the significance of the increase in the frequency of using LLSs following the instructional intervention.
- To deal with RQ 3, one-way ANOVAs were used to ascertain whether the differences in strategy use between high-, medium-, and low-anxiety participants were significant.
- To answer RQ 3, RM ANOVAs indicated whether the group differences in strategy use were significant at any given time and across times (pre/post SI).

The three subgroups of participants were created by dividing all participants into tertiles depending on the level of their trait TA on the *RTT*. This was done to answer RQ 3 concerning the possibly differential effect of affective SI on strategy use among individuals of inherently different levels of TA. We are aware that sometimes the use of parametric statistics is proscribed for Likert-scale instruments; however, this view is not universal, as revealed by Mizumoto and

Takeuchi's arguments for greater flexibility using parametric statistics with Likert-scale instruments (Chapter 5 in this volume).

We have calculated effect sizes for most of our *t*-tests and RM ANOVAs. Statistical significance testing alone reveals much about the power of a statistical test and depends to a large extent on sample size. To reveal truly meaningful results, it should be complemented by the calculation of effect sizes, which do not depend on group sizes and which show the strength of the relationship between variables (Larson-Hall 2010). We have decided to report the effect size measures that belong to the *r family* (Rosenthal 1994) because they show how much the independent and dependent variables co-vary. This in turn allows one to see what percentage of the variance of the dependent variable is explained by the independent variable (the *r* family effect size values are never higher than 1.00). For this purpose, the squared effect size measures must be used. We therefore report r^2 for the *t*-test and η^2 for RM ANOVA, the *r* family effect size measures that are conventionally reported for these tests (cf., Larson-Hall 2010). We have used the tentative guidelines for effect size interpretation offered by Cohen (1988): For r^2 as the effect size indicator for a dependent (correlated) design, i.e., a pre-post one-group design, small effect size equates with 0.01, medium with 0.09, and large with 0.25; for η^2 calculated for RM ANOVA, which showed differences for groups and times, small effect size is 0.01, medium is 0.06, and large is 0.14. Effect size interpretations will usually be at least a little different for different indicators.

In addition to these quantitative analyses, qualitative data were content analyzed in search of affective and meta-affective strategies used by the participants.

5. Results

5.1. Time 1: Trait TA

The trait TA level measured by the *RTT* ($n = 41$, $M = 2.37$) was very similar to the levels obtained in an earlier study (Mystkowska-Wiertelak, Bielak, and Pawlak 2013). This means that the students were generally characterized by a moderate and expected level of trait TA.

5.2. Time 1: Correlations between trait anxiety and strategy use

The correlations between *RTT*-measured trait TA and *SILL*-measured LLS use at Time 1 are shown in Table 11.4. All the correlations were positive, which suggests,

Table 11.4 Correlations (Pearson) between trait TA (*RTT*) and strategy use (*SILL*) at Time 1

	Strategy use measured by the SILL			
	All strategies	Cognitive	Metacognitive	Affective
Trait TA (measured by the *RTT*)	0.29	0.07	0.28	0.39*

Note: * $p < 0.05$

at first glance, that experiencing TA was associated with more frequent use of LLSs. However, looking more closely, we find that the correlation between trait TA and cognitive strategy use was nearly zero, two other trait-TA-and-strategy-use correlations were less than $r = 0.30$, and the only significant correlation occurred for trait TA and affective strategy use ($r = 0.39$), at a moderate strength.

5.3. Time 2: Correlations between state anxiety and strategy use

A very similar pattern emerged for possible links between state TA, measured by the *anxometers* and *SILL*-gauged LLSs used at Time 2. Again, all correlations, shown in Table 11.5, were positive, but only the one between state TA and affective strategies ($r = 0.33$) was significant, albeit of moderate strength. What makes these state TA results different from the trait TA ones is the fact that the use of affective strategies, together with meta-affective ones, is reported here twice. The reason is that at Time 2 the use of these strategies was measured not only by the *SILL* but also by the *SEREAS,* the 7-item survey measuring affective and meta-affective strategy use. Contrary to the significant relation between

Table 11.5 Correlations (Pearson) between state TA (*anxometers*) and strategy use (two surveys) at Time 2

	Strategy use measured by the SILL				Strategy use measured by the SEREAS
	All strategies	Cognitive	Meta-cognitive	Affective	Affective and meta-affective
State TA regarding the oral exam (measured by the *anxometers*)	0.18	0.06	0.09	0.33*	0.12

Note: * $p < 0.05$

state TA (*anxometers*) and the *SILL*-measured affective strategies at Time 2, there was no significant tie between state TA (*anxometers*) and affective/meta-affective strategy use (*SEREAS*). The latter correlation was almost negligible.

5.4. Quantitative effects of affective SI on strategy use

As mentioned, the frequency of the use of all strategies increased from before to after the instructional intervention. As clearly demonstrated by the results of dependent-samples *t*-tests shown in Table 11.6, these increases were mostly statistically significant. The effect sizes for the significant differences were either large ($r^2 = 0.30$ for all strategies) or medium ($r^2 = 0.12$ for cognitive and metacognitive, $r^2 = 0.22$ for affective strategies). Explanation of the effect size calculation is offered in section 4.6.

To discover how high-, mid-, and low-anxiety participants reacted to affective SI, the whole sample was divided into tertiles by their *RTT*-measured levels of trait TA. Descriptive statistics for strategy use before and after the intervention for low-TA, medium-TA, and high-TA participants are presented in Table 11.7. They reveal that all groups considerably increased the frequency of using all the strategies together and, except for one case, almost all strategy types, from Time 1 to Time 2.

Considering all strategies in total, the improvement in strategy use was comparable for the three groups, as graphically demonstrated by the nearly parallel plot lines representing the mean frequencies of strategy use in Figure 11.1.

The sizable improvements in the use of all strategies in total and almost all strategy types ranged for the three groups between going up by 0.13 (cognitive

Table 11.6 Descriptive statistics and dependent-samples *t*-tests for strategy use by the whole sample ($n = 41$) at Times 1 and 2

Strategy type	Time 1 M (s.d.)	Time 2 M (s.d.)	t	r^2 effect size and interpretation
All types	3.20 (0.49)	3.42 (0.53)	4.150***	0.30 – large
Cognitive	3.35 (0.57)	3.53 (0.54)	2.427*	0.12 – medium
Metacognitive	3.43 (0.72)	3.62 (0.69)	2.423*	0.12 – medium
Affective	2.70 (0.54)	2.98 (0.71)	3.373**	0.22 – medium

Note: * $p < 0.05$, ** $p < 0.01$, *** $p < 0.001$

Cohen's (1988) tentative guidelines were used for the interpretation of effect sizes using r^2: small effect = 0.01, medium effect = 0.09, large effect = 0.25

Table 11.7 Descriptive statistics for strategy use by low-TA ($n = 14$), medium-TA ($n = 13$), and high-TA ($n = 14$) participants at Times 1 and 2

Strategy type	Low anxiety ($n = 14$)		Medium anxiety ($n = 13$)		High anxiety ($n = 14$)	
	Time 1 M (s.d.)	Time 2 M (s.d.)	Time 1 M (s.d.)	Time 2 M (s.d.)	Time 1 M (s.d.)	Time 2 M (s.d.)
All types	3.15 (0.65)	3.31 (0.61)	3.11 (0.44)	3.37 (0.52)	3.32 (0.33)	3.57 (0.44)
Cognitive	3.42 (0.78)	3.56 (0.67)	3.18 (0.49)	3.43 (0.50)	3.44 (0.55)	3.57 (0.46)
Metacognitive	3.35 (0.86)	3.54 (0.78)	3.31 (0.73)	3.45 (0.72)	3.61 (0.58)	3.86 (0.54)
Affective	2.55 (0.65)	2.55 (0.79)	2.61 (0.42)	3.20 (0.69)	2.92 (0.49)	3.21 (0.44)

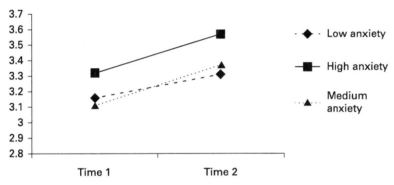

Figure 11.1 The use of *all strategies* before and after the intervention by high-TA, medium-TA, and low-TA participants

strategies, high-TA group) and by 0.69 (affective strategies, medium-TA group). This is graphically illustrated in Figure 11.2, which features the plots representing the means for the use of different types of strategies by the high-TA (top) and low-TA (bottom) groups at Times 1 and 2. The medium-TA group is not included here because of our interest in the extremes. Figure 11.2 shows that the use of most strategies increased for these two groups (this is also true of the medium-TA group), but it also shows that, in contrast to others, the frequency of affective strategies did not increase in the low-TA group.

The similarity of the improvements in the use of most strategy types for the three groups is demonstrated by the graphs in Figure 11.3, in which the plot lines representing the use of cognitive (top) and metacognitive strategies (middle) for the three groups move up in a nearly parallel fashion. However, the data for affective strategies (bottom) is very different. The frequency of their use, similarly to other strategy types, increased in almost the same way for both the high-TA

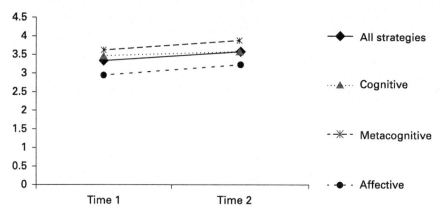

Different types of strategies before and after the intervention by high-TA participants

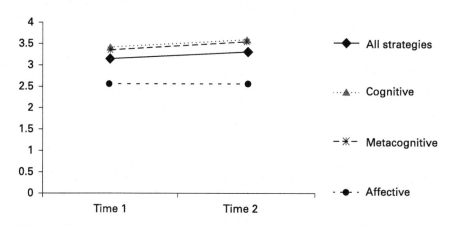

Different types of strategies before and after the intervention by low-TA participants

Figure 11.2 The use of *different strategies* before and after the intervention by high-TA and low-TA participants

and medium-TA groups, but not for the low-TA group, whose plot line, in contrast to the others, is flat.

To determine the important differences between groups in the use of all the strategies and strategy types, a series of one-way and RM ANOVAs was run. First, several one-way ANOVAs revealed no significant differences between the groups (high-, medium-, and low-TA) before the intervention with respect to all strategies together and separate strategy types. Second, for all strategies together and almost all strategy types, except for affective strategies, RM ANOVAs

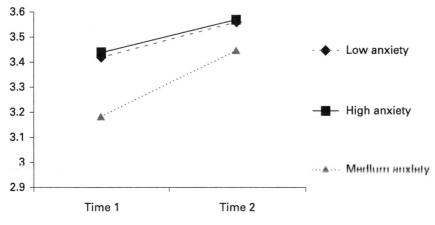

Cognitive strategies before and after the intervention

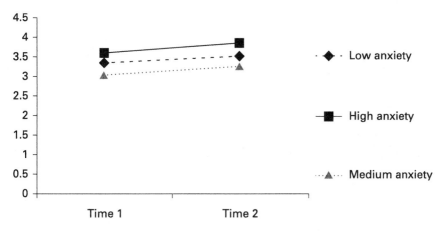

Metacognitive strategies before and after the intervention

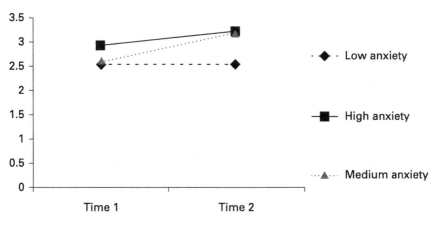

Affective strategies before and after the intervention

Figure 11.3 The use of *cognitive, metacognitive,* and *affective strategies* before and after the intervention by high-TA, medium-TA, and low-TA participants

yielded no significant effects for either (a) Group or (b) the interaction between Time and Group. However, these RM ANOVAs yielded significant effects for Time. As mentioned earlier, in contrast to other strategy types, the three groups used affective strategies differently. Regarding affective strategies, a RM ANOVA found significant effects for both (a) Time and (b) the interaction of Time and Group, with no significant effects for Group, as shown in Table 11.8. Note that effect sizes for these results were large (Time, $\eta^2 = 0.27$; Time $\times$ Group, $\eta^2 = 0.20$).

The different pattern of the use of affective strategies was demonstrated by further inferential statistics. In particular, out of several one-way ANOVAs applied to strategies in total and strategy types used at Time 2, only the one for affective strategies, the results of which are presented in Table 11.9, showed significant differences among the three groups ($F(2) = 4.50, p < 0.05, \eta^2 = 0.19$),

Table 11.8 RM ANOVA of the means for affective strategies across the three groups and at Times 1 and 2

Source	df	F	η² effect size and interpretation
Between subjects			
Group (Low TA, medium TA, high TA)	2	3.21	0.14 – large
Error	47		
Within subjects			
Time	1	14.20**	0.27 – large
Time x Group	2	4.77*	0.20 – large
Error	38		

Note: * $p < 0.05$, ** $p < 0.01$

Cohen's (1988) tentative guidelines were used for the interpretation of effect sizes using η^2: small effect = 0.01, medium effect = 0.06, large effect = 0.14

Table 11.9 One-way ANOVAs of the strategy use means of low-TA, medium-TA, and high-TA groups at Time 2

Strategy type	df	F	η² effect size and interpretation
All types	2	0.90	0.04 – small
Cognitive	2	0.20	0.01 – small
Metacognitive	2	1.34	0.06 – medium
Affective	2	4.50*	0.19 – large

Note: * $p < 0.05$

Cohen's (1988) tentative guidelines were used for the interpretation of effect sizes using η^2: small effect = 0.01, medium effect = 0.06, large effect = 0.14

Table 11.10 RM ANOVA of the affective strategies means for the three groups separately across Time 1 and Time 2

Group	df	F	η^2 effect size and interpretation
Low-TA	1	<0.001	<0.01 – small
Medium-TA	1	27.46***	0.69 – (very) large
High-TA	1	3.24[†]	0.20 – large

Note: *** $p < 0.001$, [†]$p = 0.09$.

Cohen's (1988) tentative guidelines were used for the interpretation of effect sizes using η^2: small effect = 0.01, medium effect = 0.06, large effect = 0.14.

with the post-hoc Tukey HSD test yielding the following significant differences: the low-TA group used affective strategies statistically significantly less often than both the high-TA and medium-TA groups. The effect size for these differences was large, with the trait of TA explaining 19% of the variance in the frequency scores.

Furthermore, as can be seen in Table 11.10, RM ANOVAs for the three groups yielded significant effects for Time for the medium-TA group only ($F(2) = 27.46, p < 0.001, \eta^2 = 0.69$), with a very large effect size. Although the result was not statistically significant for the high-TA group ($F(2) = 3.24, p = 0.09, \eta^2 = 0.20$; the p value approaches significance, though), what catches the eye is the large effect size for what seems to have been a desirable increase in the use of affective strategies by relatively highly anxious learners, with membership in this group explaining 20% of the variability in the *SILL* scores.

5.5. Qualitative effects of affective SI on strategy use (RQ 3)

Regarding qualitative results from Times 1 and 2 from the open-ended question attached to the *SILL*, respondents primarily listed selected strategies included in the *SILL*, especially relaxation and encouraging oneself to use English. In addition, some participants enumerated practice and preparation as antidotes to anxiety and triggers of positivity. If preparation with the intention of reducing anxiety is considered as strategic behavior of the affective sort,[1] then only one more strategy of this type was used by the participants in addition to the ones included in the *SILL*. This supports the view that the correlational analysis, which relied on the *SILL* means, did not exclude any significant aspects of the participants' strategic behavior in the affective domain.

Analysis of qualitative data from the open-ended item in the *SEREAS*, the measure of affective and meta-affective strategy use, showed some differences among the high-, medium-, and low-anxiety groups in terms of strategies reported as being used vis-à-vis the EFL exam. While only one member of the low-anxiety group used one of the specific strategic moves introduced and practiced in the treatment, namely autogenic relaxation, among the members of the medium- and high-anxiety groups there were altogether five participants using the instructed strategies, with two participants using not one but two of them. In particular, high- and medium-anxiety participants reported using autogenic relaxation, visualization, and progressive muscle relaxation.

6. Discussion

The answer to RQ 1 (Is there a relationship between strategy use (general and affective) and TA (both trait and state)? If so, is that relationship positive or negative?) resists a simple *yes/no* dichotomy. It will be a *no* with respect to general strategy use (all strategies) and the use of some strategy types as revealed by the *SILL* on the one hand and trait and state TA on the other. However, it seems that the more anxious one is, the more often affective strategies included in the *SILL* may be used. Nonetheless, a similar tendency was not captured with respect to the affective and meta-affective strategies included in the *SEREAS*, i.e., those used specifically in relation to the EFL exam. This fact may be due to insufficient refinement of the new tool. These findings further complicate the contradictory picture of the relations between anxiety and LLSs that emerges from the literature, but their unique value lies in the fact that both trait and state anxiety correlated with affective strategies. Worth mentioning is also the fact that all the strategy-anxiety relations were positive. Also, it seems that the link between the use of affective strategies and TA makes intuitive sense: being highly anxious may naturally spur one to rely on affective strategies to reduce anxiety's debilitative effect.

RQ 2 (Does affective SI relate to more frequent strategy use?) is not easy to answer given the present results and the design of this study (the lack of a control/comparison group). To some extent, they confirm the hypothesis that affective SI can be related to and perhaps even result in more frequent use of affective strategies, for which there was the greatest effect size. However, the design of the study prevents us from firmly claiming the causal relationship between SI and affective strategy use (that is why we hope to use a quasi-experimental design in the future, as described later in this chapter). The picture is complicated by the fact that, somehow, other strategy types were also used more frequently after the intervention, which did not target them at all. This constitutes a truly surprising finding. While it cannot be excluded that these effects were brought about by other factors, for example, some knowledge of strategy use gained in other university courses, it is also possible that SI targeting only one type of strategy may, in fact, trigger other sorts of strategic thinking and behaviour that may seep into new areas of language learning. Indirect evidence for this possibility comes from Kövecses and Szabó (1996), who, after encouraging language learners to consider some conceptual metaphors that motivate the meanings of several English phrasal verbs as an aid to memory, discovered that this "metaphorical thinking" mode transferred onto other phrasal verbs that were not subject to instruction. While we are fully aware of the considerable differences between strategy and conceptual metaphor instruction, it seems feasible that priming learners with SI targeting one type of strategy may result in the activation of other strategy types. This is also supported by the fact that strategies may serve multiple, sometimes unforeseen functions (Oxford 2017). For example, as we mentioned earlier, cognitive and metacognitive strategies are sometimes used for regulating emotions. However, we must acknowledge that another possible trigger of the greater self-declared frequency of strategy use at Time 2 may have been the fact that the participants were completing the *SILL* immediately after a difficult and stressful exam. This might have somehow resulted in their professing greater than real strategy use, which may have been a (subconscious) "promise" to themselves (and also the examiners) that more language learning effort will be undertaken in the future. In other words, at least some participants may have provided answers that they believed were desired by the researchers.

RQ 3 (Are high-, medium- and low-TA learners equally responsive to affective SI in terms of strategy use?) may be answered with a straightforward *no* given the results of this study. Both the quantitative and qualitative analyses suggest that high- and medium-anxiety learners are more likely than low-anxiety ones to increase the use of affective strategies in response to affective SI. The qualitative evidence is rather indirect as the use of the affective strategies introduced in the treatment among high- and medium-anxiety participants to the exclusion of low-anxiety ones was only observed at one point in time, but it is not without significance in the light of the much stronger evidence of the quantitative sort. These findings may obviously be related to the highly probable fact that low-anxiety learners simply do not need to rely on affective strategies (at least the ones targeted at anxiety reduction) given that they do not suffer from the negative consequences of anxiety. Obviously, this selective impact of SI is highly desirable as we do not want to see learners "wasting" their resources doing things that they do not recognize as beneficial. For example, it is great when an anxious learner uses progressive muscle relaxation in the restroom just before a stressful oral exam, but it is equally fortunate when a low-anxiety learner chooses to have one more look at a vocabulary list instead. The results also suggest, quite aside from the issue of whether the treatment was effective or not, that high- and medium-anxiety learners can definitely introduce affective strategies into their strategic repertoires. In other words, the finding that affective strategies are learnable receives additional support from this study. This is good news to the learners who need anxiety reduction and promotion of positive emotions.

7. Conclusions, limitations, and directions

The present research suggests that there may well be some significant links between anxiety and LLSs that should be further investigated. The positive, significant links between the use of affective strategies and anxiety may point to the possible awareness on the part of the learners in our sample, which consisted of English majors, of the need to tackle this negative emotion and the feasibility of doing so. This would speak well of their general strategic awareness hopefully fostered to a certain extent by at least some educational institutions they have attended. Despite the general lack of dedicated learning strategy programs, let alone individualized ones, in Polish schools and universities, courses offered to language majors do pay some attention to the strategic art of learning languages. It seems that in the general exam-centered climate of the Polish educational system there should be some awareness of the benefits of and some demand for counseling, which may take the form of affective SI.

The study also suggests that affective SI may bring about more frequent use of these strategies, especially among medium- and high-anxiety learners. This resonates with MacIntyre and Noels' (1996, 374) remark "that individualized strategy training programs might be more effective than those aimed at a general audience." It remains to be seen, however, whether this may be accepted and implemented in the Polish educational context where budgets are still too tight to customize teaching to small groups or individuals.

We will close by explaining the lessons learned from this study for conducting further research into the links between LLSs and affective factors, and affective SI in general, which will also expose the limitations of the present research.

Studies of the sort we have conducted should be extended in time to apply the quasi-experimental design, in a strengthened form including a control group, not only to identify strategy use tapped by general strategy surveys such as the *SILL* but also to indicate state anxiety and strategy use during specific anxiety-inducing situations such as the EFL exam taken by our participants. This means establishing at least two points of data collection separated by a whole year (the EFL exam is administered at the end of every academic year). Such designs would allow one to investigate not only the question of whether affective SI boosts strategy use but also whether it reduces anxiety and promotes positive emotions. Stretching the study considerably in this way would require more extensive affective SI used as the treatment condition, which may also find reflection in more pronounced effects on strategy use, and, possibly, anxiety.

Also, in addition to *RTT*, the application of the more often used *Foreign Language Classroom Anxiety Scale* (*FLCAS*, Horwitz, Horwitz, and Cope 1986) should be considered for greater comparability with other studies of LLSs and anxiety. Next, more qualitative data concerning not only strategy use but also state anxiety obtained within the quasi-experimental design may be needed to complement the quantitative data garnered from *anxometers*, which appear to be relatively crude instruments. Furthermore, as already suggested, the *SILL* should be administered at some time other than immediately after an anxiety-inducing event such as the EFL exam to protect the scores against the possible influence. Finally, there seems to be a need for developing and using affective strategy instruments such as the *Managing Your Emotions for Language Learning* survey (Gkonou and Oxford 2016), which would let the field improve on the now dated part of the *SILL* dealing with affective self-regulation and move into the relatively uncharted territory of positive affect.

Note

1   See Oxford (2017, Chapter 4) for flexibility in purposes and usage of a given strategy.

References

Bielak, Jakub, and Anna Mystkowska-Wiertelak. 2015. "Investigating English Majors' Affective and Meta-affective Strategy Use and Test Anxiety." Paper presented at the

Conference on Situating Stratelgy Use, Alpen-Adria-Universität, Klagenfurt, Austria, October 2015.

Cohen, Andrew D. 2014. *Strategies in Learning and Using a Second Language.* 2nd edition. Abingdon: Routledge.

Cohen, Andrew D., and Susan J. Weaver. 2006. *Styles and Strategies-based Instruction: A Teachers' Guide.* Minneapolis, MN: Center for Advanced Research on Language Acquisition, University of Minnesota.

Cohen, Andrew D., Rebecca L. Oxford, and Julie C. Chi. 2002. *Language Strategy Use Survey.* Minneapolis, MN: Center for Advanced Research on Language Acquisition, University of Minnesota.

Cohen, Jacob. 1988. *Statistical Power Analysis for the Behavioral Sciences.* 2nd edition. Hillsdale, NJ: Lawrence Erlbaum.

Cuddy, Amy. *Your Body Language Shapes Who You Are:* TEDtalks, 2012. Video file. http://www.ted.com/talks/amy_cuddy_your_body_language_shapes_who_you_are. Accessed 23 January 2014.

Dewaele, Jean-Marc. 2007. "The Effect of Multilingualism, Sociobiographical, and Situational Factors on Communicative Anxiety and Foreign Language Anxiety of Mature Language Learners." *International Journal of Bilingualism* 11: 391–409.

Dörnyei, Zoltán, and Peter Skehan. 2003. "Individual Differences in Second Language Learning." In *The Handbook of Second Language Acquisition*, edited by Catherine J. Doughty and Michael H. Long, 589–630. Oxford: Blackwell.

Gardner, Robert C., and Peter D. MacIntyre. 1993. "A Student's Contributions to Second Language Learning: Part II. Affective Variables." *Language Teaching* 26: 1–11.

Gkonou, Christina, and Rebecca L. Oxford. 2016. "Managing Your Emotions (MYE) for Language Learning Questionnaire." Version 4.1. In *Teaching and Researching Language Learning Strategies,* Rebecca L. Oxford 2017, 317–33. New York: Routledge.

Graham, Suzanne, and Ernesto Macaro. 2008. "Strategy Instruction in Listening for Low-intermediate Learners of French." *Language Learning* 58: 747–83.

Gregersen, Tammy, and Peter D. MacIntyre. 2014. *Capitalizing on Language Learners' Individuality: From Premise to Practice.* Clevedon: Multilingual Matters.

Grenfell, Michael, and Vee Harris. 1999. *Modern Languages and Learning Strategies: In Theory and Practice.* London: Routledge.

Horwitz, Elaine K. 2010. "Foreign and Second Language Anxiety." *Language Teaching* 43 (2): 154–67. doi:10.1017/S026144480999036X.

Horwitz, Elaine K., Michael B. Horwitz, and Joann Cope. 1986. "Foreign Language Classroom Anxiety." *Modern Language Journal* 70: 125–32.

Iwai, Chiaki. 2006. *Linguistic and Pedagogical Values of Teaching Communication Strategies: Integrating the Notion of Communication Strategies with Studies of Second Language Acquisition.* Hiroshima, Japan: Hiroshima City University.

Kondo, David Shinji, and Yang Ying-Ling. 2004. "Strategies for Coping with Language Anxiety: The Case of Students of English in Japan." *ELT Journal* 58: 258–65.

Kövecses, Zoltán, and Peter Szabó. 1996. "Idioms: A View from Cognitive Semantics." *Applied Linguistics* 17: 326–55.

Larson-Hall, Jenifer. 2010. *A Guide to Doing Statistics in Second Language Research Using SPSS.* New York: Routledge.

Leaver, Betty Lou. 2003. *Achieving Native-like Second Language Proficiency: A Catalogue of Critical Factors* Volume 1: Speaking. Salinas, CA: MSI Press.

MacIntyre, Peter D., and Robert C. Gardner. 1991. "Language Anxiety: Its Relationship to Other Anxieties and to the Processing in Native and Second Languages." *Language Learning* 41: 513–34.

——. 1994. "The Subtle Effects of Language Anxiety on Cognitive Processing in the Second Language." *Language Learning* 44: 283–305.

MacIntyre, Peter D., and Kimberly A. Noels. 1996. "Using Social-psychological Variables to Predict the Use of Language Learning Strategies." *Foreign Language Annals* 29: 373–86.

Mihaljević Djigunović, Jelena. 2001. "Beyond Language Learning Strategies: A Look at the Affective Link." *Studia Romanica et Anglica Zagrabiensia (SRAZ)* XLV–XLVI: 11–23.

Mystkowska-Wiertelak, Anna, Jakub Bielak, and Mirosław Pawlak. 2013. "Oral Language Tests and Test Anxiety." Paper presented at the 15th Summer School in Psycholinguistics, Balatonalmádi, Hungary, May 2013.

O'Malley, J. Michael, and Anna Uhl Chamot. 1990. *Learning Strategies in Second Language Acquisition.* Cambridge: Cambridge University Press.

Oxford, Rebecca L. 1990. *Language Learning Strategies: What Every Teacher Should Know.* Boston: Heinle & Heinle.

——. 2011. *Teaching and Researching Language Learning Strategies.* Harlow: Longman.

——. 2017. *Teaching and Researching Language Learning Strategies: Self-regulation in Context.* 2nd edition. New York: Routledge.

Pawlak, Mirosław. 2010. "Designing and Piloting a Tool for the Measurement of the Use of Pronunciation Learning Strategies." *Research in Language* 8: 189–202.

——. 2011. "Anxiety as a Factor Influencing the Use of Language Learning Strategies." In *Extending the Boundaries of Research on Second Language Learning and Teaching,* edited by Mirosław Pawlak, 149–65. Heidelberg: Springer.

Plonsky, Luke. 2011. "The Effectiveness of Second Language Strategy Instruction: A Meta-analysis." *Language Learning* 61: 993–1038.

Rosenthal, Robert. 1994. "Parametric Measures of Effect Size." In *The Handbook of Research Synthesis,* edited by Harris Cooper and Larry V. Hedges, 231–244. New York: Russell Sage Foundation.

Rubin, Joan. 1975. "What the 'Good Language Learner' Can Teach Us." *TESOL Quarterly* 9: 41–51.

Sarason, Irwin G. 1984. "Stress, Anxiety, and Cognitive Interference: Reactions to Tests." *Journal of Personality and Social Psychology* 46: 929–38.

Schmitt, Norbert. 1997. "Vocabulary Learning Strategies." In *Vocabulary: Description, Acquisition and Pedagogy,* edited by Norbert Schmitt and Michael McCarthy, 199–227. Cambridge: Cambridge University Press.

Sheorey, Ravi, and Kouider Mokhtari. 2001. "Differences in the Metacognitive Awareness of Reading Strategies Among Native and Non-Native Readers." *System* 29: 431–49.

Spielberger, Charles D., and Peter R. Vagg. 1995. "Test Anxiety: A Transactional Process." In *Test Anxiety: Theory, Assessment, and Treatment*, edited by Charles D. Spielberger and Peter R. Vagg, 3–14. Washington, DC: Taylor & Francis.

Spielberger, Charles D., William D. Anton, and Jeffrey Bedell. 1976. "The Nature and Treatment of Test Anxiety." In *Emotions and Anxiety: New Concepts, Methods, and Applications*, edited by Marvin Zuckermann and Charles D. Spielberger, 317–44. Hillsdale, NJ: Erlbaum.

Stern, Hans H. 1975. "What Can We Learn from the Good Language Learner?" *Canadian Modern Language Review* 31: 304–18.

Takač, Višnia P. 2008. *Vocabulary Learning Strategies and Foreign Language Acquisition.* Clevedon: Multilingual Matters.

Takeuchi, Osamu, Carol Griffiths, and Do Coyle. 2007. "Applying Strategies to Contexts: The Role of Individual, Situational, and Group Differences." In *Language Learner Strategies*, edited by Andrew D. Cohen and Ernesto Macaro, 69–92. Oxford: Oxford University Press.

Tseng, Wen-Ta, Zoltán Dörnyei, and Norbert Schmitt. 2006. "A New Approach to Assessing Strategic Learning: The Case of Self-Regulation in Vocabulary Acquisition." *Applied Linguistics* 27: 78–102.

Vandergrift, Larry, and Marzieh H. Tafaghodtari. 2010. "Teaching L2 Learners how to Listen Does Make a Difference: An Empirical Study." *Language Learning* 60: 470–97.

Wolpe, Joseph. 1958. *Psychotherapy by Reciprocal Inhibition.* Stanford, CA: Stanford University Press.

Woodrow, Lindy. 2006. "Anxiety and Speaking English as a Second Language." *RELC Journal* 37: 308–28.

Zeidner, Moshe. 1998. *Test Anxiety: The State of the Art.* New York: Kluwer.

12

Young Language Learners
in Classroom Contexts

The Development of Strategy Assessment Methods and Tools

Pamela Gunning
Concordia University, Canada

Carolyn E. Turner
McGill University, Canada

"It is not a straight-forward matter to get inside the 'black box' of the human brain and see what is going on."

Grenfell and Harris 1999, 36–37

1. Introduction

In a post-task reflection on students' strategy use, in a sixth grade classroom in Québec, Canada, 12-year-old Laurent reported how he uses predicting: "I predict while I read. Sometimes my predictions are right but sometimes they are wrong and I get little surprises along the way. This maintains my interest so I keep on reading to the end" (Gunning, White, and Busque 2017). Laurent's account of how predicting helps him reveals the personal nature of strategy use and the difficulty of assessing strategies in the traditional sense of assessment for scores. As Laurent's account reveals, a problematic issue with assessing strategies is that some involve unobservable mental processes. Predicting would be observable if students wrote down their predictions or color-coded a text, showing when they were predicting (Lee and Oxford 2008; see Oxford 2017 for a discussion of observable manifestations of mental processes). In Laurent's case, however, predicting would not be observable. How could one get inside of his brain and see first of all that he is using the predicting strategy, and more importantly, how he is using it in that situation? Laurent's report is indicative of the idiosyncratic nature of autonomous strategy use and how this can vary depending on the individual, task, and context.

In pedagogical contexts in which students share strategies during post-task reflections, young language learners (YLLs) provide classmates with unique perspectives regarding their strategy use, thereby making strategies context-specific and accessible to this age group (Gunning 2011; Gunning and Oxford 2014). Teachers need to capitalize on such opportunities for facilitating learning and formative assessment. Teachers would also be wise to heed the advice by Purpura (2013), who underscores the premise that the discovery of personal strategies does not always emanate from learning failures. These can also be revealed through successful learning or performance, so teachers should systematically have learners report on their strategy use. By providing YLLs with multiple practice opportunities and repeated post task reflection in which they share their strategies with concrete examples, and receive feedback, teachers can help them deepen their understanding of effective strategy use and regulate their own learning. Purpura (2013, 543) posits that "strategy sharing can be a powerful means of strategy awareness building." In addition, researchers can document this process in order to provide a contextualized framework for classroom-based strategy assessment (SA) that is oriented towards learning, in which students learn from one another through an authentic socio-cultural approach (see examples in Gunning 2011).

Assessment of strategy use has, to date, involved mainly adults and adolescents and has largely documented strategy use not linked to strategy instruction (SI). A smaller body of literature examines the effects of SI on learning, also mostly geared towards adults and adolescents (Chamot 2005; Nakatani 2005; Naughton 2006).

A few studies have focused on SI with YLLs (Gu 2007; Macaro and Mutton 2009) but there is generally a scarcity of research on SA linked to strategy instruction among YLLs in foreign and second language (L2) classroom contexts. Considering the number of children in elementary schools where the curriculum mandates SI with the intent of supporting learning, attention to assessment of YLLs' L2 strategy use in this context would be essential in helping to gauge learning. In this chapter we examine issues relevant to the context and purpose of SA in classroom settings involving SI. We provide a brief overview of the evolution of SA, and developments in the field of classroom-based assessment (CBA), in order to position our approach to classroom-based SA in its historical context. We start by situating SA along with CBA in the literature. The remainder of the chapter provides and discusses examples from classroom-based SA research with YLLs, as well as from textbook material. We have developed SA methods and tools geared towards YLLs for use in the classroom by teachers and researchers. We present some of these resources from our research and from classroom practice. These are categorized as tools: a) for teachers; b) for researchers; c) for both. We conclude with a summary of our approach to SA and reiterate SA principles that support learning.

2. Definition: What are strategies?

Purpura (2014, 533) posits that "... a *strategy* refers to a thought or behavior used by learners to regulate SFL [second or foreign language] learning or use" and that strategies "may be engaged consciously and deliberatively or unconsciously and automatically to further learners' processing while learning or while performing SFL language tasks." Oxford (2011, 12), on the other hand, states that self-regulated language learning strategies are "deliberate, goal-oriented attempts to manage and control efforts to learn the L2." Cohen (2007, 33) reports, from a survey of scholars, "some disagreement regarding the level of consciousness necessary for a process to be considered a strategy." Cohen (2011, 7) affirms, however, that strategies are "[t]houghts or actions consciously chosen by language learners to assist them in carrying out a multiplicity of tasks ...," and he adds that strategies are also "... moves which the learner is at least partially aware of, even if not being fully attentive to them." We concur with Cohen and add that learners draw upon their strategies, depending on the context and their needs, in order to solve problems and regulate their learning, so the element of strategy choice is essential.

3. Purpose and context of the assessment

The SA method will depend on the purpose and context of the assessment. There are different purposes, such as researchers assessing a phenomenon (e.g., strategies) or teachers making pedagogical decisions in the classroom. In a classroom context linked to SI, the purpose of SA is to support learning and gauge next steps. In this context, feedback is crucial in fostering self-regulation.

Both authors of this chapter have experience as elementary school teachers as a Second Language (ESL). This is particularly the case with Gunning who had a career as an elementary ESL teacher before becoming a university researcher. Both have been consultants to the Ministry of Education of Québec, for strategies (Gunning) and for assessment (Turner). We are very aware of the interface between research and classroom goals, and classroom-based assessment that assists learning, and of the fact that research and classroom goals sometimes overlap. All of Gunning's research has been situated in the context of Québec, Canada, and has focused on strategies, mainly at the elementary level (Gunning 1997, 2011; Gunning, White, and Busque 2016, 2017). Turner's research has focused on language assessment issues, and has included several studies in the context of Québec (Turner 2009; Turner and Upshur 2002; White and Turner 2005, 2012).

The Québec Education Program, or QEP, of the Ministry of Education of Québec (2001) recommends a synergistic relationship among teaching, learning, and assessment, and mandates SI and SA. Initially, the curriculum advocated a traditional approach to SA; that is, test what is taught and provide grades. Later on, however, Ministry officials realized that this was contradictory to the nature of strategy use, so they recommended instead that SA be used to promote self-regulation and life-long learning, through formative assessment that supports learning. Nevertheless, the issue of how to conduct this type of assessment remains a topic of discussion, and many teachers simply ignore SA because grades are not being assigned and/or because teachers do not have the necessary SA resources. This chapter will address these concerns.

4. Interface between SA and CBA

The recognition of the dearth of research on SA with YLLs in classroom settings is timely in that it coincides with the emerging paradigm of CBA in both general education assessment and, more specifically, in language education assessment for the purposes of this chapter (Brookhart 2003; Turner 2012). Traditionally the characteristics of classroom assessment were viewed as an interpretation of validity theory from large-scale-testing. Practice and evidence, however, have demonstrated the importance and uniqueness of the classroom learning context, and how in such settings assessment provides information to help inform teaching and learning (Fulcher and Davidson 2007). CBA is, therefore, of particular relevance to SA since it is carried out in authentic contexts and as White, Schramm, and Chamot (2007, 103) point out, "[b]ecause strategies are goal oriented and the action context has influence on these goals, the use of strategies varies greatly according to the action context." Oxford (2017) reinforces the importance of context in strategy research and states that traditional quantitative methods have viewed learners as separate from contexts. She affirms that a typical shortcoming of traditional quantitative research has been the ignoring of context as a meaningful factor. In addition, the field of language assessment has evolved beyond just the technical qualities of an assessment to currently include the use and consequences of that assessment for decision making (Purpura 2016). To those involved in strategy research, questions such as the following can arise: (a) How can YLLs' strategy use in an authentic context be assessed to enhance learning? (b) How can the effects of SI and SA on strategy use and on learning be assessed to gauge next steps in teaching? If one considers the present climate of CBA, the answers to such questions appear increasingly more feasible.

Within this context, we draw upon current research from both the strategy and assessment literature to identify efficient and effective elements needed for SA. Seeing that the elementary school classroom is a normal SA setting for YLLs, the emerging principles of CBA would appear appropriate for assessing the particularities of that context. In concurrence with the evolving assessment literature, we question and reflect upon the usefulness of conventional validity theory for guiding classroom assessment.

5. Assessing strategies: An overview of methods and tools

Because strategies involve mental processes and idiosyncratic goal-oriented learning behaviors, scholars have wrestled with the issue of how to assess them appropriately and reliably. (For thorough reviews of SA methods, see Cohen 2011 and Oxford 2011.) Various methods have been used to assess learners' strategy use (not linked to SI). These include questionnaires (Cohen, Oxford, and Chi 2005; O'Malley and Chamot 1990; Oxford 1990); verbal protocols (Anderson and Vandergrift 1996; Chamot and El-Dinary 1999), interviews (Lafontaine 2006; Naiman et al. 1978; Rubin 1975), and diaries (Ma and Oxford 2014; Oxford et al. 1996; Rubin 2003). Others have been used to assess the impact of SI on learning; for instance, color-coding (Lee and Oxford 2008), which was employed with adults in a university context. SA can serve multiple purposes and the purpose will determine the method and tools employed. Questionnaires, for example, provide a snapshot of large numbers of learners' general strategy use, whereas interviews allow for a more in-depth understanding of learners' strategies (Amerstorfer, Chapter 6 in this volume). Diary studies can provide data for students' strategy reflection and personal growth (Ma and Oxford 2014).

The purposes for SA sometimes converge. Research informs teaching and the assessment of strategy use not linked to SI can influence curriculum design, provide information to learners for personal development, and help teachers gear SI to students' needs. On the other hand, assessment of strategy use linked to SI with YLLs in the classroom aims to monitor learning through feedback, gauge what has been learned, and facilitate further learning by planning next steps. In addition, it is to help learners understand how to regulate their learning. Its goal is not to provide grades, which mainly represent levels of mastery of the material. Gkonou and Oxford (2017) posit that the assessment of learners' strategic choice and use should be based on individual learners' strategic repertoires rather than on frequencies and group averages.

The above measures involve self-report, which is subject to human error as this depends on participants' awareness of their strategy use and accurate reporting (Cohen 1998). Nevertheless, without self-report we could not have understood how the predicting strategy worked for Laurent (see introduction of this chapter). An alternative to self-report is observation (O'Malley et al. 1985; Pinter 2006). However, seeing that some strategies involve unobservable mental processes, Pinter (2006, 627) concludes that "[o]bserving task performances without asking the learners cannot give a full picture of the strategies used." Furthermore, observation of strategies can lead to misinterpretation, as observed in a pilot study by Gunning (2007; in Gunning 2011). Observation is also time-consuming for researchers (Cohen 1998), but Macaro (2001, 66) points to its potential for teachers in "looking for traces" of strategy use in classroom-based SA.

In an effort to respond to some of the above challenges, think-aloud protocols have been used. Think-aloud protocols, defined as verbal introspective self-reports consisting of "... disclosure of thought processes while the information is being attended to" (Cohen and Scott 1996, 96), have the advantage of being concurrent with the task but this procedure is cognitively demanding and training of participants is necessary. Despite training, however, this method can be problematic when used with YLLs, as revealed in an investigation by Chamot and El-Dinary (1999). Even though the learners were trained to think aloud, prompting was necessary. Gu, Hu, and Zhang (2005) also found that YLLs had difficulty verbalizing while performing a language task, so probing was essential. The degree of probing necessary with YLLs points to a fundamental problem with using this method with this age group. From the language assessment literature, we know this may be due to multiple factors (e.g., characteristics of

YLLs, context, the types of assessments they normally experience). The task demands on YLLs need to be realistic. Otherwise a task may hinder a child from performing in an optimal manner (Hasselgreen 2012).

When exploring strategy use with YLLs, in the absence of SI, Gunning (1997) also found that SA tools and methods used with older learners are not always appropriate for children, and if adapted, pilot testing is crucial. In her study, Gunning provided two examples of adaptations made to widely-used methods; namely, retrospective interviews and general strategy questionnaires.

Retrospective interviews ask learners to reflect on past learning experiences (Naiman et al. 1978, 1996; Rubin 1975). Since YLLs are centered on the here and now (Brown 2007), Gunning (1997) anchored interviews with 5th graders in the present. The participants, who had been preparing for an end-of-year oral comprehension test, were shown a practice sheet given to them earlier and asked how they had been using it to review. The unstructured interview offered the advantage of having participants talk about strategies they were using at the time of the interview, thereby avoiding the pitfall of lapses in memory and inaccurate reporting of past strategy use. This method, linked to an actual task, revealed nuances of personal strategies. The high achieving learners understood the nature of the task and adapted their strategies accordingly, whereas the low achieving learners used ineffective strategies for the task. The former practiced aloud, using idiosyncratic strategies, such as practicing with an "English-speaking" dog, playing school in English on the telephone with a cousin, pretending the study sheet was an imaginary person and engaging in a conversation with it, and practicing with a bilingual friend. The latter used strategies unsuited for the task, such as silent reading and word-for-word translation. This helped demonstrate that when there is a specific task and YLLs are commenting on their strategies related to that task, they remain on topic and report activities relevant to the research question.

General strategy questionnaires probe learners' habitual strategy use. The most widely used is the *Strategy Inventory for Language Learning* (*SILL*) by Oxford (1990). Gunning (1997) was the first to adapt this inventory for children, highlights of which will now be presented (see Gunning 1997, for details). An initial version was created and field-tested in the researcher-teacher's grade 5 class, and the children were invited to write down strategies they used that were not on the questionnaire (e.g., playing computer games in English). Modifications were made and expert comments sought (e.g., Rebecca Oxford, the developer of the original *SILL*). The final criteria used in Gunning's adaptation were simplicity, comprehensibility to children, choice of concrete, rather than abstract items, and random selection among redundant items. The resulting *Children's SILL* (Gunning, 1997) is a 30-item questionnaire, written in French for Francophone children from Québec. This version was again piloted with five grade 5 classes by another teacher from Québec, in order to confirm comprehensibility by the children. Suggestions from the piloting, such as providing an example to clarify certain items, were incorporated; e.g., *If I can't think of the expression I want to use in English, I try and find another way of saying what I want to say (e.g., synonym, description, etc.)* [translation]. The final version was administered to five other classes. The *Children's SILL* has since been translated into various languages and adapted for use with children in other contexts (Anam and Stracke 2016; Jimenez-Garrido 2010; Lan 2004; Lan and Oxford 2003).

Despite the efficiency of general strategy questionnaires, there are limitations to this method, as found in other survey studies (e.g., data are dependent on participants reporting accurately). Oxford et al. (2004) found that in the absence of a task, participants sometimes reported greater or lesser use of strategies than they would have in the presence of a task, which led them to advocate the use of task-based questionnaires, in addition to general questionnaires. Task-based questionnaires appeared to provide more reliable data. As an example, Vandergrift et al. (2006) developed the *Metacognitive Awareness Listening Questionnaire* (MALQ), a task-based strategies questionnaire to be administered following an authentic listening task. The MALQ was subjected to rigorous validation procedures. Once again, such methods were developed for older learners. Gunning (2011) reported searching in vain for a task-based L2 strategy questionnaire for YLLs.

5.1. The under-investigation of SA for YLLs

This brings us to the larger context, in which SA with YLLs is under-investigated (Gu, Hu, and Zang 2005; Macaro and Mutton 2009), especially assessment of the effects of SI on learning (Gunning 2011; Gunning and Oxford 2014). Some exceptions are Gu (2007), Macaro and Mutton (2009), and Vandergrift (2002). Macaro and Mutton (2009) used a quasi-experimental design to assess students' ability to infer meaning of French L2 words embedded in an English as a first language (L1) reading text. This rigorous study shows positive implications for the teaching of inferencing but the method is experimental and does not reflect the ecology of the classroom. Gu (2007) also used a quasi-experimental method to assess the impact of SI on writing outcomes among grade 5 students. Authentic writing tests were given to assess English language situational writing. The results show a positive impact of SI on writing but Gu did not report the actual assessment of the students' strategies. Vandergrift (2002) assessed strategies employed by intact classes of grades 4 to 6 Canadian children, using a semi-structured oral interview. In this classroom-based, French L2 investigation, the whole class did listening tasks reflecting classroom activities, and then engaged in oral group reflections about their strategy use. The results were concurrently written on a single questionnaire by each teacher. Qualitative data were analyzed for evidence of strategies that enhance L2 listening and the effect of guided reflection on student awareness of the listening process. For the teacher, this process could be useful for consciousness-raising, for noticing "traces of strategy use" (whereby the teacher observes what students are doing to help themselves learn) as suggested by Macaro (2001), and for providing feedback. For research purposes, however, reliability issues arise as the data are subject to the teacher's ability to take adequate notes while conducting the post-task reflection. An audio or video recording of the group reflection would contribute to the reliability of the procedure.

The under-examination of authentic, ongoing SA in L2 classroom contexts could be due to various reasons, but a major challenge is the lack of resources and guidance to gauge strategy use among YLLs in classroom settings (Gunning 2011). The *SILL* (Oxford 1990) and the *Children's SILL* (Gunning 1997) were ground-breaking in that they identified six categories of strategies and suggested examples of strategic behaviors to which large numbers of participants responded according to their personal strategy use. These instruments moved the field forward, but at this stage of SA evolution, we need specific assessment tools for teachers and researchers to help indicate ongoing learning among YLLs in the context of CBA.

In addition, because of the complexities of assessing strategies and of CBA, it is useful for teachers and researchers to use multiple tools to get a comprehensive picture (Amerstorfer, Chapter 6 in this volume). Sometimes the methodologies of teachers and researchers can be similar in that multiple sources of data combined are important for making decisions for future directions. A combination of self-report with observation procedures can "reveal further complexities about strategies which function as traces of cognition as in noting down, writing out, listing, and underlining" (White 1995a, in White, Schramm, and Chamot 2007, 98). Combining various methods to examine a phenomenon has been an ongoing recommendation for teachers in L2 assessment (Genesee and Upshur 1996; Turner 2012). This provides a more comprehensive profile of student progress and ability. Considering the strengths and limitations of commonly-used methods discussed above, SA could benefit from this combined approach.

For the researcher, mixed-methods research (MMR) is useful because it is "research in which the investigator collects and analyzes data, integrates the findings, and draws inferences using both qualitative and quantitative approaches or methods in a single study or program of inquiry" (Tashakkori and Creswell 2007, 4). Gunning (2011) chose MMR because of the complexity of the investigation and, as Turner (2014, 4) points out, "[t]here is growing awareness that by combining information from different sources, results (whether convergent or divergent) can often provide valuable insight into and deeper understanding of complex phenomena under study." For a description of the MMR design used by Gunning, see Gunning (2011) and Turner (2014).

For teachers, this is less straightforward, in spite of the recommendation to use a variety of assessment methods. Traditionally, assessment in classrooms managed by teachers was considered a spinoff of large-scale testing external to the classroom (e.g., provincial/state level exams, standardized tests), including the assumption that psychometric qualities also applied to all CBA. Research has, however, demonstrated the uniqueness of the classroom context, and the usefulness of diverse assessment methods including formal (quizzes/tests with psychometric qualities), but also informal (and sometimes spontaneous) activities that are frequently embedded in teaching in a formative manner to help support ongoing learning (not to necessarily generate grades). It is to be noted that SA falls into this latter category (Gkonou and Oxford 2017).

Therefore, CBA has emerged as a complex context and a paradigm to be investigated on its own merits (Fulcher and Davidson 2007; Hill and McNamara 2011; Turner 2012). Unlike current large-scale tests developed externally to the classroom, CBA is contextually bound and can also be a socially constructed activity involving different stakeholders in learning. It is "context" that creates this uniqueness. This reality has brought mounting calls in the literature to reconceptualize conventional validity theory for CBA; that is, to develop a theory for assessment that corresponds to its purpose and use in classroom settings (as opposed to large-scale test settings) (Brookhart 2003; Moss 2003). In language assessment there has been an increasing interest to explore this in both practice and theory. As has been stated above, SA in classroom settings can benefit from this interest. It is therefore useful in relation to SA to consider the different ways forward being discussed in the language assessment literature.

One example is the developing direction to promote a learning-oriented approach to CBA, where assessment is treated as a critical component of the multifaceted and dynamic process of learning. Learning-oriented assessment (LOA) builds on the many insights theoretical and empirical research in both language and academic content have provided. For example, findings demonstrate that teachers, intentionally or unintentionally, embed formal or informal, planned or spontaneous assessments within aspects of teaching. From these assessments, they are able to obtain information on learning gaps and successes, and can adjust their actions accordingly to support learning (Black et al 2004; Gardner 2012; National Research Council 2001; Stiggins 2010). Studies have reiterated how learning is incremental and student/context-specific, and that identifying ongoing learning patterns can be complex in that development may occur with no overt manifestation in performance (National Research Council 2000). To help understand how learning supported by assessment in classrooms unfolds, LOA specifically proposes a working framework that takes into account the complexities of CBA to explore the many questions concerning effective assessment in classroom settings. It helps deconstruct LOA by exploring the agents (e.g., students, teachers, peers) and interrelated dimensions that are critical factors to support learning via assessment (e.g., performance moderators such as the contextual, socio-cognitive, instructional, affective, and interactional dimensions and performance indicators such as the elicitation and proficiency dimensions) (see Purpura and Turner, forthcoming; Turner and Purpura 2016). In this chapter these same concepts are discussed in relation to SA; therefore, the fact that SA can be said to parallel developments in CBA (and more specifically in LOA) provides an opportunity to position the development of SA tools in classroom settings within the current assessment research. Gunning (2011) capitalized on this direction as she designed SA methods for YLLs in a specific context, and Gunning and Watts (2011) pursued this same direction in designing practical assessment resources for teachers and learners. The remainder of this chapter will situate this work, and provide guidelines and examples of SA methods and tools that parallel LOA in that they acknowledge the synergies across teaching, learning, and assessment.

6. Designing SA methods and tools for YLLs in a specific context

The overarching guidelines for considerations regarding SA that help YLLs learn, involve a recognition that the purpose of SA is to help students reflect on their learning, understand what they need to do to improve, and set goals for improvement (self-regulation). As such, the role of specific, descriptive feedback is crucial. SA tools must also reflect criteria shown to be appropriate for YLLs; i.e., simplicity, comprehensibility to children, choice of concrete rather than abstract strategy items, and strategic behaviors relevant to the age group (Gunning 1997). The SA tools need to be culturally appropriate and reflect the ecology of the classroom. Pilot testing of these tools in the particular context is also imperative.

Based on these guidelines, examples and advice for use of the methods and tools taken from various studies in authentic CBA settings will constitute the rest of this chapter (Gunning 2011; Gunning and Watts 2011; Gunning, White, and Busque 2015, 2016). These will be organized according to their purpose and intended audience; i.e., for teachers, researchers, or both. We will present the context in which they were used but sometimes the lines are not clearly demarcated between research and teaching purposes. The recommendations we make should be subject to decisions made by each teacher and researcher, according to their SA context.

6.1. Methods, tools, and tips for teachers

Table 12.1, designed by Gunning for a teacher-training workshop, summarizes some principles for assessing strategies in classroom contexts.

In order for SA in the classroom to promote learning, YLLs need to understand the goal of the assessment, so modeling of the expected performance is essential and learners need feedback. Examples of models of expected performance and descriptive feedback by peers are shown in a digital textbook companion, *A New Twist to Intensive English* (Gunning and Watts 2011). These 2-D animated models demonstrate three levels of speaking performance. Use of strategies, such as self-monitoring during oral presentations and asking for clarification during oral interaction, is demonstrated. Following the presentations, there are models of peers asking questions and providing descriptive feedback. Assessment rubrics are provided to help students understand the expected standards. Figure 12.1 shows an example of peer feedback following a "good" model of an oral presentation.

Whatever the method or tool used, it is important to model the expected performance in terms of content and process and to provide descriptive feedback related to performance goals. Students can also be asked to do a self-evaluation. Once YLLs understand the expected standards, they can engage in meaningful self-evaluations and regulate their learning.

Table 12.1 Teacher SA template

Principles

- Purpose: To help students regulate their learning.
- Combine more than one method.
- Focus on students' strategic behaviors.
- Allow for personal strategy choices, respecting individual differences.

SA Template

Goal: To solve reading comprehension difficulties using strategies, and explain strategies with examples.

Method	Strategy	Examples of behaviors	Procedure
Interview	*Inferencing*	• I look at English words that are similar in French (cognates). • I use visual and contextual clues.	Interview—example: • Teacher: *Which strategy did you use?* • Student: *Inferencing* • Teacher: *Can you explain inferencing?* • Student: *I look at clues. I make intelligent guesses.* • Teacher: *How did you use this strategy? Give me an example.* • Student: *I looked at English words that are similar in French.* • Teacher: (requiring <u>evidence</u>) *Which words did you find that are similar in the two languages?*

Examples of expected performance

	Advanced competency development (Excellent)	Minimal competency development (Poor)
Evaluation criterion: Use of strategies	The student • can explain his/her strategies and give examples. • chooses appropriate strategies for the task. • switches strategies, as needed, to solve learning difficulties.	• The student cannot explain his/her strategies. • The student abandons the task when faced with a learning difficulty.

Figure 12.1 Model of a good oral presentation

People we admire

Screen shot of 2-D animation presentation.

Peer feedback following the presentation:

Student 1: *Congratulations! Your presentation was complete and well prepared.*
Student 2: *Yes. You described your sister's good qualities.*
Student 3: *And you explained why you admire her.*
Student 1: *I think your presentation was very good.*
Student 2: *Me too.*

Source: This extract was authorized for reproduction per Copibec license terms

6.2. Methods, tools and tips for researchers

Interviews can be structured, unstructured, or semi-structured. With YLLs semi-structured or structured interviews are effective in keeping participants on track. Important considerations are similar to those mentioned throughout this chapter; that is, questions should be concrete, culture sensitive, and centered in the here and now. YLLs can be frank, honest, and can describe their strategies clearly. They will provide valuable information if the questions are clear, meaningful, and related to a specific task. Retrospective interviews should be avoided; see Gunning (1997). Stimulated recall, in which YLLs are shown a video of themselves accomplishing an academic task and asked to explain how they were working, is effective but organization of this can be challenging, depending on school schedules (Gunning 2011). Interviews are very informative but they should be video or audio recorded, in order to capture the rich information given and also nonverbal cues such as facial reactions. Coding and analysis of the interview data can be used for qualitative analysis (see Gunning 2011).

Video-recordings are valuable for supporting observation and recording interviews. There are, however, special considerations when using this tool with YLLs. Ethical issues involve securing parental authorization before filming a child. Affective considerations must also be addressed. The researcher should visit the class prior to filming in order to put the students at ease and to explain the purpose of the video. During the intervention, it is important to check how the children feel about being filmed, and to respect their feelings. One child told Gunning (2011) that she did not mind being filmed during group oral interactions, but she did not want to be filmed during oral presentations in front of the class.

Video-recordings can be analyzed digitally using computer-assisted software programs for analyzing qualitative data from multimedia sources, such as HyperResearch (as all studies cited in this section have used). The coding of the video data, however, needs to be consistent in order to ensure reliability of the findings. Coding can be done using a bottom-up, grounded approach, as shown in the following two studies. Gunning (2011) watched the videos for evidence of the research questions, and operationalized the findings. On the other hand, Gunning, White, and Busque (2016) observed SI in actual classrooms, identified behaviors related to specific strategies, and wrote these in a strategy table (see example for inferencing, Table 12.2, column 1). Gunning and White (ongoing) used the behaviors listed in the strategy table to operationalize the strategies identified in the video-recordings (see example, Table 12.3, column 2).

In order to operationalize the coding of the videos, Gunning and White developed Table 12.3, based on the literature and on video data from earlier investigations.

The researchers used specific examples from the video data for selective transcriptions of representative samples pertinent to the qualitative analysis. This procedure is practical for researchers using video recordings of CBA with YLLs because much of what goes on in elementary school classrooms is unrelated to the research (e.g., discipline and administrative issues). With selected transcriptions, time is not wasted transcribing irrelevant video data. Digitally tagged video clips permit double-checking of the coding for consistency, thereby enhancing the reliability of the findings.

Table 12.2 Bottom-up development of strategy table (column 1)/Top-down use of strategy table (column 2)

	Example from strategy table: Inferencing	Example of use by researchers for coding
Illustrations		• Look for evidence in videos of behaviors listed in the strategy table. • Operationalize the coding, using strategy table and guide for coding (Table 12.4).
Strategies	**INFERENCING**	
Definitions	To make <u>intelligent guesses</u> based on all available <u>clues</u> from the text.	
Examples of behaviors	(A) I look at English words that are similar in French (cognates). (B) I use what I know to guess the meaning of the words or the text. (C) I read the titles and subtitles. (D) I use visual clues. (E) I use clues from the context. (F) I look around the word.	

6.3. Methods, tools, and tips for teachers and researchers

6.3.1. Task-based questionnaires

Two task-based questionnaires for YLLs were devised by Gunning (2011) and Gunning, White, and Busque (2015) respectively, for specific, contextualized assessment of strategies. These questionnaires are suitable for researchers and teachers but for increased comprehensibility and validity, researchers should administer them in the L1, whereas teachers can administer them in the L2.

The first of these, related to oral interaction tasks, contains fourteen items that reflect strategy items associated with the oral interaction competency in the QEP (see Gunning 2011). Gunning conducted an analysis of the oral interaction competency in the QEP to ensure construct validity and created a first draft of the questionnaire. After field-testing, consulting with experts, two ESL consultants and an ESL elementary teacher from Québec, the questionnaire

Table 12.3 Operationalizing the coding of the phases of SI

Phases of SI	Operationalization (definitions and examples)
1(a). Strategy awareness-raising (by the teacher)	• Teacher helping students realize what a strategy is and how it is used.
1(b). Strategy awareness (by the student)	• Evidence demonstrating students' understanding of strategies and how to use them (declarative and procedural knowledge); e.g., students' ability to reflect upon, identify their strategies, and give examples of how they use them (Gunning and Oxford 2014).
2. Explanation and modeling	• Teacher goes through the process of the activity by thinking aloud as he/she models the strategy (based on Oxford 1990).
	• Modeling or teaching with demonstrations, making explicit the practice and the reasoning that otherwise would be implicit (Dubé, Dorval, and Bessette 2013).
3. Guided practice	• Teacher scaffolds students' strategy use. He/she proposes tasks integrating use of the strategy and accompanies students in strategy use as they complete the tasks, which can be done in lock-step by the whole class, in teams, or individually.
4(a). Independent practice (very similar to the phase immediately below)	• Students solve problems by themselves applying what they learned during the modeling and guided practice (Dubé, Dorval, and Bessette 2013).
4(b). Strategy use (very similar to the phase immediately below)	• Evidence of students visibly using strategies following instruction, or reporting using specific strategies, supporting their claims with examples (Gunning and Oxford 2014).
5. Autonomous strategy use	• Students employ strategies independently by choosing, monitoring, and flexibly orchestrating their strategies (Gunning and Oxford 2014).
6. Reflection on strategy use	• Post-task reporting of strategy use. This can be: teacher-led; student-to-student group discussion; student reporting to researcher. Examples of questions: *Which strategy did you use? Give an example. How did it help?*
7a. L1/L2 transfer of strategies (awareness-raising by the teacher)	• Teacher drawing parallels or making cross-linguistic references between strategies used in the L1 and in the L2 classes.
7b. L1/L2 transfer of strategies (by the student)	• Evidence of students transferring strategy awareness from their L1 class to their L2 class, or vice versa. They can identify and describe the strategy used as they make connections between their L1 and L2 classes.

Table 12.4 Task-based questionnaire: Reading strategies

Name _____   Date _____

| Native language: | French ☐ | English ☐ | Other ☐ |

Do you like English?   Yes ☐   Sometimes ☐   No ☐

Instructions: Read the statements and then choose one response for each statement.   1 = Yes   2 = No

If you respond *1. Yes*, indicate the time (before, during or after reading) when you use this strategy, by checking the appropriate box.

If you respond *2. No*, leave the boxes regarding the time empty.

Examples	1 = Yes 2 = No	Before reading	While reading	After reading
1. I look at the title and the illustrations to predict what the text will be about.	1	✓		
2. I go through the text quickly to get the general idea and then I go back and read it more slowly and carefully.	2			

N.B. There are no wrong answers. Different people use different strategies to help them do activities in English. **This is NOT a test.**

When I am doing an activity (like this one) based on reading a text in English . . .	1 = Yes 2 = No	Before reading	During reading	After reading
1. I look at the title and the illustrations to predict what the text will be about.				
2. I go through the text quickly to get the general idea and then I go back and read it more slowly and carefully.				
3. I ask myself questions (who, what, how) to understand what I read.				
4. I find a purpose for reading.				
5. If I don't understand everything, I don't worry. I try to understand the general idea.				
6. I look for clues to help me understand the text (punctuation marks, related words, substitution words).				
7. I use what I already know to help me understand the text; for example, my knowledge of French.				
8. I make links between the sentences and paragraphs.				
9. I look for similarities between French and English to help me understand the text.				

10.	I look for specific information that will help me to respond to the comprehension questions and complete the activity.			
11.	I use the context or words I already know to guess the meaning of some parts of the text.			
12.	If I don't understand some words, I use resources (dictionary, word banks, etc.) to help me understand.			
13.	I reflect on my strategies and adjust them as needed.			
14.	I select, organize and take notes about the important information in the text.			
15.	I reflect on my reading and I discuss my difficulties and strategies with others.			
16.	I make a mental image (in my head or on paper) in order to visualize a scene or character in the text.			
17.	I plan how to approach my reading.			
18.	I relax and enjoy the reading activity.			
Other strategies				
19.				
20.				

proved to be self-explanatory and administration time was five minutes. The second questionnaire relates to reading tasks (Gunning, White, and Busque 2015). This questionnaire (Table 12.4) is an adaptation of one used by Gunning (2011). It too included field testing similar to the oral interaction strategy questionnaire. In addition, the following adaptations were implemented to make the reading strategy questionnaire suitable for the new research context. This questionnaire evolved from two studies of L1/L2 teacher collaboration to teach the strategies in both curricula, reported in Gunning, White, and Busque (2016). A curriculum analysis was performed to identify strategies common to the French L1 and English L2 curricula, and equivalent items were added to the questionnaire. This tool was also informed by bottom-up, grounded theory as the researchers formulated some items based on examples taken from actual classrooms during these studies. An example of this procedure is that the teachers taught the learners to infer meaning of a text, based on information in the text related to *Wh-* question words, so an item added to the questionnaire was: *I ask myself questions (who, what, how) to understand what I read.* The element of time was also added; that is, whether the strategy was used before, during, or after reading, thereby reflecting the teaching. The final number of items on the questionnaire was eighteen and there were two blank spaces for students to write other strategies they might have used. Administration time was approximately ten minutes.

Special considerations used in creating these questionnaires for YLLs are similar to those outlined earlier in the adaptation of the *Children's SILL* (Gunning 1997), e.g., comprehensibility to children. The field tests revealed that the task-based questionnaires need to be administered immediately after the task being assessed, as YLLs sometimes forget what they have done if there is a time delay.

6.3.2. Strategy log

The strategy log (see Gunning 2011), adapted for YLLs from Nakatani (2005) by Gunning, was originally designed as a teaching tool. It contained the eighteen strategies in the QEP, written in simple language that is accessible to children. The process, originally used with adults by Nakatani was simplified in the following way. The teacher explained the task. The students consulted their strategy log and discussed in small groups strategies that could be helpful for that task. They then set goals by checking off on the log, in the column *I plan to use,* strategies they thought they would use. Immediately following the task, they checked off in the column *I used,* the strategies they actually used to perform the task.

The teacher then led the students in a post-task reflection, requiring them to report the strategies they had used and checked off on the log, and to support their reporting with specific examples. She rejected all attempts at simply listing strategies without examples. (See Gunning and Oxford 2014 for an example of this reporting procedure.)

The strategy log proved to be useful for the researcher. Gunning (2011) filmed the process and, upon observing the evidence and accountability required by the teacher of the participants, collected the six strategy log entries completed by the students at various intervals for quantitative and qualitative analysis. The results of the data analyses were combined in order to make inferences regarding the effects of SI on students' strategy use and on their ESL task performance. Qualitative data from the video recordings of the process were used in combination with quantitative data from the pre- and post-tests.

The strategy log had face validity because the students understood from the teaching procedure what it was supposed to measure and the strategies on it, based on the SI. The sharing of strategies and the feedback the students received from peers and teacher played an important role in helping students understand what was expected of them, how to use strategies to solve learning problems, and how to adjust their strategies when needed. They developed a wide repertoire of strategies.

6.4. The role of feedback

Based on the findings from the above study and the LOA literature, we conclude that the role of reflection, sharing, and feedback in classroom-based SA cannot be overstated. Feedback helps students understand curriculum standards and learning goals, close learning gaps, and compare their performance with the expected learning outcomes (Turner and Purpura 2016). Feedback can be given through planned interventions, such as post-task reflections, and self-evaluation of strategy use. Retroactivity, as an integral part of feedback in SA, is crucial to learning. In order for learners to progress from guided practice of strategies to autonomous use, they need to reflect on their strategy use and to receive specific, descriptive feedback that will help them understand whether their strategy use was effective in matching their performance to the expected learning outcomes. In the context of the classroom, regular post-task reflection is beneficial as learners share the strategies they used and how they used them, and all learners in the class profit from the teacher feedback. This underscores the importance of several iterations of practice opportunities, with descriptive feedback, in order to give learners many opportunities to reinvest the feedback and regulate their learning.

7. Concluding remarks

We have considered the issues about how YLLs' strategy use in an authentic context can be appropriately (according to age) and reliably assessed, and how the effects of SI and SA on strategy use and on learning can be gauged. After examination of the SA and CBA literature, we have contended that these issues can be addressed in a feasible manner, but they are contingent on the purpose and context of the assessment. We have suggested that SA be considered in a framework of LOA, in which teaching, learning, and assessment function in synergy to promote learning. This implies a revision of validity theory more conducive to assessment practice, which mirrors teaching and learning as a vehicle to further learning. We have described a variety of resources designed specifically for assessing YLLs' strategy use in classroom contexts. These can begin to fill the void of age-appropriate SA tools, but we recommend that teachers and researchers adapt them to their purposes and contexts. Whatever the method used, we have suggested combining multiple tools. In addition, SA methods and tools should vary according to pedagogical goals, and evidence needs to be collected over an extended period of time (Gunning 2011). In conclusion, classroom-based SA and CBA are complex by nature, but such assessment in authentic contexts holds potential to provide insight into exploring the impact of YLLs' strategy use on learning.

References

Anam, Syafi'ul, and Elke Stracke. 2016. "Language Learning Strategies of Indonesian Primary School Students: In Relation to Self-efficacy Beliefs." *System* 60: 1–10.

Anderson, Neil J., and Larry Vandergrift. 1996. "Increasing Metacognitive Awareness in the L2 Classroom by Using Think-aloud Protocols." In *Language Learning Strategies around the World: Cross-cultural Perspectives*, edited by Rebecca L. Oxford, 3–18. Manoa: University of Hawai'i.

Black, Paul, Christine Harrison, Clair Lee, Bethan Marshall, and Dylan Wiliam. 2004. "Working Inside the Black Box: Assessment for Learning in the Classroom." *Phi Delta Kappan* 86 (1): 8–21.

Brookhart, Susan M. 2003. "Developing Measurement Theory for Classroom Assessment Purposes and Uses." *Educational Measurement: Issues and Practices* 22 (4): 5–12.

Brown, H. Douglas 2007. *Teaching by Principles: An Interactive Approach to Language Pedagogy*. 3rd edition. New York: Addison-Wesley.

Chamot, Anna Uhl. 2005. "Language Learning Strategy Instruction: Current Issues and Research." *Annual Review of Applied Linguistics* 25: 112–30.

Chamot, Anna Uhl, and Pamela Beard El-Dinary. 1999. "Children's Learning Strategies in Language Immersion Classrooms." *The Modern Language Journal* 8: 319–38.

Cohen, Andrew D. 1998. *Strategies in Learning and Using a Second Language*. London: Longman.

——. 2007. "Coming to Terms with Language Learner Strategies: Surveying the Experts." In *Language Learner Strategies: Thirty Years of Research and Practice*, edited by Andrew D. Cohen and Ernesto Macaro, 29–45. Oxford: Oxford University Press.

——. 2011. *Strategies in Learning and Using a Second Language*. 2nd edition. New York: Longman.

Cohen, Andrew D., and Kimberly Scott. 1996. "A Synthesis of Approaches to Assessing Language Learning Strategies." In *Language Learning Strategies around the World: Cross-cultural Perspectives*, edited by Rebecca L. Oxford, 89–106. Manoa: University of Hawai'i.

Cohen, Andrew D., Rebecca L. Oxford, and Julie Chi. 2005. "Language Strategy Use Inventory." Accessed June 06, 2016. http://naunicol-e.home.amu.edu.pl/wp-content/uploads/2016/02/CohenStratInventory.pdf.

Dubé, France, Catherine Dorval, and Lyne Bessette. 2013. "Flexibles Grouping, Explicit Reading Instruction in Elementary School." *Journal of Instructional Pedagogies* 10: 1–12.

Fulcher, Glenn, and Fred Davidson. 2007. *Language Testing and Assessment.* London: Routledge.

Gardner, John. 2012. "Quality Assessment Practice." In *Assessment and Learning*, edited by John Gardner. 2nd edition, 103–?1. Los Angeles, CA: Sage.

Genesee, Fred, and John Upshur. 1996. *Classroom-based Evaluation in Second Language Education.* Cambridge: Cambridge University Press.

Gkonou, Christina, and Rebecca L. Oxford. 2017. "Formative Assessment for Language Learning Strategy Instruction and for Learners' Strategic Self-understanding." In *Learning Strategy Instruction in the Language Classroom: Issues and Implementation*, edited by Anna Uhl Chamot and Vee Harris. Bristol: Multilingual Matters.

Grenfell, Michael, and Vee Harris. 1999. *Modern Languages and Learning Strategies: In Theory and Practice.* London: Routledge.

Gu, Peter Yongqi. 2007. "Strategy-Based Instruction." In *Proceedings of the International Symposium on English Education in Japan: Exploring New Frontiers*, edited by Tomoko Yashima and Toshiyo Nabei, 21–38. Osaka: Yubunsha.

Gu, Peter Yongqi, Guangwei Hu, and Lawrence Jun Zhang. 2005. "Investigating Language Learner Strategies Among Lower Primary School Pupils in Singapore." *Language and Education* 19 (4): 281–303.

Gunning, Pamela. 1997. "The Learning Strategies of Beginning ESL Learners at Primary Level." Master's thesis. Concordia University, Montréal. Accessed June 06, 2016. http://spectrum.library.concordia.ca/517/.

——. 2007. "ESL Strategy Use and Instruction at the Elementary School Level: A Pilot Study." In Pamela Gunning. 2011. "ESL Strategy Use and Instruction at the Elementary School Level: A Mixed-Methods Investigation." PhD dissertation, McGill University, Montréal.

——. 2011. "ESL Strategy Use and Instruction at the Elementary School Level: A Mixed-Methods Investigation." PhD dissertation, McGill University, Montréal. Accessed June 06, 2016. http://digitool.library.mcgill.ca/R/?func=dbin-jump-full&object_id=103480&local_base=GEN01-MCG02.

Gunning, Pamela, and Rebecca L. Oxford. 2014. "Children's Learning Strategy Use and the Effects of Strategy Instruction on Success in Learning ESL in Canada." *System* 43: 82–100.

Gunning, Pamela, and Wynanne Watts. 2011. *A New Twist to Intensive English.* Montréal: Lidec.

Gunning, Pamela, Joanna White, and Christine Busque. 2015. *Reading Strategy Instruction in Intensive English.* Montréal. Unpublished data.

——. 2016. "Raising Learners' Awareness Through L1-L2 Teacher Collaboration." *Language Awareness* 25 (1–2): 72–88.

——. 2017. "Designing Effective Strategy Instruction, Approaches and Materials for Young Language Learners." In *Learning Strategy Instruction in the Language Classroom: Issues and Implementation,* edited by Anna Uhl Chamot and Vee Harris. Bristol: Multilingual Matters.

Hasselgreen, Angela. 2012. "Assessing Young Learners." In *Routledge Handbook of Language Testing,* edited by Glenn Fulcher and Fred Davidson, 93–105. London: Routledge.

Hill, Kathryn, and Tim McNamara. 2011. "Developing a Comprehensive, Empirically Based Research Framework for Classroom-based Assessment." *Language Testing* 29 (3): 395–420.

Jimenez-Garrido, Amador. 2010. "Effects of Bilingualism on Average LLS Use." Unpublished paper, University of Granada.

Lafontaine, Marc. 2006. "L'utilisation de stratégies d'apprentissage en fonction de la réussite chez des adolescents apprenant l'anglais langue seconde [Use of Learning Strategies of Success Learning Function in Adolescents of ESL]." *The Canadian Modern Language Review* 62 (4): 533–62.

Lan, Rae. 2004. "Language Learning Strategies Profiles of EFL Elementary School Students in Taiwan." PhD dissertation, University of Maryland.

Lan, Rae, and Rebecca L. Oxford. 2003. "Language Learning Strategy Profiles of Elementary School Students in Taiwan." *IRAL* 41: 339–79.

Lee, Kyoung R., and Rebecca L. Oxford. 2008. "Understanding EFL Learners' Strategy Use and Strategy Awareness." *Asian EFL Journal* 10: 7–32.

Ma, Rui, and Rebecca L. Oxford. 2014. "A Diary Study Focusing on Listening and Speaking: The Evolving Interaction of Learning Styles and Learning Strategies in a Motivated, Advanced ESL Learner." In "Language Learning Strategy Research in the Twenty-first Century." edited by Rebecca L. Oxford and Carol Griffiths. Special issue, *System* 43: 101–13.

Macaro, Ernesto. 2001. *Learning Strategies in Foreign and Second Language Classrooms.* London: Continuum.

Macaro, Ernesto, and Trevor Mutton. 2009. "Developing Reading Achievement in Primary Learners of French: Inferencing Strategies Versus Exposure to 'Graded Readers'." *The Language Learning Journal* 37: 165–82.

Ministry of Education of Québec. 2001. "Québec Education Program." Montréal, Québec.

Moss, Pamela A. 2003. "Reconceptualizing Validity for Classroom Assessment." *Educational Measurement: Issues and Practices* 22: 13–25.

Naiman, Neil, Maria Fröhlich, Hans H. Stern, and Angie Todesco. 1978. *The Good Language Learner.* Toronto: Ontario Institute for Studies in Education.

Naiman, Neil, Maria Fröhlich, Hans H. Stern, and Angie Todesco. 1996. *The Good Language Learner.* Clevedon, UK: Multilingual Matters.

Nakatani, Yasuo. 2005. "The Effects of Awareness-raising Training on Oral Communication Strategy Use." *The Modern Language Journal* 89 (1): 76–91.

National Research Council. 2000. *How People Learn: Brain, Mind, Experience and School.* Washington, DC: National Academy Press.

———. 2001. *Knowing What Students Know: The Science and Design of Educational Assessment.* Washington, DC: National Academy Press.

Naughton, Diane. 2006. "Cooperative Strategy Training and Oral Interaction: Enhancing Small Group Communication in the Language Classroom." *The Modern Language Journal* 90 (2): 169–84.

O'Malley, J. Michael, and Anna Uhl Chamot. 1990. *Learning Strategies in Second Language Acquisition.* Cambridge: Cambridge University Press.

O'Malley, J. Michael, Anna Uhl Chamot, Gloria Stewner-Manzanares, Rocco P. Russo, and Lisa Küpper. 1985. "Learning Strategies Used by Beginner and Intermediate ESL Students." *Language Learning* 35 (1): 21–46.

Oxford, Rebecca L. 1990. *Language Learning Strategies: What Every Teacher Should Know.* Boston: Heinle & Heinle.

———. 2011. *Teaching and Researching Language Learning Strategies.* Harlow: Pearson/ Longman.

———. 2017. *Teaching and Researching Language Learning Strategies: Self-Regulation in Context.* 2nd edition. New York: Routledge.

Oxford, Rebecca L., Yunkyoung Cho, Santoi Leung, and Hae-Jin Kim. 2004. "Effect of the Presence and Difficulty of Task on Strategy Use: An Exploratory Study." *International Review of Applied Linguistics* 42: 1–47.

Oxford, Rebecca L., Roberta Lavine, Gregory Felkins, Mary E. Hollaway, and Amany Saleh. 1996. "Telling Their Stories: Language Students Use Diaries and Recollection." In *Language Learning Strategies around the World: Cross-cultural Perspectives,* edited by Rebecca L. Oxford, 89–106. Manoa: University of Hawai'i.

Pinter, Annamaria. 2006. "Verbal Evidence of Task Related Strategies: Child Versus Adult Interactions." *System* 34: 615–30.

Purpura, James E. 2013. "Language Learner Styles and Strategies." In *Teaching English as a Second or Foreign Language,* edited by Marianne Celce-Murcia, Donna Brinton, and Marguerite A. Snow, 532–49. Boston, MA: National Geographic Learning/ Cengage Learning.

———. 2014. "Cognition and Language Assessment." In *The Companion to Language Assessment,* edited by Antony J. Kunnan, 1452–76. Sussex: John Wiley & Sons.

———. 2016. "Second and Foreign Language Assessment." *Modern Language Journal* 100: 190–208.

Purpura, James E., and Carolyn E. Turner. Forthcoming. *Learning-Oriented Assessment in Language Classrooms: Using Assessment to Gauge and Promote Language Learning.* New York: Routledge.

Rubin, Joan. 1975. "What the 'Good Language Learner' Can Teach Us." *TESOL Quarterly* 9: 41–51.

——. 2003. "Diary Writing as a Process: Simple, Useful, Powerful." *Guidelines* 25 (2): 10–14.

Stiggins, Rick. 2010. "Essential Formative Assessment Competencies for Teachers and School Leaders." In *Handbook of Formative Assessment*, edited by Heidi L. Andrade and Gregory J. Cizek, 233–50. New York: Routledge.

Tashakkori, Abbas, and John W. Creswell. 2007. "The New Era of Mixed Methods." *Journal of Mixed Methods Research* 1: 207–11.

Turner, Carolyn E. 2009. "Examining Washback in Second Language Education Contexts: A High Stakes Provincial Exam and the Teacher Factor in Classroom Practice in Québec Secondary Schools." *International Journal on Pedagogies and Learning* 5 (1): 103–23.

——. 2012. "Classroom Assessment." In *Routledge Handbook of Language Testing*, edited by Glenn Fulcher and Fred Davidson, 65–78. London: Routledge.

——. 2014. "Mixed Methods Research." In *The Companion to Language Assessment*, edited by Antony J. Kunnan, 1403–17. Chichester: John Wiley & Sons.

Turner, Carolyn E., and James E. Purpura. 2016. "Learning-oriented Assessment in Second and Foreign Language Classrooms." In *Handbook of Second Language Assessment*, edited by Dina Tsagari and Jayanti Banerjee, 255–72. Boston, MA: De Gruyter Mouton.

Turner, Carolyn E. and John A. Upshur. 2002. "Rating Scales Derived From Student Samples: Effects of the Scale Maker and the Student Sample on Scale Content and Student Scores." *TESOL Quarterly* 36 (1): 49–70.

Vandergrift, Larry. 2002. "It Was Nice to See that Our Predictions Were Right: Developing Metacognition in L2 Listening Comprehension." *The Canadian Modern Language Review* 58 (4): 555–75.

Vandergrift, Larry, Christine Goh, Catherine Mareschal, and Marzieh Tafaghodtari. 2006. "The Metacognitive Awareness Listening Questionnaire: Development and Validation." *Language Learning* 53 (3): 431–62.

White, Cynthia, Karen Schramm, and Anna Uhl Chamot. 2007. "Research Methods in Strategy Research: Examining the Toolbox." In *Language Learner Strategies: Thirty Years of Research and Practice*, edited by Andrew D. Cohen and Ernesto Macaro, 93–116. Oxford: Oxford University Press.

White, Joanna, and Carolyn E. Turner. 2005. "Comparing Children's Oral Ability in Two ESL Programs." *The Canadian Modern Language Review* 61 (4): 491–517.

——. 2012. "What Language Is Promoted in Intensive Programs? Analyzing Language Generated from Oral Assessment Tasks." In *Intensive Exposure Experiences in Second Language Learning*, edited by Carmen Muñoz, 88–110. Bristol: Multilingual Matters.

Conclusion

Lessons Learned and the Future of Situated Learning Strategies

Carmen M. Amerstorfer
Alpen-Adria-Universität Klagenfurt, Austria

Rebecca L. Oxford
University of Maryland, USA

At the beginning of this volume, we quoted poet Mary Oliver, who asked, "Tell me, what is it you plan to do with your one wild and precious life?" We connected this question to the lives of foreign and second language (L2) learners and to the processes and circumstances involved in L2 learning. This book demonstrated in each of its chapters that L2 growth is embedded in a complex and flexible network of influences and that successful L2 learning is strategic and self-regulated. Our main focus was on language learning strategies (LLS). This book clearly underlined the fact that L2 teachers should directly assist learners in the development and application of LLS. Strategy instruction (SI) presented formally or informally by teachers, as well as through workshops and through targeted LLS materials, is a boon for learners. Teacher educators also play important, active roles, while researchers energetically examine the use of LLS and the value of SI, thereby indirectly influencing L2 learners' strategic progress. The contemporary and creative studies presented in this book were built on a strong theoretical foundation honoring past research. Simultaneously, the authors of the twelve chapters sparked ideas for new research in the future.

1. The chapter authors

The powerful and innovative authorship team consisted of LLS experts and other well-known scholars whose contributions to this volume were forward-looking, theory-generating, and intellectually creative. Additionally, a group of emerging, early-career scholars shared their fresh perspectives and original thinking. The work of all these individuals contributed to the overall theme and dynamic vision of foreign and second language learning strategies.

The authors are an ethnically diverse and well-travelled group of scholars who were born in different parts of the world and have lived and worked in many countries around the globe. The diversity in the authorship team is also reflected in the many languages these scholars collectively speak, which represents one important commonality of the authors: they are all L2 learners themselves. In this book, they pooled their authentic experiences with learning one or more languages beyond their native tongues. Knowledge and skills in the authors' L2s were developed in various ways: in formal classroom settings, through intensive exposure in other countries, by tandem teaching-learning with distant partners, with technology-based language programs, or through self-instruction. All chapter authors possess personally developed knowledge of self-regulated, strategic L2 learning in practice, in addition to theoretical knowledge gained through studying related academic literature. Furthermore, most authors were or still are L2 teachers and/or teacher educators, as well as LLS researchers, with deeply rooted interests in LLS and how they can be taught, as well as in related psychological aspects of language learning, for example, willingness to communicate, anxiety, or motivation. Last but not least, many of the authors have proven to be confident and fearless in exploring the great complexity of L2 learning. The thematic wealth of this book, which is partly due to the individual backgrounds of all authors and their interests, makes this volume a fount of knowledge and experience.

2. Goals of the book

The six goals of this book, which were described in the Introduction, were

- to define LLS,
- to link LLS and self-regulation,
- to explain the fluidity of LLS,
- to show the association between individual differences and LLS,
- to explore the relationships among contexts, complexity, and strategic learners, and
- to provide insights on methods for strategy research, assessment, and instruction.

Some chapters reflected all of these goals; however, individual parts of the book emphasized specific topics. The theoretical foundation of the book was built in Part I, where the basics of individualized, self-regulated, strategic L2 learning were explained. Part II explored suitable methodologies to research LLS within a complex web of contextual influences and individual learner characteristics. This flexible and dynamic network of variables was the focus of interest in Part III. Finally, Part IV explored the flourishing topic of SI and how SI can be integrated in L2 teaching and L2 teacher education.

3. The participants of the studies

The learners of English as a foreign or second language (EFL) who participated in the studies reported in this book came from a wealth of language backgrounds: Chinese (Chapter 7), French (Chapter 12), German (Chapter 6), Greek (Chapter 4), Greek and Turkish (Chapter 8), Japanese (Chapter 5), Polish (Chapters 9 and 11), and a mix of first languages (Chapter 3). In addition to EFL, Chapter 1 addressed Spanish as an L2 and provided an example of using the South American language Quechua to raise awareness about LLS. Furthermore, experiences with learning Spanish and Chinese as L2s were shared (Chapter 2). Similar to learners' language backgrounds, the participants of the reported studies covered a wide age-span and were on different L2 proficiency levels, including beginners in primary and secondary schools (Chapter 8), more proficient L2 learners at upper secondary level (Chapter 6), and L2 learners of advanced proficiency at university level (Chapters 1, 3, 9, 5, and 11).

4. Chapter summaries

Part I presented the theoretical foundation required to understand the complexity of contextualized, self-regulated LLS. As learners purposefully apply strategies to support L2 learning, teachers should promote the use of LLS, for example, by assisting learners to focus their attention on LLS or by targeted SI. The goal is to equip learners with the ability to select and apply LLS in meaningful ways, which consequently leads to successful and enjoyable language learning and, ultimately, increased L2 proficiency. In addition to teacher practice, Part I aimed at theories regarding learner practice, research, and assessment.

In Chapter 1, Oxford, Lavine, and Amerstorfer examined self-regulated, strategic L2 learning as a complex system within further complex systems. They disclosed a new and innovative way to discover LLS by using *A*mazing *IM*ages of *S*trategies (AIMS). AIMS inspire the imagination of L2 learners and teachers and enable us to travel the depth of context and complexity related to strategic L2 learning in an innovative, entertaining way. Included in Chapter 1 was a small selection from a continuously growing pool of photographs that represent LLS. Readers can use these photographs, which are rich with colorful complexity and beloved by students, for SI and especially for its first stage, strategy awareness.

Oxford, Lavine, and Amerstorfer each conducted AIMS studies in geographically and culturally different, authentic L2 learning environments. The varying backgrounds of participants, their individual learner characteristics, and many other influential factors from participants' learning environments resulted in fascinating responses to the presented images. The diverse AIMS studies confirm that stimulating the creativity and imagination of L2 learners and teachers is a lively, meaningful way to raise strategy awareness.

In Chapter 2, Cohen investigated theoretical aspects of LLS and extended a bridge towards their practical applications. Cohen's definition of LLS highlights the element of consciousness as the main distinguishing factor between strategic and non-strategic processes, which leads the author to caution against a confusion of strategies with skills. To offer greater clarity, a number of ways to classify LLS were proposed, and Cohen introduced a classification system that specifically focuses on strategies to handle the pragmatics of an L2. An analysis of individual differences in the use of LLS and an explanation about how advanced strategy application can transform L2 learners into "super-learners" were included in the chapter.

As a pioneer in the field of LLS instruction, Cohen provided insights into handbooks for SI, related courses, and materials. He presented examples from the Center for Advanced Research on Language Acquisition (CARLA), which has pooled remarkable resources and practical tips about strategic L2 learning. Cohen also shared his personal story about studying Mandarin and ended the chapter with a number of critical questions in relation to LLS concerning the teacher's roles in L2 learning, the effectiveness of SI, and the buzzing research area of SI in general.

Chapter 3 investigated successful L2 learners who autonomously take control of their learning in different settings around the globe. Griffiths described the key qualities of "good language learners" and analyzed how strategy choice is subject to contextual influences. According to Griffiths, successful L2 learners are motivated to invest time and effort in their learning. They generally have a positive attitude towards L2 learning and the ability to regulate their learning. Griffiths emphasized that successful L2 learners make frequent use of a large repertoire of strategies that are carefully chosen according to situational demands, which distinguishes effective L2 learners from less successful ones.

In Griffiths' study, a mixed-gender group of fourteen successful EFL learners from an impressive diversity of national and cultural backgrounds was analyzed. While maintaining a holistic perception of the complexity of L2 learning in general, the study specifically focused on the participants' motivation, investment, beliefs, autonomy, and strategy application. LLS were viewed within the learning contexts in which they were used and in relation to individual learner characteristics. The study confirmed that L2 teachers should encourage learners to use a large repertoire of LLS frequently and appropriately to address individual demands. Griffiths closed with valuable recommendations for L2 teachers about how they can support strategic, self-regulated L2 learning.

The first three chapters in this volume manifested the view that L2 learning is dynamic and complex. They reminded us how important it is to pay attention to the context in which LLS are used. Educational research and particularly research about situated strategy use require thorough planning and conduct. Hence, Part II of this book was dedicated to research methodology. It presented three research projects that were carefully designed with appropriately chosen methods to fulfill focused aims and to answer specific questions.

In Chapter 4, Gkonou explored metacognitive and affective strategies for learner self-regulation with the use of two types of narratives. The qualitative research reported in this chapter was part of a mixed-methods study that investigated how highly anxious Greek EFL learners cope with L2 anxiety. Specifically, the focus was on the type of strategies used to lower anxiety and on the learner behavior to reduce stress during EFL lessons. With regard to research methodology, Gkonou described how diary entries and interviews were used in the study. For example, in-depth feedback on the participants' written diary notes was offered to raise anxious learners' motivation to participate.

The analysis of the data showed that highly anxious students used three kinds of LLS: affective strategies (relaxation and peer seeking), strategies on a meta-affective and metacognitive level (preparation and seeking practice opportunities), and strategies related to positive psychology (positive thinking). Gkonou concluded that emotional self-regulation depends on individual learner characteristics and contextual circumstances, which is in line with similar outcomes that were reflected in several other chapters. Finally, Gkonou suggested further research about strategies to lower learner anxiety, which may be accomplished through the use of different types of research methods.

At the beginning of Chapter 5, Mizumoto and Takeuchi explained that, in contrast to some claims in the related literature, LLS research has never waned since the 1970s. On the contrary, strategy research kept rising on a steep curve. Likert-scale type questionnaires have been the most popular method although there has been a noticeable increase in mixed-methods research in the field. Mizumoto and Takeuchi found that conventional analysis methods and correlation-based analysis have been predominant in studies about LLS. Following their review of popular research methods, Mizumoto and Takeuchi introduced an entirely new way of researching LLS, namely, decision tree analysis.

Decision tree analysis is a predictive modeling approach that flexibly deals with categorical and continuous data in independent and dependent variables. According to the authors, the method, which originated in marketing research, enables a more detailed way to research situated strategy use in comparison with conventional methods like questionnaires. The approach fosters the inclusion of contextual influences while demonstrating the core features of strategies. It will be interesting to observe how this innovative method will further develop in the field of LLS research.

The methods described in Chapter 6 were comparatively conventional. Amerstorfer presented a mixed-methods study that investigated self-regulated LLS in a cooperative EFL learning environment. The author explained in much detail how the original purpose of Oxford's *Strategy Inventory for Language Learning (SILL*, 1990) was expanded to evolve into a suitable tool for the study. In addition to its initial purpose to identify the strategies applied by L2 learners, the *SILL* was further used as an ice-breaker in Amerstorfer's study, to draw the participants' attention to the topic of LLS, and to elicit complementary qualitative details about strategic L2 learning in context.

The participants used a large variety of strategies that served four main purposes: to improve knowledge about and skills in the L2, to cooperate with others, to complete assignments and tasks, and to increase motivation. Strategies were often used in combination and usually aimed at multiple purposes. What was striking about the study was that contextual influences and individual learner characteristics led to situations in which the same strategies or strategy combinations fulfilled different purposes. Hence, Amerstorfer concluded that strategies should not be researched in isolation and that a mix of research methods is advisable for studies about contextualized, self-regulated LLS use.

Part II demonstrated that there is room for traditional as well as new methods in LLS research. Depending on the framework conditions (e.g., number of participants, research environment) and the aims of a study (e.g., to answer a set of research questions; to verify or falsify a hypothesis; to discover new findings), researchers carefully select appropriate methods and painstakingly plan the design of a study. The nature and aim of a study determine whether a combination of research methods may be recommendable. Additional examples of skillfully applied research methods were included in Part III of this volume, which presented three studies about strategic L2 learning with an emphasis on the diversity of contexts and individual learner differences.

Gu's Chapter 7 put the spotlight on the huge number of EFL learners in China, where English is taught with a strong focus on memorization and on studying explicit knowledge. Comparatively little attention is given to individual learner characteristics and preferences. Despite abundant publications about LLS since 1990, expected changes in L2 learning and teaching have not become evident. While findings from LLS research have been well applied in many countries of the world, hardly any practical implications are apparent in Chinese EFL classrooms. Nevertheless, strategy research has influenced the Chinese national curriculum for basic education and textbooks.

Gu reminded us that strategic L2 learning means more than striving for higher language proficiency. L2 learning also means becoming autonomous and self-regulated, balancing individual and social aspects of L2 learning, and developing an awareness of individual preferences and situational circumstances. To achieve these goals, Gu argued that LLS research has to aim higher than generating further research. It should provide understandable and detailed information on how L2 teachers can increase and improve LLS use in Chinese EFL classrooms. Moreover, Chinese EFL teachers should be motivated to conduct action research despite the pressure teachers and learners experience due to high-stakes examinations.

The study presented in Chapter 8 by Psaltou-Joycey and Gavriilidou analyzed the LLS use of more than 3,000 primary and secondary school pupils in Greece. The study examined the effect of learners' gender, education level, proficiency level, and region of residence on the application of LLS. The results showed that girls use LLS more frequently than boys, and, with the exception of compensation strategies, learners at primary level use LLS more frequently than those at secondary schools. Furthermore, a higher proficiency in the L2 correlates positively with the frequency of strategy use. And finally, the region of residence plays an important role in strategic L2 learning in Greece. Learners at schools that are located in poor socioeconomic regions show tendencies of lower strategy use in comparison with richer areas.

Psaltou-Joycey and Gavriilidou emphasized that contextual variables and individual learner differences must be taken into account when researching strategic, self-regulated L2 learning because individual and group characteristics influence learners' cognition, affect, motivation, and behavior. While the Greek curriculum generally promotes learner autonomy, and LLS are included in Greek EFL textbooks, the study confirmed that SI is in demand at Greek schools. The authors highlighted that young and adolescent learners need SI to select and use LLS effectively.

In Chapter 9, Pawlak brought to our attention a lack of research in a specific area of L2 teaching. While pronunciation instruction is comparatively well-researched, the application of pronunciation learning strategies seems to have been largely ignored. There is an acute demand for the investigation of practical aspects of LLS as they promote learner autonomy, which is the essence of self-regulated, strategic L2 learning. To fill the void, Pawlak examined a group of English majors at a Polish university who completed a form-focused and a meaning-focused pronunciation activity. The aims of the study were to analyze the kinds of pronunciation learning strategies used before, during, and after the completion of the two tasks. The study furthermore inquired into the effect of task type and the impact of gender, L2 proficiency, and learning style on the use of pronunciation learning strategies.

Pawlak found that previous studies, which frequently used questionnaires for data collection, primarily explored general strategic actions rather than practical applications concerning L2 pronunciation. In contrast, the innovative design of Pawlak's study provided new information about learners' use of pronunciation strategies. Nevertheless, the author remarked that further research, preferable mixed-methods research, is necessary to make concrete, context-sensitive, and practicable recommendations for pronunciation teaching and learning.

Part III of this volume exemplified the richness of contextual factors in LLS research. Existing circumstances like educational environment, study tradition, philosophical beliefs, geographical position, and cultural norms, shape research about self-regulated, strategic L2 learning. Despite content-related differences in the three studies, they enhanced an awareness of contextual influences on L2 learning and commonly demanded further research aimed at practical aspects of LLS application and SI.

Part IV, the final one of this volume, was dedicated to SI. It demonstrated recent research findings related to SI and on teacher education for SI. The central questions in this part were how current and future L2 teachers can actively support effective strategy application and how teacher candidates can be prepared for SI in diverse contexts.

Chamot's previous work and that of others in the field verified a strong connection between L2 learners who choose and use appropriate strategies, and increased learning success, and self-confidence. However, many L2 teachers simply do not have the time to undergo extensive autodidactic efforts to acquire knowledge and skills to teach strategic L2 learning. Other options to learn about SI, for instance, participation in workshops at conferences or collaborations in classroom-based research projects, have shown little long-term effect or have caused other problems. Therefore, Chamot advocates the integration of SI in teacher education.

In Chapter 10, Chamot presented three courses that are part of a teacher education program at a master's level. The courses integrate components about LLS and provide a variety of teaching and learning contexts. They draw on the teacher candidates' personal experience as L2 learners, manifest a solid theoretical foundation about strategic L2 learning, and create a link to practical SI in L2 classrooms. An evaluation of the program's focus on LLS instruction provided valuable information for the continuous improvement of the program design. Chamot offered a state-of-the-art way to integrate LLS instruction in teacher education; however, this particular area of strategy research is still young and requires continued inquiry and practice.

Chapter 11 was based on Bielak and Mystkowska-Wiertelak's experience as L2 examiners, who repeatedly witnessed symptoms of text anxiety during a relatively high-stakes EFL exam at a Polish university. The authors tried to find out about this issue in related academic literature and discovered that the value of affective and meta-affective SI and its influence on learners' test anxiety has not been sufficiently researched. Hence, they conducted a mixed-methods study that explored the relationship between affective SI and test anxiety.

The results of the study with 41 intermediate EFL learners showed that due to the topic's high complexity, affective components of strategic L2 learning could not be isolated from other factors. Affective SI was related to increases in the use of other types of strategies as well. Furthermore, learners with high and medium levels of test anxiety were more likely to increase the use of affective strategies after targeted instruction than were low-anxiety learners. Bielak and Mystkowska-Wiertelak recommended further research to examine the links between anxiety and LLS, as well as a continuation and expansion of the instruction of affective strategies to improve exam situations for anxious L2 learners in Poland and in the rest of the world.

In this volume's final chapter, Gunning and Turner addressed how the strategy use of young L2 learners can be assessed in a fashion that is appropriate for their age-level. As self-regulated strategy use is influenced by many variables coming from the task, the individual, and the learning environment, strategy assessment is a complicated endeavor. To gain comprehensive insights into young learners' strategic actions and, as far as possible, thoughts, Gunning and Turner suggested a variety of methods and tools for researchers and L2 teachers. They evaluated think-aloud protocols, interviews, and questionnaires and emphasized that all tools and methods must be adjusted to be appropriate for young learners.

Gunning and Turner further discussed how the effects of SI and assessment on strategy use and L2 learning can itself be assessed. They highlighted the importance of constructive and age-appropriate feedback in an L2 learning context, in which teaching, learning, and assessment promote learning in synergy. The three main purposes of strategy assessment that Gunning and Turner identified were to guide learners' reflection on their learning, to help learners explore room for improvement, and to foster young L2 learners' self-regulation.

The final part of this volume demonstrated how SI is implemented in different educational contexts around the globe and that effective SI requires thorough strategy assessment. As the chapters in Part IV showed, strategy instruction is increasingly happening in L2 classrooms, where learners are assisted in their development and improvement of appropriate strategies for self-regulated L2 learning. Equally important, SI must become a central topic in teacher education, where prospective L2 teachers are familiarized with possibilities to support the progress of learners' effective strategy use.

5. Future research and concluding remarks

There was general agreement among all chapter authors that further research is needed about LLS and related topics. Many areas are still unexplored or insufficiently researched, for example the following:

- the functions and combinations of strategies in L2 learning,
- the development of reliable tools and methods for strategy assessment for learners of different age ranges,
- the development of reliable tools and methods to investigate LLS *during* task implementation, as well as retrospectively,

- effective ways to integrate LLS into L2 teacher education programs (for instance, further examples of how future and in-service L2 teachers can be prepared to provide SI in their L2 classrooms),
- specific areas of strategic L2 learning, such as pronunciation learning strategies and grammar learning strategies,
- the strategic reduction and regulation of overall L2 anxiety and specific types of anxieties (for instance, test anxiety),
- the potential of decision tree-based methods and how they can be further used effectively in LLS research,
- the desired increase in applicability of LLS research (for example, how new findings can be presented in a fashion that is easy to understand by L2 teachers and learners and that can be practically implemented in L2 classrooms), and
- conventional research methods, for instance, survey research using strategy inventories, either individually or in combination, and how they can support studies that employ holistic perspectives of strategic L2 learning.

Putting this book together was an enriching process for the editors. We believe that the book can be an inspiration to researchers, theorists, current and future L2 teachers, teacher educators, and university faculty in many countries around the globe. We hope that the book motivates the developers of L2 learning materials, textbooks, and websites, as well as committed classroom teachers who strive to empower their students to become successful L2 learners. We also hope that it will provoke continued discussion and further research about contextualized, strategic L2 learning and teaching.

Appendices

Appendix A (Chapter 10)

Instructional Guidelines for Lessons and Units

Name_____ Date _____ Draft #_____

Grade and Language Level _____ Topic _____

STAGE 1—DESIRED RESULTS

Established Goals (Content Standards, Language Standards, and Learning Strategy Standards)

Big Idea(s) for Content and Language	Essential Question(s) for Content and Language
Examples for Content: • *The myths and fables of different cultures help us understand a people's values and beliefs.* • *Changes in climate have affected where people can live, the work they can do, and the food they can eat.*	*Examples for Content:* • *Why are myths and fables important in different cultures?* • *How have changes in climate affected people's lives in the past?*
Examples for Language: • *Myths and fables use imaginative language to explain natural phenomena or teach a lesson.* • *Informational texts use facts and scientific observations to explain causes and effects of natural or man-made phenomena.*	*Examples for Language:* • *How is the language used to tell a myth or fable different from the language of other types of stories?* • *What are three characteristics of informational texts about geography or history?*

What will students learn? (Objectives)		
Content Knowledge and Use of Content Skills	Language Awareness and Language Use	Learning Strategies Knowledge and Use
Differentiation	Differentiation	Differentiation

STAGE 2—ASSESSMENT EVIDENCE

How will students be assessed?	
Performance Assessment(s)	Other Evidence
Differentiation	Differentiation

Rubrics/Criteria for Assessment

STAGE 3—LEARNING PLAN

Materials Needed (including technology):

FIVE LESSON PHASES

QUESTIONS TO CONSIDER AS YOU PLAN ACTIVITIES

FOR THE LESSON

(PROVIDE ACTIVITIES FOR EACH OF THE FIVE LESSON PHASES)

Preparation (how you get students ready to learn): What prior knowledge/experience does each student have about the Essential Question(s), content topic, language goal, and learning strategy to be explored? What can I use as a motivator/hook? Do any concepts or vocabulary need to be reviewed or pre-taught? What advance organizer can I use to share learning objectives with students? Can students be given a choice in learning objectives?

Presentation (how you present new information, language, and strategies): What different ways can I present the new knowledge and language so that all students understand the Big Idea(s)? How can I relate the Big Idea to students' prior knowledge and interests? How will I model the new learning strategy? Do I need to differentiate and/or provide choices?

Practice (how students practice the new information and skills): What kinds of activities will help my students apply the new knowledge, language, and learning strategy and explore answers to the Essential Question(s)? How will I differentiate activities and group students so that all can learn?

Self-evaluation (how students assess their own learning): What is the best way for my students to reflect on and assess their own learning of content, language, and learning strategies? How can they evaluate their answers to the Essential Question(s)?

Expansion (how students apply the lesson to their own lives and personal backgrounds): How can I connect the Big Idea(s) of this lesson/unit to students' own lives, culture(s), and identities? How can I help students transfer what they have learned to new situations? How can parents become involved?

Assessment (your check on the planned assessments): Do I need to modify the differentiated performance assessments, other assessment evidence, and/or rubrics described in Stage 2?

Adapted from Chamot 2009; Wiggins and McTighe 2006

Checklist/Scoring Sheet for Content-based Thematic Unit

Name _____ Language and Grade Level _____ Date _____

Big Idea(s) _____ Essential Question(s) _____

Component	Description	Score	Comments
1. Big Idea(s) and Essential Question(s)	Reflect key concepts in TESOL/ACTFL and state curriculum standards		
2. Unit Plan Overview	Coherent and sequenced appropriately		
3. Objectives/ Standards/ Established Goals	Specific, teachable, measurable, aligned to specific TESOL/ACTFL and State standards		
4. Teacher Assessment Evidence	Assessment clearly based on stated objectives, performance assessment, and other evidence identified		
5. Content/Culture	Includes content knowledge and processes, higher order skills, 3 subject areas, or culture(s) for FL		
6. Language	FL: 3 Communicative Modes; ESL: 4 Language Modalities; All: language awareness of grammar, vocabulary, discourse		
7. Learning Strategies	Appropriate to task, metacognitive awareness developed, guided strategies practice		

8. Materials	Appropriate to task and proficiency level; copies provided, sources identified, worksheets included		
9. Preparation Phase	Students' prior knowledge elicited, topic vocabulary developed, advance organizer provided		
10. Presentation Phase	Comprehensible, motivating, teacher modeling, explicit strategies instruction; addresses Big Idea and related language structures		
11. Practice Phase	Cooperative learning/ hands-on/ inquiry; uses content, academic language, learning strategies; responds to Essential Question(s)		
12. Self-Evaluation Phase	Student self-evaluation of content, language, strategies and of the Big Idea(s) and Essential Question(s)		
13. Expansion Phase	Applications to students' lives, connections to other subjects, cultural and linguistic comparisons, parent involvement		
Summary Rating (maximum score = 39)			

Scoring: 3 = *Target*   2 = *Acceptable*   1 = *Unacceptable*   0 = Item not present

Appendix B (Chapter 10)

Teaching Language Learning Strategies in the Second/Foreign Language Classroom

Questionnaire

In your language teacher preparation courses at GWU, you have studied learning strategies from various perspectives. For example, in CPED 6557: Second Language Acquisition, you read about and discussed current research on language learning strategies. In CPED 6551: Second Language Instruction and in CPED 6627: Teaching Reading and Writing in a Second Language, you were asked to include learning strategy instruction in your lesson planning and microteaching.

Please reflect on what you have learned about teaching language learning strategies by answering the following questions:

1. What is your personal definition of a learning strategy?

    _____

    _____

2. To what degree have/would you incorporate learning strategy instruction into your language teaching?

    _____ Rarely   _____ Occasionally   _____ Frequently

3. How confident do you feel in your ability to teach learning strategies to language learners?

    _____ Not at all confident   _____ Somewhat confident   _____ Very confident

4. In learning about language learning strategies and how to teach them, what activities are most helpful to you? Please rank order the following list of activities by writing a 1 next to the most important, a 2 next to the second in importance, and so on. If two activities are of equal value, please assign them the same number.

    __ reading about research on language learning strategies

    __ writing a 1-week diary about my own learning strategies

    __ reading about how to teach language learning strategies

    __ listening to lectures on language learning strategies

    __ classroom discussions about teaching language learning strategies

    __ watching demonstrations about how to teach language learning strategies (for instance, with props like stuffed animals or plastic tools)

__ watching videotapes of language teachers teaching learning strategies

__ observing a language teacher teaching learning strategies

__ role-playing the parts of ESL or FL students in a demonstration of teaching language learning strategies

__ planning lessons that include learning strategy instruction

__ presenting learning strategy lessons to the class (microteaching)

__ trying out strategy instruction with my students

__ getting feedback from my students about my strategy instruction

__ other (please describe) _____

5. Please describe the challenges you have faced/will face in teaching learning strategies to language learners. Then describe the steps you have taken/will take to meet these challenges.

_____

_____

_____

_____

_____

Thank you very much for sharing your ideas about learning how to teach language learning strategies! Please feel free to add any additional comments below:

_____

_____

Appendix C (Chapter 11)

Survey of Exam-Related EFL Affective Strategies, or *SEREAS* (English translation)

In relation to today's EFL exam (immediately before the exam, but also much earlier, during, and after the exam):

1. I have tried to notice the emotions (such as stress, anxiety, self-confidence, etc.) which I experienced.	1	2	3	4
2. I have tried to somehow plan my emotions.	1	2	3	4
3. I gained access to resources (e.g. relaxing music, Internet sites about relaxation) that favorably influence emotions.	1	2	3	4
4. I have somehow affected the examination situation (e.g. asked other students for a relaxing conversation just before the exam) in order to improve my emotions.	1	2	3	4
5. I have tried to determine whether I was experiencing the right emotions.	1	2	3	4
6. I have tried to determine whether I should change the way I influence my emotions.	1	2	3	4
7. I have tried to experience the right emotions.	1	2	3	4

1—Not at all true of me, 2—Only somewhat true of me, 3—Quite true of me, 4—Very true of me

Write in your own words what you have done before (immediately before, but also much earlier), during, and after the exam to experience favorable emotions (low level of stress/anxiety, self-confidence, self-efficacy, etc.)

....

....

....

....

....

Appendix D (Chapter 11)

Anxometers (English translation)

In the *anxometers* below indicate (circle the right number) the level of your anxiety (nervousness, stress) experienced immediately before, during, and immediately after the exam that you have just taken.

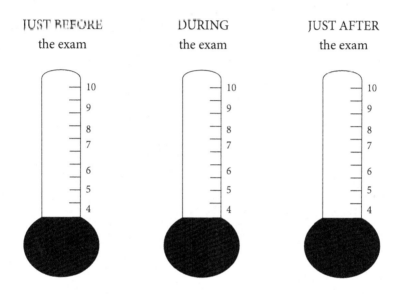

JUST BEFORE
the exam

DURING
the exam

JUST AFTER
the exam

Index of Names

Adonis, Mary 214
Agathopoulou, Eleni 37, 170
Aida, Yuki 81, 83
Alexiou, Thomaï 37, 170, 172
Alonso-Tapia, Jesús xxv, 49
Al-Saraj, Taghreed M. 81
Amerstorfer, Carmen M. xviii–xx,
    xxiii–xxxiv, 2, 5–29, 75–6, 101, 111,
    114, 123–40, 204, 237, 266, 269, 287–97
Anam, Syafi'ul 268
Anderson, Neil J. 189, 213, 265
Anstrom, Kristina 214
Anton, William D. 238
Aphek, Edna 43
Ardasheva, Yuliya 171, 179
Arroyo, Alan A. 107, 170

Bai, Rui 36, 151
Bailey, Kathleen M. 81, 83, 91
Bailly, Sophie 7
Bandura, Albert xxvi
Barcelos, Ana Maria F. 86
Barkhuizen, Gary 86
Barnhardt, Sarah 152
Barraza, Ruth A. 222
Bartels, Nat 214
Bedell, Jeffrey 238
Belcher, Dianne 56
Benson, Phil 86
Berkil, Gulcin 189, 191, 193
Bessette, Lyne 277
Bielak, Jakub 179, 210, 237–60, 295
Bielska, Joanna 80
Black, Paul 271
Boekaerts, Monique 81
Bond, Trevor 105
Borg, Simon 216, 218
Bown, Jennifer 91
Breiman, Leo 111
Bronfenbrenner, Urie xxviii–xxix, 7
Brookhart, Susan M. 264, 270
Brown, H. Douglas 148, 267

Burden, Robert L. 83
Busque, Christine 261, 264, 272, 275–6, 279
Butler, Deborah L. 42
Butler, Emily A. 82
Butler, Yuko Goto 172, 181

Cameron, Lynne 125
Canagarajah, Suresh 146
Carifio, James 106
Chamot, Anna Uhl xxv, xxxi, 1, 36–7, 49,
    55, 69, 124, 130, 152, 158, 171–2, 179,
    181, 191, 194, 210, 213–35, 237, 262,
    264–6, 269, 295, 301
Chan, Letty 10
Chen, Mai-Lin 180
Cheng, Bing 153, 168
Chi, Julie C. 43, 102, 197, 233, 237, 265
Chik, Alice 86
Clément, Richard 81, 83
Cohen, Andrew D. 2, 31–53, 55, 69, 102,
    109, 124, 189–90, 197, 213–14, 217, 219,
    232–3, 237, 261, 263, 265–6, 290
Cohen, Jacob 237, 239, 246, 248, 252–3
Cope, Joann 80–1, 83, 85, 87, 91, 193, 238,
    257
Cortazzi, Martin 148
Cotterall, Sarah 56
Coyle, Do 201, 237
Crabbe, David 158
Creswell, John W. 85, 129, 270
Csíkszentmihályi, Mihály 92
Cuddy, Amy 240, 242

Dai, Zhongxin 153
Daley, Christine E. 83
Daniloski, Kim 108
Davidson, Fred 264, 270
De Boer, Hester 118
De Bot, Kees 7
Deci, Edward L. 169
DeKeyser, Robert M. 190
Derwing, Tracy M. 189

De Silva, Radhika 46
De Waal, Ton 172
Dewaele, Jean-Marc 81, 83, 91–2, 238
Diamantopoulos, Adamantios 102
Dignath-van Ewijk, Charlotte 118
Donato, Richard xxv–xxvi
Donker, Anouk S. 118
Dörnyei, Zoltán xxvi, xxviii, 8, 10, 32, 35,
    49, 56, 59, 65, 83, 91–92, 100–3, 108,
    130, 237
Dorval, Catherine 277
Droździał-Szelest, Krystyna 191
Dubé, France 277

Eckstein, Grant T. 192–3
Edmonds, I. G. 222
Egbert, Jesse 104, 111
Egloff, Boris 82
Ehrman, Madeline E. xxvi, 57, 181, 194
El-Dinary, Pamela Beard 152, 171, 214,
    265–6
Ellis, Gail 152
Ellis, Rod 57, 190, 192, 216
Erickson, Elisabeth A. 82

Feuerstein, Raphael S. xxv
Feuerstein, Reuven xxv
Falik, Louis xxv
Fox, Christine M. 105
Frangoudaki, Anna 172
Frank, Eibe 116
Freud, Sigmund 79
Friedman, Jerome 111
Fröhlich, Maria 75, 124, 267
Fu, Yurong 153
Fuchs, Christoph 102
Fulcher, Glenn 264, 270
Furnham, Adrian 92

Gabryś-Barker, Danuta 80
Gao, Xuesong Andy 43, 56, 101
Gardner, John 271
Gardner, Robert C. 81, 108, 193, 238, 244
Gavriilidou, Zoe 75, 142, 167–187, 201,
    210, 237, 293–4
Ge, Bingfang 153
Genesee, Fred 269
Gkonou, Christina xxx, 76, 79–97, 237,
    257, 266, 270, 291

Goh, Christine C. M. 101, 213
Goleman, Daniel 92
Graham, Suzanne 46, 239
Graves, Kathleen 216
Green, John M. 170–1, 179, 181
Gregersen, Tammy 57, 80–1, 83, 91, 124,
    141, 209, 240
Grenfell, Michael xxvii, 35, 172, 213–14,
    217, 219, 228, 231, 237, 261
Griffiths, Carol xxv–xxvi, 2, 32, 48–49,
    55–73, 99, 101, 104, 118, 170–2, 189,
    201, 216, 237, 290–1
Gross, James J. 82
Grotjahn, Rüdiger 128
Gu, Peter Yongqi 36, 42–4, 46, 48–9, 100,
    103, 108, 112, 114, 142, 145–66, 170,
    210, 213–14, 262, 266, 268–9, 293
Guba, Egon G. 87
Gunning, Pamela 44, 49, 69, 75, 124, 179,
    210, 214, 237, 261–86, 296

Hakuta, Kenji 181
Hall, Mark 116
Han, ZhaoHong 7
Hancock, Gregory R. 118
Harris, Vee xxvii, xxxi, 35, 44, 69, 172,
    210, 213–214, 217, 219, 228, 231, 237,
    261
Harrison, Christine 271
Hasselgreen, Angela 267
Hastie, Trevor 111
Hatch, Evelyn 105
Hayes, Jasmeet P. 82
He, An E. 43
He, Lianzhen 149
He, Mengyi 153
Henry, Alistair xxviii
Herrington, Richard 104, 111
Hill, Kathryn 270
Hiromori, Tomohito 108
Hiver, Phil 1, 9
Ho, Belinda 170–1
Hodis, Flaviu A. 118
Holliday, Adrian xxviii, xxxii
Hong-Nam, Kyunsim 170, 179
Horwitz, Elaine K. 80–1, 83, 85, 87, 91, 193,
    238, 257
Horwitz, Michael B. 80–1, 83, 85, 87, 91,
    193, 238, 257

Hosenfeld, Carol 141
Hou, Yali 153
Hsiao, Tsung-Yuan 108
Hu, Guangwei 44, 46, 151, 266, 268
Hu, Hsueh-chao Marcella 32, 49
Huberman, A. Michael 87
Hulstijn, Jan H. 160

Inceçay, Görsev 57
Ishihara, Noriko 36
Isoda, Takamichi 108
Iwai, Chiaki 239

Jaccard, James 108
James, Scott E 82
Jarvis, Scott 112
Ji, Peiying 153
Jimenez-Garrido, Amador 268
Jin, Lixian 148
John, Oliver P. 82
Johnson, Karen E. 216, 218
Johnson, Robert K. 103, 108, 112, 114

Kaiser, Sebastian 102
Kalaja, Paula 86
Kantaridou, Zoe 37, 170–1, 179–80
Kappler, Barbara 233
Katsikas, Christos 172
Kavvadias, Georgios K. 172
Kawahara, Tatsuya 111
Kazamia, Vassilia 37, 170, 179
Keatley, Catharine W. 214, 231
Kim, Hae-Jin 43
Kitano, Kazu 81
Kojic-Sabo, Izabella 108
Kondo, David S. 84, 91, 239
Kostons, Danny 118
Kotsiantis, S. B. 111
Kövecses, Zoltán 255
Kramsch, Claire 6
Kubanyiova, Maggie 91
Kumaravadivelu, B. 153
Küpper, Lisa 69, 124, 214, 266

LaBar, Kevin S. 82
LaFlair, Geoffrey T. 104, 111
Lafontaine, Marc 265
Lakoff, Robin 170
Lan, Rae 21, 23, 25, 28, 170–1, 179, 268

Larsen-Freeman, Diane xxviii, 1, 6–10, 57, 125
Larson-Hall, Jenifer 104, 106, 111, 246
Lassegard, James P. 233
Lavine, Roberta Z. 2, 5–29, 111, 125, 237, 290
Lazaraton, Anne 105
Leavell, Alexandra G. 170, 179
Leaver, Betty Lou xxvi, 194, 239
Lee, Clair 271
Lee, Kyoung Rang 189, 190, 261, 265
Lee, Kyung O. 171, 179
Levin, Ben 154
Lightbown, Patsy M. 108
Lin, Chien-Yu xxxi
Linck, Jared A. 35
Lincoln, Yvonna S. 87
Littlewood, William 148, 153, 161
Liu, Dianzhi 153
Liu, Jinkai 160
Liu, Rongjun 149
LoCastro, Virginia 130
López y Fuentes 222
Lu, Zhi 150

Ma, Rui 265–6
Ma, Xiaomei 158
Macaro, Ernesto 32, 48, 55, 114, 167, 189, 194, 213, 239, 262, 266, 268–9
MacIntyre, Peter D. xxviii, 2, 57, 80–1, 83, 91–2, 124, 141, 193, 209, 238–40, 244, 256
McArdle, John J. 111
McCarthy, Gregory 82
McCormick, Dawn E. xxv–xxvi
McDonough, Stephen H. 194
McGonigal, Kelly M. 82
McNamara, Tim 270
Magno, Carlo 180
Mak, Barley 81
Manchón, Rosa M. 219
Mareschal, Catherine J. 101
Márquez, Xiomena 214
Marshall, Bethan 271
Martinez-Pons, Manuel 49
Masgoret, Anne-Marie 108
Mattheoudakis, Marina 172
Mazur, Amy 214
McTighe, Jay 219, 301
Menezes, Vera 86

Meng, Yaru 158
Meng, Yue 151
Mercer, Sarah xxvi, xxviii, 80, 83, 91–2, 125, 128, 141–142, 209
Meza, Mario 81
Mihaljević Djigunović, Jelena 239
Miles, Matthew B. 87
Miller, Ann 191
Mitits, Lydia 37, 171–2, 175, 179–80
Mizumoto, Atsushi 1, 71, 76, 99–122, 130, 245, 292
Mokhtari, Kouider 237
Morey, Rajendra A. 82
Morris, Pamela A. xxviii, 7
Moss, Pamela A. 270
Moyer, Alene 56
Munro, Murray J. 189
Mutton, Trevor 262, 268
Mystkowska-Wiertelak, Anna 179, 210, 237–60, 295

Naiman, Neil 75, 124, 191, 265, 267
Nakatani, Yasuo 262, 280
Nassaji, Hossein 32, 49
Naughton, Diane 262
Nguyen, Le Thi Cam 44
Nilsson, Jeff 10
Nisbet, Deanna L. 107, 170
Noels, Kimberly A. 81, 83, 239, 256
Norton, Bonny 56
Norton Peirce, Bonny 56
Nunan, David 128, 181
Nyikos, Martha 38, 170, 180, 233

Oliver, Mary xxiii, 287
Olson, Tucker 81
O'Malley, J. Michael 1, 49, 55, 69, 124, 191, 213–14, 217, 219, 222, 237, 265–6
Onwuegbuzie, Anthony J. 83
Ortega, Lourdes 7
Osburne, Andrea G. 192
Oxford, Rebecca L. xviii–xx, xxiii–xxxiv, 1–2, 5–29, 32, 35–7, 42–4, 48–9, 55–6, 75, 82–3, 91, 93, 99–102, 104, 107–8, 111, 118, 124–5, 128–33, 145, 148, 158, 168–72, 175–81, 189–91, 193–4, 197, 201, 210, 213–14, 217, 219, 228, 231, 233, 237, 240–1, 243, 255, 257, 261–3, 265–70, 277, 280, 287–97

Paige, R. Michael 233
Panadero, Ernesto xxv, 49
Papadopoulou, Iris 37
Papanis, Alexandros 170
Parkhurst, Helen 127
Pawlak, Mirosław 56, 118, 142, 189–207, 237, 239, 246, 294
Peacock, Matthew 170–1
Peng, Renzhong 153
Pennycook, Alastair 146, 148
Perla, Rocco 106
Perry, Nancy E. 49
Peterson, Susan S. 191
Petrides, K. V. 92
Petrogiannis, Konstantinos 175, 180
Petty, Christopher M. 82
Pinilla-Herrera, Angela 41, 45, 190
Pinter, Annamaria 266
Plano Clark, Vicki L. 129
Platsidou, Maria 171, 179, 180
Plonsky, Luke xxxi, 44, 104, 106–7, 111, 117–18, 210, 239
Popham, W. James 161
Psaltou-Joycey, Angeliki 37, 75, 124, 142, 167–87, 201, 210, 233, 237, 293–4
Purpura, James E. 262–3, 265, 271, 281

Rand, Yaacov xxv
Rees-Miller, Janie 69
Robbins, Jill 152
Robinson, Peter xxvi
Rokoszewska, Katarzyna 193
Rose, Heath xxv
Rosenthal, Robert 246
Rubin, Joan 1, 49, 55, 70, 124, 149–50, 191, 213–14, 219–20, 228, 231, 233, 237, 265, 267
Russo, Rocco P. 69, 124, 266
Ryan, Richard M. 169,
Ryan, Stephen xix, xxi–xxii, xxvi, 10, 32, 65, 80, 83, 92, 100, 103, 128, 141–142, 209

Saldaña, Jonny 87
Samalieva, Marina 192
Sarafianou, Anna 37
Sarstedt, Marko 102
Schmitt, Norbert 101, 108, 112, 237
Schneider, Jack 154

Schramm, Karen 124, 130, 172, 194, 264, 269
Schunk, Dale H. xxv, 49, 169
Scott, Kimberly 266
Seth, Srishti 82
Sheorey, Ravi 237
Si, Jianguo 153
Şimşek, Erdi 92
Sinclair, Barbara 152
Sipitanou, Athena 171, 179, 180
Skehan, Peter xxvi, 56, 237
Smith, Benjamin K. 35
Smith, Nancy C. 82
Smith, Richard C. 153
Smoski, Moira J. 82
Song, Yichang 160
Sougari, Areti-Maria 37, 170, 172, 175, 179, 180
Spielberger, Charles D. 80, 238
Srivastava, Sanjay 82
Stern, Hans H. 75, 124, 149, 237, 267
Stewner-Manzanares, Gloria 69, 124, 266
Stiggins, Rick 271
Stracke, Elke 268
Strauss, Anselm L. 87
Sunderland, Jane 57
Szabó, Peter 255
Szpyra-Kozłowska, Jolanta 189, 195
Szyszka, Magdalena 191–3

Tafaghodtari, Marzieh H. 101, 239
Taguchi, Tatsuya 100, 102
Takač, Višnia P. 237
Takeuchi, Osamu 1, 71, 76, 99–122, 130, 201, 237, 246, 292
Tamir, Maya 82
Tannen, Deborah 170
Tashakkori, Abbas 85, 270
Teddlie, Charles 85
Thompson, Irene 233
Thompson, Jonathan R. 41, 45
Thompson, Marilyn S. 107
Tibshirani, Robert 111
Tindall, Evie R. 107, 170
Todesco, Angie 75, 124, 267
Tono, Yukio 111–12
Toohey, Kelleen 56
Tragant, Elsa 107, 170
Tremblay, Paul F. 108

Tretter, Thomas R. 171, 179
Tseng, Wen-Ta 101, 108, 112, 237
Tsui, Amy B. M. 83
Turner, Carolyn E. 69, 75, 179, 210, 237, 261–86, 296

Upshur, John A. 264, 269
Ushioda, Ema xxviii, 6, 35, 56

Vagg, Peter R. 238
Vandergrift, Larry 101, 213, 239, 265, 268–9
Van der Werf, Margaretha P. C. 118
Van Lier, Leo 6
Victori, Mia 107, 170
Vitanova, Gergana 191
Vrettou, Athina 170–1, 179, 180, 233
Vygotsky, Lev S. xxv, 128

Walqui-van Lier, Aida 222
Wang, Fang 152
Wang, Hongcui 112
Wang, Isobel 49
Wang, Lifei 148–51
Wang, Maohua 160
Wang, Qiang 146, 156–7
Wang, Xiaowei 149
Waple, Christopher J. 112
Watts, Wynanne 271–2
Weaver, Susan J. 37–8, 232, 237
Wen, Qiufang 146, 148–50, 160
Wenden, Anita 49, 55, 217
Wenger, Etienne 5
Wharton, Glenn 170–1, 179
White, Cynthia 56, 130, 194, 264, 269
White, Joanna 261, 264, 272, 275–6, 279
Wiggins, Grant 219, 301
Wilczynski, Petra 102
Wilhelm, Fank H. 82
Wiliam, Dylan 271
Willenborg, Leon 172
Williams, Marion 80, 83, 92, 128, 141–2, 209
Winne, Philip H. 49
Witt, Daria 181
Witten, Ian 116
Wittrock, Björn 154
Wittwer, Helga 127
Witzig, Lance E. 41, 45

Wolpe, Joseph 241
Woodrow, Lindy 108, 238
Wu, Weiping 153

Xiang, Juping 152
Xu, Jinfen 153

Yamamori, Koyo 108
Yan, Jackie X. 81
Yang, Jianding 151
Yang, Ming-Nuan 171, 179
Yang, Shuxian 149

Yao, Meilin 146
Yin, Tiechao 149
Ying-Ling, Yang 84, 91, 239
Young, Dolly J. 80

Zeidner, Moshe 238, 240, 243
Zhang, Jie 160
Zhang, Jun 151
Zhang, Lawrence Jun 36, 44, 46, 266
Zhang, Xuan. 149
Zhao, Jizheng 153
Zimmerman, Barry J. xxv, 49, 169

Subject Index

action research 161, 293
affective function 39
affective strategy/strategies xxiix, 79–80,
    82–3, 85–7, 92–3, 130, 153, 171, 210,
    237, 239, 241, 243–57, 291, 295
Amazing IMages of Strategies (AIMS) 2,
    11–27, 290
anxiety xviii, 57, 76, 79–93, 180, 193, 210,
    237–49, 253–7, 288, 291–2, 295, 297,
    306–7
    anxiety-coping strategies 84
    classroom anxiety 79–80, 85, 193, 257
    language anxiety (LA) 79–93, 238–9,
        244
    state anxiety 80, 244, 247, 254, 257
    state test anxiety (state TA) 244, 247–8,
        254
    test anxiety (TA) 210, 237–9, 241,
        243–55, 295, 297
    trait anxiety 80, 246
    trait test anxiety (trait TA) 244–8, 254
Anxometer(s) 237–60, 307
autonomy xx, xxv, 32, 49, 56, 58, 62, 70,
    101, 146, 148, 150, 153, 179, 189,
    291, 294

Center for Advanced Research on
    Language Acquisition (CARLA) 2,
    37, 40, 43, 290
classroom-based assessment (CBA)
    262–5, 269–72, 275, 281–2
cognition-focused instruction 240
Cognitive Academic Language Learning
    Approach (CALLA) xxxi, 219–20
cognitive restructuring 240
cognitive strategy/strategies xxix, 1, 33, 48,
    65, 82, 103, 130, 150, 153, 155, 171,
    181, 191–2, 238, 243, 247–51, 255
Common European Framework of Reference
    (CEFR) 18, 21, 70, 85, 129, 195
communication strategies 65, 149, 151,
    155–6, 200, 239

communicative language teaching 128,
    219
compensation strategies 130, 171, 176, 180,
    193, 243, 293
complex systems/complexity theory xxviii,
    2, 6–10, 14, 24–5, 27, 290
Content and Language Integrated
    Learning (CLIL) xxxi, 56
content-based language instruction
    219
context xviii, xx, xxii–xxxii, 1, 2, 5–10,
    17–18, 21–5, 32, 38, 43–4, 55–6,
    58, 66–7, 69–70, 76, 83–4, 93, 99,
    101, 109, 112, 116–17, 124, 126–7,
    133, 135, 141–2, 148, 150, 157,
    167–73, 175, 179–80, 182, 192,
    198, 204, 220, 224, 228–229, 232,
    237–8, 256, 261–5, 267–72, 276,
    279, 281–2
    classroom context xxviii, 169, 261–3,
        269–70, 272, 281
    contextual factors 8, 35, 55, 294
    cultural context 168, 170, 182
cooperation 123, 127, 131–3, 135–8
cooperative learning 128, 131, 220, 303
CoOperative Open Learning (COOL)
    127–8, 131–2
corrective feedback (CF) 195–6, 198,
    201–2
cover strategies 33
curriculum integration 154

decision tree analysis 111–12, 114, 115,
    116, 292
decision tree-based methods 99, 110–12,
    116–18, 297
descriptive feedback 272, 281

emotion-focused instruction 240
English as a Medium of Instruction (EMI)
    56
English for Specific Purposes (ESP) 56

Foreign Language Classroom Anxiety Scale (FLCAS) 85–6, 193, 257

goal-orientation 62
good language learner(s) xxii, 34–5, 55–7, 61, 68–70, 75, 171, 191, 237, 290
grammar learning 40, 190, 204, 297

imagination xx, xxiii, xxxi, xxxii, 5–6, 10, 17, 18, 24, 25, 290
individual differences (ID) xviii, xx, xxvi, xxvii, xxix, xxxi, xxxii, 2, 32, 35–36, 55–6, 75, 107, 109, 114, 116–17, 118, 141, 189–90, 192–4, 197, 201, 203–4, 237, 273, 288, 290
   affect xvii, xxvii, 8, 38, 56–7, 79–84, 154, 167, 169, 173, 182, 217, 240–1, 257, 294
   age xxvii, xxxi, 8, 18, 20, 34, 39, 44, 56, 85, 129, 145, 155, 167, 170, 171, 175, 179–80, 210, 240, 262, 266, 272, 281, 289, 296
   gender xxvii, xxix, xxxi, 8, 11, 34, 36, 45, 56, 58, 67, 129, 142, 167, 169–70, 174, 176–7, 179, 182, 194, 201, 203, 291, 293–4
   language proficiency xxiv, xxxi, 5, 9, 18, 21, 34–35, 42–4, 46, 70, 85, 129, 142, 145, 148–9, 160, 167, 169–71, 174–82, 193–5, 197, 201, 203, 216, 219, 221, 223, 225, 229, 240, 271, 289, 293–4, 303
   learning style(s) 8, 35–6, 40, 42–3, 56–7, 67, 142, 158, 167, 194, 197, 201–3, 216, 229, 294
   motivation xvii, xxv, xxvi, xxvii, xxxi, 2, 8, 10, 20, 35, 38, 42, 56, 58, 60, 67, 70–1, 81, 91, 108, 133, 136, 138, 158, 167–72, 180, 182, 204, 216–17, 221, 229, 288, 291–2, 294
   personality xxvii–xxviii, xxxi, 7, 35, 56–7, 80–1, 88, 90, 129, 158, 170
inference strategies 35
inferences 32, 35–7, 151, 222, 270, 280
interaction 1, 6–9, 14, 22–3, 34–5, 128, 141, 169, 191, 195, 217, 237, 252, 272, 275–6, 279
   peer interaction 8
   teacher–student interaction 8

Language Learning Strategy Instruction (LLSI) 213–14, 216, 219, 225, 227, 229–31
Language Strategy Use Inventory and Index (LSUII) 102–3
learner-centered teaching 214, 231
learner-context ecosystem 6
learning goals 7, 55–7, 61, 62, 169, 281
learning-oriented assessment (LOA) 271, 281
life-long learning 264

Managing Your Emotions for Language Learning Questionnaire (MYE) 257
memory 35, 37, 39, 65, 125, 130, 133, 134, 135, 159–61, 171, 175–8, 192–3, 197, 203, 226, 243, 245, 255, 267
   associative memory 35
   working memory 35, 203
memory strategies 33, 130, 135, 159–61, 176
meta-awareness 75
metacognitive awareness 83, 179, 225, 302
Metacognitive Awareness Listening Questionnaire (MALQ) 268
Metacognitive Control of Strategy Use (MCSU) 112, 114
metacognitive function 34, 39
metapragmatic function 39
metastrategies xx, 82–3
   meta-affective strategies 79, 82–3, 87, 92–3, 240, 243, 246–8, 254
   metacognitive strategies 33, 65, 79, 87, 91–3, 130, 149, 151, 153, 171, 176, 179, 181, 191–2, 200, 217–18, 230, 238, 243, 248, 249, 251, 255, 291
mixed-methods research xxix, 101, 270, 292–4
mnemonic keyword strategy 43

operationalizing strategies 32

peer feedback 38, 272, 274
pronunciation xx, 34, 63, 125, 142, 189–204, 240, 294, 297
pronunciation learning strategies 142, 189–94, 197–204, 294, 297

Reactions to Tests (RTT) 242–8, 257
regulation strategies 155
rehearsal strategies 33
resource strategies 155–6
retrieval strategies 33

second language acquisition (SLA) xviii,
    79–84, 91, 100–1, 216–17, 219, 221,
    232, 304
second language instruction 216, 219, 221,
    232, 304
self-assessment 202
self-evaluation 132, 209, 218–19, 224–5,
    228, 232, 272, 281, 301, 303
self-reflection xxvi, 27, 218
self-regulation xviii, xx, xxiv–xxv, xxxii, 5,
    8–9, 32, 49, 76, 79, 81, 84, 92, 101,
    127, 169, 209, 237, 257, 263–4, 272,
    288, 291, 296
social strategies 33, 65, 130, 171, 176, 192,
    243
socio-affective/socioaffective strategies
    192, 239
*Strategic Pronunciation Learning Scale
    (SPLS)* 193
strategy assessment xx, 2, 43, 101, 210,
    261–73, 281–2, 296
strategy awareness 2, 6, 11, 14–15, 24–25,
    27, 262, 277, 290
strategy-enhancing activities 2
strategy guidance 152
strategy instruction/strategies-based
    instruction xx, xxxi, 2, 8–11, 20, 25,
    31, 36–46, 69, 107, 117–18, 135,
    148–53, 161, 169, 182, 191–4,
    209–10, 213–14, 220–1, 223–32,
    237–45, 248, 253–7, 262, 264–9, 275,
    277, 280–1, 287, 289–90, 294–6,
    304–5; see also strategy training,
    strategy intervention, styles- and
    strategies-based instruction

strategy intervention 151–2
*Strategy Inventory for Language Learning
    (SILL)* 43, 75–6, 101, 106, 130–8, 168,
    175–6, 242–8, 253–5, 257, 267–9,
    280, 292
*Strategy Inventory for Learning
    Pronunciation (SILP)* 193
strategy research xxxii, 47, 75–6, 99,
    101, 117–18, 128–9, 142, 146,
    149, 172, 210, 228, 265, 282, 288,
    292–3, 295
strategy sharing 262
strategy training 148–53, 161, 256
styles- and strategies-based instruction
    (SSBI) 36, 38
*Survey of Exam-Related EFL Affective
    Strategies (SEREAS)* 237–260,
    305
systematic desensitization 83, 240–1

task-based instruction 219
task-based strategies 217–18, 268
teacher education 15, 17–18, 152, 158, 162,
    210, 289, 294–7
teacher preparation xx, 214, 216, 225,
    231–2, 304
*Teaching Language Learning Strategies
    in the Second/Foreign Language
    Classroom Questionnaire*
    304–5
teaching strategies 83–4, 218, 226, 228
test-management strategies 41–2
test-wiseness strategies 41–2
textbook integration 156
THALES project 168, 175–6, 182–3

vocabulary learning strategies 1, 103, 108,
    112, 160

young language learners (YLLs) 210,
    261–82

CPSIA information can be obtained
at www.ICGtesting.com
Printed in the USA
LVOW13*1626130318

569708LV00010B/225/P

9 781350 005044